Studies in Historical Archaeoethnology

Volume 5

THE SCANDINAVIANS
FROM THE VENDEL PERIOD TO THE TENTH CENTURY

AN ETHNOGRAPHIC PERSPECTIVE

Studies in Historical Archaeoethnology

FOUNDING EDITOR: † GIORGIO AUSENDA

THE SCANDINAVIANS

FROM THE VENDEL PERIOD TO THE TENTH CENTURY

AN ETHNOGRAPHIC PERSPECTIVE

Edited by

Judith Jesch

THE BOYDELL PRESS

Center for Interdisciplinary Research on Social Stress
San Marino (R.S.M.)

First published 2002
The Boydell Press, Woodbridge

ISBN 9780 85115 867 9 hardback
ISBN 9781 84383 728 2 paperback

The Boydell Press is an imprint of Boydell & Brewer Ltd
PO Box 9, Woodbridge, Suffolk IP12 3DF, UK
and of Boydell & Brewer Inc.
PO Box 41026, Rochester, NY 14620–2731, USA
website: www.boydellandbrewer.com

*This volume contains the papers presented
at the third conference on 'Studies in Historical Archaeoethnology'
organized by the Center for Interdisciplinary Research on Social Stress,
which was held in San Marino from 2nd to 6th September 1995*

A CIP catalogue record of this publication is available
from the British Library

Library of Congress Catalog Card Number: 98–39983

This publication is printed on acid-free paper

CONTENTS

LIST OF MAPS

INTRODUCTION

JUDITH JESCH

School of English Studies, The University of Nottingham, University Park, Nottingham GB-NG7 2RD

Despite many books about Vikings, and many general surveys of the Viking Age, Scandinavia itself is still relatively unknown territory to international, English-language scholarship on the early Middle Ages. The expansion of the Scandinavian peoples to regions as far apart as North America in the west and the Caspian Sea in the east, where they indulged in the typically Viking activities of raiding, trading and settlement, have been thought to be the most dramatic and most interesting aspects of this period. This book aims to return our gaze to the Viking homelands and to set the scene for Viking expansion by presenting recent research into the economic, social, political and cultural life of Scandinavia in the three centuries from around AD 700 to the turn of the millennium.

Problems and questions of dating and chronology are central to many of the chapters below, as they were to the discussions in San Marino, recorded in part in this volume. Archaeologists often wish to date the beginning of the Viking Age somewhat earlier than 793 (the raid on Lindisfarne), or the conveniently round 800, both favoured by historians, not only because they see no sharp break in the material culture of Scandinavia, but also because they find archaeological evidence of Scandinavian activities outside Scandinavia before this time. However, the nature and significance of this evidence remains controversial. On the other hand, historians and philologists suffer not only from a paucity of sources which can confidently be dated to before 793, but also from the fact that almost all written sources for the period 800-1000 are from outside Scandinavia. Scandinavian sources (especially runic inscriptions) become more copious towards the millennium, and especially so in the eleventh century, which many would still reckon as the Viking Age. But it is not possible to study the Viking Age in Scandinavia without taking some account of the vast body of evidence recorded after 1100 (skaldic and Eddic poetry, laws, even sagas), though how to use this evidence is a knotty question that still occupies students of the period. This volume recognises these approaches and dilemmas. It is not simply another book about the Viking Age, but explores the continuities between pre-Viking Age and Viking Age Scandinavia (however those are defined). And it both admits the value of and explores the possibilities of the later evidence for developing our understanding of Scandinavia in the first millennium.

The chapters by Bente Magnus on the characteristics of settlements and dwellings, by Lise Bender Jørgensen on the rural economy, and by Svend Nielsen on the urban economy, set the scene by surveying the archaeological evidence for daily life and its organization. The importance of kinship and inheritance in social

1

© C.I.R.O.S.S.
SAN MARINO (R.S.M.)

organization is explored by Birgit Arrhenius using DNA testing on grave finds from central Sweden, and Elisabeth Vestergaard using an anthropological approach applied to a variety of legal and literary sources. Stefan Brink draws attention to some contemporary evidence for legal organization in Scandinavia and shows that it often accords with the more copious evidence of later law codes and literary sources, reaffirming their value for the reconstruction of early Scandinavian law. Lena Holmquist Olausson's case study of Birka shows the importance of military functions and the assertion of power in that place, alongside its better-known functions of trade and craft production. Judith Jesch explores the symbolic expressions of military success in skaldic and other poetry. Towards the end of the Viking Age, power coalesced in the alliance between the nascent monarchies of Scandinavia and its growing Church, and Niels Lund explores the potency of this combination in Adam of Bremen's ideologically-charged, and retrospective, narrative of Harald Bluetooth. David Dumville surveys the problems and the possibilities of the evidence for Viking activities in Britain and Ireland, showing how the Viking Age in England must be understood in the context of Viking activity elsewhere. On the European continent, Dennis Green illustrates the Viking effect, by showing how a poem on a Frankish defeat of Vikings inaugurated new literary genres.

The chapters and the discussions return repeatedly to the main themes of this period: urbanization (Magnus, Nielsen, Olausson); Christianization (Brink, Green, Lund); the growth of literacy (Brink, also in Sørensen's paper not printed here); the development of rulership and monarchies (Arrhenius, Brink, Dumville, Green, Lund, Nielsen, Olausson); and parallels and contacts with the rest of Europe (Dumville, Green, Jesch). Other, minor, themes emerge between the lines: the social and symbolic uses of pagan mythology (Arrhenius, Jesch, Magnus); the roles of women (Arrhenius, Jørgensen, Vestergaard); contacts with near neighbours such as the Saami (Arrhenius, Magnus); forms of orality (Brink, Jesch); and technology (Jørgensen, Magnus, Nielsen, Olausson). Several papers and their subsequent discussion highlight the importance of continual source criticism (Brink, Dumville, Jesch, Lund) and the need for precision of terminology and clarity of definition (Dumville, Green, Magnus, Nielsen).

At the symposium, Preben Meulengracht Sørensen gave a paper on 'Religion and writing in pre-Christian Scandinavia', and Frands Herschend on 'Political structures - 6th to 10th century'. It is a matter of regret that their papers could not be made available for publication, though their participation in the symposium is reflected in their contributions to the discussions. It is with sadness that we record here Preben Meulengracht Sørensen's death in December 2001.

Thanks are due to Giorgio Ausenda, guiding light of the symposium, who transcribed all the discussions, and whose gentle persuasion and substantial editorial assistance ensured the completion of this volume.

Nottingham
February 2002

Map of Scandinavia in relation to the north-western Roman *limes*

4

Map of Scandinavia with names of places mentioned in the papers.
(Note: place names are the modern ones).

BENTE MAGNUS

Saltmätargt. 6, SE-111 60 Stockholm

On archaeology and landscape

Settlement archaeology is a field of research of long standing in Scandinavia. Gudmund Hatt, C. J. Becker and Sten Hvass in Denmark, Mårten Stenberger and Björn Ambrosiani in Sweden and Jan Petersen, Anders Hagen and Bjørn Myhre in Norway are archaeologists who in different ways have had a profound influence on the development of settlement archaeology. One of the modern pioneers was Anders Hagen who in 1946 began his excavations of a deserted farm from the Migration period in southern Norway as part of his doctorate (Hagen 1953). It was the first totally excavated farm site in Scandinavia (Myhre 1988:310). Earlier investigations, which were concentrated more on single elements like the house foundations and the graves and their furnishing, were replaced in the 1960s by a more holistic view where the organization of the agrarian settlements and the cultural landscape came into focus and interdisciplinary research strategies were developed. Catchwords were *society, economy* and *human adaptation to the natural environments*. In Sweden there developed a close interdisciplinary cooperation between Human geography and Settlement archaeology, where man in prehistory was seen as a mediator between nature and culture. In line with functionalist archaeology, the disciplines which cooperated with archaeology in projects were mostly from the natural sciences. The excavations were large-scale and mostly results of rescue archaeology. Two factors have revolutionized settlement archaeology, the possibility to remove the topsoil mechanically over large areas and metal detectors which have led to the discovery of important sites without any recognizable features above ground level.

The necessity for a long-term perspective when working with archaeological fragments of early societies has from the 1980s also brought forth a new trend in interdisciplinary research projects on settlement and landscape where archaeology has renewed and deepened cooperation with the humanities: onomastics, history of religion, history, folklore and ethnology. This type of comparative approach was begun in the 1920s. In 1926 the Norwegian linguist Magnus Olsen published a series of lectures under the heading *Ættegård og helligdom* (Ancestral farm and Sanctuary) where he, particularly by way of farm names and the position of the farms in the landscape, but also place-names, medieval written sources, ethnology and well dated archaeological sites, attempted a reconstruction of the social development of the late Iron Age in Norway. Olsen stressed the importance of the lineage (*ætt*) in this process before the formation of the state. He compared the

5

farm with its extended family to a small realm with the farmer as its king. Little by little this system was dissolved and replaced by one-family farms. Olsen coined the concepts *gårdens, bygdens og veiens navn* (place-names given from the farm, from the settled area, from the road), meaning all the different designations given to features in the landscape, whether man-made or not, from the viewpoint of the farming family, the neighbourhood and the travellers on land or on sea and which in one way or another testify to the development of the society (Olsen 1926). Magnus Olsen's research on place-names as a historical source material has had a strong impact on settlement archaeology particularly in Norway (Myhre 1972, 1978, 1987). His conclusion that late Iron Age society was one of freeborn farmers who owned their land has been long-lived (Opedal 1999), but recent historical and archaeological research has altered this view (cf. Skre 1998 with references). Stefan Brink (this volume) during the last decade has followed in Olsen's footsteps regarding the importance of onomastics in archaeological research on settlements and landscape (Brink 1990, 1994, 1996, 1997; cf. Strid 1999; Fabech & Ringtved 1995; T. Zachrisson 1994; Burström 1994, 1995).

Women and men in prehistory perceived the landscape in a very different way from people in modern urban societies. Their sense of time was different, bound to seasonal changes and the movements of celestial bodies. People in the Iron Age organized and dominated the landscape so that their settlements and burial mounds expressed legitimacy, hierarchy and power. The landscape, however, was not only where the settlements were located and people did their daily chores, lived and died, but also a mythical landscape where incidents and events had occurred to mankind, heroes, gods and giants long ago, in a distant past. It was a cognitive landscape where the ancestors still lived and the gods had their special places where people could come in contact with them (cf. Magnus 1990).

Natural preconditions for subsistence and surplus

Present-day Scandinavia comprises the territories of Denmark, Norway and Sweden. Albeit often regarded as more or less one homogeneous region from 'the outside', the three countries present a profound variation as regards geology, climate, soils, topography which since the end of the last glaciation have presented man with different conditions for settlement and usage of land: *Denmark* ('land of the Danes') consists of the peninsula of Jutland, which is a continuation of the European continent, and 483 islands, the largest being Zealand, Fyn and Lolland. The island of Bornholm situated further east has belonged to Denmark only since 1660. There are big differences between East and West as regards both climate and frostfree periods. Eastern Jutland, the islands and the Scanian plain have fertile moraine soils, while western Jutland has less fertile regions, but large tracts of man-made Atlantic heath landscape (P. E. Kaland 1986). No place in Denmark lies more than *ca* 52 km from the coast, and the coastline is in constant change because of marine erosion and accumulation.

The Scandinavian peninsula, shared by Norway and Sweden, is *ca* 1850 km long, extending southwards from the Barents Sea to Kattegat and Skagerrak and the Norwegian and North seas. *Norway* ('the northern way') is located at almost the same northern latitudes as Alaska, but with a mild climate made possible by the Gulf Stream. Nearly 2/3 of the country are occupied by mountains, massifs and tablelands. The average height above sea level is 500m and 15% lies above 975m above sea level. Characteristic for the landcape are also the extended valleys. The very long coastline is unique in Europe, and on the continental shelf outside lie more than 50,000 islands (more than 2000 still have permanent settlements). The climate is markedly maritime, moist and warm-temperate along the coast and cold-temperate inland. Due to the variable geographic conditions with deep fiords and high mountains there are profound climatic differences. The proximity to the ocean and the prevailing west and southwest winds bringing in mild airmasses warmed by the ocean currents plus the differences in altitude govern the climate. The main agricultural regions lie in the Northeast, East and Southwest, but the coastal heath landcape has made husbandry and agriculture possible also on the outer coast (S. H. H. Kaland 1987).

Sweden ('land of the Svear') has a topography very similar to Norway's and Finland's excepting parts of Scania in the south which resemble Denmark. A really high mountainous region is found only in a narrow zone along the Norwegian border. Typical for the country are deep rivers running NW–SE splitting the landcape and enormous glacial gravel ridges, deep valleys and tableland. Large regional woods like Kolmården ('the coalblack wood'), Tiveden ('the gods' wood') and others formed natural barriers between settled areas at least since the Iron Age. The climate is temperate and moist with ample precipitation and relatively small differences between summer and winter. The proximity to either the Baltic or the Norwegian Sea and the west winds bring deep climatic differences. Moraine and moraine clay with a high content of calcium are the most common types of soil, particularly in the landscapes surrounding lake Mälaren. This region which has benefited from the constant land elevation, has always been densely settled.

The long coastlines and thousands of islands, the numerous lakes large and small and the great variations in soils have had a considerable impact on the inhabitants' subsistence means and possibility to produce a surplus. Even though a near relationship to ancestral land and to a sedentary lifestyle based on husbandry and agriculture was the pivot on which life and death for the Germanic Scandinavian population was centred, it is evident that marine products as well as freshwater fish must have played a more important role for subsistence and economic surplus in Scandinavia than is testified by paleoarchaeological investigations. Cold, rainy summers could easily destroy the harvest of cereals. But as sheep and, to a certain extent, cattle and horses could find their own fodder outdoors most of the year and there always was fish, seabirds and ducks to be caught, a coastal or island-based farming population would seldom starve. A regional perspective on settlement archaeology is therefore all the more important in order to bring out both the similarities and the variations over this vast area to understand the economic and political development in Scandinavia during the late Iron Age.[1]

But there is also a problem of terminology. The archaeological literature is rife with terms like 'king', 'chieftain', 'warlord', 'élite', while on the rune stones and in place-names one finds terms like *þegn, drengr, rinkr, bryti, karl*. Where do they fit in the settlement hierarchy? In this paper the term 'chieftain' is a translation of Scandinavian *høvding*, the Old Norse *hǫfðingi*, a secular as well as a religious leader, and used as such. The term 'king', translating Old Norse *konungr*, means 'son of a man of rank' (Hellquist 1980), an inherited title and office above that of chieftain. The term seems to be later than Old Norse *þjóðann*, 'folk leader', and *dróttinn*, 'warlord' (Hellquist 1980; Falk & Torp 1991). With the profound societal changes that took place during the sixth and seventh centuries, it is probable that the titles and the roles of the leaders changed as well.

Literary illustrations

When writing about the Viking Age, it is always tempting to search for literary material which may add some information. There are runic inscriptions from eastern Scandinavia which are particularly numerous, there are skaldic poems and sagas from western Scandinavia and Iceland, Anglo-Saxon chronicles and epic poems and Frankish annals. Two examples often figure when discussing settlements: the creation myth from *Gylfaginning* (the beguiling of Gylfi) of the *Prose Edda* by Snorri Sturluson, and the eddic poem *Rígsþula*.

The cosmological myth found in *Gylfaginning* has a 'horizontal' and a 'vertical' aspect: the world is circular like a disc and surrounded by the mighty ocean where the Midgard serpent lives. The giants live on the fringe of the world, close to the ocean, in Utgard, 'outside the fence'. Midgard, the safe home of mankind lies in the centre surrounded by a fence or a wall against the supernatural beings and the giants. The gods built an enormous fortified settlement for themselves, called Asgard somewhere inside Midgard, where each god had his own hall, and some even had two. The 'vertical' aspect of cosmos is the World Ash, Yggdrasil, 'Odin's horse', which represents the ultimate mediation between life and death. Yggdrasil connected the sky, the earth and the underworld. The creation myth reflects the Norse spatial organization in the cultivated and the wild (Hastrup 1985:141 ff.). The farm was the centre of the people's life, surrounded by cultivated fields and pastures. Further out lay the dangerous wild, wooded or mountainous landscape and the wide ocean beyond man's control. The myth also reflects the people's place in the social

---

[1] A quick chronological table follows, early Iron Age: *ca* 500 BC – AD 1 (Pre-Roman Iron Age); middle Iron Age: *ca* AD 1–*ca* AD 550 (Roman and Migration periods); late Iron Age: *ca* AD 550 – *ca* AD 1050 [Vendel (or Merovingian) & Viking periods]; early medieval period (early Middle Ages): *ca* AD 1050 – AD 1250).

hierarchy which was marked by the distance from the centre, the settlement of the king or chieftain, like wave rings on water (Thomasson 1998:73 ff.).

A mythical explanation of how society was created and organized can be found in *Rígsþula*, a problematic Old Norse poem (Dronke 1997:162 ff.). Here we are introduced to the enigmatic Norse god Heimdallr, here called 'Rígr', who on his way visits three dwellings, the thrall's hut, the spacious house of the farmer and his wife, and the hall of the earl and his wife. During his stay with the three couples he gets the three wives with child. After nine months each one bears a child who in turn becomes the origin of the social strata of slaves, farmers and earls. From the poem we learn that slaves lived in a house with an open door and a fireplace on the floor; their meagre food was served on a table. The farmer's abode was a hall, *skáli*, where the door was ajar, a fire burned on the floor, plentiful food was served on a table and the guest was seated at the table. The large hall of the earl and his wife had a door facing south and it was closed, but could be opened by pulling a ring handle; the floor was strewn with rushes; a lavish meal was placed on a table covered with a patterned linen cloth, and the hosts as well as the guests were seated at the table. In many ways, the archaeological material of settlements and dwellings corroborates the picture presented by *Rígsþula* (cf. below).

Not only farmers

The Scandinavian peninsula then as well as today is ethnically and culturally a dual region with a Saami minority speaking languages belonging to the Uralian language group and a majority population belonging to the Germanic language group. During the period in question the semi-nomadic Saami inhabited the vast wooden and mountainous areas of central and northern Scandinavia as well as the inner fiord regions of northern Norway. The sedentary north-Germanic agrarian population lived along the coast up to *ca* 70° North. This was explained traditionally by this being the natural limit for barley to ripen. The Norwegian archaeologist A. Schanche (1989) has questioned this dogma: she maintains that, although the inner fiord districts offered more favourable conditions for agriculture than the coast, the distribution of Iron Age burials confirms the concentration of north-Germanic settlements along the coast. The avoidance of the inner fiord areas must have had cognitive causal connections as to the north and east of this 'boundary' only Saami settlements are found. How far south in the Scandinavian peninsula the Saamis dwelled during the late Iron Age is a hotly disputed issue, likewise the degree and kind of interaction between the sedentary, mostly agrarian north-Germanic population and the Saamis. This has recently been the basis for an interdisciplinary research project (I. Zachrisson 1997). The main result of the final publication of this important project is the overall impression, given by the various sources, of close relations and cooperation between the two ethnic groups of central Scandinavia during the Viking Age and the early Middle Ages. The piece of information given by the Viking chieftain Ohthere (Ottar) of northern Norway to King Alfred of Wessex in AD 890, according to which he lived further north than all 'northmen', probably close to present-day Tromsø, and collected tribute in the guise of furs from northern Saamis, is not corroborated by archaeological investigations (I. Zachrisson 1997:218 ff.). Future research, particularly DNA analyses on human osteological material from late Iron Age graves in the border areas, will probably show that the interaction between the two ethnic groups was much more complex than envisaged at present.

In a land where the sea, rivers and lakes were the main arteries of traffic, and riding paths criss-crossed the landscape, it was during the winter, when lakes, rivers, and even the sea were frozen, that people in the Scandinavian peninsula had a real opportunity to travel overland, to meet and hold markets, particularly on large lakes like Lake Mälaren, outside Birka. Bone skates were common as were skis, and possibly a sort of snowshoes, and frost nails for horses that pulled sleighs. Wooden skis ^{14}C-dated from the Neolithic to the Middle Ages have been found in fens and moors in the Scandinavian peninsula and in Finland (I. Zachrisson 1997:66, 215 ff.; cf. Berg 1993). The Norse myth of the giantess Skadi, an able skier and archer, and her marriage to the fertility god Niord, may be taken as an indication of the problematic relationship between Saamis and the Scandinavian Germanic population. In this paper, I will concentrate my presentation to settlements and dwellings belonging to the Scandinavian agrarian population.

The prelude

The cultural expressions from the first five hundred years of the first millennium AD are amazingly homogeneous in Scandinavia, Holland and northern Germany, a fact which has made it possible to compare phenomena from widely different locations. The reason for this homogeneity must have been that the pagan agrarian population of this large area shared the same ideologies and cognitive aspects concerning land and settlements, and that the contact networks were wide and fine-meshed. The house, the farm, and the 'village' together formed the social and economic basis which reflected 'real life' more than anything. Viewed in a long-time perspective, changes in the settlements reflect changes in the whole society (Hvass 1993:187; Pedersen & Widgren 1998). Settlements and dwellings reveal social differences, but until recently archaeology was mainly concerned with the social strata of the free born who had special inherited rights to land. The slaves and the *leysingjar* (freed slaves) who must have been major contributors to the surplus that was necessary for landowners, chieftains and kings to come to power and retain it, are late-comers in archaeological publications (Skre 1998).

The archaeological material of settlements from the period *ca* AD 200–600 is vast and steadily increasing compared to the relatively meagre material from the Vendel and Viking periods. Accordingly, it seems wise to begin with a presentation of the settlements of the sixth century as a background to the changes which led to the different society of the Viking Age.

Farms and villages

The farm with its buildings, the land belonging to it with infields and outfields, and the ancestral graves were the centre of people's life. It was of utmost importance to be able to prove the families' legitimate right to their land. The inherited land and the family's rights to make use of special resources which were not defined as common lands is linked to the Germanic concept of *óðal* (KLNM XII:493 ff.). The principle of the *óðal* right was that the land was not the property of one single man or woman but that they administered it on behalf of the lineage (*ætt*) and ancestors. During the Viking Age the power of the lineage over land had diminished. As corroborated by the rune stones, there was also access to agricultural land through channels other than inheritance, such as purchase, gift giving, *landnám* in previously unsettled or even settled regions, or administration of someone else's property. Slaves may have been set to break new land and till it for their master and maybe in the end acquire the status of a freed slave (*leysingr*).

From around AD 200 until the late sixth century there are numerous traces of deserted stable rural settlements all over Scandinavia. There are distinct regional differences, but a general feature is the existence of several models of cooperation. There are single farms bound together by enormous lengths of stone fences, villages or village-like settlements within a common enclosure, single farms located in the landscape at a relatively short distance from each other, fortified settlements and central places. Most commonly there is one farm which is bigger than the others in each settled area indicating some sort of dominance. In some regions the farms are enclosed, in other regions fences are lacking.

The centre of each farm was the three-aisled longhouse with two rows of parallel posts running lengthwise through the building carrying the roof. The general width of the house was *ca* 5 to 7 m, and the main entrances to the house were either placed in the middle of both the long sides or closer to the gabled ends. These entrances gave access to the byre and storage room on one side and the living quarters on the other. This general plan varies depending on how the weight of the roof was divided between the walls and the inner posts (Herschend 1989:83 ff.). Walls were thick and rather low, built of wattle and daub, or wooden planks in a bulwark construction, or standing directly on a sill or in a wall ditch, and, in some regions, with an insulating wall of stones on the outside. One living room was bigger than the others and had a central fireplace. The three-aisled longhouse represented a very special way of life, a sort of 'compact living' with all the functions of a farm assembled under one roof. The longhouses had ample room for stalled cattle, and animal husbandry seems to have had higher status than the cultivation of cereals. The fields were relatively small and scattered in between clearance cairns and burial mounds. The same fields were heavily manured and sowed every year due to the lack of a crop rotation system.

Vorbasse: a wandering village and a reference

Between 1974 and 1987 Steen Hvass directed excavations at the settlement site Vorbasse in central Jutland where altogether 260,000 m^2 were cleared. A unique material of a group of farms was revealed, each farm and its infield marked by a rectangular enclosure. Due to a system of relocation and reorganization of the farms after a number of generations on the same spot, it became possible to follow the development of the farm group from the third to the eleventh century within the same resource area (Hvass 1980, 1988, 1993). For a number of years Vorbasse was considered a norm, but further research has shown that it must have been rather exceptional. For many years Vorbasse was the only completely excavated village (or village-like settlement) in Scandinavia that had existed within the same resource area for about 800 years, and thus it became a material of reference to which one could easily turn.

Hvass has shown how the farms in the 'village' underwent very slight alterations from the third to the sixth century. Every farm consisted of one main three-aisled longhouse and one or two smaller rectangular storage buildings all surrounded by a fence which separated the manured fields from the pastures. One farm was distinguished by having the largest longhouse, a greater number of smaller buildings and a larger enclosed infield than the others. This farm rested more or less on the same location through ten generations. "The picture provided is of a thriving agrarian society producing for a steadily growing population of specialists like warriors, artisans, tradesmen and servants" (Hvass 1993:194). The remaining farms were relocated only slightly. At the beginning of the sixth century, the settlement was relocated 100-200 m to the north and remained there until the eighth century when the settlement was relocated again (Hvass 1993:194). Although there is no discernible break in the settlement, the number of farms was reduced and the remaining were organized in a different way, this time in a long row (Hvass 1988, fig. 23).

This change in the sixth-century settlement at Vorbasse is connected with other profound changes observable in the Iron Age material from the whole of agrarian Scandinavia, a sort of dividing line which has been termed the Migration period crisis. The idea of a devastating crisis caused by pestilence, etc., is no longer tenable, but one can see that there were regions more deeply affected than others and that the period of change can be said to cover a period from the third to the seventh century, i.e. from the late Roman period to the early Vendel period (Näsman 1988:277 ff; Widgren 1988:273 ff.). The visible traces of this change are the number of deserted farms which even to-day constitute distinct features in the landscapes of the islands Gotland and Öland, and southwest Norway, due to the use of stone for insulation of houses and fences. In Östergötland and northern Uppland in Sweden, strings of stone boundaries still bind together the agrarian landscape of the Migration period and, on the southern coast of northern Sweden, house terraces reveal the previous existence of 1500 year-old farm sites. They are all remains of a system built on an extensive use of the landscape for husbandry and agriculture. During a period of approximately two to three generations this system was replaced by one based on intensified agriculture involving the cultivation of cereals. The three-aisled longhouse became a special-purpose building, a hall, whilst other functions moved out to ad hoc buildings, i.e., byre, stable and barn. However, in western Scandinavia, the multifunctional longhouse lived on in the periphery. It was brought by Viking Age settlers to Iceland and other North Atlantic islands (Myhre 1982:206 ff).

Village problems in the middle Iron Age

During the last 20 to 30 years the use of metal detectors and large scale excavation have brought to light a great variety of Iron Age settlements. Due to the varied conditions for agriculture and husbandry existing in the different regions of Scandinavia, different terms and concepts pertaining to settlements difficult to compare have developed through the centuries, not to mention the difficulties in translating terms, for example, into English. One problem concerns the concept of *village*, *by* in Swedish, but *landsby* in Danish and Norwegian, where *by* means town. The Vikings had no word for town. To them the farm *garðr* was the standard settlement and, consequently, the metropolis of Constantinople became *Miklagarðr*, 'the large farm'. How does one define an Iron Age 'village'?

It has been almost a dogma that Iron Age villages existed only in Denmark, and only one 'village' until now was located in Norway. Landa at Forsandmoen in south-west Norway was excavated during the years 1979 to 1987. The history of the settlement goes back to the early Bronze Age and continues without a break until the end of the sixth century AD (Løken 1987:155 ff.; 1988:177 ff.; 1991). During the last 400 years of the settlement, it consisted of at most 15 units with one main three-aisled longhouse and a couple of smaller houses in each unit.

But in south-west Norway and in Östergötland and Uppland, Sweden, there also existed 'composite farms' (Myhre 1972:21) consisting of two or more single farm units connected by common fences. In Östergötland the cultural landscape is characterized by a net of linear stone walls linking large areas and dividing them into enclosed lots which comprise single farm settlements, cemeteries, infields and outfields in much the same way as in south-west Norway (Widgren 1983). The question is whether such a system of linked single farms can be labelled 'village'? Danish archaeologists have shown that enclosed villages as well as non-enclosed villages and single farms could exist within the same area (Hvass 1993:194). According to the traditional, ethnological definition of a village, two or more farms should be located in a limited area of fields, in which all the neighbours possessed their land separately or in mixed property. Danish archaeologists have maintained the need for three farms to exist simultaneously, "so that they had common rules for their provision" (Fallgren 1993:61). Discussions are complicated because definitions for historical villages have been applied to prehistoric material. The problem is that, even though several deserted Iron Age single farms may be lying in close proximity to each other, it is impossible for the archaeologists (or others) to know whether their kind of cooperation was in any way near that of historical villages. Another important question is how a village was formed. Fallgren noted that Iron Age villages on Öland have a very irregular form compared to the Jutish villages and the Norwegian village of Landa, but points to irregular villages both in Denmark (Sejlflod in North Jutland) and in Sweden. The question is whether the composite Iron Age farms of south-west Norway, the irregular farms of Öland, Östergötland and Uppland in reality are comparable to the village systems of Vorbasse in Jutland. Do the inequalities noted result from differences in modes of cooperation, land use and ownership (or right to disposal) of land? Only further debate and research may clarify the picture. Composite farms, 'villages' and even single farms within a local area (*bygd*) must have had some sort of cooperation which was organized according to tradition.

The military aspect

The war-booty finds from fens in Denmark and Sweden, the numerous weapon-graves, the hill-forts and the large boat houses testify to the martial aspect of the period from the third to the sixth century. Hill-forts are numerous on the Scandinavian peninsula, and some of them have proved to be fortified settlements. One of the best investigated is the hill-fort of Runsa in Uppland, Sweden situated on the crest of a hill surrounded by two harbours and a large cemetery. Within a system of double walls seven house terraces have been found with remains of smithing, metal casting and textile work (Olausson 1997:175 ff). According to Olausson, the fortified settlements and hill-forts are expressions of individual power and should be viewed in a spatial context together with large burial mounds and chamber graves. Lack of datable finds seem to indicate that the old hill forts lost their importance in the Vendel and Viking Ages. However, a new hill fort was constructed when Birka was founded. During recent excavations of the broad wall, a chamber grave for a man and his horse was discovered underneath the wall. A large building erected on a terrace within the walls has been interpreted as a garrison building (cf. Holmquist Olausson, this volume).

Among the 16 to 20 ring fortresses on the island of Öland in the Baltic, at least ten are dated to the period between the fourth and the seventh century. A few of them were reused in the late Viking Age and the "High Middle Ages" (Näsman 1997:149). In nine of the fortresses there are finds and structures testifying to occupation. The largest fortress, Ismantorp, shows remains of 83 long houses, while Eketorp, the fortress on southern Öland, which was excavated between 1964–1974 had 53. In the Migration period, Eketorp held thirteen farmsteads including a residential hall within its walls. It was also inhabited during the early Middle Ages.

The change

From the late sixth to sometime in the seventh century, the Scandinavian farming societies experienced a period of restructuring. The Vorbasse village in Jutland underwent only minor changes which are discernible in the seventh-century settlement consisting of two groups of farms. The houses were built with slightly curved walls with a straight gable end strengthened by two posts, a construction hailing the Viking Age longhouse (Hansen *et al.* 1991).

The extensive farming system with longhouses, cemeteries, infields, outfields and fences so characteristic of southwest and north Norway, Östergötland, Uppland, the islands of Gotland, Öland, and southern Norrland in Sweden was abandoned and the cultural landscape slowly changed (Näsman & Lund 1988). Due to a set of different methods ranging from aerial photography, the mechanical removal of topsoil over large areas, metal detection, phosphate mapping, geomagnetic prospecting, soil drilling, pollen analyses, etc., the picture of the development of settlements in Scandinavia is clearer than a decade ago. During the period from the third to the seventh century, the farms were part of an economic system built on redistribution—a power system resting on the acquisition and distribution of luxury goods. Grave finds and gold hoards point to the existence of well developed social hierarchies centred around a chieftain's family and their large farm. A number of farming units at varying distances from the chieftain's farm produced a surplus for the chieftain in return for protection, gifts and participation in splendid rituals to secure the chieftain's power as well as fertility and re-generation (Myhre 1987; Ramqvist 1987; Fabech & Ringtved 1995). Foreign imports and war booty of gold and silver, vessels of glass and bronze, weapons and colourful clothing were among the prestige goods necessary to keep up this system. When it collapsed, a large number of families left their homes. What happened to them and to their animals? All we know is that in many regions the farms were never rebuilt and people never returned to their homesteads and ancestral graves. During several generations they had invested much in clearing fields and pastures, building fences and houses and holding on to their legitimate right to their farm and the use of the land. Did the land remain the possession of the family? Burial mounds built several generations later on top of the remains of a Migration period farm house in Stavanger, Norway could point in that direction (Myhre 1987, fig. 9).

Long-lived farms and central places

There are a number of settlements which bridge the period of restructuring and continue throughout the later Iron Age, and there are settlements established in the sixth century which continue all the way into the Middle Ages. In the Mälar region several single farms were established in the middle of the eighth century. At the site of Pollista in Uppland two farms were established around AD 760. They were similarly organized with three to four longhouses surrounding an open courtyard. Until the twentieth century the spatial structure of Pollista remained unchanged. There continued to be two farms which in the course of the centuries moved only slightly within the original site (Hållans & Svensson 1999:87). Another important site is Sanda in Uppland, which was completely excavated in the 1990s (Åqvist & Flodin 1992; Lamm & Åqvist 1997). An area of 10,000 m² was cleared and traces of more than 50 houses, enclosures and a well came to light spanning a period of 1100 years during which the settlement underwent major changes. In the northern part of the site a large three-aisled hall was built during the seventh century. It underwent at least two rebuildings, but remained in use for nearly 500 years! Sanda was obviously a manorial settlement with important cultic functions. A similar farm with cultic functions is Borg in Östergötland excavated to give room for a new motorway in the early 1990s (Lindeblad & Nilsen 1997). At least five house foundations were found. One of the houses, possibly a timber house standing on a sill, measured 6 m x 7.5 m and was open towards the west. It must have been a kind of temple. It was erected within a courtyard measuring about 1000 m² covered with flat stones. West of the building a depot of 98 amulet rings of iron was found, and spread within the courtyard were some 75 kg of bones of dogs, pigs, horses and cats which had been ritually slaughtered on the spot. Both iron extraction and smithing had taken place in the courtyard as well. The cultic activities have been dated to the tenth century. The farm at Borg was founded in the seventh or eighth century and in the eleventh century it underwent restructuring. From cadastral sources we know that Borg was a royal demesne in the fourteenth century, but it was abandoned in the sixteenth century probably in connection with the foundation of the town of Norrköping. The strategic location of Borg by a waterfall on the important river Motala ström flowing into the Baltic Sea must be one of the reasons why it lived on for eight centuries. But its religious importance was probably of short duration.

Metal detectors have led to the discovery of sites characterized by a distinct accumulation of hoarded gold, metal objects and workshop material which is not found in ordinary agrarian settlements. These sites have been termed *central places* and seem to have functioned as economic, political and particularly religious centres for a whole region. They take up much land as they consist of a number of farms. Some central places, such as Gudme-Lundeborg on Funen and Sorte Muld (Ibsker) on Bornholm, go back to the late Roman period and existed up to the early Medieval period. The central places have a strategic location in relation to important lines of communication both by sea and by land, and the settlements were stationary for the whole period of occupation. The hall, the main building of the largest farm, occupied a conspicuous location and was the cultic centre. Other important sites besides Sorte Muld (Ibsker), Bornholm (Watt 1991, 1991), Gudme on Funen (Thrane 1998, Jørgensen 1994, 1995) with their most important period during the mid-Iron Age, are Tissø on Zeeland (Jørgensen 1998), and Boeslunde/Neble, Toftegård in Zealand (Tornbjerg 1998:217 ff.) which flourished in the late Iron Age. In Sweden we know of Helgö in Uppland

(Lundström 1988), Uppåkra, Vä, and Ravlunda in Scania (Hårdh 1998; Fabech 1997, 1998 with references) and Slöinge in Halland (Lundqvist 1997). The Norwegian central places at the moment include Borg in Lofoten (eighth to tenth century), Åker in Vang (sixth and seventh centuries), Avaldsnes on Karmøy (from *ca* AD 300 to well into the Middle Ages) and Anda–Tu in Klepp (middle Iron Age).

Research on the central places and their importance in the development of the Scandinavian regions into medieval kingdoms is flourishing at the moment. The central places constituted a topographic hierarchy which left its imprint particularly on place-names. But it has become clear that what constituted a central place in southern Scandinavia may differ from what characterized those further north. The site of Borg in Lofoten, north of the Arctic circle (see above) belongs in this group of manorial farms controlling trade, production, and cult, and having military power (O. S. Johansen 1979, 1982; Munch *et al.* 1985, 1986). The three-aisled longhouse, 81m long with slightly curved walls, overlay another long-house (67 m long) of Migration period date. The later longhouse had five entrances, two leading into the dwelling section and the hall respectively, one leading into a storage room and two giving access to a byre 32 m long. In the section called 'hall' there were traces of benches along the walls and a large open fireplace in the middle of the room. In one of the post holes in this section three *'gullgubber'*, tiny stamped gold foils with a representation of an embracing couple, came to light. *Gullgubber* are associated predominantly with ritual activities connected with manorial farms and central places like Gudme, Sorte Muld, Helgö, Eketorp, Slöinge and Anda–Tu (Watt 1988:94 ff.; 1991:89 ff.). Sherds of various glass vessels of very high quality, golden objects as well as sherds of tinfoil and Rhenish jugs, add to the general impression of Borg as a central place for the region. The place-name 'Borg' means 'fortress', 'stronghold' and the location of the main building on a high promontory in the landscape was well chosen. Three large boat houses, burial mounds and a so-called 'court site' (see below) in the vicinity testify to the importance of Borg.

In the Viking Age, the island of Vestvågøy, where Borg is located, was densely populated and is still one of the best farming districts in northern Norway. The rich fisheries (which in the Middle Ages made Lofoten famous), abundant grazing land, eider down, sealing, whaling and a relatively mild Atlantic climate have formed the basis for the establishment in the late Iron Age of a chiefdom or regional kingdom this far north. Contrary to the conditions in south-west Norway, finds and pollen diagrams from Vestvågøy indicate a continuous settlement without a break in the sixth century (O. S. Johansen 1982:45 ff.).

Central places from the early and middle Iron Age respectively belong to different 'centralities'. The early ones like Gudme, Sorte Muld and Helgö had all the important economic, religious and political functions within one relatively restricted area ruled by one leading family. All kinds of activites from handicrafts to splendid public religious sacrifices were centred on their farms. In the changing society of the late Iron Age the leading families seem to control a much wider geographical area. They controlled several farms which produced a surplus of different goods for consumption that could be traded on a market, probably under their control. The hall was the centre for religious as well as political and economic transactions, and contained the family's living quarters and possibly those of the retinue.

A different landscape

The agricultural landscape that emerged around 700 AD was different. The houses of the settlements were smaller, the byre had room for fewer animals and only special persons were buried under mounds. An intensified agriculture, possibly with crop rotation, had taken the place of the former extensive system. Fewer animals were kept and stalled through the winter months, which again meant a need for less grazing land and pastures. But the change was a process which took time, and there were distinct regional differences. Through subsequent generations the redistribution system was replaced by a system built on the production and exchange of goods for daily consumption, such as grain, iron, soapstone vessels, slate hones, textiles etc. New families came into power. Such a system meant that the securing of personal rights to agricultural land, grazing land, as well as rights to timber, iron bogs, hunting grounds, seal skerries and salmon fishing became important for each farm unit. The emergence of manorial farms and a stratum of landholders who strived to acquire as much land as possible in order to control the production of subsistence and surplus is characteristic of the late Iron Age. Runic inscriptions on stones and solid rock from the latter part of the Viking Age give a vivid impression of this. On one Swedish rune stone up to six generations are accounted for (Brink 1994:145–162). To keep a body of armed men, a retinue, was a matter not only of prestige, but vital so as to secure dominance. To be able to organize raiding and trading expeditions, the landholders were dependent on slaves, and *leysingjar* who could produce a surplus. Social relations during the Vendel and Viking periods seem to have had a personal basis. The regional kings and mighty landholders depended on the *þing*s and repeated collective rituals and ceremonies to be able to exercise power, and the spacious hall provided their most important scene of action. Generosity and hospitality were their primary assets, and the system of gift giving was a powerful instrument. The Icelandic sagas and the Old English epic poem *Beowulf* offer examples of this system and of the importance of social and ritual life in the hall. The establishment of trading places and urban centres, which is characteristic particularly of the eighth century, testifies to the emergence of powerful individuals (regional kings and allied landholders) with an important social and political network also outside of the pagan communities of Scandinavia. Urban centres like Ribe, Hedeby, Birka and Kaupang were established in all likelihood by regional kings on their private property.

Trading places

Coastal trading places from after *ca* 700 AD are numerous in southern Scandinavia, but have not yet been found in Norway (Sognnes 1979). Trading places were strategically located in relation to transport routes and are characterized by workshop material, particularly bronze casting, glass beads and traces of the production of beads, brooches of many kinds, coins, and imported goods like ceramic pots, soapstone vessels, iron tools etc. Trading places must have had a lively activity during the summer season, whilst only a few seem to have been permanent settlements. Early urban centres like Ribe in West Jutland and Birka in Lake Mälaren may have begun as trading places. Dankirke in southwest Jutland (S. Jensen 1991:73ff), Sebbersund, situated on the Limfiord in north Jutland (Christensen & Johansen 1992:199–225) and Åhus in Scania (Callmer 1991b:29 ff.; 1998:27-37) are good examples of trading places centred on the coast with a semi-permanent settlement of longhouses and 'Grubenhäuser'. Abundant traces of specialized handicrafts and trade with imported products make it probable that craftsmen and tradesmen travelled from one place to another staying for a longer or shorter period but having winter quarters of a more permanent character, such as a farm somewhere else. The relationship between the central places and the trading places is far from clear. According to Callmer (1998:36) it is unlikely that all tradesmen and craftsmen were dependent on kings and magnates but likely that craftsmen were dependent on tradesmen.

Urban centres

There are four sites in Scandinavia which have been defined as early towns, Ribe which was established in the early eighth century, Birka in Lake Mälaren and Kaupang in Vestfold, Norway (Blindheim *et al.* 1998), sometime in the latter part of the same century, and Hedeby established about 800 AD on the east side of the root of the Jutish peninsula. The structures of the settlements have much in common: standard sized plots in rows running up from the shore (of the river or fiord) and the entire settlement enclosed by a semicircular wall; cemeteries with well furnished graves outside the wall. Each plot, enclosed by a wooden fence, had room for one house which was either built in wattle and daub, or of wood in bulwark technique, and contained both living quarters and/or workshops. The rows of plots were divided by ditches. An entire house which had collapsed and was buried in mud clay was found at Hedeby. It measured 12 m by 5 m and had three rooms but only one with a hearth. The walls were made of wattle and daub on a wooden frame and had external supports. It was dendrochronologically dated to 870 AD (Schietzel 1981:31 ff.). The urban houses were without internal posts and the weight of the roof rested on the walls.

All the urban centres are mentioned in a number of different contemporary written sources (i.e. Frankish annals, Archbishop Rimbert's hagiography of the archbishop Ansgar, Adam of Bremen's *History of the Hamburg See*, King Alfred's enlarged edition of Orosius' world history, Lund 1983). There is still a problem whether these sites come under the concept of 'town', and they will be referred to as urban centres in the following discussion (Helle 1994).

With the establishment of the earliest urban centres one may say that the urban individual was born. For the first time in Scandinavian history people had the possibility of living and working in a community basically different from the mostly self-supporting farm and village. In an urban centre the population consisted of craftsmen and their families, tradesmen, the king's representatives and a military force, captives and slaves, representatives of the Christian Church, none of which produced their own food or raw materials. Very little is known of the relationship between the early Scandinavian urban population and the surrounding population of magnates and farmers, not to mention the relationship between craftsmen and tradesmen. What we can deduce from the archaeological material from the excavations in Ribe, Hedeby, Birka and Kaupang is that urban centres generated specialization, production and trade on different levels in Scandinavian society. They are intimately connected with a phase of urban development in north-west Europe. During the late tenth century, three of the four urban sites were deserted and new towns were founded by kings allied with the Church. In Ribe the new settlement was established on the other side of the river, and Schleswig on the other side of the fiord Schlei replaced Hedeby by mid-eleventh century. The relationship between pagan Kaupang and the establishment of the Christian town of Tønsberg, or pagan Birka and the establishment around AD 980 of the Christian town of Sigtuna *ca* 45 km further to the northeast, is far from clear. From Rimbert's *Vita Anskarii* we know that the see of Hamburg-Bremen was very active in both Hedeby and Birka and churches were built. Until now, no traces of churches have been found, apart from a church bell discovered during the excavation of the port of Hedeby (Drescher 1984:56–7). It may have belonged to Ansgar's church mentioned in *Vita Anskarii*, ch. 32.

Farms and villages of the Viking Age

The knowledge of settlements and dwellings of the late Iron Age and early Medieval period is still scanty compared to the mid-Iron Age. Turning to Vorbasse once again, a thorough change occurred during the first two decades of the eighth century (dendrochronologically dated). The village was moved 400 m away and completely restructured. Only seven farms, built on both sides of a common road, remained (Hvass 1988). Each farm was allotted a much larger and almost square infield area marked by an enclosing fence. The main building, a three-aisled long-house with slightly curved walls was erected in the middle of the enclosed area surrounded by three or four smaller houses and a few sunken feature buildings (Grubenhäuser). Hvass sees the almost total redistribution of cultivated land as a strong indication of the introduction of the 'toft'. According to Danish medieval law, 'toft' was the part of the total resources of the village that was allotted to each farm. He also sees a connection between this altered structure and the existence of a central political state power which could guarantee a certain amount of trade. "The villages must have produced an agricultural surplus that enabled this trade to take place and brought supplies of food to the budding towns" (Hvass 1988:90).

The aisled longhouse was still the main type of building in the Viking Age with the curving of the walls becoming more prominent. Separate buildings for humans and animals became common also in Denmark, and 'Grubenhäuser' were important elements of the farm structure. Important Danish sites like Trabjerg (Bender Jørgensen & Eriksen 1995), Omgård (L. C. Nielsen 1980) and Sædding (Stoumann 1980) belong here.

The Scandinavian settlements in Iceland, the Faeroes, Greenland, Newfoundland, the Isle of Man, Scotland, Orkney and Shetland have left a large number of deserted farms from the Viking Age and early Middle Ages with material which, in many ways, is superior to what is known at least from Norway and Sweden (for references see articles in Myhre *et al.* 1982; Batey, Jesch & Morris 1993; Arneborg & Gulløv 1998).

Relatively few sites from the Viking Age have been found in Sweden. The reason may be that they are underneath existing villages and, until 1991, only a few of these sites were available for excavation. Both research and large-scale rescue excavations have revealed a number of important settlement sites in southern and central Sweden. Often these are found close to village sites known only from cadastral sources. Recent investigations have shown that a number of such sites have had continuous settlements since the late Iron Age, some even since the mid-Iron Age (Lamm & Åqvist 1997; Broberg 1992). The single farms may have moved slightly during the centuries but within the same resource area. Settlements of southern Scandinavia, established in the seventh century, continued until the eleventh, and there seemed to be a connection between manorial farms and the oldest churches. Longhouses with slightly curved walls were the most common building type, but the size and building techniques differed (Tesch 1992; Callmer 1992).

The importance of large halls in the late Iron Age is shown by a number of excavations, sagas and the poem *Beowulf.* Among the very few halls which may be connected with early kingship is the large one erected on a terrace, Kungsgårdsplatån, close to the later medieval church at Old Uppsala, Uppland (Nordahl 1993:59-63). Another enormous building from the latter part of the tenth century is the hall, measuring 48 by 11.5 m, of the large manorial estate at Lejre, Zealand (Christensen 1997:47 ff.). The hall was divided into six sections with an entrance for each. The largest room with the long hearth covered 200 m^2.

In Norway a number of important locations with single house foundations from the late Iron Age were known from pre-war excavations (Myhre 1982:195 ff.). But few sites have been investigated during the last 30 years. The site of Ytre Moa, found on a huge gravel terrace above an arm of the inner Sognefiord consisted of six small, three-aisled houses having different functions, all with the entrance in one of the gabled ends, and 16 burial mounds. The organization of the buildings may indicate the existence of two different farm units (Bakka 1965). The farm at Lurekalven which was established in the eighth century on a small island on the coastal heath landscape north of the city of Bergen, was investigated in the course of an interdisciplinary project (P. E. Kaland 1986). The farm had at most three longhouses from 10 to 20 m in length and 6–7 m wide. At Borg, in Lofoten, north of the Arctic circle (Munch *et al.* 1985, 1988) the three-aisled longhouse of 81 m had a Migration period-type plan with living quarters, hall, storage and byre under the same roof. The house was erected in the sixth century and rebuilt in the eighth century on the same site. Other coastal farm sites in northern Norway indicate that the region was well settled from the early Iron Age into the Middle Ages (O. S. Johansen 1979:95–116). Place-names and archaeological finds show that there was an inner *landnám* in Norway during the Viking Age when considerable numbers of new farms were established in the inner regions of the fiords and valleys. Lately, the mechanical removing of topsoil over large areas has disclosed farm sites in the central agricultural regions of Norway (Skre 1998).

The settlement sites of the Viking Age represent a varied picture of adaptation to regional conditions. The profound changes at Vorbasse in Jutland may have a connection with the growing royal power.

Exploitation of resources

In the Norwegian high mountain areas there are examples of 'marginal' settlements with an aisled longhouse dated to the Viking Age and early Medieval period. These settlements were permanent and based on husbandry and iron extraction or some other specialized craft and the products could be traded for grain and other necessities at a market (Martens 1987, 1995; Indrelid 1988). The mountain areas were not only frequented to dig for bog iron and as hunting grounds, but also for pastures where cattle, sheep, goats and horses could graze from midsummer till the end of September. A shieling system with permanent buildings for the farmhands who milked cows and goats and produced butter and cheese was established to exploit those mountain resources. Pollen analyses indicate that transhumance with intensive grazing of the mountain pastures began in the late Bronze Age, but the system with permanent small buildings, with the entrance at one gabled end and enclosures where the animals could be kept during the night, may have begun in the late sixth century (Magnus 1983:93-103, 1985; Kvamme 1988:94 ff.). The shieling system had a twofold function, namely to keep the animals away from the grazing land close to the farms and to exploit the fertile mountain pastures. It created a cultural landscape characterized by intensive grazing and a vegetation devoid of trees and bushes. The transhumance system differed from region to region depending on the distance from the farms to the mountain pastures. In western Norway the way up was short, steep and dangerous and took only a day, while eastern Norwegian farms were located miles away from the pastures so that the expedition took much longer. On the other hand, the inland farmers could collect and store hay and fodder in the mountains and transport it to the farm during the winter. The shieling system was something that people emigrating from the Scandinavian peninsula took with them to Iceland, Greenland and the Faeroes (Mahler 1989:164-6, 1993:487 ff.).

The coastal resources were intensively exploited as well, and along the archipelago of the Scandinavian peninsula there are traces of seasonal maritime occupation from the mid-Iron Age into the High Middle Ages. On islands along the Norwegian outer coast the stone walls form square huts (5 m by 4 m) grouped together close to the water, often with a clearance of stones nearby for pulling up boats on shore. The maritime location and finds from excavated sites consisting of iron fishing hooks, different sinkers of soapstone, iron knives etc. and fishbones make it reasonable to interpret the settlements as part of a system by which the farms further inland and along the fiords could exploit the rich coastal fisheries in the early spring (Magnus 1974). This system is documented from the eighteenth century and the men fishing were then called 'fjæremenn', shore men. Judging from the numerous and different sites with stone walls of huts, this type of exploitation of maritime resources with permanent huts began during the Migration period and continued until the twentieth century. In all likelihood, the system changed with the economic and political development throughout the centuries, both regarding the rights to the best places and the social status of the individuals who actually did the fishing.

The Swedish counterparts in the exploitation of maritime resources, called *tomtningar*, have been found along the Swedish west coast, on the southeast coast of Blekinge and in Norrland (Stibéus 1997 for further references). On the coast of Norrland the *tomtningar* are located high up and relatively unsheltered on islands furthest out to sea, mostly used in connection with sealing. In western Sweden they are located close to the water at a relatively low altitude and show a great diversity of shape and size. Most of the *tomtningar* have been dated to a period between the year 1300 and the eighteenth century; only investigations in Norrland have yielded dates going back to the Viking Age.

Military structures

The wealthy landholders and kings of the Viking Age were surrounded by a retinue of sworn men who were professional warriors. In addition, the kings could call men to arms when in need of greater forces. At times this required housing facilities for a large number of men. The four Danish ring fortresses Trelleborg (Zealand), Nonnebakken (Funen), Aggersborg and Fyrkat (Jutland), are constructed on the same principle of four quarters with four large buildings, 30 m by 8 m arranged in a square in each quarter, all surrounded by a circular wall with wide gates. Aggersborg measures 240 m across, the others 120 m and 137 m respectively. The Roman foot of 29.33 cm was the unit of measurement used for the construction of all the ring fortresses. The houses were used as dwellings as well as for storage. By way of excavations, ^{14}C-datings and dendrochronology, the Danish fortresses have been dated to *ca* AD 980 and connected with the historically documented martial activities of King Harald Bluetooth. The buildings, in use for a few years only, may also have been used for royal administration (Roesdahl 1987:208-26). The only ring fortress found in Scania, at Trelleborg, was never completed as no traces of buildings were found within its walls. ^{14}C-datings confirm that it was contemporary with the Danish ring fortresses. At Fyrkat one of the large buildings has been reconstructed and gives the visitor an overwhelming impression of the size of a royal hall. It is built of oak with curved walls, external supports, straight gables and broad benches along the walls.

The north-Norwegian 'court sites' belong in this connection (Johansen & Søbstad 1978; Herteig 1988:402-14). The court sites consisted of a number of three-aisled buildings (5 m to 17 m) arranged around an oval open space with one gabled end facing the open space. The houses had curved walls and varied in dimensions from 3.5 m by 7 m to 16 m by 5 m. The 'court sites', of which 15 are known along the coast, are variously dated from the first to the tenth century AD and their use is disputed. Their different sizes may have been determined by the retinue of the regional chieftain and thus may have served to house people in connection with military, economic and religious activities within the centre of the chiefdom (Johansen & Søbstad 1978:9-56). The seven north-Norwegian 'court sites' seem to have been connected with central places like Borg in Lofoten with one or more large boat houses in the vicinity as additional indicators of political organization (Myhre 1985). Herteig (1988:412) has argued that the north-Norwegian 'court sites' were instrumental in housing the armed men which the chieftains (like Ohthere) needed for collecting trading furs and walrus tusks from the Saamis and other indigenous populations in the far north.

Wealth built on slavery?

Settlements and dwellings in Scandinavia during the last 4-500 years of the pagan era show, more than anything else, the rise of influential families demonstrating their power by monumental buildings. A system built on tribute must have been the backbone of the manorial estates around which central places grew. Tribute could be in form of service, products or special goods like furs. Large farms with herds of cattle, pigs, sheep and horses must have been based on work being done by men and women in various forms of serfdom and dependence on the owners.

Returning to the poem *Rígsþula*, what it narrates in colourful terms is that, in a hierarchical society, slaves do the hard and dirty work for the free farmers, earls and kings. Traces of their huts are probably to be found among the 'Grubenhäuser' and the small buildings on the outer coast. Within history and settlement archaeology it has been somewhat of a dogma for generations that the Scandinavian agrarian population consisted of free born farmers only, with inherited rights to their land (the *óðal*). The social difference between them was a matter of quantity and quality only. As Dagfinn Skre has shown, this concept of the Scandinavian free farmer who was never enslaved goes back to a doctrine which should be assigned to German ideological conceptions, the *Gemeinefrei*-doctrine (Skre 1998). It was long-lived particularly in Norway, but also in Sweden, and had a profound influence on archaeology as well as history and human geography.

In a recent thought-provoking article Mats Widgren (1998:281-96) argued for an integration of the archaeology of chiefs with the human geography of peasants. He asked how the surplus of the chieftains of the central places was accumulated and whether the 'Scandinavian free farmer', to some extent, was a myth. On the one hand we can discern a basic equality between free-born farmers, expressed in equally large farm units, the same size in houses and equal burial customs, while on the other hand there are basic features testifying to an unequal distribution of power and wealth. The upper strata, often called élite in archaeological literature, had a cross-regional culture of their own, different from the native, regional culture (Widgren 1998a:283 ff.). How the surplus which was the foundation of their power and wealth was accumulated is still an open question. In his work on settlement and ownership in Romerike (200 to 1350 AD), Skre (1998) has shown that the rights to land use and to surplus were regulated within an institutional framework where, not only slavery, but also a patron-client relationship, friendship, kinship, cult, lavish meals and military protection were important aspects.

References

[Abbr.: *AmS* = *Arkeologisk museum*, Stavanger; KLNM = *Kulturhistorisk leksikon for nordisk middelalder*].

Textual sources:

Adam of Bremen
    Gesta Hammaburgensis ecclesiæ pontificum: see Trillmich & Buchner (eds.) 1978.
Orosius
    King Alfred's edition of Orosius' world history: see Lund 1983.
Rimbert
    Vita Anskarii: see Odelman (trans.) 1986.

Bibliography

Åqvist, C., & L. Flodin
  1992   Pollista och Sanda - Två tusenåriga byar i Mälarregionen. In *Gård-tettsted-kaupang-by. Seminar i Bergen 11-13 desember 1991.* S. Myrvoll *et al.* (eds.), pp. 227-234. (N.U.B. Nytt fra utgravningskontoret i Bergen, 3). Bergen: Riksantikvaren.
Arneborg, J., & H. C. Gulløv (eds.)
  1998   *Man, Culture and Environment in Ancient Greenland.* Report on a Research Programme. Copenhagen: The Danish Polar Centre and The Danish National Museum.

Arrhenius, B.
1998   Bebyggelsesstrukturen i det förhistoriska Vendel och järnålderns
            mångmannagårdar. In *Centrala platser - Centrala frågor. Samhälls-
            strukturen under järnåldern.* (Uppåkra studier 1). L. Larsson & B. Hårdh
            (eds.), pp. 179-188. (Acta Archaeologica Lundensia, Series in 8°, No.28).
            Lund: Almqvist & Wiksell International.
Bakka, E.
1965   Ytre Moa. Eit gardsanlegg fra vikingtida i Årdal i Sogn. *Viking* 29: 121-145.
Batey, C. E., J. Jesch & C. Morris (eds.)
1993   *The Viking Age in Caithness, Orkney and the North Atlantic.* Edinburgh:
            Edinburgh University Press.
Baudou, E.
1989   Hög - gård - helgedom i Mellannorrland under den äldre järnåldern.
            Arkeologi i norr 2: 9-49.
Bender Jørgensen, L., & P. Eriksen
1995   *Trabjerg. En vestjysk landsby fra vikingetiden.* (Jysk Arkæologisk Selskabs
            Skrifter, XXXI:I). Århus: Jysk Arkæologisk Selskab.
Berg, K.
1993   *Ski i Norge.* Oslo: Aventura forlag.
Blindheim, C., B. Heyerdahl-Larsen & R. L. Tollnes
1998   *Kaupangfunnene.* (Norske Oldfunn 18). Oslo: Universitetets Oldsaksamling.
Brink, S.
1990   *Parish-formation and Parish-names: Studies in Early Territorial Division in
            Scandinavia.* (Studier till en svensk ortnamnsatlas, 14). Uppsala: Gustav
            Adolph Akademien.
1994   En vikingatida storbonde i södra Norrland. *Tor* 26: 145-162.
1996   Political and social structures in early Scandinavia. A settlement-historical
            pre-study of the central place. *Tor* 28: 235-281.
1997   Political and social structures in early Scandinavia II. Aspects of space and
            territoriality – The settlement district. *Tor* 29: 389–437.
Broberg, A.
1992   Archaeology and East-Swedish agrarian society AD 700–1700. In *The
            Medieval Town. Riksantikvarieämbetets arkeologiska undersökningar.*
            O. Kyhlberg (ed.), pp. 273–309. (Skrifter, 3). Stockholm: Riksantikvarieämbetet.
Burström, M.
1994   Forna jättar ger landskapet mening. *Kulturmiljövård* 5: 46-49.
1995   Gårdstankar. In *Hus och gård i det förurbana sämhället. Rapport från ett
            sektorforskningsprojekt.* O. Kyhlberg & H. Göthberg (eds.), pp. 163-178.
            (Arkeologiska Undersökningar, 14). Stockholm: Riksantikvarieämbetet.
Callmer, J.
1991   Platser med anknytning till handel och hantverk i yngre järnålder. Exempel
            från Sverige. In *Høvdingesamfund og kongemagt. Fra stamme til stat i
            Danmark. 2.* P. Mortensen & B. M. Rasmussen (eds.), pp. 29-47. (Jysk
            Arkæologisk Selskabs Skrifter XXII:2). Århus: Jysk Arkæologisk Selskab.
1992   A contribution to the prehistory and early history of the South Scandinavian
            manor. In *The Archaeology of Cultural Landscape.* L. Larsson *et al.* (eds.),
            pp. 411-457. (Acta Archaeologica Lundensia, Series in 4°, no. 19).
            Stockholm: Almqvist & Wiksell.
1997   Aristokratiskt präglade residens från yngre järnåldern i forskningshistorien och
            deras problematik. In *"...gick Grendel att söka det höga huset..."* J. Callmer &
            E. Rosengren (eds.), pp. 11-18. (Hallands Länsmuseers Skriftserie No. 9/
            GOTARC C. Arkeologiska Skrifter 17). Halmstad: Hallands Länsmuseer.

1998 Handelsplatser och kustplatser och deras förhållande till lokala politiska system. Ett bidrag till strukturen i den yngre järnålderns samhälle. In *Centrala platser - Centrala frågor. Samhällsstrukturen under järnåldern.* (Uppåkrastudier 1). L. Larsson & B. Hårdh (eds.), pp. 27-37. (Acta Archaeologica Lundensia, Series in 8°, No. 28). Lund: Almqvist & Wiksell International.

Christensen, T.
1997 Hallen i Lejre. In *"...gick Grendel att söka det höga huset...." Arkeologiska källor till aristokratiska miljöer i Skandinavien under yngre järnålder.* J. Callmer & E. Rosengren (eds.), pp. 46-54. (Hallands länsmuseers Skriftserie No 9/GOTARC C. Arkeologiska Skrifter No 17). Halmstad: Hallands Länsmuseer.

Christensen, P. B., & E. Johansen
1992 En handelsplads fra yngre jernalder og vikingetid ved Sebbersund. *Aarbøger for nordisk oldkyndighed og historie* [1991]: 199-229.

Drescher, H.
1984 Glockenfunde aus Haithabu. In *Berichte über die Ausgrabungen in Haithabu*, Vol. 19. K. Schietzel (ed.), pp. 9-63. Neumünster: Wachholtz Verlag.

Dronke, U.
1997 *The Poetic Edda*, Vol. 2. (Mythological poems). Oxford: Clarendon Press.

Ersgård, L.
1996 Two magnate's farms and their landscape – a postscript. In *Slöinge och Borg. Stormansgårdar i öst och väst.* Pp. 116-122. (Arkeologiska Undersökningar. Skrifter No. 18). Stockholm: Riksantikvarieämbetet.

Fabech, C.
1997 Slöinge i perspektiv. In *"...gick Grendel att söka det höga huset...." Arkeologiska källor till aristokratiska miljöer i Skandinavien under yngre järnålder.* J. Callmer & E. Rosengren (eds.), pp. 145-160. (Hallands Länsmuseers Skriftserie No.9/GOTARC C. Arkeologiska Skrifter No. 17). Halmstad: Hallands Lansmuséer.

1998 Kult og samfund i yngre jernalder - Ravlunda som eksempel. In *Centrala platser - Centrala frågor. Samhällsstrukturen under järnåldern.* (Uppåkrastudier 1). L. Larsson & B. Hårdh (eds.), pp. 147-163. (Acta Archaeologica Lundensia, Series in 8°, No. 28). Lund: Almqvist & Wiksell International.

Fabech, C., & J. Ringtved
1995 Magtens geografi i Sydskandinavien – om kulturlandskap, produktion og bebyggelsesmønster. In *Produksjon og samfunn.* H. Resi (ed.), pp. 11–37. Beretning fra det 2. nordiske jernaldersymposium på Granavolden 7.–10 mai 1992. (Varia 30). Oslo: Universitetets Oldsaksamling.

Falk, H., & A. Torp
1991 *Etymologisk ordbog over det norske og det danske sprog.* [First edition, 1903-06]. Oslo: Bjørn Ringstrøms Antikvariat.

Fallgren, J.-H.
1993 The concept of the village in Swedish archaeology. *Current Swedish Archaeology* 1: 59-86.

Göthberg, H.
1995 Huskronologi i Mälarområdet, på Gotland och Öland. In *Hus och gård i det förurbana samhället. Rapport från ett sektors- forskningsprosjekt.* H. Göthberg, O. Kyhlberg & A. Vinberg (eds.), pp. 65-109. (Arkeologiska undersökningar. Skrifter No. 14). Stockholm: Riksantikvarieämbetet.

Hagen, A.
1953 *Studier i jernalderens gårdssamfunn.* (Universitetets Oldsaksamlings Skrifter IV). Oslo: Universitetets Oldsaksamling.

Hallans, A. M., & K. Svenson
1999 *Pollista: bo och bruka under 1200 år.* Stockholm: Arkeologiska undersökningar, Riksantikvarieämbetet.

Hansen, T. E., D. K. Mikkelsen & S. Hvass
1991 Landbebyggelserne i 7. århundre. In *Høvdingesamfund og Kongemagt. Fra Stamme til Stat i Danmark.* 2. P. Mortensen & B. M. Rasmussen (eds.), pp. 17-26. (Jysk Arkæologisk Selskabs Skrifter XXII:2). Århus: Jysk Arkæologisk Selskab.

Hårdh, B.
1998 Preliminära notiser krig detektorfynden från Uppåkra. In *Centrala platser - Centrala frågor. Samhällsstrukturen under järnåldern.* (Uppåkra studier 1). L. Larsson & B. Hård (eds.), pp. 113-127. (Acta Archaeologica Lundensia, Series in 8°, No. 28). Lund: Almquist & Wiksell International.

Hastrup, K.
1985 *Culture and History of Medieval Iceland.* Oxford: Clarendon Press.

Helle, K.
1994 Descriptions of Nordic towns and town-like settlements in early literature. In *Developments around the Baltic and the North Sea in the Viking Age.* B. Ambrosiani & H. Clarke (eds.), pp. 20-31. (Birka Studies 3. The twelfth Viking Congress). Stockholm: Central Board of Antiquity & Statens Historiska Museum.

Hellquist, E.
1980 *Svensk etymologisk ordbok.* Lund: Liber läromedel/Gleerup.

Herschend, F.
1989 Changing houses. Early medieval house types in Sweden 500-1100 A.D. *Tor* 22: 79-103.

Herteig, A. E.
1988 *De nordnorske tunanleggene fra første årtusen e. Kr. Sentrale ledd i en hedensk høvdingeinstitusjon.* Arkeologiske Skrifter fra Historisk Museum 4, pp. 402-414. Bergen: Historisk Museum, Universitetet i Bergen.

Hvass, S.
1980 Vorbasse. The Viking-Age settlement at Vorbasse, Central Jutland. *Acta Archaeologica* 50: 157-208.
1982 Huse fra romersk og germansk jernalder i Danmark. In *Vestnordisk byggeskikk gjennom to tusen år. Tradisjon og forandring fra romertid til det 19 årh.* Myhre et al. (eds.), pp. 130-145. (AmS Skrifter 7). Stavanger: Arkeologisk Museum i Stavanger.
1988 Jernalderens bebyggelse. In *Jernalderens stammesamfund. Fra stamme til stat i Danmark.* 1. P. Mortensen, & B. M. Rasmussen (eds.), pp. 53-92. (Jysk Arkæologisk Selskabs Skrifter, XXII:1). Århus: Jysk Arkæologisk Selskab.
1993 Bebyggelsen. In *Da Klinger i Muld... 25 års arkæologi i Danmark.* S. Hvass & B. Storgaard (eds.), pp. 187-194. Århus: Universitetsforlag.

Indrelid, S.
1988 *Jernalderfunn i Flåmsfjella. Arkeologiske data og kulturhistorisk tolking.* Arkeologiske Skrifter fra Historisk Museum 4, pp. 106-119. Bergen: Historisk Museum Universitetet i Bergen.

Jensen, S.
1991   Dankirke-Ribe. Fra handelsgård til handelsplass. In *Høvdingesamfund og Kongemagt. Fra Stamme til Stat i Danmark. 2.* P. Mortensen & B. M. Rasmusssen (eds.), pp. 73-87. (Jysk Arkæologisk Selskabs Skrifter XXII:2). Århus: Jysk Arkæologisk Selskab.

Johansen, O. S.
1979   Jernaldergårder i Nord-Norge. In *På leiting etter den eldste garden.* R. Fladby & J. Sandnes (eds.), pp. 95-117. Oslo: Universitetsforlaget.

1982   Viking Age farms: Estimating the number and population size. A case study from Vestvågøy, North Norway. *Norwegian Archaeological Review* 15 (1-2): 45-69.

Johansen, O. S., & T. Søbstad
1978   De nordnorske tunanleggene fra jernalderen. *Viking* 41: 9-56.

Jørgensen, L.
1998   En storgård fra vikingetid ved Tissø, Sjælland - en foreløbig præsentation. In *Centrala platser - Centrala frågor. Samhällsstrukturen under järnåldern.* (Uppåkra studier 1) L. Larsson & B. Hårdh (eds.), pp. 233-248. (Acta Archaeologica Lundensia, Series in 8°, No. 28). Lund: Almqvist & Wiksell International.

Kaland, P. E.
1986   The origin and management of Norwegian coastal heaths as reflected by pollen analyses. In *Anthropogenic Indicators in Pollen Diagrams.* K.-E. Behre (ed.), pp. 19-36. Rotterdam: A. A. Balkema.

Kaland, S. H. H.
1987   Viking/Medieval settlement in the heathland area of Nordhordland. In *Proceedings of the Tenth Viking Congress, Larkollen, Norway, 1985.* J. Knirk (ed.) pp. 171-190. (Universitetets Oldsaksamlings Skrifter, Ny rekke 9). Oslo: Universitetets Oldsaksamlings.

KLNM
1956-78   *Kulturhistorisk leksikon for nordisk middelalder, I-XXII.* Copenhagen: Rosenkilde og Bagger.

Kvamme, M.
1988   Lokale pollendiagram og bosetningshistorie. In *Folkevandringstiden i Norden.* U. Näsman & J. Lund (eds.), pp. 75-113. Århus: Universitetsforlag.

Lamm, K., & C. Åqvist
1997   Long-lived settlement units in central Sweden. *Studien zur Sachsenforschung* 10: 179-194.

Lindeblad, K., & A.-L. Nielsen
1997   Centralplatser i Norrköpingsbygden - förändringar i tid och rum 200-1200 e.Kr. In *"...gick Grendel att söka det höga huset...." Arkeologiska källor til aristokratiska miljöer i Skandinavien under yngre järnålder.* J. Callmer & E. Rosengren (eds.), pp. 99-118. (Hallands Länsmuseers Skriftserie No 9/GOTARC C. Arkeologiska Skrifter No. 17). Halmstad: Halland Länsmuseer.

Lund, N.
1983   *Ottar og Wulfstan: to rejsebeskrivelser fra vikingetiden.* (Trans. from Old English and commented). Roskilde: Vikingeskibshallen.

Lundqvist, L.
1997   Central places and central areas in the Late Iron Age. Some examples from South-western Sweden. In *Visions of the Past: Trends and Traditions in Swedish Medieval Archaeology.* H. Andersson *et al.* (eds.), pp. 179-197. (Lund Studies in Medieval Archaeology, 19). (Arkæologiska undersökningar Skrifter, No. 24). Stockholm: Riksantikvarieämbetet.

Lundström, A. (ed.)
1988   Thirteen Studies on Helgö. (Statens Historiska Museum. Studies 7).
            Stockholm: Statens Historiska Museum.
Løken, T.
1987   The Settlement at Forsandmoen - an Iron Age Village in Rogaland,
            SW-Norway. Studien zur Sachsenforschung 6: 155-168.
1988   Forsandmoen - et samfunn i blomstring og krise. In Folkevandringstiden i
            Norden. En krisetid mellem ældre og yngre jernalder. U. Näsman & J. Lund
            (eds.), pp. 169-186. Århus: Universitetsforlag.
Magnus, B.
1974   Fisker eller bonde? Undersøkelser av hustufter på ytterkysten. Viking 37: 68-109.
1983   Seterdrift i Vest-Norge i yngre jernalder? Foreløpig rapport fra en
            undersøkelse. In Hus, gård och bebyggelse. G. Olafsson (ed.), pp. 93-103.
            Föredrag från det XVI nordiska arkeologmötet, Island 1982. Reykjavík:
            Þjóðminjasafn Íslands.
1985   Bygda, fjorden och fjellet. Systrond i nær og fjern fortid. Utstillingskatalog.
            Bergen: Historisk Museum.
1990   Om våre forfedres syn på landskapet. In Kulturminnevernets teori og
            metode. Status 1989 og veien videre. Seminarrapport. NAVFs program for
            forskning om kulturminnevern, pp. 160-172. Oslo: Norges almenviten-
            skapelige forskningsråd.
Mahler, D. L .D.
1989   Argisbrekka: Nye spor efter sæterdrift på Færøerne. Hikuin 15: 147-170.
1993   Shielings and their role in the Viking-Age economy. New evidence from the
            Faroe Islands. In The Viking Age in Caithness, Orkney and the North
            Atlantic. C. Batey, J. Jesch & C. Morris (eds.), pp. 487-505. Edinburgh:
            Edinburgh University Press.
Martens, I.
1987   Iron Extraction, Settlement and Trade in the Viking and Early Middle Ages
            in South Norway. In Proceedings of the Tenth Viking Congress, Larkollen,
            Norway, 1985. J. Knirk (ed.) pp.69-80. (Universitetets Oldsaksamlings
            skrifter, Ny rekke 9). Oslo: Universitetets Oldsaksamlings
1995   Deltidsspesialist og utkantbonde. Presentasjon av et forskningsprosjekt. In
            Produksjon og samfunn: om erverv, spesialisering og bosetning i Norden i
            1. Årtusen e. Kr. H. G. Resi (ed.), pp. 180-182. (Varia 30). Oslo:
            Universitetets Oldsaksamling.
Munch, G. S., et al.
1986   A chieftain's farm at Borg, Lofoten, N. Norway. Medieval Archaeology 30:
            88-90
1988   Borg in Lofoten. Norwegian Archaeological Review 21: 119-126.
Myhre, B.
1972   Funn, fornminner og ødegårder: jernalderens bosetning i Høyland
            Fjellbygd. (Stavanger Museums Skrifter 7). Stavanger Museum.
1978   Agrarian development, settlement history and social organization in South
            West Norway in the Iron Age. In New Directions in Scandinavian
            Archaeology. K. Kristiansen & C. Paludan-Müller (eds.), pp. 225-272.
            (Studies in Scandinavian Prehistory and History, 1). Copenhagen:
            Nationalmuseet.
1982   Bolighusets utvikling fra jernalder til middelalder i Sørvest-Norge. In
            Vestnordisk bygeskikk gjennom to tusen år. B. Myhre, B. Stoklund &
            P. Gjærder (eds.), pp. 195-217. (AmS Skrifter 7). Stavanger: Arkeologisk
            Museum i Stavanger.

1985 Boathouses as indicators of political organization. *Norwegian Archaeological Review* 18 (1-2: 36-60).
1987 Chieftains' graves and chiefdom territories in South Norway in the Migration Period. *Studien zur Sachsenforschung* 6: 169-187.
1988 "Materielt som åndelig i pakt med tida". In *Festskrift til Anders Hagen*. S. Indrelid *et al.* (eds.), pp. 310-324. (Arkeologiske Skrifter fra Historisk Museum, No. 4). Bergen: Universitetet i Bergen.

Näsman, U.
1988 Den folkvandringstida krisen i Sydskandinavien, inklusive Öland och Gotland. In *Folkevandringstiden i Norden. En krisetid mellem ældre og yngre jernalder*. U. Näsman & J. Lund (eds.), pp. 227-255. Århus: Universitetsforlaget.
1997 Strategies and tactics in Migration period defence. In *Military Aspects of Scandinavian Society in a European Perspective, AD 1-1300*. A. Nørgård Jørgensen & B. L. Clausen (eds.), pp. 146-155. Copenhagen: Nationalmuseet.

Näsman, U., & J. Lund (eds.)
1988 *Folkevandringstiden i Norden. En krisetid mellem ældre og yngre jernalder*. Århus: Århus universitetsforlag.

Nielsen, L. C.
1980 Omgård. A settlement from the Late Iron Age and the Viking Period in West Jutland. *Acta Archaeologica* 50 (1979): 173-208.

Nordahl, E.
1993 Södra Kungsgårdsplatån: utgrävningarna 1988-1991. In *Arkeologi och miljögeologi i Gamla Uppsala*, vol. I. W. Duczko (ed.), pp. 59-63. (OPIA 7). Uppsala: Department of Archaeology.

Odelman, E. (trans.), A. Ekenberg *et al.* (comm.s)
1986 *Boken om Ansgar*. (Skrifter utg. av Samfundet Pro fide et christianismo 10). Stockholm: Proprius.

Olausson, M.
1997 Fortified manors during the Migration period in eastern middle Sweden. In *Military Aspects of Scandinavian Society in a European Perspective, AD 1–1300*. A. Nørgård Jørgensen & B. L. Clausen (eds.), pp. 157-168. Copenhagen: Nationalmuseet.

Olsen, M.
1926 *Ættegård og helligdom. Norske stedsnavn sosialt og religionshistorisk belyst*. (Instituttet for sammenlignende Kulturforskning, Serie A, Forelesninger; 9a). Oslo: Instituttet for sammenlignende Kulturforskning.

Opedal, A.
1999 *Arkeologiens gårdsforskning og utformingen av norsk identitet*. (AmS Varia, 35). Stavanger: Arkeologisk museum i Stavanger.

Pedersen, E. A., & M. Widgren
1998 Järnålder 500 f.Kr. - 1000 e.Kr. In *Det svenska jordbrukets historia. Jordbrukets første år*. J. Myrdal (ed.), pp. 239-459. Stockholm: Natur och kultur/LTs förlag.

Ramqvist, P.
1987 Mellannorrland under äldre järnålder. Några aspekter på samhällsstrukturen. *Bebyggelsehistorisk tidskrift* 14: 105-126.

Roesdahl, E.
1987 The Danish geometrical Viking fortresses and their context. *Anglo-Norman Studies* 9: 208-226.

Roesdahl, E., & U. Näsman
1993   Yngre germansk jernalder og vikingetid. In *Da Klinger i Muld... 25 års arkæologi i Danmark*. S. Hvass & B. Storgaard (eds.), pp. 181-186. Copenhagen: Det Kgl. Nordiske Oldskriftselskab, Jysk Arkæologisk Selskab.

Schanche, A.
1989   Jernalderens bosetningsmønster i et fleretnisk perspektiv. In *Framskritt for fortida i nord. I Povl Simonsens fotefar*. R. Bertelsen et al. (eds.), pp. 171-183. (Tromsø Museums Skrifter, XXII). Tromsø: Tromsø Museum.

Schietzel, K.
1981   *Berichte über die Ausgrabungen in Haithabu*. Vol.16. Neumünster: Karl Wachholtz Verlag.

Skre, D.
1998   *Herredømmet: Bosetning og besittelse på Romerike 200-1350 e. Kr*. Oslo: Scandinavian University Press.

Sognnes, K.
1979   *Arkeologiske modeller for Vestlandets vikingtid*. (Gunneria, 34). Trondheim: Det Kgl. norske videnskabers selskap. Muséet.

Stibéus, M.
1997   Medieval coastal settlement in Western Sweden. In *Visions of the Past. Trends and Traditions in Swedish Medieval Archaeology*. H. Andersson, P. Carelli & L. Ersgård (eds.), pp. 513-538. (Lund Studies in Medieval Archaeology 19. Riksantikvarieämbetet Arkeologiska Undersökningar Skrifter 24). Stockholm: Central Board of Antiquities, Institute of Archaeology, University of Lund.

Stoumann, I.
1980   Sædding. A Viking Age village near Esbjerg. *Acta Archaeologica* 50 (1979): 95-118.

Strid, J. P.
1999   *Kulturlandskapets språklige dimension: ortnammen*. Stockholm: Riksantikvarieämbetet.

Tesch, S.
1992   House, farm and village in the Köping area from Early Neolithic to the Early Middle Ages. In *The Archaeology of Cultural Landscape*. L. Larsson et al. (eds.), pp. 283-344. (Acta Archaeologica Lundensia, Series in 4°, no. 19). Stockholm: Almqvist & Wiksell.

1993   *Houses, Farmsteads and Long-term Change. A Regional Study of Prehistoric Settlements in the Köping Area in Scania, South Sweden*. Uppsala: Dept. of Archaeology, Uppsala University.

Thomasson, J.
1998   Domus terrae Scania. In *Centrala platser - Centrala frågor*. (Uppåkra studier 1). L. Larsson & B. Hårdh (eds.), pp. 73-94. (Acta Archaeologica Lundensia, Series in 8°, No. 28). Lund: Almqvist & Wiksell International.

Thrane, H.
1991   Om Gudmes funktion. In *Samfundsorganisation og regional variation*. C. Fabech & J. Ringtved (eds.), pp. 259-267. (Jysk Arkæologisk Selskabs Skrifter, XXVII). Århus: Jysk Arkæologisk Selskab.

1998   Overvejelser af kultindholdet i Gudmes bebyggelse. In *Centrala platser - Centrala frågor*. (Uppåkra studier 1). L. Larsson & B. Hårdh (eds.), pp. 249-261. (Acta Archaeologica Lundensia, Series in 8°, No. 28). Lund: Almqvist & Wiksell International.

Torbjerg, S. Å.
1998   Toftegård - en fundrig gård fra sen jernalder og vikingetid. In *Centrala platser - Centrala frågor*. (Uppåkra studier 1). L. Larsson & B. Hårdh (eds.), pp. 217-232. (Acta Archaeologica Lundensia, Series in 8°, No. 28). Lund: Almqvist & Wiksell International.
Trillmich, T., & R. Buchner (eds.)
1978   *Quellen des 9. und 11. Jahrhunderts zur Geschichte der hamburgischen Kirche und des Reiches*. Ausgewählte Quellen zur deutschen Geschichte des Mittelalters. Freiherr vom Stein-Gedächtnisausgabe, Band XI. R. Buchner (ed.). Darmstadt: Wissenschaftliche Buchgesellschaft.
Watt, M.
1991   Sorte Muld. Høvdingesæde og kultcentrum fra Bornholms yngre jernalder. In *Høvdingesamfund og kongemagt. Fra stamme til stat i Danmark 2*. P. Mortensen & B. M. Rasmussen (eds.), pp. 89-107. (Jysk Arkæologisk Selskabs Skrifter, XXII:2). Århus: Jysk Arkæologisk Selskab.
Widgren, M.
1983   *Settlement and Farming Systems in the Early Iron Age: A Study of Fossil Agrarian Landscapes in Östergötland, Sweden*. (Stockholm Studies in Human Geography, 3). Stockholm: Almqvist & Wiksell International.
1988   Om skillnader och likheter mellan regioner. In *Folkevandringstiden i Norden. En krisetid mellem ældre og yngre jernalder*. U. Näsman & J. Lund (eds.), pp. 273-287. Århus: Universitetsforlaget.
1998   Kulturgeografernas bönder och arkeologernas guld–finns det någon väg till syntes? In *Centrala platser - Centrala frågor. Samhällsstrukturen under järnåldern*. (Uppåkra studier 1). L. Larson & B. Hårdh (eds.), pp. 281-296. (Acta Archaeologica Lundensia, Series in 8°, No. 28). Lund: Almquist & Wiksell International.
Zachrisson, I.
1994   Saamis and Scandinavians - examples of interaction. In *Developments around the Baltic and the North Sea in the Viking Age*. B. Ambrosiani & H. Clarke (eds.), pp. 173-179. The Twelfth Viking Congress. Birka Studies 3. Stockholm: Central Board of Antiquities a Statens Historiska Museum.
1997   *Möten i gränsland. Samer och germaner i Mellanskandinavien*. Statens Historiska Museum Monographs 4. Stockholm: Statens Historiska Museum.
Zachrisson, T.
1994   The odal and its manifestation in the landscape. *Current Swedish Archaeology* 2: 219-238.

Discussion

BRINK: You are citing Magnus Olsen (page 5) and one could believe that nothing happened before Magnus Olsen. A very long history much discussed. When you talk about these matters it is especially from the Norwegian point of view, and it is impossible to get away from Magnus Olsen who set up the theoretical framework that we followed. If it is outdated today we have to return to previous models.

GREEN: I have difficulties when you are talking about Asgard and Midgard (page 8) as farms. The Germanic term *garð* has a wide semantic spectrum of meanings, 'fence', 'yard', 'farm', 'court', 'house', 'stronghold', 'domain'. Because of that I think it is linguistically very tricky to restrict the meaning of this word in this context arbitrarily to one stage in its semantic development. That is a question of principle.

MAGNUS: I feel that especially in view of what was said during the discussion of the fisher-farmers, that you could have farms where no cereals would ripen, you would keep cattle because, since these farms were located at high altitudes, there was plenty of grazing land. So, there is something about a farm and the land belonging to it which is essential, in my opinion, to the growing population of Scandinavia.

GREEN: I don't deny that. I question the application of that terminology and the concept it carries to Asgard and Midgard.

BRINK: But that is socially correct. Professor Green all this is what every young archaeologist, especially in Sweden, is writing about, i.e. what we are discussing: Scandinavia as a society.

AUSENDA: How far south of present-day Saami settlements (page 9) were those in the third century?

ARRHENIUS: We only know they were the closest neighbours to the Svear, so they could have been as far south as Uppland.

AUSENDA: Does that mean that before the Indo-European migrations the Saami populated all of the Scandinavian peninsula?

MAGNUS: We don't know.

HERSCHEND: All we know is that the Saami seem to have been there first.

ARRHENIUS: On this subject we must be very careful with the research. Officially the Saami people are what we call 'indigenous', and they have the official status of being the oldest settlers, but we still don't know these things well and there are a lot of problems in all the sources. So I think we must be very careful not to say anything before we have much more evidence.

BRINK: And different sources and place-names. We have in the north of the area absolutely no traces of Saami place-names. In other areas there are hybrids and so forth. There are many problems with them, so the correct answer is: "We just don't know".

DUMVILLE: Now you suffer the problems about the questions of terminology. Can you describe what a 'Viking chiefdom' is (page 9)? (Laughter).

MAGNUS: The way of avoiding the term 'kingdom'.

DUMVILLE: Yes, but what about the word 'viking'. This is a purely chronological marker?

MAGNUS: We don't know the social position of Ohthere, but at least he was a chieftain having both power to extract tribute from the Saamis and wealth to have a large ship built to sail to England.

DUMVILLE: You are using the word 'viking' for purely chronological purposes.

MAGNUS: Yes.

GREEN: You use the term 'semi-nomadic' (page 9). From my Germanistic angle concerned with relationships between language and history, I use terminology, such as 'nomadic', 'migratory' and 'settled'. Do you mean 'semi-nomadic' as the equivalent of what I call 'migratory'?

MAGNUS: The Saami population were moving during the summer season between their permanent winter dwelling sites and their summer dwelling sites to exploit different kinds of resources.

GREEN: So that is different then from 'migratory'.

MAGNUS: Yes.

GREEN: Migratory would be a tribe on the move, but settling whenever it can for as long a period as it can. And then perhaps forced to migrate further.

MAGNUS: They are not 'migratory', they are moving between summer and winter settlements. What would you call that?

GREEN: I would accept semi-nomadic in that case. I wanted to know what you meant.

ARRHENIUS: It would be good to have special names for this kind of nomadism.

VESTERGAARD: There are various technical terms. In the Middle East, you have corporate groups and social organization in the winter encampments, and during summer they diperse to the available pastures at some distance from their winter quarters. That would be semi-nomadic.

NIELSEN: In the Middle East according to anthropological knowledge, nomads had to interact with settlements; this is important because it is not the case here. According to anthropology it is a symbiotic relationship.

ARRHENIUS: And here there is no such relationship. It is only that they had to draw their livelihood from a nomadic existence.

BRINK: Transhumance.

MAGNUS: But they did interact with the permanent settled agrarian populations on the coast of northern Norway and also traded with them. If Ohthere's information to King Alfred is right, there must have been special places where they assembled to exchange goods and where chieftains like Ohthere collected tribute. Because these are vast regions.

HERSCHEND: Ohthere was a settled peasant. He was a high status peasant.

GREEN: You talk about interdisciplinary work between the Saami and Germanic. Has anything been done on linguistic interaction between Saami and Germanic?

MAGNUS: The publication I refer to, edited by Inger Zachrisson, is an interdisciplinary work where those linguistic problems are discussed.

MEULENGRACHT: The linguistic aspect of this relationship has been studied since the nineteenth century, and it is very much clarified in the loanwords.

AUSENDA: Could the Migration period crisis (page 12) be due to the decline in the purchasing power of the Roman empire?

VOICES: Yes, yes.

MAGNUS: There are many components but that could be one, yes.

GREEN: Was there a provision, such as a stone chimney to decrease the risk of fires? You mention (in the original draft) a spark-arrester; can you describe one?

MAGNUS: This in is an interpretation that has been put forward mostly by Per Ramqvist on the basis of burnt clay from remains of burnt down Iron Age buildings, with imprints of wooden construction details on the fragments of burnt clay. He maintained that the clay fragments found over the fire-place must belong to a 'spark arrester' or some sort of hood above the fire-place.

AUSENDA: Is there a reconstruction?

MAGNUS: Not that I know of.

HERSCHEND: But there is another one from the Iron Age where the hearth is below a burnt clay layer, actually a square frame, which reminds one of what it looked like in historical times in the Baltic, where above the hearth there was a square frame, a dome with a clay layer.

ARRHENIUS: Have you had a look at the dating? Is it quite clear?

HERSCHEND: From the house type in that region the houses built are pre-Roman with an insulating wall which doesn't carry the weight of the roof.

NIELSEN: About settlement history in northern Sweden. I don't understand your point because you write here that the Gene longhouse was abandoned in the sixth century, and there was an earlier longhouse, when did that start? The second century AD or later?

HERSCHEND: It gave such ancient dating, due to the fact that posts were dated, but when this farm was made there was a virgin forest. I mean that the trunks were pine and they divided them into four parts and cut away in round pieces, and then they burnt the posts in order to get them charred so they would keep better. So, when you date that, you have the possibility that you get a date which is more than 300 years older than the actual house, that is some 80% of the period. When they dated the house, they got obviously fourth century, so that's the correct date, I think. Dating the posts gives you 300 years too ancient. It is very common when you cut down virgin forest.

NIELSEN: I think that there would be periods where the site was deserted. I mean, experience shows that such a post buried into the ground might last only one or two generations. Of course, if you char it, it lasts longer, but still I think 200 or 300 years is too long.

HERSCHEND: That is not correct, they have been rebuilt and moved twice in the long direction. It is not an unreasonable thing to say that they started in the late fourth century and ended in the middle of the fifth.

BRINK: That is the problem, and it was not published.

HERSCHEND: No, it looks exactly like the Gene house, excavated and published by Per Ramqvist (1985) and you could put it in above it, and there also the posts give you fourth century due to the fact that there are such dense ancient woods.

BRINK: With reference to 'single farms', 'composite farms', 'villages': you touch upon a very big problem under discussion which is so important. Because as you know, the older view is that they were single farms, that was Olsen's theoretical framework.

ARRHENIUS: It is very important to mention the regions here, because it is different in different regions and I think we must recognize that. You cannot talk about the whole of Scandinavia.

HERSCHEND: The old hypothesis is that archaeological material cannot lie because it is just artefacts. I think it can lie. The Iron Age is a very typical period where they actually display things that aren't true. We were too naive about history.

LUND: We recognize that to the extent archaeological data can speak, they can lie.

HERSCHEND: I did mention that new large farms in Jutland (page 13) that are single farms start somewhere in the sixth century. What about saying that they are the result of the Danes occupying Jutland? What do you think of that? Are there migrations within Scandinavia, the Franks crossing the Rhine, or the Danes crossing the sea?

MAGNUS: They could have migrated somewhere else within Scandinavia, of course they could.

HERSCHEND: That is what anthropologists think. You mentioned that that could have occurred long before and that they are much earlier than what would have been nuclear Danish territory, Zealand and Scania. But they are unknown until the sixth century, and they actually come in the new large farms settled outside the villages. It is a typical phenomenon.

MAGNUS: Internal migration, which you mentioned, an interesting problem. Internal migration from SW Norway to N Norway in the fourth, fifth, and possibly even in the sixth century has been postulated by several late Norwegian scholars like Gjessing, Petersen, and Sjøvold.

BENDER: When do the house types appear? What is the basis for this house typology? You theorize on the development in Denmark based on a reference to Steen Hvass, the excavator of Vorbasse. This site is very central to the unravelling of house typologies. Steen Hvass has published his house typology, but the arguments behind it have never been published yet. And I would like to see them. In western Sweden house types don't fit quite into the Danish house typology. I think we have to do a bit more work to get the arguments published and not only the typology.

MAGNUS: I think you are perfectly right there and, as I say at the beginning of my paper, I used it deliberately as a sort of starting point to discuss these differences in other regions.

HOLMQUIST: I have a short comment about houses from the Viking Age in Central Sweden, you have mentioned two of them (page 16). I think it is important to point out that there are very few Viking Age houses, excavated in Central Sweden, five houses in all. So our knowledge is not so great.

HERSCHEND: Going back to the later Iron Age I think that the ideological centres in society clearly departed from trade centres (page 16). Like the Romans, the upper classes and the aristocracy in Scandinavian countries did not find trade interesting so they deliberately moved the trading places off the premises of the essential settlements. Not until the late eighth century can we actually say that there is a sort of cohabitation between these and some sort of production and the hall buildings. And I think that the essential point is that when trade is somewhat more developed it needs some sort of contract idea, and it is much more effective if you believe in contracts. And I think that is the whole idea that in the early Iron Age they did not enter into contracts in this way without obligations into the future and that's where the ideological problem actually creates the situation where they have both settled contracts and trade contracts.

MAGNUS: What do you base that on apart from your opinion?

HERSCHEND: Oh well, I would base that on expectation, of course. But I think it is an essential point to see the possibility of that model.

BRINK: You discuss trading places, central places, and so forth. And as Frands [Herschend] just said, the only cause for you to separate these, is only because you decided to see them that way. For example, on page 20 you discuss Kaupang in Norway, a place which has been excavated. They have found lots of interesting things. Therefore, it becomes very important for archaeologists, and Kaupang could be the example in this picture. A couple of hundred metres north of it there is a place called Huseby. I think it is impossible in my work to separate Huseby from Kaupang, and therefore if you look at all these trading places you will find these complexes, again and again and again. So, they are linked to each other in some way.

MAGNUS: Yes, what you are talking about is the port or trading place on the coast and the main farm with a hall further inland.

BRINK: Yes, it constitutes a complex. It is a complex during the Iron Age and then, later on, you can have the same situation again and again in southern Scandinavia. If you read archaeological literature, they are discussing places where they excavated and especially for recent years they are discussing places that have been excavated because of exploitation. Taking in different kinds of sources perhaps we can be better off. For instance, if one includes archaeology and place-names, one can see that these complexes become very eminent during the Iron Age.

MAGNUS: You mean that this is a pattern?

BRINK: I take it that it is in Denmark, in southern Sweden and in Norway.

DUMVILLE: How do cod fisheries provide a basis for the establishment of a chiefdom or a petty kingdom (page 17).

MAGNUS: I have done that on the basis of very thorough investigations which were carried out by Dr. Johansen for years in the region of Vestvågøy in the Lofoten Islands. He was able to show that there are several types of ancient monuments from the Iron Age on the island, deserted farms and boat houses, burial mounds and court sites (O. S. Johansen 1979). On a promontory at Borg, in the middle of the island, the remains of this enormous house were excavated by an international team *ca* 15 years ago. Nobody expected to find a settlement of this kind so close to the Arctic circle: there is good grazing for sheep and cattle but not enough warm days for growing barley or other cereals even if the Atlantic climate is fairly mild. Since the cod fisheries were so important in Lofoten from the early Middle Ages, Johansen maintained that they had been important even in the Viking Age and could have been one of the reasons for a centre like Borg with its building more than 80 m long, with cattle and people under the same roof, and exceptional archaeological finds of gold foils and sherds of various goblets of decorated glass.

DUMVILLE: So, in essence, the dating range is established archaeologically and there is nothing there before the seventh century.

MAGNUS: Between the seventh and tenth centuries.

DUMVILLE: Oh, we are in the period where there is major transition.

MAGNUS: Yes, there is a rise in activities, the large boat houses and the house being rebuilt. The interesting thing is that the house is not Norwegian at all. It is an exact Jutish house [laughter]. Yes, built in a very typical southern Scandinavian way. With a central entrance into the living quarters and right into the byres. In middle Scandinavia you go diagonally into the house. There were two entrances, one to the byre and one to the living quarters. And there are several hundreds of examples of that.

DUMVILLE: And what conclusion does one draw from that?

MAGNUS: It gave them higher status to build a house of a different kind than other powerful men in that northern part of the country.

HERSCHEND: The byre is exactly how Ohthere described it. It has room for 40 cattle.

MAGNUS: Ohthere says that he is living further north than any other Norwegian, but he doesn't say anything about his hall.

MEULENGRACHT: You mentioned (page 17) Borg as a central place for the region having "cult" and "military power". Yes, you or Gerd Stamsø Munch are probably right about cult in Borg (1991). The hypothesis is very much based on the *guldgubber* found in a post-hole.

MAGNUS: Well, I don't feel any more comfortable with that than you do.

MEULENGRACHT: I don't feel comfortable about it because it may be a proof of ritual activities but not of being a centre of cult: two different things.

MAGNUS: Yes, but they have been found in post-holes at other sites.

ARRHENIUS: Yes, but I don't think that all places where you find *guldgubber* are cult centres, but I think that when you have 2,000 and more *guldgubber* in a place, as at Sorte Muld, Bornholm, then you might think of a cult centre.

MAGNUS: It has to do with their number.

MEULENGRACHT: It has to do with the post-holes. You seem to build this hypothesis on the place-name 'borg'.

MAGNUS: No, also on the evidence of the so-called 'court sites'. Johansen interprets these court sites as some sort of military garrisons.

MEULENGRACHT: Anyway, you say 'borg' is a fortress.

MAGNUS: No, just what I tried to say. I tried to link it to the rest of the ancient monuments but also to the very place of the longhouse at Borg. It is lying there on this sort of promontory in the landscape.

MEULENGRACHT: A sensible farmer would never have built his farm on that place. But why is it on this small hill? Certainly not as big as San Marino. Is it easy to defend this place? There are other explanations, if this is in a central farm—I think you are right there—then this is also a question of honour, you want to live high if you have a high status. So, if I have to put this as a question, are there any signs of fortifications?

MAGNUS: No, none whatsoever.

GREEN: You make reference (page 21) to the hall at Lejre now being equated with the hall of Heorot in *Beowulf*. Is there any comparative research linking archaeological with linguistic and literary evidence?

HERSCHEND: There is a big difference. When Beowulf enters Heorot, he is directly in the hall. If he entered a longhouse, he would be still in an anteroom.

GREEN: So you would not attempt the equation.

LUND: And the underwater archaeologists haven't found the place where Beowulf slew Grendel's mother [laughter]. I wonder whether we shouldn't be more cautious about how we use our evidence, they seem to serve too many purposes today. We don't know what the ring fortresses were. Sometimes they are garrisons, sometimes they are for administration.

MAGNUS: They were built for martial purposes.

LUND: Yes, but we don't know how long it served them.

MAGNUS: Two years [laughter].

LUND: We really don't know whether an artefact deposited in them, say thirty years after the time of construction, may have been brought there by squatters.

MAGNUS: Yes, that might be so. What I was after was the site that had been at least tentatively interpreted as a military site, where people lived for a short while.

LUND: Yes, but we cannot really use it for military purposes with one hand and for administrative purposes with the other.

MAGNUS: No, but if it had been used for military purposes and it had been been built for military purposes and used that way for a couple of years, then you have with one hand the military purpose and with the other hand something else which comes after it.

LUND: Yes, but as I read your text, you go along with the old garrison interpretation and use that as evidence of the military strength of the Danish kings at a time where really the original purpose had been forgotten and you are really into the next period of royal administration and not a garrison any more.

AUSENDA: Did Scandinavian societies have age grades?

MAGNUS: Yes they did. At age 12, when they were still boys they were given weapons and considered grown-up men.

AUSENDA: Did they have different terms for each grade and did they have initiations and so forth?

MEULENGRACHT: They probably had initiations.

AUSENDA: In fact age grades are widespread among 'military' societies.

ARRHENIUS: There is also evidence for them in archaeological grave finds.

AUSENDA: What is a shieling system (page 22)? Could you give a description of a shieling system? Is it a pasture or a shepherd's hut, or a cottage?

MAGNUS: It is transhumance. A very essential component of farming in the Scandinavian peninsula was to bring the cattle and sheep up into the woods or mountains to graze in the summer to lighten the pressure on meadows and pastures around the farms. The season lasted from after mid-summer until September, and each farm had one or more permanent cottages in a certain area with ample grazing. In the high mountain regions of West Norway, the walls of such buildings have been found often in groups and are chronologically covering a period from the late Migration period until the early Middle Ages. In certain Icelandic sagas it is said that women from the farm, often the farmer's wife and daughters, assisted by shepherds, were responsible for this part of the farming economy. From the eighteenth to the twentieth century, the administration of shielings, the animals and the production of butter and cheese was the responsibility of women of high status in the peasant society.

BRINK: And in the historical system there are vast regional differences and variations, every possible pattern.

AUSENDA: Would that be what in the Alps they call 'alpeggio', where in the summertime the families go up to the mountains where they have houses and cow sheds. The men make cheese and the cattle graze on the high pastures.

MAGNUS: Not quite, but something similar.

BRINK: Geographers dealing with Scandinavia use the Norwegian term *seter* in scholarly papers.

AUSENDA: There was a considerable export of stockfish (page 23) to central and southern Europe, which warranted an expansion of maritime occupations. When did that happen?

MAGNUS: The production of stockfish, which is a North Norwegian phenomenon, started sometime in the early Middle Ages or probably in the late Viking Age.

HERSCHEND: There are osteological samples from the twelfth century where cod is found, never the heads, just the spines. And those are large deposits.

AUSENDA: At a previous seminar Sven Schütte said (1995:167, 170) that in Cologne they had stockfish in the late sixth century, and it must have come from Scandinavia.

ARRHENIUS: Olav Sverre Johansen thought (pers. comm.) that this trade started much earlier than the twelfth century, as a matter of fact in the Merovingian period, and then there is a doctoral thesis about fishing along the east coast.

MAGNUS: The trade in stockfish developed, among other things, because of a growing European demand for fish in connection whith the Christian Church's rules for fasting in addition to a general development of trade.

ARRHENIUS: Yes, but there was trade also earlier.

AUSENDA: Is there any substantiation of early deep-sea fishing in Scandinavia (page 23), in the sense of boats or settlements close to the sea? In fact, my experience along the east coast of Sudan is that cattle and other livestock-raising populations seldom go fishing. This is because, in the absence of a market economy, cattle and land represent a capital investment, whereas fishing equipment might not.

MAGNUS: Well, it is different from Sudan. A fishing boat (or a ship) was a major investment and so was fishing tackle. The Scandinavian agrarian population which lived on the coast, along the fiords or on islands were dependent on their boats. But their life was based on agriculture and husbandry. In North Norway the agrarian population had fewer animals and smaller fields where cereals hardly would ripen even during a good summer. Their living was to a larger degree dependent on the outcome of the sea. In modern times they have been called 'fiskebønder' (fishing farmers).

ARRHENIUS: It is all discussed when we talk about the neolithic immigration into Scandinavia. The analysis which has gone on shows that for these so-called farmers one of the main food sources was fish. So farming was an extra luxury, and not the main subsistence strategy. This seems to develop all over Scandinavia.

MAGNUS: The men went out to fish or hunt sea mammals, the women did the rest of the work. They did the farming, looked after the cattle, looked after children and did their household chores. So the women were the farmers and the men the fishers.

HERSCHEND: Bente [Magnus] was referring to the Norwegian northwest coast where there is a special thing called 'farm-mounds', small 'tells' resulting from the accumulation through the centuries of refuse from fisheries, household rubbish, building activities, etc.

MAGNUS: The farm mounds (or middens) are found along the northwest coast of Norway, and the majority belong to the late Viking Age, and the Middle Ages when the large scale fisheries led to the abandonment of agriculture. Husbandry was still important, though, but the dung from the stalled animals was not used for manuring the fields but was left in heaps around the houses.

JESCH: This idea of the élite farmers you are describing (page 24), people who are farmers, but are better than other top peasants, I think there is some support from other kinds of evidence here. A word which has been much discussed, it is another one of these words that is difficult to translate, the word *þegn* used in Danish runic inscriptions I do think describes exactly this class, and I think there is evidence for that in skaldic poetry as well. Probably the people who call themselves *þegn* or are called *þegn* on Danish rune stones are precisely powerful people with some kind of local power, and a strong interest in genealogy, in land and I don't know whether I can go any further than that. So I think that is something that could be profitably developed in an interdisciplinary way.

BRINK: Mats Widgren stressed that our ancient society was a stratified society (1995, 1998). So the idea that more or less free farmers existed has not been on the agenda. However, we should not forget free farmers on the Scandinavian scene.

MEULENGRACHT: It is very important when we discuss these things to be sure of what we mean. Equality and freedom are two different things. Freedom doesn't mean freedom in our modern sense. You can be economically free or politically free, but to be free is also to have a certain personal integrity, and on that level you can talk about free people, free farmers, in opposition to slaves. To be free in this sense has nothing to do with social or economic status in Viking or early medieval times, and it is not the same as to be equal.

MAGNUS: I know that. That is a difficult problem, especially when discussed from an archaeological point of view.

BRINK: However, there are also independent farmers. Skre is dealing with Romerike, one of the central areas in Norway, and Dagfinn agrees that if we go to other more peripheral areas there are independent farmers.

MEULENGRACHT: You can be free but not independent, for example.

LUND: Well, I think that we can throw some light on this question of the peasants and the size of their holdings, as well as their freedom, from a Danish point of view. It is at the centre of a dispute I am involved in about the character of Danish military obligation. They used to be interpreted as a peasant system, a system devised for the peasants. The question is what were these peasants? And we look at them from the time when we get evidence for them, that is the thirteenth century. But some evidence is emerging now that they were, what we could call exactly *þegnar*, large landholders, squires, if you like, in English, who held estates that were later divided into seven, eight, ten little villages. So, if you had a peasant *leiðangr*, as we call it, in the early eleventh century, it would consist of that sort of peasant. If you had a peasant *leiðangr* in the thirteenth century, it would consist of peasants who held much less; the villages had by then been split up, but only those who still held land on old type estates would go on serving personally and would now become, or continue to be, thanes in a more modern sense of the word. While the others would have to go Dutch to come up with even one member of the army. I think when we are talking about their freedom, a free man was somebody who would appear for himself in court, all those who depended on him could not, they needed his protection and they might at this stage, at the early stage, have been all those who inherited the land and became leaders. I shall return to that when we come to talk about slavery.

JESCH: Am I right in thinking that what you call a 'court site' (page 24) is a translation of *tunanlegg*?

MAGNUS: Yes.

JESCH: Could I please then suggest some Norwegian linguistic imperialism here and suggest you keep the term *tunanlegg*? Because 'court site' has the wrong connotation and it is a very misleading term. Use 'courtyard site' if you must.

GREEN: Your mention of freedom and protection in your last sentence (page 25) reminds me of the etymology of the word 'free', connected with the word *fridu* which we translate as peace, but its original meaning was 'peace guaranteed by protection' rather than simply 'peace'. So that freedom and protection go together linguistically too.

MEULENGRACHT: But the crucial word may be *helgi*, the Old Norse word that means 'to have one's integrity' and nobody is allowed to attack you or to offend you and that goes for many more people than those farmers. And in the laws this was the right secured by everyone except slaves.

VESTERGAARD: And this holds true with regards to the earlier discussion. Does it have to be either yeomen or élite farmers, as the combination of both together might constitute the basic social structure.

References in the discussion

Textual sources:

Beowulf: see Klaeber (ed.) 1941.

Bibliography:

Hvass, S.
1993   Bebyggelsen. In *Da klinger i muld... 25 års arkeologi i Danmark*. S. Hvass
              & B. Storgaard (eds.), pp. 187-194. Aarhus: Aarhus Universitetsforlag.
Johansen, O. S.
1979   Jernaldergårder i Nord-Norge. In *På leiting etter den eldste garden*.
              R. Fladby & J. Sandnes (eds.), pp. 95-115. Oslo: Universitetsforlaget.
Klaeber, F. (ed.)
1941   *Beowulf and the Fight at Finnsburg*. New York: Heath.
Munch, G. S.
1991   Hus og hall. En høvdinggård på Borg i Lofoten. In *Nordisk Hedendom*.
              (Et symposium). G. Steinsland *et al.* (eds.), pp. 321-333. Odense: Odense
              Universitetsforlag.
Ramqvist, P.
1985   See References at end of paper.
Schütte, S.
1995   Continuity problems and authority structures in Cologne. In *After Empire:
              Towards an Ethnology of Europe's Barbarians*. G. Ausenda (ed.),
              pp. 163-175. Woodbridge: The Boydell Press.
Skre, D.
1998   See References at end of paper.
Widgren, M.
1995   Individuellt eller kollektivt ägande i bondesamhällen? In *Äganderätten i
              lantbrukets historia*. M. Widgren (ed.), pp. - 5-16 Stockolm: Nordiska
              museets förlag.
1998   See References at end of paper.
Zachrisson, I.
1994   See References at end of paper.

KINSHIP AND SOCIAL RELATIONS IN THE EARLY MEDIEVAL PERIOD IN SVEALAND ELUCIDATED BY DNA

BIRGIT ARRHENIUS

The Archaeological Research Laboratory, Greenska Villan, Stockholm University, S-106 91 Stockholm

Cemeteries with non-cremated boat graves have long been known from central Sweden and have been seen as emanating from leading families connected to the royal dynasty of the Svear in Uppsala, the so-called *Ynglingar*. Most recently Bengt Schönbäck (in Nylén & Schönbäck 1994) has discussed these graves and emphasized their symbolism as a dynastic manifestation of a cult attached to Freyr/Freyia. He also claimed that the boat graves were the graves for the ruling persons, men or women, in each generation. The dynastic manifestation suggests that petty kingdoms in Svealand were hereditary. That there existed a hereditary right to land is a concept which has been discussed recently. Connected to this concept is the word *óðal* which means the inherited right to land property (cf. Zachrisson 1994). The occurrence of cemeteries close to the farmsteads where the ancestors were buried is one of the indications of an *óðal* right. The other one is, as noted by Stefan Brink in his paper, the ability to name five generations of forefathers (Brink, p. 103, this vol.). However, the second concept in inheritance, the right of the oldest son to be the head of the family and inherit the farm or estate, is not clear. This means that, even if the family right is accepted, the inheritance of a kingdom is not at all clear if there exist several sons. In Swedish medieval history we can follow fights between brothers right up to the seventeenth century and we can also note that this was a problem among the Franks as well as the Goths.

I think it is of importance to recognize the problem that the concept of the special rights of the oldest son seems not really to be a Germanic legal concept, but a Christian one. As long as the land was considered to be family property, it belonged to all the brothers and the unmarried sisters, whereas the married sisters were paid off with a dowry. In another paper I have tried to show that the gold bracteates were an important element in both dowries and morning gifts (Arrhenius 1992).

To examine the hypotheses of the development in Svealand the research programme SIV, Svealand in the Vendel and Viking periods: Settlement, Society and Power was started. The programme is a collaboration between the Institute of Archaeology in Uppsala and the Archaeological Research Laboratory in Stockholm led by professor Frands Herschend of Uppsala and myself (professor Birgit Arrhenius) in Stockholm with the help of 14 scientific collaborators. Within this programme a DNA project was initiated that included Dr. Kerstin Lidén, a biologist who graduated in archaeology, Anders Götherström, a graduate student in laboratory archaeology, and a few undergraduate students. The work has now gone on for five and a half years and given some results that I will discuss briefly here.

45

© C.I.R.O.S.S.
SAN MARINO (R.S.M.)

In the boat-grave cemetery at Tuna in Alsike (Arne 1934), with 12 boat graves, for both males and females, two male lineages could be observed (Götherström 2001:24). Here also a marker for a male relation to the Saami people was found (Götherström 2001:24). That means that one of the buried men had a Saami father. These results contradict the hypothesis that the boat graves were reserved for the ruling members of one selected family. The find of a Saami marker is not surprising considering that both Tacitus and Jordanes wrote about Saami people close to the Svear. Also, in the *Ynglinga saga,* a Saami woman is said to be the mother of the mythical king Visbur. It is quite natural that there was an intermingling of the two groups of people in a border zone, but the result obtained here, in which the father was a Saami, is of course not a result expected by those who contend that the boat graves were arranged for rulers from the Yngling dynasty. As has recently been argued by Svante Norr (1998), the *Ynglingar* were originally named *Scilfingas*, the name occurring in *Beowulf* (an idea often repeated in earlier research). That Skialf could be the ancestress is, I believe, extremely important. Skialf was possibly one name of Freyia (cf. Brate 1913, cf. also, however, Björkman 1919 who explains Skialf as a term meaning 'elevated') and I believe that Freyia was one of the most important goddesses in the early Germanic Iron Age in Svealand, and also on the continent, especially among the Langobards (cf. Näsström 1995). The boat graves, as well as the occurrence of huge button-on-bow brooches with garnets, too large to be worn by a normal woman, but otherwise corresponding to normal button-on-bow brooches are, according to my investigations, symbols of Freyia (Arrhenius 1997). These symbols can also be traced back to a late Roman cult of the goddess Isis where sacrifices of loaded boats as well as garnet jewellery are important items in the cult (cf. Arrhenius 1997 & 2001b).

Norr underlines in his work the role of counsel in the development of Germanic kingship. I think this structure also influenced the structure of families, where the authority of the *pater familias* was not as strong as we tend to believe. The role of women was stronger than in Roman culture and we, therefore, find both males and females in rich graves as well as in the boat graves. An example of this is the cemetery at Tuna in Badelunda, situated in a central region, close to the present town Västerås in Västmanland to the west of Uppland. The cemetery was found as a result of the building of a foundation for a cellar which was placed into a chamber grave from the later Roman Iron Age. The cemetery consists of 64 cremation graves, 5 chamber graves, and 8 boat graves. It seems to have been in continuous use from AD 300 until the eleventh century and the earliest dated graves are two boat graves from around 1050. With the duration of more than 700 years, the number of burials per generation is only about two (when it should at least have been three), indicating that the cemetery was arranged only for a selected part of the population. Some graves contain more than one person, and children are only found together with adults.

The osteological examination showed a dominance of males in the cremation graves whereas there was a total dominance of females in the boat graves. This, however, had to be determined from the grave goods, as the female skeletons were very fragmentary. However, the DNA analyses in the three cases examined could prove the assumption that graves with female grave-goods also contained females (Götherström *et al.* 2001a, table 1). With Schönbäck we might ask, are the rich female graves a typical trait for this cemetery, where this tradition can be followed back to 300 AD? However, one also should note that one cremation from the late Viking Age had rich contents belonging to a horseman.

Two of the boat graves which could be analysed with DNA (Götherström 2001a:4) appeared to be very closely related, either a mother and her daughter (or granddaughter) or two sisters. These two graves were richly equipped with beads and brooches. A remarkable brooch in the earliest grave was a garnet-inlaid button-on-bow brooch of the type I have mentioned above as especially attached to the cult of Freyia. In this case the brooch was very worn and had lost the button on the bow and only the 'crown' of the button, obviously mounted on a replacement made of organic material, was left. These high-value brooches are often found as antiquities, for example in Gotlandic finds of treasures from the Viking period. It is, however, of interest that the necklace with beads and the two small brooches seem to be of the same date as the brooch, i.e. the later Vendel period. The corpse was that of a young girl. In the other grave an old woman was buried with three brooches belonging to the early Viking Age and a splendid necklace with blue glass beads and millefiori beads, together with silver pendants made of copies of Arabic coins from around 750. The brooches and the necklace give a very fresh impression, as if they were newly made for the burial. This burial also contained a great number of wooden items among which a wooden goblet is especially remarkable. Schönbäck (in Nylén & Schönbäck 1994:36, 44) dates grave 35 with the young girl to the later eighth century whereas grave 75 should be dated to around 850. If we accept the new date of the beginning of the Viking period at around 750 and also a ^{14}C date, which when calibrated would come to the end of the eighth century, then I consider the graves to be very close to each other, perhaps more or less contemporary. It could easily be a mother and daughter, where the more prestigious mother got the new jewellery and the daughter the worn jewellery.

However, the boat-grave cemeteries of Vendel and Valsgärde in Uppland were the first to indicate that these graves might belong to ruling members of the Yngling dynasty. A characteristic trait in both Vendel and Valsgärde is that the boat graves are arranged only for men, equipped as warriors and horsemen. The female graves which occur in the same cemeteries are cremation graves. But, and this is of importance, male cremation graves also occur in these cemeteries. Finally, in Old Uppsala, undoubtedly the seat of the Yngling dynasty, the boat graves found there are for both females and males (Nordahl 2001), but the most important male graves are the large mounds, which are cremation graves.

Thus the picture of the boat graves as an exclusive burial mode for the ruling class is not at all as clear as is sometimes pretended. Early in my treatise on the boat graves, I underlined the possibility that these graves were sacrifices rather than graves (Arrhenius 1983).

How can one distinguish between ordinary graves and sacrifices? This is of course a question of judgement, easier to express than to prove. In my opinion a sacrifice is an action which is meant to be an event for a greater public, whereas a burial is primarily an event for the mourners, i.e. the family. Of course there is a difference when the deceased is a king, as the mourners in that case will be many more than only the close family. A sacrifice, however, has to exaggerate an event and, therefore, repetition is an important aspect which does not affect a burial. When I proposed that the boat graves were sacrifices rather than proper graves, it was based on the observation that the boat-grave cemeteries often show groups of graves, two or three that are more or less contemporary. In Vendel this is the case with Vendel grave X and XIV as well as XI and XII. In Valsgärde, it is especially graves 5-6, but grave 7 may also belong to the same group. In Tuna Alsike, Arne already had observed a certain contemporaneity in the Viking Age boat graves, having them in groups of three and even four (Arne 1934:71). Although there has to be some revision of the final dates in the boat-grave cemetery due to the more advanced Viking Age chronology we have today, I think that in the main Arne was right. This observation also fits well with the DNA analyses where a family of three could not be constructed but the groups within the cemetery had some kind of relations (Götherström 2001:23).

Another important trait in a sacrifice is the spectacle and here I see the boat-grave ceremony in itself as an event. We can note that both in Vendel and in Valsgärde the strait on which the boats were transported was clearly visible from the top of large mounds, in the case of Valsgärde from the mounds in Old Uppsala and in the case of Vendel from Ottar's mound. On the flat top of these mounds the people could gather and follow the boats on their way to the cemetery situated 2.5 km north of the mounds.

The new biological examinations, I think, also hint at a kind of sacrifice. If we look at these structures as sacrifices rather than graves, we get an explanation of why the bodies are so decayed, a typical trait for many of the boat graves that can be seen clearly at Vendel and Valsgärde. In these cemeteries the human skeletons are so destroyed that no DNA analyses could be done. At the same time and in the same graves the animal remains (horses and dogs) are in excellent condition. The fragmentary state of the human bodies should perhaps be explained by the fact that the bodies had taken part in ceremonial rites such as hanging, as described by Adam of Bremen in connection with the ceremonial rites in Old Uppsala.

Human sacrifices are events that can occur when a society is in a crisis and, therefore, the boat graves may tell us that early medieval society in Middle Sweden was often in crisis, as we find boat graves more or less irregularly used from 550 to the tenth century. This is not surprising, considering that this was the period when a kingdom tried, but did not succeed, to become established in this part of Sweden.

This evidence makes it necessary to turn to the cremation graves to get clearer analyses of family relations. In these cases, however, DNA analysis is not the method one would primarily choose, as cremation destroys the organic part of the bones and DNA is bound to that part. A careful examination of some cremation graves, however, has given evidence that also in a cremation, at any rate in the type of cremation that was used from early medieval times, some of the bones and especially teeth were spared by the heat and have, therefore, kept the DNA more or less intact. In reality, bones only slightly heated (below 200 degrees) give a better opportunity to prevent the decay of the organic matter than unburnt bones. The preliminary analyses here seem to be very fruitful, but they require much more detailed analysis of the cremated bones themselves than earlier osteological research had understood.

In Svealand, cremation burial is the dominant grave ritual and, therefore, the material will be rich. I think, however, that one has to apply theoretical considerations when choosing the material for further analyses. The typical cemeteries in Svealand are situated close to settlements. From the excavations in Vendel, which belong to our research project, we have learned that there is a kind of settlement, belonging together not in a village but in a setting with one settlement of higher status and some minor settlements gathered within the same estate (Arrhenius 1998, cf. also Seiler n.d.). Here it is of vital interest to know the relations between those buried in the high status graves and those in the simpler graves. Do they all belong within an extended family or do they represent a diversified group of persons gathered around a leader? In Vendel we can also note that the settlers seem to have come to the area during the Migration period, after which we can follow them into medieval times. When these settlers arrived, the area, a woodland, probably was used only by hunters or those making charcoal. Was this population driven away, or enslaved, or incorporated into the new families? Are the traces of Saami people evidence of this original population? I believe that future DNA analyses will be very helpful in answering these questions.

Thus we are only at the start of being able to give a clear picture of family relations in the early medieval period in Svealand. It is in my opinion of great importance to do these studies directly on the source material, i.e. the grave finds and settlements, and not do too far-reaching analogies with the Christian peoples on the continent or the British Isles. The conversion to Christianity, I believe, did much to change the family pattern from earlier times and to recognize this change is an important task.

References

[Abbr.: *AUN* = monographs published by the Institute of Archaeology in Uppsala; *KVHAA* = Kungl. Vitterhets Historie och Antikvitetsakademien; *Opia* = minor monographs published by the Institute of Archaeology in Uppsala].

Textual sources:

Snorri Sturluson
        Heimskringla: see Hollander (trans.) 1964.
Ynglinga saga: see Snorri Sturluson, *Heimskringla*.

Bibliography:

Arrhenius, B.
1983   The chronology of the Vendel graves. In *Vendel Period Studies*. J. P. Lamm
              & H.-Å. Nordström (eds.), pp. 39-70. (The Museum of National Antiquities,
              Studies 2). Stockholm: Museum of National Antiquities.
1992   Smycken som diplomati. In *Föremål som vittnesbörd. Festskrift till Gertrud
              Grenander Nyberg på 80: årsdagen den 26 juli 1992*. Pp. 18-25. Stockholm:
              Nordiska museet Stockholm.
1997   Stora kvinnor och små män. In *Till Gunborg; arkeologiska samtal*.
              A. Åkerlund, S. Bergh, J. Nordbladh & J. Taffinder (eds.), pp. 175-188.
              Stockholm University, Theses and papers in Archaeology. Stockholm:
              Stockholm University.
1998   Bebyggelsestrukturen i det förhistoriska Vendel och järnålderns
              mångmannagårdar. In *Centrala platser - Centrala frågor. Vänbok till Berta
              Stjernqvist*. L. Larsson & B. Hårdh (eds.), pp. 179-187. (Acta Archeologica
              Lundensia., Series in 8°, N°. 28). Lund: Lund University.
2001a   The belief behind the use of polychrome jewellery in the Germanic area. In
              *Roman Gold and the Development of the Early Germanic Kingdoms.
              KVHAA conferences* 51: 297-310.
2001b   Previous and recent research on the Svear. In *Kingdoms and Regionality*.
              B. Arrhenius (ed.), pp. 5-12. (Theses and papers in Archaeology, B:6).
              Stockholm: Stockholm University.
Björkman, E.
1919   Skialf och Skilfing. *Namm och Bygd* 1919: 163-181.
Brate, E.
1913   Betydelsen av ortnamnet Skjälv. *Namm och Bygd* 1913: 102-108.
Götherström, A.
2001   *Acquired or Inherited Prestige? Molecular Studies of Family Structures and
              Local Horses in Central Svealand during the Early Medieval Period*. (Theses
              and Papers in Scientific Archaeology, 4). Stockholm: Stockholm University.
Götherström, A., H. Malmström & K. Lidén
n.d.   Matrilinearity? Female boat burials in Tuna in Badelunda, Central Sweden.
              (Submitted). *Tor* (In press).
Götherström, A., M. Arvidsson, H. Hermansson & K. Lidén
n.d.   One cemetery, many kin: Molecular analysis of the remains from the
              cemetery in Tuna in Alsike. (Submitted). *Antiquity*
Hollander, L. M. (trans.)
1964   *Heimskringla: History of the Kings of Norway*. Austin, TX: University of
              Texas Press.
Näsström, B.-M.
1995   *Freyja the Great Goddess of the North*. (Studies in History of Religions, 5).
              Lund: Lund University.
Nordahl, E.
              Båtgravar i Gamla Uppsala. Spår av en vikingatida högreståndsmiljö.
              (AUN 29). Uppsala: Institute of Archaeology.

Norr, S.
1998   *To Rede and to Rown: Expressions of Early Scandinavian Kingship in Written Sources.* (Opia 17). Uppsala: Institute of Archaeology.
Nylén, E., & B. Schönbäck
1994   *Tuna i Badelunda, del I och II.* (Västerås kulturnämds skriftserie, 27). Västerås: Västerås University.
Seiler, A.
2001   *Vendel i skuggan av båtgravfältet.* (Theses and papers in Archaeology, B:5). Stockholm: Stockholm University.
Zachrisson, T.
1998   *Gård, gräns, gravfält. Sammanhang kring ädelmetalldepåer och runstenar från vikingatid och tidig medeltid i Uppland och Gästrikland.* (Stockholm studies in Archeology, 15). Stockholm: Stockholm University.

Discussion

AUSENDA: I saw in your transparencies that you have found ancient graves in a churchyard. Does that mean that there was continuity in the choice of a sacred location?

ARRHENIUS: No, there is no continuity as the church was erected at the end of the thirteenth century (1280-1290), whereas the graves and the prehistoric settlement end in the later part of the eleventh century.

DUMVILLE: Could I ask you to explain contextually why you see the organizational situation in Svealand to be at this time. You suddenly introduced us to kings and petty kings, but what is the overall picture as you see it, the governance to which you are relating the graves?

GREEN: What evidence leads you to associate these kingdoms with petty kings in particular?

ARRHENIUS: In Old Uppsala we know that kings and kings' graves existed. But Vendel, which I talked about now, is located 30 kilometres north of Uppsala and there we have one mound that has a size comparable to that of the royal mounds in Old Uppsala. We also have a settlement of some resemblance to Old Uppsala. The boat graves and grave-goods in Vendel are very close in arrangement to those found in Valsgärde which is located only 2.5 km from Old Uppsala and, therefore, belongs to the kings in Old Uppsala and most probably, therefore, also the boat-grave cemetery in Vendel is under the influence of the Uppsala dynasty. And then you can ask the question whether the petty kings ruling in Vendel wanted to copy those in Old Uppsala or the Uppsala kings extended their rule and built these tombs.

GREEN: Forgive my ignorance, but what is the difference in dating between the graves at Uppsala, at Valsgärde, and at Vendel?

ARRHENIUS: At Valsgärde, the boat graves start a generation later than in Vendel. However, the big mounds in Old Uppsala are of the same date as the earliest boat graves in Vendel.

GREEN: The closer these are in dating, the more possible is the linking of the graves to the same dynasty.

ARRHENIUS: Yes. And it is also so that, within the boat-grave cemetery, which was part of a larger cemetery with cremation graves there, are boat graves which are contemporary. It is difficult to date precisely in archaeology, because we always have the danger that some artefacts are old at the time of burial. But if you look closely at the finds in some of the boat graves they appear to be contemporary.

HERSCHEND: If I may comment, what is a generation among Anglo-Saxon kings? It is 11 years. They don't last any longer.

DUMVILLE: That is not a generation though.

HERSCHEND: No, but, if they are considered petty kings, we shouldn't feel it is strange that the three graves are as good as contemporary. There might be just 15 years between them.

DUMVILLE: Or they may have been ruling simultaneously.

ARRHENIUS: Yes, the interesting thing is that when you have two or three graves which are, if you so call them, contemporary, then you often find also items which are made by the same goldsmith.

DUMVILLE: So, if I attempt to summarize, you see different levels of kingship and the contemporaneity of material within one cemetery may allow you the possibility that there is multiple kingship at the lowest level.

ARRHENIUS: I have not dealt with multiple kingship but with ritual burials — where more than one can have been arranged on the same occasion.

GREEN: I don't think there is any reference to different levels of kingship. We are talking about different petty kings on one level, so far. I think you are including something which hasn't been said here.

DUMVILLE: Then there is a misunderstanding. The relationship between Old Uppsala and Vendel, is it not one of different status?

ARRHENIUS: Yes, if you take the royal graves in the big mounds at Old Uppsala, there is a great difference between these and the boat graves at Vendel. But the boat graves at Valsgärde cemetery belonging to Old Uppsala did not differ in status from those of Vendel.

DUMVILLE: Right, so are we then talking about different statuses within a kingship defined in unit of rule or are we talking about different units of rule, or what?

ARRHENIUS: I think they are different units of rule.

GREEN: Of the same status, or not?

ARRHENIUS: Well, then you have the problem of those at Uppsala because it is only one generation that we have there for the big mounds, perhaps two. Then we have kings in Uppsala but we don't find them in the graves. So it could be that there was an attempt in Old Uppsala in the sixth century to establish a real kingdom and they had these big mounds.

HERSCHEND: I will just say that we are very fortunate to be able to see status at some given points in the landscape, which are all rural centres. If you take Vendel and Valsgärde, they are two out of some seven or so. From that point of view, even from the fact that they are boat graves, where such things as gender and age are separated, there they are at the same level. One of them might be the overall king, but of course you couldn't see that. And there are slight differences too, for instance the use of regalias is obvious in the mounds in Old Uppsala. In the Valsgärde boat graves, the helmet and the spear are placed in the outer part, not next to the bodies as in Vendel, which might suggest some sort of royalty other than that in Vendel.

ARRHENIUS: And then, of course, I don't think that the boat graves in Vendel are true graves!

MEULENGRACHT: You say that "a marker for a male relation to Saami was found. That means that one of the buried men had a Saami father" (page 46). My question is, what is a marker for a male relation and why can this one buried not have a mother with a Saami father?

ARRHENIUS: The Saami have in their DNA a very typical marker which is very specific. In the whole of Europe you will only find it among the Saami people.

MEULENGRACHT: Is it sex specific?

ARRHENIUS: It is found in the Y chromosome, so it is male specific.

VESTERGAARD: But then there might be in this case another explanation, that distinguishes between biological and classificatory kinship. So the father might not know that the biological father was a Saami. So, therefore, he was not buried as a Saami.

ARRHENIUS: Yes, that may be. In that cemetery, Tuna i Alsike, we quite clearly have two lineages, and the same is evidenced at Tuna i Badelunda, where we have perhaps even three lineages. That means that in these cemeteries we have the descendants of more than one family.

AUSENDA: Have any parallels been made to contemporary agro-pastoral societies? In such societies prevailing marriage is between close parallel cousins, with occasional marriages between clans, or even between tribes only for alliance purposes. Have similar studies on DNA been carried out on contemporary societies?

ARRHENIUS: No, no, DNA has not been done so much. It is only in Sweden that DNA surveys have been made on archaeological material from the early medieval period. There is some DNA research done on Eskimos, but in our kind of society no DNA research has been carried out at all.

AUSENDA: It would be interesting to see what is going on in contemporary societies in response to mixed marriages.

ARRHENIUS: Yes, but for comparison we have looked at some early Christian cemeteries from northern Sweden, and there it appears that those buried in one cemetery were all very closely related.

AUSENDA: I agree, but if you do the same study on living people you would know what they call each other, and at the same time you could see what their DNA relationship is. It would be interesting to find out whether the Saami were considered as having the same status level as Scandinavians or a lower one, because if they were at the same status level, the mixed marriage would certainly represent an alliance, if on a lower level, the offspring might have had the status of a slave.

ARRHENIUS: In late medieval times they had a much lower status level, but what it was at this time we don't know. It would be very important to clarify the situation. But when we read about the travels of Ohthere in the ninth century, he said that in the North of Norway they were not human, so he obviously thought that the Saami had very low status. But we don't know how it was at this particular time in Sweden. I am not at all sure that it was so. I think it has to do with the spread of Christianity that the Saami were considered as having a much lower status, because heathens in general were considered as having lower status.

GREEN: There is a possible linguistic connection, not uncontested, in that the word for Finn has been seen as a Germanic word, primitive Germanic *finþan* 'to find', suggesting a hunting and gathering culture only.

BRINK: We find the element Finn in several place-names in Scandinavia. In parts of southern Scandinavia, where obviously these names are very ancient, they are given to the herders in contrast to the sedentary population. You find Saami names only in something like thirty or forty among all Scandinavian place-names.

ARRHENIUS: That doesn't say anything about status.

BRINK: It doesn't say anything even if they were Lapps or Saami. Most probably they were living in contrast to people living in sedentary clusters.

MAGNUS: The Norwegian king Harald Finehair had a Saami wife called Snæfrid, daughter of Svasi. With her he had a son who was practicing *seiðr*. Even if this is a story interpolated later, it means something. Why, otherwise, would the tradition relate that the king had a son with a Saami woman?

ARRHENIUS: If you go into the *Ynglinga saga* you find intermarriages between *Ynglingar* (the ancestors of Swedish and Norwegian kings) and Saami women.

MEULENGRACHT: Yes, this theme is frequent in the story of the Norwegian kings.

MAGNUS: Why?

MEULENGRACHT: According to the hypothesis of the alien woman, in Scandinavian mythology the king is thought to marry a woman from the aliens, that is a woman you usually cannot marry.

ARRHENIUS: But it doesn't fit with the Saami father.

MEULENGRACHT: No, that's why this is interesting: it is the other way round, it is prohibited. In mythical and historical thinking, you can't let a Saami father marry a 'white' woman without giving rise to social problems.

ARRHENIUS: I am not sure that it was forbidden at that time. This is later.

GREEN: It is good to know that Scandinavians were politically correct [laughter].

ARRHENIUS: We also have analyses of the trace elements, stable carbon isotopes, in the skeletons. These analyses show what they have been eating, obviously reindeer, because they had a high selenium content compared to a high nitrogen content, which also shows contact with the Saami (cf. Lidén & Nelson 1994).

HERSCHEND: But I think it is more interesting to see these cemeteries or whatever they are as a sign of a social change. What it means to be Saami does not have so much to do with patrilineality or matrilineality any more; there is much more of a social idea to what it means to be an aristocrat. You might be good at fighting which would make people forget about your being a Saami, especially if you are good at killing people.

MEULENGRACHT: The 'Kings' Sagas' are important stories. They are explanatory stories about the origin of Scandinavian kings. They don't contradict your material.

ARRHENIUS: I want to add why I don't believe in the interpretation of the couple depicted on gold foils as hierogamous, a holy wedding which was the origin of the Scandinavan kingship, as told in the myth of Freyr and Gerd. This story is not contemporary with the pictures, which are much earlier. And on the gold foils we also have the image of a woman with the big garnet jewel. Altogether the images on the so-called gold foils fit much better with what we know about the Isis cult which we know was practised by some Germanic people in the fifth century. I think it is extremely important to use sources which are contemporary with the images.

MEULENGRACHT: Yes, but why should the myth not be as old as the pictures?

ARRHENIUS: Because it is only known from Snorri in the thirteenth century.

BENDER: I wonder what the genetics would be of Snæfrid's son? How Saami would he be? Could someone like him be the father of your man in the Tuna i Alsike boat grave?

ARRHENIUS: Yes, we have been discussing that, but the DNA researchers are not quite convinced by that as they believe the relation is closer between the first and the second generation.

MAGNUS: You maintain that these people in the boat graves were sacrificed (page 48). That means they were ritually killed some time before they were buried. Do you consider that typical for just this part of Sweden?

ARRHENIUS: No, I have just been talking of the Upplandic boat graves because I haven't had time to go through the other material. But we also have cremated boat graves.

GREEN: Talking about graves, you say 'sacrifices' rather than graves, and my string of questions arising from this is: sacrifices of whom, to whom, why and what are the grounds for assuming this?

ARRHENIUS: Half of the fallen warriors went to the god Odin, and half to the goddess Freyia. The large bog sacrifices date back to the Roman Iron Age and the Migration period. And then after that we have no recognized sacrifices before we can read Adam of Bremen. He tells us about the holy tree at Old Uppsala where all kinds of sacrificed animals and humans were hanging.

HERSCHEND: Can we trust Adam of Bremen? This is the main question. There is a problem, the fact that you don't find the bodies or the skeletons in the boat graves. It could be explained in those graves that were not filled with earth and were left open. And the corpses and the animals are not in the boat graves, they are outside.

ARRHENIUS: The animals, horses, cattle, as well as dogs, were aligned along the gunwales.

GREEN: Your remark about the horses sacrificed outside the grave is, of course, reminiscent of the discovery of Childeric's grave with horses sacrificed outside.

ARRHENIUS: There are lots of horses sacrificed around Childeric's grave, but this is also known from a row of graves in Westphalia, where sacrificed horses are known as late as the early Viking period.

HERSCHEND: Also in the Lombard tradition.

ARRHENIUS: Yes. And at the same time as we have these horses, we also have chamber graves in Birka, and the skeletons there are very well preserved, so we have been able to take out DNA and so we don't have these problems. The problems concern only the decayed skeletons of humans in the boat graves.

HERSCHEND: And in Sutton Hoo.

ARRHENIUS: In Sutton Hoo only the phosphate of the skeleton is left and nothing more.

HERSCHEND: But about these sacrifices could we say that they rebelled and offered sacrifices as a sign of defiance?

ARRHENIUS: I think that is open to question.

VESTERGAARD: Yes, à propos of these horse sacrifices—well, this is of course very far away, but I thought it could be interesting for you to note that in Luristan, up in the westernmost Himalayas, the very steep mountains, there lives an Indo-European people. They have always had horses connected with their burials. It is not possible to keep horses in Luristan, which means that every time someone was buried, they had to travel down the mountains and, with great effort and expense, lead the horses high up into the Himalayas to sacrifice them. They never used horses for anything but taking them up the mountain and sacrificing them at funerals. I wanted to comment here on sacrifices and crises. You argue that sacrifices are held only at certain times and not always because the society is in crisis. I would not deny the possibility that it might be an explanation, but I would object that there is no need for sacrifices and crises to go together; you have just as much evidence of sacrifices with no crises as crises with no sacrifices. I think that it is not sufficient to state that sacrifice coincides with crises as there might be other explanations.

ARRHENIUS: Well, I collected a lot of quotations from anthropological literature which I haven't referred to in my paper. They claimed sacrifices went together with societies in crisis. The best known examples are from the Aztecs of Mexico and the Inca of Peru where they started a wave of human sacrifices when they were invaded by the Spaniards.

VESTERGAARD: Yes, but these were done to keep the gods fed and the world going on, so it was directly connected with the needs of everyday life.

DUMVILLE: This is not so much a comment but a request for a story. I was sure that archaeology was about telling stories and I have a test. Could you tell the story of the archaeological history of human sacrifices in Scandinavia?

ARRHENIUS: It starts in the Iron Age but not before, although we have a lot of sacrifices before. I think the bog finds in the Iron Age were huge sacrifices of weapons, but we also found animals and human beings sacrificed. And then we have the bog finds where you only find humans. There are also the graves Lena [Olausson] described this morning, where humans were sacrificed, sometimes as beheaded people put in the upper layers of the grave. I myself have dug an enormous mound with a cremated warrior and then in a little pot there were the cremated bones of an eighteen year-old girl. This perhaps was not a sacrifice, but a gift placed in the grave.

DUMVILLE: One of the reasons I am asking is the question of continuity. You strongly imply in what you have written that there is a discontinuous history to this practice. Therefore, we have to find it, we have to seek a special explanation.

ARRHENIUS: Yes, because we don't have any sacrifice in the bogs and lakes from the early Vendel period.

DUMVILLE: How big is the gap?

ARRHENIUS: Some hundred years.

HERSCHEND: But there are also several signs, for instance, of animals, of remains of meals, where the only human elements are some used bones, a thumb, a fibula, something like that. And they were obviously used for a long time. They carried them in their satchels, with skulls and that kind of thing. So obviously they were philacteries. There is a discontinuity: they are really not very common when you come up to the Migration period and later.

GREEN: Why do you think there is this distinction between cremation graves, mound graves for men, and boat graves for women? Because one thinks of the English example for boat graves at Sutton Hoo, maybe that was for a king of East Anglia, but certainly for a man. Why this distinction between Uppland and East Anglia?

ARRHENIUS: No, there is a misunderstanding. In central Svealand some boat graves, especially in Vendel and Valsgärde are only for men, but others, as at Tuna i Badelunda, were for a woman, while in Old Uppsala and Tuna in Alsike both men and women were buried in boats.

GREEN: So the fact that the boat grave at Sutton Hoo is for a man could be purely fortuitous, or not?

ARRHENIUS: Well, all the men's graves were recognized first and then the boat grave with the queen Oseberg in Norway was found. The female boat graves were thus recognized much later in the history of research. They were never discussed in connection with Sutton Hoo. And, as far as I know, from the phosphate content in the Sutton Hoo grave, you can't really say whether it was a man or a woman. However, all the items found there are for a man.

GREEN: Yes, but you wouldn't expect those items to be added to a grave for a woman?

ARRHENIUS: No. There are too many things which belong to a man.

References in the discussion

Textual sources:

Snorri Sturluson
    Edda: see Faulkes (trans.) 1987.
    Heimskringla: see References at end of paper.
Ynglinga saga: see Snorri Sturluson, *Heimskringla*.

Bibliography:

Brate, E.
  1913   See References at end of paper.
Faulkes, A. (trans.)
  1987   *Snorri Sturluson Edda*. London: Dent.
Hollander, L. M. (trans.)
  1964   See References at end of paper.
Lidén, K., & D. E. Nelson
  1994   Stable carbon isotopes as dietary indicators in the Baltic area. *Fornvännen*
       89: 13-21.

KINSHIP AND MARRIAGE:
THE FAMILY, ITS RELATIONSHIPS AND RENEWAL

ELISABETH VESTERGAARD

The Danish Institute for Studies in Research and Research Policy, Finlandsgade 4, DK-8200 Aarhus

Introduction

The bilateral kinship organization is considered by several scholars to be the old Germanic kinship organization whereas the patrilineal kinship system is held to be a later development which became predominant in Europe in the early Middle Ages (Chadwick 1912; Phillpotts 1913).

Briefly stated, the discussion about Germanic kinship has to a great extent taken place between the two following evolutionary schools:

1. An original *matrilineal* society developed over time into a *bilateral* or *cognatic* society which in turn developed into a *patrilineal society.*

2. An original *matrilineal* society developed over time into a *patrilineal* society which in turn developed into a *bilateral/cognatic society.*

It has been argued that the bilateral system followed after the matrilineally-organized Germanic societies (Chadwick 1912; Phillpotts 1913). Tacitus has been used frequently to support the argument for the development from a matrilineal to a bilateral kinship organization in Germanic societies (Tacitus, *Germania* XX):

Sororum filiis idem apud avunculum qui ad patrem honor. Quidam sanctiorem artioremque hunc nexum sanguinis arbitrantur et in accipiendis obsidibus magis exigunt, tamquam et animum firmius et domum latius teneant. Heredes tamen successoresque sui cuique liberi, et nullum testamentum.[1]

The argument in favour of matrilineality is based on the close relationship between sister's son and mother's brother and on the preference for receiving the enemy's sister's son in the exchange of hostages—as stated by Tacitus—not the enemy's own or his brother's son.

On the other hand, anthropological kinship studies show that a close relationship between sister's son and mother's brother is a common feature even in patrilineal organizations. This relationship is outside the frame of authority and inheritance interests because the sister's son belongs to a different group from that of the mother's brother, which explains the above-mentioned hostage exchange system.

---

[1] *"Sisters' sons are held in as much honour by their maternal uncle as by their fathers. Some regard this consanguine tie as more holy and strong and when they receive hostages they primarily demand such* [sisters' sons] *perceiving this to grant them a stronger grip on the family. Still, they choose their own sons as heirs and successors, and they have no testament"* (Tacitus, *Germania* XX).

The strongest guarantee that a hostage giver would keep his promises was to make him responsible for a life belonging to another group. To sacrifice a member of one's own group was, in spite of the tragedy, a matter of concern only to one's own group. To risk the sacrifice of a member of another group was a matter involving at least two groups. Thus the quotation from Tacitus does not necessarily point to a matrilineal kinship organization, but allows for the existence of a patrilineal structure in Old Germanic society.

However, kinship is neither tangible nor static. It is a social process in which the given preconditions and strategic considerations give actions their significance, as can be demonstrated for Iceland and Norway. Medieval Icelandic society was organized according to a bilateral system whilst Norwegian medieval society was organized according to a patrilineal one, but the systems should not be seen as mutually exclusive. Rather, they were processes which created different patterns of action and organization from the same basic model. Or, as Barth would argue (1966), interaction related to vital resources and descent rights gives rise to the particular form in which the kinship system is expressed, and to the formation of relations of solidarity, possibilities of exploitation and of joining in action against external threats.

Norwegian and Icelandic medieval laws

It has been generally accepted that early medieval laws were only valid from the time in which they were written down. The argument goes that they were written down precisely because they differed from the laws of the preceding period and were too complicated to memorize due to the advent of a more complex social order. Such an argument for committing legal texts to writing is a simplistic explanation which regards writing as nothing but a technical instrument.

Yet, writing itself may confer a new kind of authority upon the same law previously transmitted orally (Lévi-Strauss, 1976:388-394). The attempt to detach his authority from popular legal assemblies would be ample reason for a king to want the laws written down. Research into the Norwegian laws has shown that they contain vestiges of mnemotechnical rules, which in many cases would preclude any change of detail except at the cost of whole sets of rules falling apart. These rules were gradually obliterated as writing took hold (T. Vestergaard 1988).

In the *Gulathing Law* (1163 AD) a number of legal rules are enumerated in series that are literally numbered. The numerical order is linked to the contents of the rules in such a way that three rules of thumb are sufficient to assign 23 types of kinsmen to their right place as heirs in a series of 13 categories (T. Vestergaard 1988:168). The Icelandic law *Grágás* mentions that the first 13 heirs are named *the counted ones*, but there is no ordered relationship between numbers and type of heir. The more recent law of Magnus 'Law-mender', (1274 AD) retains the numbering of 13 categories of heirs, but as a formality. There is no systematic relationship between numbers and content. This later list contains 80 types of kinsmen including exceptional and unlikely varieties of relationships, and all together it would be impossible to memorize. In the law of Magnus 'Law-mender', this is no obstacle since the law was committed to writing from its inception (T. Vestergaard:192-3).

There is a structural difference between the early Norwegian inheritance rules and Roman law as regards the closeness of kinsmen as heirs. In the Norwegian rules reciprocal kinsmen are categorized together whether they are in the same generation or not, for instance:

> *Son _____ father*
> *son's son _____ father's father*
> *father's brother _____ brother's son*
> *father's agnatic cousin _____ agnatic cousin's son*

Within each category the heir of the descending generation inherits before the heir of the ascending one, and both inherit before the heirs of the next distant category (T. Vestergaard 1988:165). Father's brother and brother's son belong to the same category. In the kinship reckoning of Roman law, brother's son would be a sideline descendant of one's father, whilst father's brother would be a sideline descendant of one's father's father. They would not be in the same kinship group.

For all we know, the Gulathing and the Frostathing laws are codifications of an oral tradition, and the formalization of many rules is such as to make them easily reproducible. The inheritance rules, especially, are thoroughly structured and in harmony with numerous other rules concerning kinship and property. Thus they could not have been changed without extensive concomitant changes in the domain of kinship. This situation would support the argument that important parts of the law could have applied for a long time before its codification in writing.

Comparisons between the Norwegian *Gulathing Law* and the Icelandic *Grágás* show a marked difference in organization with respect to inheritance and penalties. The *Gulathing Law* is considered to be the oldest of Scandinavian laws. It originates from western Norway and is generally believed to date back to around 900 AD. It was committed to writing in the twelfth century and copied in 1274 into a still existing manuscript. All Icelandic laws dating back to before 1263 share the common name *Grágás*. Icelandic legislation was committed to parchment from the year 1117.

The Norwegian system—as it appears from the *Gulathing Law*—shows clear patrilineal preferences whereas *Grágás* operates on a more bilateral basis or an indiscriminate network. It even includes affinal relations in incest prohibition categories. The Icelandic deviations show not only on the legal level: social organization and power relations differed on major points from Norway—the Icelanders' land of origin—with its *óðal* system.

Icelandic studies have often concentrated on the marked difference between Iceland and Norway stressing the bilateral or cognatic character of Icelandic society and the importance of ties other than kin ties, like political alliances and friendship. The descriptions of feuds in the sagas have supported this line of research. In Icelandic feuds even close kin may fight each other, which could lead to the conclusion that kinship was weak or at least subordinate to other forms of social bonds.

The Icelandic family sagas supply apt illustrations of the course of feuds which reveals the same pattern of succession of events:

Following an initial conflict, the opponents seek support and/or advice. Support and advice may be sought from men well-reputed for wisdom or power, from men related through blood ties or marriage, from men related through contractual bonds or bonds of friendship, or men whose support is available as a result of gifts, money or threats. Persons with whom the actors in one situation would have sided, for various reasons, could be found among the opponent's supporters in another situation. No constellation of groups—no matter the character of ties among the individuals—could be expected to last longer than the actual event, and maybe not even that long. Even the peacemaker, who was expected to solve the dispute, might change his position, which was an acceptable act in the social domain since what was sought was not objective justice, but a viable, commonly-acceptable justice or settlement of affairs (Miller 1984). In conclusion, everything seems to point to a bilaterally organized Icelandic society with some patrilineal traits on the operative level that could indicate either a development to come or that they were vestiges of a Norwegian inheritance. Family ties often seemed weak, and friendship and economic or political relations were of great importance in disputes.

With a theoretical grounding in Barth's generative models, this paper argues that actors always sought the most advantageous alliances. In Norway the system of descent, inheritance and óðal rights made patrilineal ties by far the most advantageous, and members of the lineage would join in action with their allies against threats from other groups. In Iceland, common interests of economic and political importance with persons outside the descent group would often overcome ties within the descent group. All over Scandinavia one finds a kinship system with patrilineal preferences regarding inheritance and succession, and with matrilineal or cognatic relations of secondary relevance to inheritance and succession. Yet, matrilineal and cognatic relationships were of primary importance as the basis of alliances between groups. The difference between Iceland and Norway depends on differing perceptions of the most advantageous choice of action, so to make a comparison one has to look at the range of possibilities that in those societies determine the actors' 'choice':

1. Norway was a kingdom with the king as the guarantor of law. Iceland had no king and the decisions of the þing were dependent on the strength of the parties involved to a greater extent than in Norway.

2. Norway had óðal[2] rights. The individualized settlement process in Iceland did not include the network of óðal rights (Magerøy 1965). The incorporation relations into the patrilineal group in Norway protected an óðal in which one had rights

---

[2] óðal (Lat.: allodium). In medieval Norwegian law óðal is the patrimony for which agnates had privileged inheritance and redemption rights.

whether or not one actually possessed the land. In Iceland similar rights only covered the minimal family and not a wider range of relatives.

3. However, the possibilities of taking someone else's land were much greater in Iceland, as no *óðal* ties existed, and as the legal protection of the robbed was not dependent on royal power, but on the decisions of a *þing* (legal assembly) which was open to influence. It follows that it was more profitable to mobilize support even outside the patrilineal group.

All of Scandinavia shared the same ideology of kinship relations, but the terms for a choice varied within Scandinavia. By acting differently, following the most profitable choice, the pattern turned out differently in Iceland and Norway. The Icelandic and the Norwegian kinship system were thus not two mutually exclusive systems: they were processes creating different patterns of action from the same basic model.

Kinship in the Poetic Edda and in German heroic epic

A marriage is an alliance in that it creates a social link between two groups whether between someone and his neighbour or between two royal houses. The social function of such an alliance depends on circumstances, and it obviously makes a difference whether it is a marriage alliance between two poor neighbours or between powerful chiefs. Very close forms of endogamy like the Middle Eastern marriage to one's father's brother's daughter almost neutralize the alliance aspect. It makes sense in circumstances where it serves to hinder the fission of groups of close agnates. A case in point is the conflictual relationship between agnatic cousins (*tarbur*) among the Pashtun. It also makes sense when there is an alternative system of solidarity between groups (e.g. a segmentary lineage and clan system) that should not be jeopardized. Marriage customs are always both endogamous and exogamous. There is a limit to how distant it is socially convenient to contract a marriage (endogamy) and there is a limit to how close one can marry outside one's nuclear family (exogamy).

In pre-industrial societies, the purpose of marriage is not based on the legitimization of love between two persons; it is an alliance or a contract that serves the aim of uniting the two kin groups to which the bride and groom belong, and also to affiliate the offspring to a kin group thus giving the child an acknowledged social existence. These traditional functions of marriage make the question of love between the spouses a minor point. Obligations and duties are in this case more important than personal sentiments. This point will be illustrated with examples from the heroic lays in the *Poetic Edda* and from the German *Nibelungenlied*.

The heroic lays depict a clear-cut patrilineal descent system. Roughly categorized, fights or battles take place as revenge for a slain father or patrilateral relative, or are matters of honour, or are caused by the hero's marrying against the will of his antagonized father-in-law. Often all aspects are combined as in the lays of Helgi Hundingsbani and in the Volsung cycle. Here, generation after generation in the patriline are involved in fights with their wives' families, and sisters will have their solidarity vested in their own patrilineal kin group, not in the one into which they have married. Though love might be so strong that the woman disregards her father's will, she will not interfere if her husband is slain by her kinsmen. However strong, love is a personal emotion whereas kin solidarity is a group duty in situations of conflicting ties with other social links.

The examples are drawn from *Atlakviða* and *Atlamál*. *Atlakviða* is one of the oldest eddic lays, perhaps pre-Viking Age and at least not more recent than the last half of the ninth century.[3] *Atlamál* is approximately three hundred years later, that is from the end of the twelfth century.[4] *Atlakviða* and *Atlamál* both recount the same series of events, yet they relate the events differently.

In *Atlakviða* Gudrun warns her brothers in vain, and she stays indoors during the fight and the slaying of her brothers. She kills her sons—how, is not described—and serves them for Atli to eat. After having revealed this to Atli she kills him, squanders his gold by giving it to everyone present before burning Atli and all his men to death.

Atlamál is different. After having tried in vain to warn her brothers and then in vain to dissuade them and Atli from fighting each other, Gudrun joins her brothers in the battle and fights fiercely. Then, after the death of her brothers, she slaughters her sons and prepares a meal with their spoils. Later at dinner she reveals to Atli that he just devoured his children's hearts. Finally she kills Atli aided by her brother Hogni's son.

Having been given in marriage to Atli, Gudrun's duty and obligation is to be faithful and loyal, and to bear his children. This she fulfils according to the lays which describe her marriage as happy as well as to the lays which tell of an unhappy marriage. To this duty Atli appeals in *Atlamál* and Gudrun responds without any opposition:

> *Gørðu nú, Guðrún, af gæzco þinni*
> *okr til ágætis, er mik út hefia.*
> *Knǫrr mun ek kaupa ok kisto steinda,*
> *vexa vel blæio at veria þitt líki,*
> *hyggia á þǫrf hveria, sem við holl værim.*
> (*AM* 100-102).

*   *   *

---

[3] *Atlakviða* belongs to the oldest eddic poems. According to Holtsmark it reached Scandinavia before the Viking Age (KLNM VI:415-16, KLNM XV:228-29). Dating is no later than the end of the ninth century (see also Genzmer 1947:9; Dronke 1969:44).

[4] Classified by Holtsmark as a late poem as kings are described as small farmers and the heroism is grotesque (KLNM VI:416, KLNM XV:228-29). Dronke (1969:107-11) dates *Atlamál* to the twelfth century, Helgason (1934:43-4) says no later than the twelfth century. The dating used here is the end of the twelfth century.

Do now, Guðrún, of your goodness,
what befits our honour when they bear me out.
I shall purchase a ship and a painted coffin,
wax well the shroud to wrap your corpse.
Think of every need, as if we were at one (Trans. Dronke 1969:97).

Gudrun's solidarity with her husband Atli would never have come into question had not a stronger demand on solidarity come to the fore: the inescapable blood ties. The suspense of both *Atlakviða* and *Atlamál* is based on the dual role of Gudrun who behaves as both sister and wife until, in *Atlamál*, she joins her brothers in the battle and, in *Atlakviða*, she reveals that she has killed the sons she bore Atli and served them to him as a meal. From then on, she is unambiguously the sister.

A marriage is a contract that ties together both two persons and two kin groups. The affinal relationships between Gudrun and Atli, and between Atli and the brothers of Gudrun, are therefore contractual. In killing his affinal partners, Atli has laid violent hands on Gudrun's patrilineal kinship group. Gudrun's revenge strikes the essential parts of Atli's relations of solidarity as in *Atlamál* she sides with her brothers, slays one of Atli's men and cuts Atli's brother's foot off, and finally serves Atli their sons as a dreadful meal.

In *Atlakviða* she first slaughters her sons, squanders Atli's gold, kills Atli, and finally burns his kinsmen and his men to death. The description of her acts shows that in this domain the affinal, contractual relationship yields to blood ties. The killing of her own sons reveals that inside the consanguine group, the patrilineal affiliation is the most basic relationship of solidarity. Her status as a mother is subordinate to the fact that her sons belong to the most intimate part of the patrilineal group of Atli. Hence the boys become the most obvious and effective means for Gudrun to avenge her brothers. She humiliates Atli as father and king.

In the heroic lays, Gudrun's acts appear as logical consequences of Atli's provocation. Also the killing of the children is a logical act. My interpretation, that in situations of conflicting obligations the patrilineal kin group will be dominant is supported by *Atlamál*, st. 89 and *Vǫlsunga saga*, ch. 40; here Gudrun's brother's son, i.e. Hogni's son, is involved as her helper in carrying out her revenge. Because of the unavoidable duty to avenge one's brothers—a duty so strong that it outweighed all personal concerns and emotions—the lays become tragic. According to the social and moral universe of these poems, Gudrun had no other choice but to kill her sons as they now belonged to an enemy patriline.

A characteristic trait in the German *Nibelungenlied* as compared to the Norse Volsung cycle is that kinship relations are not as strong as contractual or affinal relations. In situations of conflicting solidarity, the solidarity between spouses has precedence over the solidarity between siblings. And in these situations of conflict, the relationships between a lord and his vassal—which were political and contractual relationships—also had precedence over the kinship relations of the individuals concerned. Most of the mighty vassals surrounding Gunther were his kinsmen, but conjugal ties were considered to be the more binding obligations vis-à-vis one's feudal lord than ties of kinship.

However, kinship relations are not without importance in the *Nibelungenlied*. In situations where close relations between persons are stressed, there is a frequent use of words like 'friend', *oheim* (maternal uncle), *mag* (brother-in-law), 'brother', 'sister'. But in situations of conflict one chooses sides according to contractual affiliations, and one's schemes against one's counterpart are in favour of one's contractual partners, not of one's agnates.

Kriemhild stays in Worms after Siegfried's death in spite of her knowledge of her brother's involvement in the slaying of Siegfried, and in spite of Siegmund's, Siegfried's father's, earnest attempt to beseech her to return with him to Xanten in his kingdom (*NL*, 1084-1090), Kriemhild refuses. In spite of her grief and her expressed intention to take vengeance, at this stage of the impending tragedy, Kriemhild prefers to stay with her patrilineal kin group as a widow rather than as a ruling queen in the country of her late husband's family and of her own son. The son she entrusts to Siegmund, his father's father, which means that the son stays with his patrilineal group, and the mother with hers (st. 1090, v. 3-4).

Grief and tension are present now, but the conflicts are yet to come. In this state of grief Kriemhild feels a need for the love of her own mother and brothers. Kinship relations are also of great importance of the *Nibelungenlied*, but only as long as they concern personal matters.

In *Atlakviða* and *Atlamál* Gudrun's slaughter of her sons contains an important clue to the understanding of the most basic relations of solidarity. Kriemhild has two sons, one with Siegfried and one with Etzel, but the sons are of hardly any importance in the *Nibelungenlied*. The figure of Kriemhild does not include the mother's role. The surrounding men place her in the role of sister, wife, and enemy. In Kriemhild's response to events, and in her choice of solidarity, the clue is in the understanding of the kind of ties which are the mainstay in situations of conflict in the universe of the *Nibelungenlied*.

The patrilineal relationships were the basis for the moulding of groups of solidarity in *Atlamál* and *Atlakvida*. In the *Nibelungenlied* contractual ties constitute the dominant features of social organization, and they have precedence in situations of conflicting obligations. The dramatic sequences of the last half of the *Nibelungenlied* illustrate this:

The killing of Siegfried in the 16th Âventiure leads to the violent events in Âventiure 31-39. Gudrun is in deep grief because of the killing of Sigurd by her brothers. She curses them, but takes no steps towards vengeance. Siegfried's death causes Kriemhild grief, too, and she is filled with thoughts of revenge. Out of fear for the expected revenge, Hagen deprives her of the Nibelungen hoard that might otherwise have been used by Kriemhild as a means for buying allies. Later, and for the same reasons, Hagen feels called upon to prevent her marriage to the mighty King Etzel, but in vain (*NL*, 1205, 1210, 1212). Such a fear would be unthinkable in the social universe of the Volsung cycle. Here, whatever happened, Gudrun would have remained the faithful sister in conflicting solidarities. In contrast, Hagen's fear suggests the likelihood of Kriemhild's vengeance on her own kin. In this case the solidarity of the wife is more binding than her commitment to her consanguineal kin group. The ties of contractual relationship here show their strength, and not only in Kriemhild's association with Siegfried; Hagen, Kriemhild's uncle, is also a striking example of this. He is the highest in rank of all Gunther's vassals; his political importance and influence at court could in practice even exceed that of Gunther. To him the main duty in life is to protect the royal family, that is, his nephews. When his niece by blood Kriemhild insults Brünhild, Gunther's wife and thus Hagen's lord, Hagen immediately strikes Kriemhild a severe blow: he murders Siegfried. His loyalty towards his queen exceeds that of his loyalty towards his consanguineal niece.

The part of the *Nibelungenlied* which corresponds to *Atlakviða* and *Atlamál* begins with the 23rd *Âventiure*. Kriemhild has now for several years been married to Etzel and lives with him in Huneland. She proposes to Etzel that her family in Worms get an invitation to visit them. The king happily agrees with this. Secretly Kriemhild instructs the messengers that Hagen has to be among the guests (*NL*, 1419). The execution of her revenge starts with the 31st *Âventiure* and is directed towards her father's brother Hagen. But, as we saw in *Atlakviða* and *Atlamál*, revenge is not confined to the slaying of the actual offender. Vengeance aims at striking the essential parts of the opponent's relations of solidarity in order to reach the maximal results. Kriemhild persuades Blödel, Etzel's brother, to organize the killing of the 9000 pages who accompany her family on the visit to Huneland and in this connection she refers to her family as her enemies:

> *Si sprach: "du solt mir helfen, herre Blœdelîn!*
> *jâ sint in diesem hûse die vîande mîn,*
> *die Sîfriden sluogen, den mînen lieben man.*
> *Swer mir daz hilfet rechen, dem bin ich immer undertân"* (*NL*, 1904).
> * * *
> Sie sagte: "Herr Blödel, Du mußt mir helfen! In diesem Haus
> sind meine Feinde, die Siegfried, meinen lieben Gemahl, er-
> schlagen haben. Wer mir hilft, das zu rächen, dem bin ich auf
> Alle Zeit treu ergeben."

Kriemhild makes use of a person attached to her by contract, in this case affinal ties (Blödel), in order to wreak vengeance on a person with whom she is connected by consanguineal ties (Hagen). The act of revenge is to murder the pages who, as pages, are related to their lords by contractual, i.e. political ties. Just as the killing of Siegfried was an offence directed towards Kriemhild, the killing of the pages is an offence against her brothers and, most of all, against Hagen. Their relations of solidarity and not their own persons become the victims:

> *"Jane darftu mich niht grüezen", sô sprach Blœdelîn,*
> *"wan diz komen daz mîne daz muoz dîn ende sîn,*
> *durch Hagenen dînen bruoder, der Sîfriden sluoc.*
> *des engíltest du zen Hiunen und ander degene genuoc"* (*NL*, 1923).
> * * *

"Du hast wirklich keinen Grund, mich zu grüßen", sagte Blödel,
denn mein Kommen wird Dich das Leben kosten, und
zwar deswegen, weil Dein Bruder Hagen Siegfried erschlagen
hat. Dafür mußt Du und viele andere Helden heute bei den
Hunnen büßen".

They managed to kill the 9000 pages and 12 knights; only Dankwart (whom
Blödel addressed in the above stanza) survives, goes to the banquet hall and
informs Hagen. Hagen takes up the gauntlet, and again it is not the very person,
here Kriemhild, who is attacked. Hagen beheads first Ortlieb, the son of Kriemhild
and Etzel, then the child's teacher, and finally he smites the messenger who
brought the invitation. Joined by the other Burgundian vassals and Kriemhild's
three brothers Hagen starts a massacre of everyone present at the banquet:

Dô sluoc daz kint Ortlíeben Hágen der hélt gúot,
daz im gegen der hende arme swérte vlôz daz bluot
und daz der küneginne daz hóubet spránc in die schôz.
dô huop sich under degenen ein mort vil grimmec unde grôz (NL, 1961 ff.).
* * *
Da erschlug Hagen, der treffliche Held, das Kind Ortlieb, so
daß ihm am Schwert entlang das Blut auf die Hände floß und
der Königin der Kopf in den Schoß flog. Da hob unter den
Helden ein Grimmiges, schreckliches Morden an.

Etzel is absolutely innocent and knows nothing of the conspiracy against the
Burgundians. Because he is married to Kriemhild, Etzel becomes one of the targets
of Hagen's vengeance for the murdered pages. Hagen aims at the greatest possible
humiliation of Kriemhild, and to achieve that he attacks her most important circle
of solidarity. This circle is represented by her relations through Etzel. He is both
her husband and the king who entitles her to the rank of queen. Through Etzel,
Kriemhild's affinal as well as her political solidarity groups are defined. Kriemhild
now exploits these solidarity ties of hers in the fight against her consanguineal
kinsmen and their men. Only Gunther and Hagen survive the fierce battle. In her
attempt to force Hagen to reveal where the Nibelungen hoard is hidden she has
Gunther beheaded, but like Atli in *Atlakviða* she is fooled and learns nothing about
the hoard.

Before she beheads Hagen, they have a final dialogue in which there is a
complete lack of the kinship terminology they had used earlier in addressing each
other (*NL*, 2367-2372). He styles her 'queen' and refers to her brothers, i.e., his
nephews as his 'lords'. In the final scene the affinal and political relations clearly
take precedence over consanguineal relations.

To avenge her brothers, Gudrun killed her sons and her husband. To avenge her
husband Kriemhild took the initiative which led to her brothers and their men
being killed. Which of these deeds was the more heroic or the more monstrous is
neither to be decided nor of any particular interest. What is of interest is that
changed social conditions gave rise to changed reactions, and changed ties of

solidarity in the face of the same kind of events. From this point of view Gudrun's and Kriemhild's responses to events are in structural accordance with each other. The differences, although in opposite directions, are the same. In both cases the heroines have to choose between solidarity ties of the utmost importance to them as persons and to society as a whole. In both cases their choice was dictated by the very ties which had precedence in situations of conflicting obligations in the social organization of the society in which they lived. Their choice was dearly paid, but inevitable in order that they might not lose their honour.

The Faeroese tradition

I argued earlier that kinship is a social process in which acts take place in preconditions and strategic considerations, and that differences were due to a process which created different action patterns from the same basic model.

The analysis of *Atlakviða* and *Atlamál* showed that the organizing social principles survive even radical social change as long as the basic structure remains the same. *Atlakviða* took shape in a pre-Christian society in which the political organization could be characterized as that pertaining to a primitive state. *Atlamál* is more recent by three hundred years and it got its present form in a Christian society that was developing into a semi-feudal political organization. But the ideological and legal connections of kinship, *óðal* and inheritance remained unchanged during the period in spite of the drastic changes at a higher political level.

The *Nibelungenlied*, in the versions we know of, was shaped in a fully-fledged feudal society in which contractual relations were the main organizing political and social principles. Kinship ties, especially the patrilineal were, however, not without importance and almost all the main episodes of conflict in the *Nibelungenlied* involve a clash between these two organizing principles. The importance of patrilineal relations did not vanish in German feudal society, but in situations of conflicting obligations they were subordinate to contractual relations.

The Faeroese version of the Volsung/Nibelungen tradition is generally believed to have reached its present form in the fourteenth century (see e.g. Lockwood 1983). The ballads were orally transmitted and were not committed to writing until 1800-1850 (see e.g. á Kroki 1968; Grundtvig 1872-76; Lockwood 1983). Figures 4-1 to 4-4 shown below constitute both a summary of the chain of events and an interpretation of the kinship structures as they appear in the ballads. The interpretation is taken to give meaning to the period in which the ballads were written down, namely the first half of the nineteenth century. Apart from the king's farmers, land was *óðal* and transmitted as bilateral inheritance; all children disregarding gender inherited an equal share.

The analysis shows that in the Faeroese farmer's universe the main social unit is the nuclear family, husband, wife, and children. No matter which one of the spouses may have the final word inside the family, in all social and public relations the husband is the only one responsible.[5] Gudrun avenges her first husband by killing her brothers. Her brother's son strikes back, not at Gudrun but at her husband.

The Faeroese version of the Volsung ballads

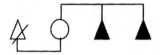

Fig. 4-1: Gudrun's two oldest brothers kill her husband.

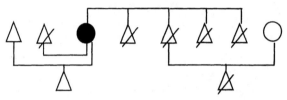

Fig. 4-2: Gudrun's revenge: she kills all four her brothers and her brother's son.

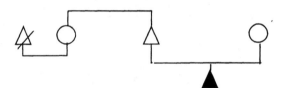

Fig. 4-3: Høgne is avenged by his son who is responsible for Artalas' death.

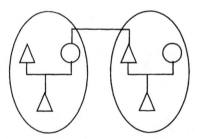

Fig. 4-4: The main solidarity group is the core family: father, mother and child with a weak patrilineal preference.

---

[5] The husband was responsible to such an extent that until the present day, in spite of the fact that some women were also landowners, only men would be present at the village meetings concerning the administration and use of the village commons.

Kinship in modern Europe

With Emanuel Todd we will assume that present-day European kinship systems all originate from the same stem. This stem is divided into four main branches:

Type I - The ***exogamous community family*** characterized by *equality* between brothers defined by rules of inheritance and cohabitation of married sons and their parents (Todd 1988:33).

Type II - The ***authoritarian family***. Here one finds *inequality* between brothers laid down by inheritance rules, transfer of an unbroken patrimony to one of the sons, and cohabitation of the married heir with his parents (Todd 1988:55).

Type III - The ***egalitarian nuclear family***. The same as in the exogamous community family, the egalitarian family is characterized by equality between brothers laid down by rules of inheritance, but in this family type, married children do not cohabit with their parents (Todd 1988:99).

Type IV - Finally, ***the absolute nuclear family*** is defined by no precise inheritance rules, a frequent use of wills, and no cohabitation of married children with their parents (Todd 1988:99).

The four family types are defined by degree of equality between siblings or brothers, inheritance rules, and cohabitation of grown-up family members. All four family types have been represented in Scandinavia, too. However, Todd does not distinguish between possession and property.

Possession and ownership are not necessarily synonymous: by definition, one does not necessarily own what one possesses, but an individual controls her or his possessions. Property, on the other hand, concerns ownership and rights. In Norwegian society, the mere fact of belonging to a patrilineal group gave one *óðal* rights whether or not one actually possessed the land. The difference could be further illustrated by pointing to the distinction between the *Queen's personal property*: jewels and estates of which she can dispose freely and then the crown jewels, regalia and castles which are the *property of the office,* but the queen's *possessions as long as she holds that office.*

With a focus on possession, Old Norwegian society would be based on the family type III, i.e. *the egalitarian nuclear family.* The farmer would possess his farmland, but he would not be able to dispose freely of the land nor of the rights. Here the wider *óðal* group would have a say.

If we choose property as the determining factor, the Old Norwegian family would be family type I, *the exogamous community family.* In this family type, stress is on equality between heirs. The Norwegian and Swedish society later developed into family type II, *the authoritarian family* in terms of possession due to primogeniture. The same holds for the Faeroese King's farmers. Here the oldest son inherited the tenure and unmarried siblings would often stay at the farm as cheap labourers. In this family type inheritance stays unbroken.

Old Icelandic society and Faroese *óðal* farmers belong to *the egalitarian nuclear family*: the inheritance is distributed evenly among the heirs leading to an ongoing fragmentation process of land and other belongings.

Latter-day Danish society was characterized as family type IV, the *absolute nuclear family* with no precise inheritance rules and no cross-generational cohabitation.

All present-day Nordic countries have moved towards family type IV with its absolute nuclear family. But again, the shifts and developments over time should not be interpreted as radical changes from one system to another, rather—as stated earlier—the different systems are not to be seen as mutually exclusive, but as processes which create different patterns of action and organization from the same basic model.

Conclusion

This paper has argued that kinship should be considered as processes creating different patterns of action from the same basic model. The processes and actions are not random. Availability of land or of other vital resources, political conditions and types of resource limit the choices and channel social processes into different patterns of possession, cohabitation, solidarity and authority structure. They create variations in formal rules relating to kinship such as those of inheritance. Despite these variations the fundamental notion of kinship may still be the same. The European, and here specifically the Scandinavian kinship structures, appear to be ever-shifting systems within the same basic model for maybe more than two thousand years

References

Textual sources:

[Abb.: *AM = Atlamál*; *KLNM = Kulturhistorisk Leksikon for Nordisk Middelalder*; *NL = Nibelungenlied*]

Atlamál: see Dronke (ed. & trans.) 1969.
Atlakviða: see Dronke (ed. & trans.) 1969.
Gulatingslovi: see Robberstad (ed. & trans.) 1968.
Landnámabók: see Benediktsson (ed.) 1968.
Laws of the Salian and Ripuarian Franks: see Rivers (trans.) 1986.
Nibelungenlied: see Brackert (ed. & trans.) 1970.
Norges gamle love indtil 1387: see Keyser & Munch (eds.) 1846-1895.
Tacitus
          De origine et situ Germanorum: see Bruun & Lund (eds. & trans.) 1974.
Vǫlsunga saga: see Olsen (ed.) 1906.

Bibliography:

á Kroki, J. (ed) ,
     1968   *Sandoyarbók*. Tórshavn: Mentunargrunnur Føroya Løgtings. (Ms. collected
                 1819).

Ausenda, G.
1995 The segmentary lineage in contemporary anthropology and among the Langobards. In *After Empire: Towards an Ethnology of Europe's Barbarians*. G. Ausenda (ed), pp. 15-50. Woodbridge: The Boydell Press.
Barth, F.
1966 Models of Social Organisation. *Royal Anthropological Institute. Occasional Paper, 23*. London/Glasgow: Robert MacLeHose & Co. Ltd./Glasgow University Press.
Benediktsson, J.
1968 *Landnámabók*. Íslenzk Fornrit 1. Reykjavík: Hið íslenzka fornritafélag.
Boor, H. de (ed.).
1972 *Das Nibelungenlied*. Nach der Ausgabe von Karl Bartsch. Wiesbaden: Brockhaus.
Brackert, H. (ed. & trans.).
1970 *Das Nibelungenlied*. Mittelhochdeutscher Text und Übertragung. Vols. I-II. Frankfurt am Main: Eischer Taschenbuchverlag. [Repr. 1976].
Bruun, N. W., & A. A. Lund (eds. & trans.).
1974 Tacitus, *De Origine et Situ Germanorum*. Århus: Wormianum.
Chadwick, H. M.
1912 *The Heroic Age*. Cambridge: Cambridge University Press.
Corpus Codicum Islandicorum Medii Ævi.
1937 Vol. X. Copenhagen: Einar Munksgaard.
Corpus Codicum Islandicorum Medii Ævi.
1940 Vol. XIV. Copenhagen: Einar Munksgaard.
Dronke, U. (ed. & trans.).
1969 *The Poetic Edda*. Vol. I. Oxford: Clarendon Press.
Ehrismann, O.
1973 *Das Nibelungenlied: Abbildungen, Transkriptionen und Materialen zur gesamten Handschriftüberlieferung*. Göppingen: Kümmerle.
Genzmer, F.
1926 Der Dichter der Atlakviða. *Arkiv för nordisk filologi*. Vol. XLII. Lund/Malmö: Liber Läromedel.
1947 *Eddische Heldenlieder*. (Heidelberg Ausgaben zur Geistes- und Kulturgeschichte des Abendlandes, 9). Heidelberg: Carl Winter Univ. Verlag.
Grundtvig, S., & J. Block (eds.)
1872-76 *Føroya kvæði. Corpus Carminum Færoensis*. Copenhagen: Einar Munksgaard. [Repr. 1951-68].
Helgason, J.
1924 *Færøske studier; I. i Maal og minde*. Kristiania: Gyldendal.
1934 *Norrøn litteraturhistorie*. Copenhagen: Munksgaard.
1952-1964 *Eddadigte*. Vol. I & III. (Nordisk filologi, Serie A: Tekster). Copenhagen: Einar Munksgaard.
Holtsmark, A.
1968 "Atlaqviða" & "Atlamál" in "Codex Regius". In *Kulturhistorisk leksikon for nordisk middelalder* (KLNM). Vols. VI:415-416; XV:228-229. Copenhagen: Rosenkilde og Bakker.
Keyser, R., & P. A. Munch (eds.)
1846-95 *Norges gamle love indtil 1387*. Vol. 1-IV. Kristiania: Kongelige Norske Videnskabers Selskab.
Lévi-Strauss, C.
1955 *Tristes tropiques*. Paris: Librairie Plon. (Eng. trans. *Tristes Tropiques* by J. & D. Neightman. London 1976).

Lockwood, W. B.
1983   Die Färöischen Sigurdlieder nach der Sandoyarbók. Tórshavn: Føroya
          Fróðskaparfelag.
Long, R.
1968   Jóannes à Króki. Sandoyarbók. Tórshavn: Mentunargrunnur Føroya
          Løgtings.
Magerøy, H.
1965   Omstridde spørsmål i Nordens historie III. Norsk - islandske problem.
          (Foreningene Nordens historiske publikasyoner, IV). Gjøvik:
          Universitetsforlaget.
Miller, W. I.
1984   Avoiding legal judgement: The submission of disputes to arbitration in
          Medieval Iceland. American Journal of Legal History 28: 95-134.
Neckel, G., & H. Kuhn (eds.).
1962   Edda. Die Lieder des Codex Regius nebst verwandten Denkmälern. I-II.
          Heidelberg: Carl Winter Universitätsverlag. [Repr. 1983].
Olsen, M. (ed.).
1906   Vǫlsunga Saga ok Ragnars Saga Loðbrókar. S.T.U.A.G.N.L. Vol. XXXVI,
          hæfte 1. Copenhagen: S. L. Møller.
Phillpotts, B.
1913   Kindred and Clan. (Cambridge Archaeological and Ethnological Series A).
          Cambridge: Cambridge University Press.
Rivers, Th. J. (trans.)
1986   Laws of the Salian and Ripuarian Franks. New York: AMS Press.
Robberstad, K. (ed. & trans.)
1968   Gulatingslovi. Oslo: Det norske Samlaget.
Todd, E.
1985   The Explanation of Ideology. Family Structures and Social Systems. Oxford:
          Basil Blackwell. [Repr. 1988].
Vestergaard, E.
1990   Space and gender at the Faroe Islands. In North Atlantic Studies. Vol. I (1).
          S. Dybbroe, E. Vestergaard & V. Wåhlin (eds.), pp. 33-37. Århus: SNAI-
          North Atlantic publications.
1991   Gift-giving, hoarding, and outdoings. In Social Approaches to Viking
          Studies. R. Samson (ed.), pp. 97-104. Glasgow: Cruithne Press.
1994   Germanske transformationer: et antropologisk perspektiv på nibelunge- og
          vølsungedigtningens forskningshistorie. In Traditions and Innovations.
          Papers presented to Andreas Haarder. Odense: PEO Odense University.
Vestergaard, T. A.
1988   The system of kinship in early Norwegian law. Mediaeval Scandinavia
          12: 160-193.

Discussion

GREEN: You say that the matrilineal argument focuses on the close relation
between the ZS (sister's son) and the MB (mother's brother). Here there is one
small linguistic point which lends support to that thesis. It is the occurrence in
three early Germanic languages, OHG *oheim*, OE *eam*, Middle Dutch *ôm*. It does
not mean an uncle, but more specifically MB; and the etymology of this word is

very clear, I think, and is supported by Tacitus, whom you also adduce here. The etymology of this formation would suggest someone who occupies the homestead of the maternal grandfather, with special responsibility to protect his sister and his ZS, so that would tie up closely with the point you are making.

DUMVILLE: There is a complex issue where you say (page 60) "writing itself confers a totally new kind of authority... been orally transmitted so far". Are you as determined as that, or do you wish to say, "may confer" this may happen, that is one possibility. Are you determined to say "it will"?

VESTERGAARD: I would say, "it is most likely". But of course, this is not to say always. But it is most likely also if you compare it with similar situations elsewhere.

GREEN: Would it be safer to say, "can confer", "could confer"?

DUMVILLE: Does this depend upon the kind of authority which would enforce it? You take literacy as a sufficient condition to do this.

VESTERGAARD: No, there is a reference I have, here. It is from *Tristes tropiques* by Lévi-Strauss.

DUMVILLE: Yes, who is a generalizer by nature.

VESTERGAARD: The freezing of the words which also happens, is also of importance. You can interpret the word, but it is no longer possible for the same sort of manipulation which could be argued could have taken place before.

DUMVILLE: I would suspect that if you had two manuscript copies of the same medieval law code, you would rapidly find that not to be true. It seems to me that a generalization is very dangerous.

HERSCHEND: From a chronological point of view it doesn't matter how many copies there are as in front of the copy there can only be one reader. There is the logical fact that you can produce another copy—you could call it a fake—but from the theoretical point of view the fact that there are several copies does not make orality come back.

DUMVILLE: No, no. Neither can it freeze the text.

HERSCHEND: Oh, of course, the copy is a frozen text, a frozen word.

DUMVILLE: No, because the text can change.

HERSCHEND: No, not in the copy. Keeping to the chronological aspect, you can only take one text in front of you each time. What you can say is that you can look at another copy, but that is another situation in time.

LUND: It started as the leading authority whether it was the first version or a later one, isn't that what you were saying Frands [Herschend]?

HERSCHEND: No, I said that if you present to me an oral text and I say: "It doesn't say so", I say it at one time. But if you produce another text and you say, "that is another text", that is also another time, and the text cannot be discussed in the same way. I think Lévi-Strauss pointed out that actual writing refers to a given time.

DUMVILLE: Yes, but that wasn't the point of difficulty. The point of difficulty was the relation which by the very fact of writing, we have a new kind of authority.

And that kind of authority changes the situation wherever literacy begins to apply. I mean, by nature, I am hostile to broad generalizations like this. And so my objection will have to be taken within those terms of reference.

LUND: It is the same argument as Patrick Wormald (1977:105-38) advanced many years ago, isn't it, when he described the earliest Kentish laws as status symbols of newly Christianized kings.

DUMVILLE: Which is itself a very extreme statement.

LUND: Yes. Do we still believe in this old stuff about the mnemotechnical rule?

VESTERGAARD: It is part of my husband's thesis. Here I refer to his article on 'Mnemotechnical rules and writing' that he wrote ten years ago.

AUSENDA: There are some instances in Langobardic law which are both examples of antiquity and of mnemotechnical rules. These concern the payment of compensation for bodily injuries. In Langobardic law, as also in early Anglo-Saxon law, in Alamannic and other laws, compensations for bodily injuries are listed from head to foot. That seems to me mnemotechnical. They also must be very ancient and related to customary law, because injury compensations vanished completely from the more recent law codes. I think that this is evidence of the fact that there were mnemotechnical systems in customary law, which eventually surfaced in later written versions as they had been enunciated in the ancient oral laws of the 'barbarian' chiefdoms.

GREEN: There is a snag there Giorgio [Ausenda]. I come back to my distinction between what is oral mnemonic practice, and written rhetoric. Now, I know that rhetoric obviously mainly started off by being meant for the oral dimension, but then it was taken over into written Latin poetics, and by the time it reached the twelfth century, it is written poetics. In other words, when one comes across a description proceeding from head to foot, one has no idea from that fact alone, whether it goes way back in orality or is connected with written rhetoric. That's the problem.

BRINK: Concerning the laws, during the early period they had the Roman law and the continental Christian one and some kind of early provincial law. Similarities in the continental laws were considered too easy because it was too simplistic an approach.

HERSCHEND: The point is that what is changing in the written laws is the logic, it is not head to toe, it's head, knees, elbows, feet. That's the whole point. There are no roots in rhetoric, that's what changes with the Scandinavian laws in the thirteenth century. I have been interested in the Icelandic theme and in whether you can consider the Icelandic society old-fashioned in terms of lineage (page 62) or whether you just consider the typical *landnám* situation, people out in a virgin country forced to do something with the lineage.

VESTERGAARD: In a *landnám* situation you would have places where people for one reason or another move into and make new settlements and, therefore, they move into an open area, where the old system is not in force, and there they build those bilateral organizations which are found in Iceland. You may find the same development problem in the Middle East. Here you would normally have endogamous societies, but when people move into new areas where they have no family connections, then for some generations they might have exogamous families in a bilateral society. However, nothing else changed, the access to resources, the kind of resources available, etc. This means that, after a couple of generations, they go back to the erstwhile patrilineal society. But Iceland was different in this perspective, as it did not go back to the traditional Norwegian system, because it was not the most viable way of organizing that society.

HERSCHEND: I think there is an interesting parallel to your studies about honour, the ever-negotiated idea of what honour means is typical of the Icelandic society. It is a very dangerous model for understanding Iron Age society and Viking Age as well.

AUSENDA: On the question of endogamy and exogamy, I disagree with Dr. Vestergaard. To me it is indubitable that several barbarian groups, if not all Germanic ones, were 'endogamous', for the simple reason that they lived in a society where close marriage made living much easier for the new couple. That is because they were very small communities, hence when one married a close relative, one didn't have such high bridal payments as one would if one would marry someone less closely related. Supporting evidence comes also from religious laws issued from the sixth century onwards forbidding so-called incests, i.e. close cousin marriages. This is a written clue that 'endogamy' was practiced. The *Libellus responsionum* with Gregory the Great's answers to Augustine's inquiries about the possibility of marrying close parallel cousins among the newly converted Anglo-Saxons, shows that, on the strength of their recent conversion, the pope allowed Augustine's missionaries to marry the Anglo-Saxons even when related in the third generation, i.e. through their grand-parents. The Anglo-Saxons, the Langobards, and other Germanic populations can be seen to have practiced 'endogamy' during the pre-Christian and early times after conversion. I would like to know on what basis you can say that every population in Europe was exogamous?

VESTERGAARD: When you speak about endogamous and exogamous societies, it doesn't mean that everyone matched the model like that. But if you had more than 60% of the marriages being either exogamous or endogamous, you then could say that you had respectively an exogamous or an endogamous society.

AUSENDA: Have you quantified it?

VESTERGAARD: No, but....

AUSENDA: This is one of the reasons I am so interested in Professor Arrhenius research on DNA, since I hope that she will soon find out whether these people were endogamic.

VESTERGAARD: Of course there are limits to our knowledge, how far back you can trace the laws, but even in the oldest Scandinavian laws such as the *Gulathing*[6] law you find marriage prescriptions and prohibitions for marriage to close kinship relations.

AUSENDA: When was it written down?

---

[6] *þing* is the Scandinavian term for the locus of legislative power.

BRINK: It was formulated in the twelfth century and written down later.

AUSENDA: I am talking about the fifth, sixth, and seventh centuries.

VESTERGAARD: We have no evidence whatsoever about Scandinavian marriage prescriptions or preferences at that time.

AUSENDA: I believe that both State and Church made big efforts to prohibit close marriages. So, I agree with you that after a certain time these marriages were forbidden, although they might still have taken place in smaller numbers. It is quite probable that they were forbidden in Scandinavia as in all of western Europe, because the Church wanted to make inroads into the countryside where these marriage customs prevailed, and needed to break down tightly knit kinship groups. You cannot go back from the twelfth century to the fifth, sixth and seventh centuries and say that the laws and even less the customs were the same.

VESTERGAARD: I said that I would never claim validity for the sixth century because I have nothing to base it on. But you can compare the tenth century with the twelfth century and then Church interference becomes visible. The result is that they had to go to much more distant kin before being allowed to marry them. I have forgotten how far, maybe the tenth degree or even further.

AUSENDA: No, no. The closest allowed by the Church was the seventh degree of kinship, which corresponds to cousins with the same ancestor at the fourth ascending generation, i.e. the great-great-grandfather.

ARRHENIUS: Yes, one thing is law and the other is social practice. What we know is that in one Christian cemetery in northern Sweden the DNA examinations revealed that the corpses belonged to individuals who were closely related. And so it is quite clear that they didn't follow the law. This is from the twelfth century. If we could look at Icelandic graves of the same time, maybe we could obtain comparative material.

AUSENDA: Both Church and king wanted to assert their authority on villages by trying to break up the allegiance of closely knit kin groups. Both institutions didn't want close kin marriages because they strengthened the kinship group which had its own elders who tended to be independent.

VESTERGAARD: I do not disagree with Arrhenius. There would be situations with only few people in the neighbourhood. What I say is that there may be a difference between practice and theory, in this case the law. In those societies where there is a preference for alliances with other groups....and that's where one gets exogamy.

AUSENDA: Where did you do your fieldwork?

VESTERGAARD: In the Faeroe Islands.

AUSENDA: Maybe people there needed to make alliances with other groups. Usually the individuals who make alliances with other groups are those who represent the groups, i.e. the chiefs or the elders of the groups in question. However, individuals at the lower tiers of society usually do not make alliances with other groups. If they did they would become suspect of making alliances to overthrow their chiefs or elders. Ian Cunnison, who worked with the Baggara

Arabs in southern Sudan in the 1960s, wrote a chapter on why those people married within each encampment, the *surra*, hence with very close relatives (Cunnison 1966:89). When they married out, they lost many privileges, they could not inherit their wife's cattle because they had no rights in the other encampment.

The same is true also of both populations I studied in eastern Sudan, the Hadendowa Beja, and the Tigré-speaking Beni Amer, and of most populations in the Middle East.

HERSCHEND: I was just thinking that there might be a class perspective to this idea whether you are marrying in or out.

AUSENDA: It is an idea, but you would have to have a class society.

HERSCHEND: Certainly not in Scandinavia, because there was nothing of an egalitarian society within sight and there are several exogamic archaeological samples of nordic female graves in Thuringia. And in *Beowulf* too. What about the Finns in Bergen?

AUSENDA: I am not referring to the Saami. Indeed, in that case that was a chief who married a Saami girl probably to make an alliance. Ordinary people did not.

HERSCHEND: Obviously if you live in a village in Jutland, there can be no question of marrying except at the next village at most. There are no great class differences in the Iron Age, I am sure. But I think that the odd class represents an idea of how it ought to be.

AUSENDA: I hope that the DNA research Professor Arrhenius is carrying out will vindicate me soon [laughter].

GREEN: At the end of the first paragraph on page 62, talking about Iceland, you say that "kinship was weak or at least subordinate to other forms of solidarity relations". Well, of course, that is true elsewhere in *Germania*, and in particular of its subordination to the war band or to kingship. Neither of these applies though in Iceland, and so I wonder what you are thinking of when you say that.

VESTERGAARD: When I say it is weak, I say it because it is not the kin group which is the basic group in situations of conflict.

GREEN: Why is that the case then?

VESTERGAARD: Well, what I have tried to argue here is that in such a situation based on the social system, on the organization of society, on the access to resources and the rules of inheritance, there was no sense in relying on the kin group, as you do not have an *óðal* system which would create a greater group of kinsmen sharing common interests. In societies without the concept of *óðal* the relation to land is different and the land is not to be seen as a sort of collective.[7] And that means that kinship ties are weaker because other things might turn out to be more profitable.

AUSENDA: When Christianity produced a break-down in kinship ties and when the transfer of landed property began to be based on written contracts and was divided according to inheritance practices based on individual dispositions,

---

[7] *Óðal* (Lat. *allodium*), in medieval Norwegian law is the patrimony for which agnates had privileged inheritance and redemption rights.

then close kin could become very unfriendly [laughter].

HERSCHEND: No one is going to argue with that.

AUSENDA: On page 61, you mentioned "the bilateral or cognatic character of Icelandic society". This bilaterality is not borne out in the generalized use of patronymics among men and women as, if I am not mistaken, to this day all women are called 'so-and-so's' 'dóttir'.

VESTERGAARD: No, not today. I have Icelandic friends where the daughters can be named either daughters of the man or of the wife. Legislation has changed recently.

AUSENDA: Then bilaterality in names is only recent.

NIELSEN: Yes, I thought about the Icelandic situation and the period you were talking about. It fascinates me because there is a difference from the period of the *landnám* and later. So I think kinship relations may have changed drastically and you have to consider this problem, isn't that right?

VESTERGAARD: The period I am speaking about here is the early centuries of the Icelandic settlement. It is not later than the millennium.

NIELSEN: Pre-eleventh century? OK.

GREEN: The antiquity, the importance of the *óðal* (page 62) lies in the fact that it is the name given to one of the characters in the common Germanic runic system of writing. So it goes back to considerable antiquity. My other point is a small one, where you translate *thing* by 'court'. I think 'court' is very ambiguous here. What you possibly mean in this context would be better expressed by 'legal assembly' or something like that. 'Court' is in itself too ambiguous.

JESCH: Or even *thing*.

BRINK: To you love is a late social construction (page 63)?

VESTERGAARD: No, I think it is a very fundamental and vital thing among all societies of the industrialized world. At that level's perspective it is not a social construct, I think it is absolutely valid. People are dying for it. But from the acknowledgement of this to the acknowledgement of love as a structuring principle in social organization there is quite a step.

HERSCHEND: The great problem with love is that there must be social directing mechanisms as soon as it can be detected. It is such a personal thing that in a society it must be regulated.

GREEN: On page 65 you begin your movement from the poetic *Edda* to the German *Nibelungenlied*, seeing the latter as a focus of love and wider social obligations in marriage. In connection with German literature around 1200 when the *Nibelungenlied* was composed in writing, there is a broader range of examples possible. I don't know if you are aware of some of the publications in this field in German medieval scholarship. I can give you three titles afterwards if you are interested. But the point is that they deal precisely with this problem. Not in the context of the heroic epic, but in the context of the contemporary Arthurian romance. And that is moving into a totally different field.

AUSENDA: In so-called primitive society love is not a factor in social cohesion. Where there is close kinship relationship, sons and daughters marry who they are told to, and one might say that marriage choice is dictated by custom. The man has sexual rights on his wife and the wife has supporting rights from her husband. However, in Beja encampments men eat together at the *shafatt* (a hearth on the ground at the edge of the encampment), the men's place, and women congregate together in one of their tents. The impression is that, apart from defined sexual rights, women constitute a community in binary opposition to the community of men. If for any reason a woman gets angry at her husband, she may throw him out of her tent—women erect their own 'tents'—and the husband will have to sleep on the ground outside the encampment or at the *shafatt*. So the relationship is not the kind we are accustomed to; it is a completely different one, for which, despite the fact that I lived there for a long time, I never was able to penetrate completely, as I am not a Hadendowa. The trouble with anthropologists is that they can never completely understand the feelings of the people they are interacting with. I believe this supports your proposition.

With reference to *Atlakviða*'s preferential consanguineal ties (page 65), one should remember that, if a woman gets slighted by her husband or his kin, her consanguines are the only defenders of her honour and welfare. In simple society a woman relies on her brother if something happens to her, so she has to keep a viable relationship with her consanguineal relatives, because she might get into trouble with her affinal kin, and that is an occasion when she would have to fall back on them.

ARRHENIUS: I am a bit worried that you use *Atlakviða* or *Atlamál*, to show how the society behaved. Indeed, even after the dramatic events in these poems two different constraints clash with each other: the mother's love and the unfolding of the drama itself.

VESTERGAARD: If I had confined myself here and elsewhere only to those two poems, I would say the same. It would not be possible to say what happens or rather what was accidental and if there was any logic. Therefore, I compared it with the German *Nibelungenlied*, which narrates exactly the same events, the same individuals, conflicts, etc., which you can put into a structure, into a logical and coherent system. And in order to see how far it was possible to go, I included also the Faeroese version of the same story. It is very short so you can see that in that society it was markedly different. I have no space here, but there are some very marked differences where you can discern all the logical systems of transformation or comparison in the two medieval texts, which are totally deconstructed when you go to the Faeroe Island version: they are completely different statements. And then it is possible to say, that you have a logical system where you can go to and fro and say what happens here, so that's the reason you can say that "Gudrun chooses this and that relation and... behaves differently" because you not only have these two, but you have a third text in a different time and space where you can see how and at which points it deconstructs. But I agree with you, taking those two texts alone would have been just a flight in the air.

GREEN: When talking at this stage about the poetic *Edda*, and the *Nibelungenlied*. It is more than ever necessary that you avoid what in literary terms is a contradiction. One can talk about the poetic *Edda*, containing heroic lays, and in the context of the *Nibelungelied* about a heroic epic, but you cannot conflate the two because they are totally different.

HERSCHEND: Yes that was about this idea of exogamic marriage and whether one should see the idea of taking hostages perhaps in the society, that the women are actually the hostages in the late Iron Age. While I have this idea, that in the late Iron Age, the rather big battles disappeared, and in the late Iron Age it was a matter of fighting over the hall. It was political fighting, where in fact women were the hostages. And what do you think about women hostages instead of men.

VESTERGAARD: I never thought of this but it makes excellent sense. And it's well that you can say that, in some way, women of that time might represent the kings who also were somehow hostage to the society.

HERSCHEND: Yes, it was systematic as women and children were used as hostages in the late Iron Age.

VESTERGAARD: I think it is a very useful suggestion.

AUSENDA: I would like to remark that subsequently (page 66) you recognized that the *Nibelungenlied* society was completely different from the *Atlakviða* and *Atlamál* societies, in that the former was urbanized, while the other two were still mostly rural.

VESTERGAARD: It is the very difference between the societies which is one of the main points.

GREEN: This is a more general question about your bringing in the *Nibelungenlied* (page 66). It is a question which came to my mind right through the second half of your paper. How relevant do you think the position of the *Nibelungenlied* in Germany around 1200 is to the period we are considering in Scandinavia?"

VESTERGAARD: I would say that it doesn't matter. What matters here is to show what happens with kinship structures in different social organizations, and how you can see that in a social organization like the one you had in Scandinavia around the millennium, among societies which had the same roots with regards to the ideology of descent, but it is a society which is structured around contractual bases. What happens then? So it is in order to show that for people, even if the have the same ideology, the social organization is important to what solidarity relation is the most dominant in conflict situations.

GREEN: My problem with that approach is this: you are arguing in terms of a two-dimensional contrast, one in time and the other in geography. I don't know how many imponderables these two dimensions bring in. If you concentrated on only one dimension, one in time or one in geography, the imponderables would be fewer.

VESTERGAARD: Yes, and it would have been quite uninteresting [laughter].

LUND: Well, perhaps this is the same sort of question that I wanted to raise but which I would have saved to the very last page, where you conclude that kinship is dynamic. If that is so, it probably changes and adapts to changing situations. How can you confidently assume then that information you can distill from sources that are basically post-twelfth century will apply to the period you are dealing with, which is sixth to tenth century?

VESTERGAARD: I am not dealing with the sixth century, therefore, I would never say anything about that period.

LUND: Well, the translation that we were given this morning belonged in the Vendel period.

VESTERGAARD: Being an anthropologist, I would never presume to comment on 'pure' archaeological evidence. At most, therefore, I could argue that in given circumstances it would be most likely for a given situation to prevail, but I would not presume to do an anthropological study of populations in the Vendel period or earlier.

ARRHENIUS: What period are you working with?

VESTERGAARD: It is around the millennium.

LUND: Well, I think my objection is still valid. If your sources are high medieval, it narrows down, I would think, a little bit, but if it is such a dynamic process, can you really take evidence from such a wide chronological frame, and treat it as if it applied to the same thing?

VESTERGAARD: No, again I found it interesting to take two versions of the same event, where you know that no matter how you date them, there were the same centuries between them. One was pre-Christian and the other was post-Christian. The aim was to see whether and how they differed or were related. What happened to the ideology of kinship: did it change during that period when a lot of traumatic changes at state level and in the political system that inpinged on customs took place? There was a period from the ninth, tenth century to the eleventh or twelfth century when a lot of things were going on. What happened then to kinship ideology? Was it transformed or changed, or broken down or did it develop more or less in the same form?

DUMVILLE: This is a question to the Old Norse literature specialists. What is the basis for the very different datings of *Atlamál* and *Atlakviða* (page 64)?

JESCH: I think it is problematic but it comes under several headings, partly linguistic, partly of content; and I think probably one of the best clues is that if you look at scholars who disagree about the dating of every other eddic poem, nevertheless all agree that *Atlakviða* is one of the oldest...but they cannot prove it.

DUMVILLE: But can you state what the evidence is?

JESCH: Language and the content.

DUMVILLE: Yes, and what are contents?

MEULENGRACHT: Very impressionistic dating, in fact. Every criterion you can put forward for dating this or that, this or that time, will be challenged by some other scholar. The language, for example, we know that it is possible to use archaic language at any time. The minimalistic point of view is of course that this was written down in the thirteenth century. And one cannot really say that *Atlakviða* in the extant form is a ninth-century poem, because then you totally ignore the fact that it was orally transmitted through 400 years or something.

DUMVILLE: Is that a fact?

MEULENGRACHT: If you say it is from the ninth century, then it is a fact that the poem has been transmitted from that time to the thirteenth century.

DUMVILLE: It is a hypothesis.

GREEN: And by the same argument, the same is true for the *Nibelungenlied*.

MEULENGRACHT: What does it mean to say that *Atlamál* is from, say, the thirteenth century? Anyway it is built on this old history. Something in *Atlamál*, to my mind, looks like a parallel, that is a conscious use of the old story in a new form. But the old story is there, and the old story is in *Atlakviða*. You don't have an ancient poem like *Atlakviða* living alongside a later poem like *Atlamál* without people being aware of this contradiction.

GREEN: I am not quite convinced that people must have been aware of a difference between the *Atlakviða* and *Atlamál* (again I speak from the position in Germany in the thirteenth century). We have an incomplete love poem by Gottfried von Strasbourg, which has been transmitted alongside it, completing it, two versions utterly different in spirit and in comprehension. Now the people who commissioned the scribe to have these in the same manuscript and presumably to be recited on the same occasion to the same audience, were interested in the thematic continuation of the earlier story and were not necessarily aware that there was a difference in spirit. So it may be a thematic interest, two versions of the same story, rather than an awareness of difference.

VESTERGAARD: Then if I may add one thing, pictures show that no matter in which form, the plot itself was known long before. Something else which I think is important here, is that one thing is to know when this was written down and the whole discussion about that, but I think the main difference between those two *Atli* poems and *Gísla saga* is that here they just act. The element of reflection in Icelandic saga is very important and actually supports also what I was writing about the social organization in Iceland based on the bilateral kinship system. The importance of these kinship ties is borne out by the fact that in Iceland you have to weigh kinship relationships when you make a choice, whereas in a patrilineal kinship system it is irrelevant to weigh relationships because you are bound by kinship ties and obligations.

JESCH: Just briefly to support that in a way. I think the reflection that you see in Iceland, whether it is in the composition of a piece of a saga in two versions or these two poems, is that it is a reflection, it is being aware of the difference. The saga is set in the tenth century, even though it is written in the thirteenth century. Maybe they didn't recognize one poem was older than the other, but I think that they certainly did recognize them as different. I think a lot of that is precisely the historical awareness, in thirteenth-century Iceland, when they knew they had a lot of old sources. Our problem is actually pinning down how old and how they got them. But as far as the Icelanders in the thirteenth century being aware that their material was old, I am certain of that.

LUND: Could I just ask one question? When is the first evidence that these poems were known to other writers? When were they used in other texts, when are the first traces that they existed?

VESTERGAARD: You can find the plots of these epic lays on the picture stones of Gotland dated to about 850. And so these plots have been referred to in skaldic poetry. I deal with Faeroese society at the time the ballads were written down at the beginning of the nineteenth century, at which time the ballads were quite popular.

The *Sjurðar kvæði* was the most popular of all ballads. It is generally believed that this material arrived in the Faeroe Islands from Norway in the fourteenth century. However, I chose to analyse the ballads at the time they were taken down in writing, and also to analyse the societies which wrote them down.

References in the discussion

Textual sources:

Gísla Saga: see Loth (ed.) 1974.
Libellus responsionum: see McClure & Collins (eds. & trans.) 1994:42-54.
Sjurðar kvæði: see Lockwood (ed.) 1983
Venantius Fortunatus
        Carmina: see Leo (ed.) 1881.

Bibliography:

Cunnison, I.
   1966   *Baggara Arabs: Power and the Lineage in a Sudanese Nomad Tribe.* Oxford: Clarendon Press.

Leo, F. (ed.)
   1881   *Venanti Honori Clementiani Fortunati presbyteri Italici Opera poetica. Monumenta Germaniae Historica. Auctores antiquissimi*, 4, 1. Berlin: Weidmann.

Lévi-Strauss, C.
   1955   See References at end of paper.

Lockwood, W. B. (ed.)
   1983   *Die Faröischen Sigurlieder nach der Sandoyarbók.* Tórshavn: Føroya Fróðskaparfelag.

Loth, A. (ed.)
   1974   *Gísla saga Súrssonar.* (Series: Nordisk filologi, A. Tekster, vol. 11). Copenhagen: Munksgaard.

McClure, J., & R. Collins (eds. & trans.)
   1994   *Bede: The Ecclesiastical History of the English People. The Greater Chronicle. Bede's Letter to Egbert.* Oxford: Oxford University Press.

Vestergaard, T. A.
   1988   See References at end of paper.

Wormald, P.
   1977   *Lex scripta* and *Verbum regis.* Legislation and Germanic kingship from Euric to Cnut. In *Early Medieval Kingship.* P. H. Sawyer & I. N. Wood (eds.), pp. 105-138. Leeds: School of History, Leeds University Press.

LAW AND LEGAL CUSTOMS IN VIKING AGE SCANDINAVIA

STEFAN BRINK

*Department of Archaeology and Ancient History, Uppsala University, St Eriks torg 5,
SE-753 10 Uppsala*

Önund carried on violently for a time. But once Egil could see that Önund wanted no fair
solution of the case, he summoned him to the Thing, referring the suit to the Gulathing Law.
[- - -]

The winter passed away and it grew time to go to the Gulathing. Arinbjörn took a crowd of men
to the Thing, and Egil kept him company. King Eirík was there too, and had a big body of men.
Bergönund was in the king's troop with his brothers, and they had a strong following. And when
there should be decision in men's lawsuits, both sides proceeded to where the court was
established, to set out their proofs. Önund was now all big talk. Where the court was established
there was a level field, with hazel poles set down in the field in a ring, and ropes in a circuit all
around. These were called the hallowed bands. Inside the ring sat the judges, twelve out of
Firthafylki, twelve out of Sognfylki, and twelve out of Hördafylki. It was for these three twelves
to reach a verdict in men's lawsuits. Arinbjörn decided who were the judges from Firthafylki, and
Thórd of Aurland those from Sogn. They were all in the one party. Arinbjörn had brought a
powerful body of men to the Thing. He had a fully-manned snekkja, and had a lot of small ships,
skútur and rowing-ferries of which his tenants had control. King Eirík had a big force there too,
of six or seven longships. There was also a big gathering of farmers there.
    Egil began his suit by calling on the judges to pronounce lawful judgment in his suit against
Önund. He then set forth what proofs he had for his claim to this property which had belonged
to Björn Brynólfsson. He stated that Ásgerd, the daughter of Björn and own wife of Egil, had
title to the inheritance and that she was odal-born and landed-born in all branches of her
family, and born of princes early in her line. He asked the judges to award Ásgerd half of
Björn's inheritance, both lands and movable goods.
    But once he stopped talking, Bergönund set to work.
[- - -]
    At that Askman and the men of his troop ran to the court, cut through the hallowed bands
and broke down poles, scattering the judges abroad. A great uproar broke out at the Thing, but
everyone was weaponless there.
    "Can Bergönund hear my words?" asked Egil then.
    "I hear", said he.
    "Then I am challenging you to holmgang, that we fight here at the Thing. Let him have the
property, land and movable goods, who wins the day. And be every man's dastard if you dare
not" (*Egil's saga*, chap. 56; trans. Jones 1960:138 ff.).

Introduction

What do we know of law in Scandinavia before the appearance of our provincial
laws? Were there any laws at all? After reading about Egil's performance at the
famous Gulathing in western Norway in the year 946 AD (according to *Egil's*

87

Saga), the question seems to be settled: Viking Age Scandinavia was a society with a legal framework, with legal institutions such as *þing* assemblies, judges and special *þing* sites enclosed with *vébǫnd* (the 'hallowed string').

However, these rather odd questions and statements *may* be raised, firstly bearing in mind the (accurate) scepticism regarding the sagas as historical sources emphasized especially by the literary historians of our time, and secondly—and primarily—seen against the writings of some legal historians in Scandinavia during the last few decades. The burden of the 'Germanenrechtschule' (i.e. the nineteenth-century idea of a *germanisches Urrecht*) has been very heavy for legal history in Scandinavia (Fenger 1991:156 f.), and the settlement with this 'legacy' by later scholars has resulted in the expression of, in some cases, fierce statements (Sjöholm 1988 *passim*), that have led early Scandinavian legal history research into a state of shock, or perhaps better, an annoying and obtrusive silence. The 'Stand der Forschung' of today seems to be that all provincial laws were written down for the purpose of the crown, the nobility and the Church during the early Middle Ages, and it all goes back to earlier Continental law. The first Scandinavian laws were thus a mirror of Roman law (and of the Law of Moses!).

Scholars working with Scandinavian culture before the Middle Ages must, in the light of this, repeatedly have asked themselves in recent years: did the Scandinavians have any kind of law, and if so, what did it look like, and are there any links to the known provincial laws? In spite of the bold statements by the legal historian Elsa Sjöholm in particular, some have continued to discuss law and legal practice in pre-medieval Scandinavia, first and foremost the Danish legal historian Ole Fenger (1971, 1983, 1987, 1991), but also others have continued dissecting the provincial laws for older, perhaps prehistoric, strata (e.g. Foote 1987; Ruthström 1988; Stein-Wilkeshuis 1982, 1986, 1998:313, 321; cf. also Bagge 1989; Hagland & Sandnes 1994: IX ff.; Rindal 1994). The philologist Peter Foote (1987:54) has commented on this state and situation in a very eloquent and elegant way, accepting the tendency of lawbooks to be "normative and unreal, a derivative image-building exercise, ideologically motivated", however wrapping up the discussion with a sigh, "but we should not be so busy reading between the lines that we fail to tackle the lines themselves".[1]

According to the (of course dubious) Old Icelandic sagas, there were laws, lawmen and assemblies in Viking Age Scandinavia. We have had one testimony from *Egil's Saga* (above) and in the same saga there is the famous dispute at a *várþing* between Thorstein and Steinarr, the sons of the two old friends Egil and Ǫnund Sjóni, that Egil settles (chaps. 80 ff.).

Famous is also Snorri's story of Thorgny lawman among the Svear and their assembly in Uppsala (*Óláfs saga ins helga*, chap. 78), in a sub-province in Uppland. His forefathers had been lawmen for generations, according to Snorri.

---

[1] Judith Jesch has recently (1998) discussed law in Viking-Age Scandinavia, especially in the case of homicide and treachery. Many of the sources mentioned by me below are also referred to in her very useful and interesting article.

Thorgny was known as a rich, important and wise man and he had a large military escort (*hirð*).[2] In the same episode Snorri gives us his description of an assembly meeting at the Uppsala *thing* (*Upsalaþing*, chap. 80):

> On the first day, when the thing was opened, king Olafr sat in his chair and his *hirð* around him. On the other side of the thing site sat Rǫgnvaldr jarl (from Västergötland) and Thorgny in a chair, and in front of them sat the *hirð* of the jarl and the housecarls of Thorgny. Behind the chair and around in a circle stood the peasant congregation....

After a persuasive speech by Thorgny, that appealed to the congregation, the people made noise with their weapons: "*Þá gerði lýðrinn þegar vápnabrak ok gný mikinn.*

In *Óláfs saga ins helga* there is also the story of the sly lawman Emundr from Skara amongst the Västgötar, the most influential man in Västergötland, next to the jarl Rǫgnvaldr.[3] In this episode Emundr has a meeting with the king of the Swedes in Uppsala where he tries to settle a problem, in which the law of the Götar differed from the law of the Svear: "*er lǫg vár greinir ok Upsala-lǫg*". Thus, at least for Snorri in the thirteenth century, the Västgötar had their law in the early eleventh century, and the Svear theirs.

From these episodes, in Snorri's *Heimskringla* and *Egil's Saga*, there are several important features relating to *þing* and law to be noted. We hear of lawmen, normally rich and important men. They had their own *hirð*, i.e. military escort; thus, we may assume that, for Snorri, lawmen were part of the uppermost stratum in society. It is also interesting to note that Snorri thought the lawman institution was inheritable; but we don't know if he is correct on this point. Snorri and the author of *Egil's Saga*[4] take the *þing* for granted and build heavily on these assembly meetings occurring in several layers in society. At these *þing*s the people could collectively make their opinion heard by rattling their weapons (*vápnabrak*, *vápnatak*). Thus, the congregation must have been allowed to have their weapons at the *þing* assembly. In the *Gulaþing* episode in *Egil's Saga*, however, there were no weapons at the *þing* (cf. also below). Finally, when Emundr *lǫgmaðr* from Västergötland meets with the king of the Svear, he, or more correcly Snorri, states that the Västgötar had a law and the Svear had theirs, thus, different people (Svear and Västgötar) had their own laws.

---

[2] *Þá var á Tíundalandi sá lǫgmaðr, er Þorgnyr hét; faðir hans er nefndr Þorgnyr Þorgnysson. Þeir langfeðgar hǫfðu verit lǫgmenn á Tíundalandi um margra konunga ævi. Þorgnyr var þá gamall; hann hafði um sik mikla hirð, hann var kallaðr vitrastr maðr í Svíaveldi....* (Snorri's *Heimskringla*, *Óláfs saga ins helga*, chap. 78).

[3] "*Maðr er nefndr Emundr af Skǫrum; hann var þar lǫgmaðr í Gautlandi vestra ok var manna vitrastr ok orðsnjallastr; hann var ættstórr ok frændmargr, stórauðigr; hann var kallaðr undirhyggjumaðr ok meðallagi trúr; hann var maðr ríkastr í Vestra-Gautlandi, þá er jarl var á brot farinn*" (*Heimskringla*, *Óláfs saga ins helga*, chap. 94).

[4] I am aware that it has been proposed that Snorri Sturluson may also have written *Egil's Saga* (see R. M. Perkins in *RGA* 6:473 f.). I find the arguments for this opinion quite convincing myself; however, as I would not bet my last penny on it, I write "the author of *Egil's Saga*".

The above is, of course, literature, and we have to take the stories for what they are, literary constructions, but if we can qualify statements and details by Snorri and others with information from other sources than literary sagas, then it should be obvious that from a historical point of view we are on much safer ground, and again may listen to the authors of the sagas in a more historically observant way.

From what we know, it seems obvious that in early Scandinavia it was the custom to make a noise with weapons at *þings* for expressing opinions, this the divisions of *wapentakes* in the Danelaw tells us, but the custom is also mentioned in the much later Magnus Lagabøter's Law (*landslǫg*) (I:5; *NGL* 1:409), where it says that a verdict is not legally valid unless the people at the *þing* assembly, who stand outside of the judges in the *lǫgrétta*, give their consent to the verdict by rattling with or raising their weapons in the air (*vápnatak* or *þingtak*).[5] In this case it is somewhat confusing that in the same chapter in *ML*'s *landslǫg* we read of the prohibition against carrying weapons at *þings*. This contradiction is explained by Arne Bøe (1965: col. 180) by the fact that this prohibition did not apply to all weapons, a solution to the problem that does not seem very convincing. Instead, the most logical solution is that men with weapons were present at the assembly, however, not in the actual, consecrated *þing* site, within the round circle marked out by the *vébǫnd*, where all weapons were banned, but outside the *vébǫnd*, as Magnus Lagabøter's Law hints at (above).[6]

Is the mentioning of *vébǫnd*, enclosing the *þing* site at *Gulaþing* in *Egil's Saga*, a fictitious literary spice invented by the author without any historical bearings? Most probably, it is not. In the *Gulathing Law* itself (chap. 91) it says that the *þing* site should have a round shape (*Þingring*; cf. Robberstad 1937:198; Schledermann 1974: col. 374), and in the early *Frostathing Law* (I:2) the word *vébǫnd* is actually used; it says that the *ármen* (bailiffs) from all *fylki* shall with *vébǫnd* enclose the place of the men in the *lǫgretta*. In the so called *Hundabrævið* from the Faeroe Islands *vébǫnd* are mentioned in a context with *lagþing*: *Var þetta gort a logþingi innan vebanda* (Barnes 1974: col. 386). Finally, the regulation of the use of *vébǫnd* is also in Magnus Lagabøters *landslǫg* (3:2) and *bylǫg* (town law) (3:2). The background of the usage of hazel poles to fasten the *vébǫnd* on, mentioned in *Egil's Saga*, may also be non-fictitious. This custom is known, for example, from Frankish Law (*Lex Ribuaria* 67:5) in the eighth century.

Regarding the legal assemblies in Viking-Age Scandinavia, we know for certain of their existence (cf. Jesch 1998). A most famous contemporary evidence for this is the Bällsta rune monument in the parish of Täby, just north of Stockholm. On two rune stones erected here one can read **[ulfkil] uk arkil uk kui þir kariþu iar þikstaþ**, "Ulvkel and Arnkel and Gye, they made here a *þing* place (*þingstaðr*)"

---

[5] For *vápnatak*, *wapentake*, see Hertzberg 1889:356–8, and *KL*.

[6] This plausible hypothesis was mentioned by Prof. Jørn Sandnes, Trondheim, at a seminar I gave at the Centre for Medieval Studies, Trondheim, in the spring of 1998. According to Prof. Sandnes, this is regulated in the *Frostathing Law*.

(Jansson 1987:120). Several other *þing* sites are known from rune stones and place-names in Sweden. It is also possible to reconstruct *þing* sites through archaeological excavations. One of the most startling ones in recent time was the excavation at *Þingnes* outside Reykjavík in Iceland. This may be the site of the famous *Kjalarnesþing*, mentioned in *The Book of Settlements*. Founded by Þorsteinn Ingólfsson, the son of the first settler of Iceland, Ingólfr Arnason, this *þing* may have served as a kind of general assembly until 930, however, with no legislative role. A reminiscence of this is that the chieftains of Kjalarnes and the descendants of Þorsteinn Ingólfsson held the honorary title *Allsherjargoði*, the supreme chieftain, whose function was to hallow the National Assembly at Thingvellir every year. Exept for the sparse information we get in *The Book of Settlements* and Ari's words in *The Book of the Icelanders*, very little is known of the *þing* assembly in Kjalarnes. Therefore, it is most interesting that recent archaeological excavations at Elliðavatn by *Þingnes* probably have revealed this first assembly site (Ólafsson 1987).

How old then was the *þing*-institution in Scandinavia? Well, we cannot be certain. However, in a "Stand der Forschung" article, Per Sveaas Andersen (1974: col. 347) finds it plausible that it went back to the early Iron Age (i.e. before AD 600).

Admitting the possibility of having different laws for different regions, as mentioned by Snorri, we do not have any contemporary sources to confirm this, but as will be discussed below, it is my belief that legal customs and legal traditions differed between the provinces of Scandinavia. This was probably the background for the later provincial laws.

The provincial laws of Scandinavia were compiled and written down during the twelfth and thirteenth centuries in western Scandinavia, and during the thirteenth and fourteenth centuries in the eastern parts. Fairly recently it was suggested that these laws mirror society only at the time of depreciation and codification, i.e. the early and mid-Middle Ages. Some even state that the legal text is not a mirror of society at that time, but shows the intentions and ideology of those who instituted those written laws. In particular Elsa Sjöholm (1988:50) has declared that the provincial laws of Scandinavia are useless for reconstructing prehistoric society. I do not understand how she then copes with, e.g., the early *Law of Gulathing*, that, at least according to tradition, is believed to have been edited and written down during the late eleventh century (Hertzberg 1905:92 ff.; Knudsen 1960: col. 560), but presumed to have been conceived and formulated already during the early tenth century (Rindal 1994:7). Still, there are scholars (see above) who penetrate our old provincial laws and find old strata, and even obviously prehistoric phenomena and enactments.

For an analysis of our oldest legal sources in Scandinavia an obvious start would be the famous *Baugatal* in *Grágás*, i.e. rules concerning the duty to pay and to accept payment for injuries; however, although this law-rule is truffled with archaic words, it is very dubious, highly controversial and even uncertain if it was ever in use (see Phillpotts 1913; Ingvarsson 1970:223 ff.; Fenger 1971; Barlau 1981; Sawyer 1982:44; 1987; Meulengracht Sørensen 1992:169 f.).

Another possible departure could be the Old Danish *Vederlov* (*Witherlogh*), the penalty law of the king's *hirð*, with manuscripts from the late twelfth century, except in two of these, stated to be from 'old Knut's days' (understood as being from the time of Canute the Great, thus in the early eleventh century). However, this law is also problematic regarding origin and age (Kroman 1975; Fenger 1983:63.).[7]

Also the Old Swedish so-called *Hednalag*, i.e. 'Pagan Law', as the title of the fragment indicates, has been assumed to be very old. The codex, in which the *Hednalag* has been written, is from the middle of the thirteenth century, but the age of the actual law-rule is not known. The law discusses and regulates *einvígi*, the settling of disputes by fighting, and some phrases have been considered as very archaic (see Nelson 1944:57; Ståhle 1954:130 f.; Wessén 1968:51).

In an interesting study, Peter Foote (1987:63) analyses the Icelandic *Grágás*, especially *Landabrigðis þáttr* and *Reka þáttr*, and his conclusion is that these parts of the law should be dated to the eleventh century. He also concludes that other parts of *Grágás* must be just as early, perhaps even earlier, i.e. from the pre-Christian period (cf. Meulengracht Sørensen 1992:112 f.).

Thus, there are reasons to believe that the provincial laws have earlier roots, respectively in their different provinces, than the twelfth or thirteenth centuries. The editing and writing down of the provincial laws in books between the twelfth and fourteenth century has seen, of course, the use of Continental law and legal knowledge as the basis for the new product, and the transferring of laws to other regions, as in the case of the *Hälsinge Lawbook*, which is practically a copy of the *Uppland Lawbook*. These facts have been established by Elsa Sjöholm and others. However, for the tracing of older strata and details in the lawbooks, one has to look for aspects that *differ*. For example, the *Hälsinge Law* has taken over the administrative structure from the *Uppland Law*, but used (retained!) a terminology totally unknown in the *Uppland Law*, a fact which must have an explanation.

But, for the sake of not being too controversial from the perspectives of literary and legal history, let us keep the much-debated Scandinavian provincial laws out of the discussion, and also the much-discussed Old Icelandic sagas, and instead look for other legal evidence from prehistoric Scandinavia. As a starting point we can assume that the old proverb (or prudence), *ubi societas, ibi jus* (where there is society, there is law), was also valid in the case of early Scandinavian society. This seems to be a good departure point. We can thus assume that there was some kind of law there. The question is, are there any reminiscences in the contemporary source material that reflect this?[8]

---

[7] For the Old Danish *Vederlov* see also Hjärne 1979:151–208.

[8] The first source to be mentioned would be Tacitus' *Germania*, where in chapters 11 and 12 the *þing* institution and the judicial system as well as the German tribes are described (Tacitus, *Germania*, cf. Much 1967 *passim*), but this work predates the Viking Age. The fact that Elsa Sjöholm

Contemporary evidence for Viking Age law in Scandinavia

a) *The Oklunda runic inscription*

In the hamlet of Oklunda in Östra Husby parish in the eastern part of the province of Östergötland in Sweden a remarkable runic inscription was discovered in the year 1929. In the hamlet, on a solid rock, someone in the early Viking Age carved a small runic text that, when found, created a scholarly stir and has been discussed ever since (Nordén 1930, 1931; von Friesen 1933; Jansson 1987:37; Salberger 1980; Ruthström 1988; Peterson 1993; Lönnqvist & Widmark 1997; Jesch 1998). The reason for this is that this is an early legal document, considered to be the oldest information in Scandinavia on the right of asylum, in this case at a pagan cult site. According to Salberger (1980:19) the runes are as follows:

> • þitta faþi kunar • faþi runaʀ þisaʀ • in sa flau sakiʀ • suti ui þita • in sa afʀ la nruþ þan • in sa bat uifin •

which normally is translated as:

> Gunnar cut this, cut these runes. And he fled guilty (of homicide), sought this pagan cult site (*vi*). And he has a clearance thereafter, and he tied Vi-Finn.

The text is still under heated discussion. Normally the inscription has been dated to the ninth or tenth century, but Olov Lönnqvist and Gun Widmark (1997:151) have presented strong evidence for a dating to the first half of the ninth century. The start of the text and the readings of some parts are still not obvious. For example the part **in sa afʀ la nruþ þan** is very problematic. Lately several have preferred to read there **in sa afr landruð þan**, 'and he owns the *landruð* then', a somewhat incomprehensible statement, in my opinion. I think this interpretation may be dismissed, since a word **landruð* has presumably never existed. Such a compound is virtually impossible and nothing similar has been found in old Scandinavian languages.

Both words *land* and *ruð* (or *rjóðr*) are well known in Old Scandinavian for arable land and clearances, respectively. However, the compound **landruð* is

---

(1988) has totally dismissed Tacitus' *Germania* as being absolutely useless as a historical source for early Scandinavia, would demand a painstaking treatment and discussion on this topic. However, I cannot agree with Sjöholm's view of Tacitus' work. There are some extremely interesting features that we find in later periods, and which certainly have their roots in the Roman Iron Age.

The second source to pay attention to is the runic inscription on the *Eggjum stone* in western Norway. However, this rune stone also predates the Viking Age since it has been dated to *ca* 700 AD, and, furthermore, the inscription is extremely difficult to interpret (cf. Olsen 1919; Jacobsen 1931; Grønvik 1985; Buti 1987; G. Høst in *RGA* 6:460 ff.). At least one scholar, Otto Springer, assumes that the runic text comprises some sort of legal information. In a damaged part of the inscription, Springer (1970:40 f.) amends the missing text as *sakʀ*, which he identifies with OWN *sekr* (< **sakjaʀ*). In, e.g., the *Gulathing Law* this word has the meaning 'obliged to pay a fine' or the more general meaning 'punishable, guilty'. However, in the Old Icelandic sagas the word *sekr* frequently has the meaning 'outlawed'. As also Springer (1970:45) observes, it is notable that this word occurs on the Oklunda inscription (*sakiʀ*).

never found. To qualify a kind of 'land', one would use a compound with *land* and an attribute as a first element, such as the case with *myrland, röjningsland* or OSw. *ruðskogher,* etc., but never the other way round. There is a large number of words for cultivated land that are compounded with *-land,* but none where *land-* is the qualifier, first element (cf. Sdw, *SAOB*).[9] Therefore, when Lena Peterson (1993:35) in a most polemical way dismisses an interpretation by Bo Ruthström (1988:70 f.), who here reads **(i)n sa fik kruþ þan**, "and he got free safe-conduct (to the assembly) then (or later)", she is, in my opinion, too quick on the trigger. The OSw word. *gruþ* or *griþ* is well attested in early legal language in Scandinavia (cf. von See 1964:166 ff.), and in assuming that a rune is wrongly carved, Ruthström shows parallells in the same text. This interpretation must therefore, in my opinion, be considered in future discussions of the text. Thus, it is more or less certain that new interpretations and readings of this rune inscription will be presented in the future. However, the part of interest to us, namely that *Gunnarr...fló sekr* and that he *sótti vé þetta...,* seems to be fairly evident and has never been disputed.

Bo Ruthström (1988), as already Arthur Nordén (1931), has argued that this runic legal document has reflections in the early Swedish provincial laws, in both the *Guta Law* of Gotland and the *Östgöta Law* of Östergötland. He notices that the legal procedures, according to the provincial laws, for preventing vengeance for a homicide were:

1) A serious crime (a homicide) has been committed.
2) The escaping perpetrator goes to a protected place.
3) The perpetrator is reconciled with the family of the injured party.

As the Oklunda inscription thus shows, a malefactor was allowed protection after committing homicide at a *vi,* that is if he managed to get there before his enemies managed to 'legally' kill him, and—one should perhaps add—also after officially announcing his crime. We know this custom from Christian laws, where the church was regarded as the place of special legal sanctity where people had right of asylum (Nilsson 1991). It is probably impossible to ascertain whether the right of asylum in Scandinavian churches is a transformation of the pagan custom of right of asylum at cult and *thing* sites, or if it is simply taken from Canon Law (Nilsson 1991).

As both Nordén (1931) and Ruthström (1988) have noted, the Oklunda inscription has an apparent parallel in the *Guta Law,* where the three churches in Fardhem, Tingstäde and Atlingbo were regarded as asylum-churches. The latter also points to the *Östgöta* Law (DrB VII:1 and EdsB III:2) which contained a provision whereby a killer was protected from vengeance by the victim's relatives within the churchyard, and that killing a man in a church was looked upon as a serious crime (*epsørisbrut*). Olov Lönnqvist and Gun Widmark (1997:155 ff.) continue a discussion started by Nordén and focus on the word **bat**, probably

---

[9] As in: *avradsland, betland, bodland, fäbodland, fälleland, gräftland, hack(e)land, lökland, morland, myrland, plogland, risland, röjeland, röjningsland,* etc. (*SAOB*).

band(a), that is used also in the *Guta Law* for a "protected space (literally: something enclosed)", and they believe that this *banda,* "protected space", was defined by the malefactor himself. They connect the word *banda* in the *Guta Law* with **bat** in the Oklunda inscription and thus they see here a prehistoric reminiscence in the *Guta Law*.

The word *sakiʀ* is central in the inscription. There is a consensus that the word is the adjective OWN *sekr* 'guilty', OSw *sæker* (< **sakiaʀ*), a formation to *sak, sǫk* (< **sakō-*), 'case, suit, dispute', cf. Goth. *sakjo,* 'fight, dispute', that in turn is a formation to the Pr-Germ verb **sakan,* 'accuse, process, dispute', etc. and related to Sw, OSw *saker,* 'legal dispute' (cf. e.g. Turville Petre 1977:769; de Vries 1961:469; Olson 1916:364). Olov Lönnqvist and Gun Widmark (1997:151) have commented on the form of this word, suggesting that the linguistic entity represents an early stage of the language. In commenting on this word **sakiʀ** in the inscription Otto Springer (1970:45 f.) discusses Gunnar's status as a refugee:

> There is no doubt that Gunnar's state immediately upon his commitment of the crime, his state of being *sakiʀ* [...], cannot be identified with the officially imposed, *de jure* outlawry, a penalty inflicted only under certain circumstances. On the contrary, it is precisely Gunnar's avoidance of such *de jure* outlawry—by virtue of making a settlement after he has become *sakiʀ* but has found temporary refuge in a sanctuary— that has occasioned the preliterary document of Oklunda....

The exact semantic content of the word **sakiʀ** is difficult to find. Scholars have translated it as 'guilty' (von Friesen *et al.*), 'outlawed' (Springer), 'under penalty' (Foote), etc. In any case, the overall meaning, which must be 'guilty', unless Springer's arguments are valid, seems to be clear.[10]

Ruthström (1988:73) also asks why a perpetrator should seek asylum in a cultic grove, and not on a *þing* site. His answer is that law and cult were intimately tied together in early times, something he thinks he can trace in the Old Swedish legal process, which is imbued with religious conceptions. Hence, a question of guilt was in early times not decided by an independent assessment by the judges in a court, but through a regulated system of allotments of right to give evidence, the so-called process of *eþgærþismæn*, where the taking of oaths was the determining factor. When taking an oath, after an invocation to the gods, one adduced an established oath formula (cf. Brink 1996b:46), as recorded in the early *Västgöta Law* (Dråpsbalken I:2):

> *Sva se mær guð hol ok vattum minum. at þu bart a han od ok æg. ok þu ær sændær bani hans*

> The gods (or god) be with me and my witnesses, that you carried on him point and edge, and you are his true murderer.

I believe Ruthström is correct on this point, but think it is possible to qualify this connection between law and cult even more. As I shall discuss below, it seems

---

[10] For outlawry and *sekr* in early Iceland, see Breisch 1994:133 ff.

perfectly possible to assume that legal matters were performed and a *þing* assembled at a *vi*. In my opinion cultic and legal (as well as probably also skaldic) matters were so intimately connected (cf. Rehfeldt 1954; Gurevich 1973:81 f.), that it is impossible to separate one phenomenon from the other during pre-Christian times in Scandinavia.

To sum up, the Oklunda inscription is obviously a legal document from the early ninth century that has the aim of announcing that a certain Gunnar followed the law or the legal custom in a correct legal way after committing a crime, a homicide. He escaped to a *vi*, an assembly site, and there got asylum and perhaps drew up a protected space (Sw *fridskrets*) where he was safe.

b) *Forsaringen – the oldest 'law' in Scandinavia*
In the parish church of Forsa in the province of Hälsingland, northern Sweden, an iron ring with a runic inscription has been hanging on a door for centuries. The ring was observed and mentioned in a text already in 1599 and the inscription was published and translated around 1700 by the famous Olof Celsius. The ring measures 43 cm in diameter and contains nearly 250 runes.

Traditionally and ever since an important and influential analysis of the inscription by the Norwegian Sophus Bugge in 1877, it has been called the oldest legal inscription (legal rule) in Scandinavia. There has been a consensus regarding the fact that the inscription contains an ecclesiastical legal rule, regulating either tithe, or the protection in a church, or the omission of giving service. The main argument for this being a law of the Church has been the occurrence of two key words, **staf**, '(bishop's) staff' and **lirþir**, 'the learned (clergy)', so read and translated by Bugge. The ring and the inscription has therefore been assumed to be from the Christian period. Even though the runes on the ring are very archaic, the same kind found on, e.g., the famous Rök rune stone in the province of Östergötland (from *ca* 800 AD), scholars placed the Forsa rune ring in the first half of the twelfth century.

In an important analysis of the inscription in the 1970s, the Norwegian runologist Aslak Liestøl was able to prove that Bugge's reading *lirþir* was wrong. Instead one should read *liuþir*. This removes the foundation of the traditional interpretation and dating of the ring. There is nothing that forces us to tie the ring to a clerical context anymore.

The inscription reads:

> : uksatuiskilanaukauratuastafatfurstalaki :
> uksatuaaukaurafiurataþrulaki :
> : inatþriþialakiuksafiuraukauratastaf :
> aukaltaikuiuarʀifanhafskakiritfuriʀ
> : suaþliuþiʀakuatliuþritisuauasintfuraukhalkat :
> inþaʀkirþusikþitanunratarstaþum :
> : aukufakʀahiurtstaþum :
> inuibiurnfaþi:

this may be normalized as:

> *Oxa at vis gil[d]an ok aura tva staf at fyrsta lagi,*
> *oxa tva ok aura fiura at aðru lagi,*
> *en at þriäia lagi oxa fiura ok aura atta staf;*
> *ok allt äigu i värr, ef hann hafsk äkki rett fyriʀ,*
> *svað liuðiʀ äigu at liuðretti, sva vas innt fyrr ok hälgat.*
> *En þäirʀ gärðu sik þetta Anundr a Tarstaðum*
> *ok Ofagʀ a Hiortstaðum.*
> *En Vibiorn faði.*

and in translation:

> One ox and two *aura* [in fine] to the *staf* for the restoration of a *vi*
> in a valid state for the first time;
> two oxen and four *aura* for the second time;
> but for the third time four oxen and eight *aura*;
> and all property in suspension, if he doesn't make right.
> That, the people are entitled to demand, according to the law of
> the people, that was decreed and ratified before.
> But they made themselves this ('ring' or *sigþ*), Anund from Tåsta
> and Ofeg from Hjortsta.
> But Vibjörn carved.

There have been several odd conceptions in the traditional interpretation and dating of this runic inscription. The most obvious are the runes themselves. They are of the kind called 'Norwegian–Swedish runes', or *kortkvistrunor* (Norw. *stuttruner*), that we find on several rune stones, among them the Rök stone, that normally are dated to *ca* 800 AD or the ninth century. But the pressure from the words *staf* and *lirþiʀ* was so strong that scholars saw themselves forced to place the ring in the twelfth century. To save their hypothesis they produced an *ad hoc* explanation, saying that the province of Hälsingland was a relict area, where archaic words and ninth century runes had survived. However, regarding the conversion to the new Christian religion, the province, on the other hand, was supposed to have been totally unique in the opposite direction. A Christian society, and an established ecclesiastical organization with churches, were assumed to be present already around the year 1100 AD. Of course these arguments are not valid; not only are they full of contradictions, they are historically impossible.

Instead the Forsa rune ring most probably should be dated to the ninth century, which makes the old attribution "the oldest law rule in Scandinavia" even more accurate. I shall not go into any detailed discussion concerning the ring and the inscription. For anyone interested in the matter, I have done so in the Swedish language (Brink 1996b). I will just briefly comment on some details by stating that we have here a legal text, a kind of law rule, from the early Viking Age. Most probably it regulates the maintenance of a *vi*, i.e. an assembly site (Ruthström 1990). The comparison with the Oklunda inscription is then evident. For failure to restore the *vi* in a legal way, one must pay a fine, one ox and two *aura* (*ørar*) the first time, two oxen and four *ørar* the second time, and four oxen and eight *ørar* the third time; in case this was not done, all the culprit's property was to be suspended. Perhaps the most important part of the inscription is the phrase *svað liuðir æigu at liuðretti*, "that, which the people are entitled to demand according to the people's right (the law of the *land*)". Thus, we have here evidence of a special kind of law of the people or the *land* (most certainly Hälsingland), a *liuðrettr*, cf. OWN *lýðrettr* (cf. von See 1964:57 ff.). To my knowledge, this statement is unique for Viking Age Scandinavia, and it actually supports the statement by Snorri (above) that, in early Scandinavia, different peoples had different laws.

Two men, Anund and Ofeg living in Tåsta and Hjortsta, are mentioned in the inscription. Neither of these settlements are in the parish of Forsa, but in the neighbouring parish of Hög. This fact, together with an old legend that places the ring in Hög, makes it very plausible to assume that the ring originally had been kept in Hög, known during the Middle Ages as the *þing* assembly for all of the people of Hälsingland and where we also have one of the royal farms in northern Sweden, *Kungsgården*. As described below, the place-name *Hög* refers to a large mound from the early Iron Age, called *Kungshögen,* 'the king's mound', situated beside the church. Probably this was the *þing* assembly site in early times and to this *þing* I think one is entitled to assign the rune ring.

Therefore, it is very tempting to look at the rune ring as a kind of oath ring, that was used at the *alþing* for the *hælsing(i)ar* at Hög. In the light of scholarly writings during the last decades, this is a somewhat controversial statement, but I believe that the possibility should be mentioned and taken into consideration. In any case, the Forsa rune ring must be seen as one of the most important artefacts from the early Viking Age that can shed light on early Scandinavian society.

c) Scandinavian law in a tenth-century treaty from Russia
In the famous Nestor Chronicle from Russia, three tenth-century charters or treaties between Rus and Greeks are mentioned. The most comprehensive is a treaty of 911, signed by Rus' princes and Scandinavian merchants, at least bearing Scandinavian names, containing articles on the legal position of merchants with respect to some kind of legal procedure in case of offences (Stein-Wilkeshuis 1998:312).

In several interesting articles, the legal historian Martina Stein-Wilkeshuis (e.g. 1991, 1994, 1998) has analysed these treaties, which had earlier been seen as having traces of Byzantine law. She found striking resemblances with early Scandinavian law. One of the features mentioned is the statement in public of the offence. This way of publicly announcing one's abuses, and also the fact that the injured parties were allowed to state in public that they had been abused, was basic in early Scandinavian law, although also found in several continental *leges*. Facts, agreements, injuries, etc., must be stated to the public. As Stein-Wilkeshuis (1998:313) writes, this procedure, with a declaration in public, announcing contracts, conflicts, actions or abuses, is typical of an illiterate society. One should note that this case has an obvious resemblance with the Oklunda runic inscription, in which Gunnar makes a public announcement.

Among other aspects mentioned in the treaty of 911 is oath-taking, well known for early Scandinavia, a procedure that is very elaborately described in the early laws, and also the right to revenge. In the treaty one is allowed to kill a thief caught red-handed, a procedure also known from, e.g., the Icelandic *Grágás*. The correct legal steps foresaw that one was allowed to kill the thief on the site of the crime where one had been injured; however, if the malefactor had been able to announce his crime 'officially' to the victim or his family, or to any other trusted person, and then voluntarily go the *þing* assembly, or if he managed to reach a protected site or area of asylum, as was the case mentioned in the Oklunda inscription, one was not allowed to lay one's hand on the culprit.

In her analysis of these treaties, Martina Stein-Wilkeshuis (1998) states that she can probably trace early Scandinavian law rules in this agreement between Rus and Greeks regarding some crimes and their correct penalties. She argues that the law rules found in the treaties have direct counterparts in early provincial laws of Scandinavia. If Stein-Wilkeshuis is correct, we have here a very interesting case were judicial matters, known from Scandinavian provincial laws, may be traced back to as early as *ca* 900 AD, i.e. to the Viking Age. This observation totally contrasts with Elsa Sjöholm's negative views (1988) on the age of the provincial laws and the possibility of tracing earlier reminiscences in these lawbooks.

Place-names in *-lǫg,-lag*

The name *Danelaw* refers to the northern and eastern parts of England, where the Vikings had established themselves, and it means 'the area where Danish law was applicable' (see e.g. Kisbye 1988:52). In a Latin document from 1324 it is stated that England was divided into three laws (*leges*), namely *Essexenelaga, Mircenelage et Denelaga* (Calissendorff 1980:13), also *Westseaxenalag* for Wessex is recorded (Kisbye 1988:52). From this, we may conclude that during the Viking Age a certain kind of law, identified as Danish law and rules, was used in the part of England known as *Danelaw*. This name in *-lǫg, -lag* is however not unique (cf. von See 1964:193; Calissendorff 1980).

In Norway we are familiar with the territorial names *Gulaþingslag* and *Frostaþingslag*, referring to the areas where the *Gulaþing* and the *Frostaþing* were in use. A semantically similar name is the Swedish *Bergslag(en)*, that most probably means 'the area where a special law for the mining district of central Sweden is valid' (Calissendorff 1980). Equivalent to this is also certainly the name *Roslagen*, denoting the eastern strip of land in the province of Uppland, where a special kind of law, the so called *roþarætt*, was used (Hjärne 1947:125). This is perhaps reflected in Kristoffer's Law (*landslag*) of 1450, where the Uppland Law is called *Gamble rodz lagh*. Both *Bergslagen* and *Roslagen* are known from fairly recent times, from the fourteenth and fifteenth centuries, but at least the latter may be earlier than that. In the Middle Ages *Roslagen* was known as *Roden* (< OSw *Roþ(r)in*), where the *rosþiggar* (< *roþsbygghiar*) lived. The name *Ludherlag*, a name on a medieval *skeppsreda*, a naval district, in the province of Bohuslän, comprising the parishes of Tanum and Lur (Brink ms.) is more problematic.

Apart from these, more or less obvious place-names in *-lǫg*, *-lag*, there are some elusive names, such as the Norwegian *Njarðarlǫg* (= *Tysnesøy* in Sunnhordaland), *Freyslǫg* (= *Frøyslog* in Rogaland) and *Tyslǫg* (= *Tislauan* in Sør-Trøndelag). All three have the name of a pagan god (or goddess) as the first element of the compound. The question is how this should be interpreted. Magnus Olsen (1905) assumed that the first name referred to the area (here an island) were a special kind of law was in use and were the god *Njǫrðr* was worshipped. This interpretation is complicated by the fact that the legal district (the *lǫg*) was dedicated to Njǫrðr, but the name of the island itself reveals that it was dedicated to the pagan god Týr, probably indicating that Týr had some sacral affiliation to this island or that this god had some special worship here. However, there is also the possibility that the second element of the compound in *Njarðarlǫg*, *Freyslǫg* and *Tyslǫg* is OWN *laug* f. 'lake' or **lókr* m. 'calm, shallow water', which is also an interesting interpretation, because then these names may be assigned to a set denoting probable sacred lakes (see Brink 1997:430; cf. Stjernquist 1987, 1998).

Anyhow, if we are to see the word *lǫg*, 'law' in these three theophoric place-names, which is probable, they can be assigned to another small but interesting set of names, namely district names with a pagan god as the first element. We have the obscure Swedish *Frösthult* (< *Frøstolpt*), i.e. the *tolft* district dedicated to the god Frö, and the Danish *Frøsherred* on Jutland. From these names we may assume that administrative districts also could be some kind of cult districts, where a specific pagan god had a special position. This is the old idea of the Swedish legal historian Gerhard Hafström (1949, 1964), i.e. that the parishes and also the *þing* districts originated in prehistoric pagan cult districts. This idea has been criticized in later years (cf. Brink 1991:124), but for the interpretation of these few district names, Hafström's idea should be still considered. In this case it is interesting to note that the above mentioned three Norwegian names in *-lǫg* may bear witness to the fact that in prehistoric Scandinavia the cult and the law were tied together.

Thing mounds – place-names in *-haug*, *-hög* – and thing sites

The famous mound called *Tynwald Hill* on the Isle of Man has been in use as a *þing* mound for over a thousand years. From this hill, the election of new kings was proclaimed, as e.g. in the years 1393 and 1408. Even nowadays laws which were passed during the previous year are ratified here. *Tynwald Hill*, that in a medieval chronicle is written *Tingualla* and goes back to a OWN *þingvǫllr* 'assembly site', has several counterparts in Scandinavia. The most famous one is, of course, *Þingvellir* in Iceland, the ancient site where the *Alþing* was held. Others are *Dingwall* in northern Scotland, *Thingwall* on Orkney and *Tingvalla* at Karlstad in the province of Värmland in Sweden (Fellows Jensen 1993; Brink 1997:403). At least Tynwald Hill and *Þingvellir* are prehistoric, showing that the use of *þing* mounds and the practice of locating *þing* assemblies on special hills or mounds was a prehistoric phenomenon (cf. Lindqvist 1925; Schledermann 1974; Barnes 1974).

This observation makes several Scandinavian place-names in *-haug*, *-hög* of interest. As mentioned above, the unique Forsa rune ring may be tied to *Hög* in the province of Hälsingland. Hög's distinction is being the focal place for the entire province. We know that, in the Middle Ages, this was the *þing* assembly site for all Hälsingar, and here we also find *Kungsgården*, one of the royal farms in northern Sweden. The name *Hög* refers to the so called *Kungshögen*, an imposing mound from the early Iron Age, which obviously was a focal point and where probably legal matters took place.

The same background probably applies to the place-name **Hög* (> *Högsby*) in the district of Handbörd in eastern Småland, and also the famous *-haug* sites in Trøndelag: *Sakshaug*, *Alstahaug* and *Haug* (Brink 1990a:272 ff.; 1996a:262), all prominent centres in three of the four *fylki* in Inn-Trøndelag.

When hearing that kings were elected or proclaimed on *þing* mounds like these, as in the case of Tynwald Hill on Man, it is interesting to cite Snorri in *Haralds saga ins hárfagra*, who in chapter 8 tells us how king *Haraldr* got his hand on Namdal (*Naumdœlafylki*):[11]

North in Naumu Dale two brothers, Herlaug and Hrollaug, were kings. They had been three summers about fashioning a funeral mound. This mound was constructed of stones, mortar, and timber. But when this mound was completed, the brothers learned that King Harald was marching against them with an army. Then King Herlaug had much food and drink brought to the mound, and then entered it with eleven other men, whereupon he had it walled up [from the outside].

King Hrollaug went up on the mound on which the kings were wont to sit. There he had a king's high-seat prepared for himself, and seated himself on it. Then he had down pillows laid on the footstool where it was the custom of earls to sit. Thereupon King Hrollaug rolled himself down from the king's high-seat and onto the earl's seat and gave himself the title of 'earl'. Then he went to meet King Harald and gave to him all his realm, offering to become his follower and informing him about the

---

[11] Norðr í Naumudal váru brœðr ii. konungar, Herlaugr ok Hrollaugr. Þeir hǫfðu verit at iii. sumur at gera haug einn; sá haugr var hlaðinn með grjóti ok lími ok viðum gǫrr; en er haugrinn var algǫrr, þá spurðu þeir brœðr þau tíðendi, at Haraldr konungr fór á hendr þeim með her; þá lét Herlaugr konungr aka til vist mikla ok drykk. Eptir þat gekk Herlaugr konungr í hauginn með xii. mann; síðan lét hann kasta aptr hauginn. Hrollaugr konungr fór upp á haug þann, er konungar váru vanir at sitja á, ok lét þar búa konungs hásæti ok settisk þar í; þá lét hann leggja dýnur á fótpallin, þar er jarlar váru vanir at sitja; þá veltisk konungr ór hásætinu ok í jarlssæti, ok gaf sér sjálfr jarlsnafn. Eptir þat fór Hrollaugr á móti Haraldi konungi ok gaf honum alt ríki sitt ok bauð at gerask hans maðr ok sagði honum alla sína meðferð. Þá tók Haraldr konungr sverð ok festi á linda honum, þá festi hann skjǫld á háls honum ok gerdi hann jarl sinn ok leiddi hann í hásæti; þá gaf hann honum Naumdœlafylki ok setti hann þar jarl yfir {Snorri's *Heimskringla*, Haralds saga hárfagra, chap. 8; Hollander (trans.) 1964:64}.

procedure he had taken. Then King Harald took a sword and fastened it in Hrollaug's belt. He hung the shield around his shoulder and named him his earl and led him to the high-seat. He gave him the District of Naumu Dale to rule, setting him as earl over it.

Firstly Snorri relates how a *konungr* could abdicate or resign in a formal way and instead appoint himself to a lower title, in this case a *jarl*, probably by placing himself in the high seat upon the mound in full official vestments and then rolling over and down to the foot-stool, "where *jarl*s where used to sit". Secondly Snorri describes how a mound of this kind, on which kings used to sit, was furnished and organized (*búa konungs hásæti*). A *hásæti*, a 'high seat', was placed on the top of the mound, then cushions were placed on the foot-stool below, which was the place of the *jarl*. All of this most probably must be seen as a literary construction by Snorri, but at least, according to him, mounds could have had this use in Scandinavia in the ninth century, and I am inclined to believe him on this point.

It is possible to assign other Scandinavian place-names referring to assemblies and *þing* meetings to the same semantic sphere. I will show this with the name *Tjølling*, a parish in southern Norway (Brink 1996a:271 ff.). This parish is famous for the grand excavations at Kaupang, which prove this site to be a kind of counterpart to Birka on lake Mälaren, Sweden. Between the church in Tjølling and Kaupang by the sea, we find the hamlet of *Huseby*, an old royal farm. Thus, this small settlement district, which in the Middle Ages was named also *Skíringssalr*, has an unusual history. It is not surprising that the actual name *Tjølling* goes back to a OWN *þjóðalyng*, meaning 'the ground (heath) of the *þjóð* (i.e. the people)', which refers to people assembling on this site, most probably for communal matters.

The first notice we have of *þing*s in Scandinavia is found in Rimbert's *Vita Anskarii*, and here we get a most vivid and interesting description of pre-Christian *þing* sites and *þing* rituals. These take place in the early town of Birka in central Sweden during the ninth century. In chapter 19 Rimbert describes an event when a *þing* is going to take place and the Christian *praefectus* over Birka, *Hergeir*, attends it. "Once he sat at a *þing*, where a hut was erected on the ground or field for the session" (*Vita Anskarii*, 19 [p. 35–41]). Later Rimbert narrates the well-known episode when King Björn, because he did not dare to decide on his own whether Ansgar should be allowed to spread the Christian word in Birka, submitted the question to the *þing* assembly. Before the actual *þing* took place, King Björn convened his chieftains to discuss Ansgar's case. "They decided then to find out the attitude of the gods by casting lots". Rimbert writes: "Then when the day for the *þing* came, a *þing* that was held in Birka, the king let his herald shout what was going to be decided". There are several very interesting cases in this narrative that make it historically probable, the hut on a field, the *þing* on a field, and the casting of lots to communicate with the gods, showing that cult and law were intimately connected.

Inheritance and the right to *óðal* – the enumeration of pedigrees

Genealogies and the knowledge of one's forefathers were vital in early Scandinavian society. Genealogies even came to constitute a literary genre of itself called *áttvísi, mannfrœði* or *langfeðgatal*. The royal pedigrees were called *konungatal*, of which several are known to us, such as *Ynglingatal* and *Noregs konungatal*. To prove the right to one's *óðal*, the ancestral landed property, one had to be able to enumerate the forefathers in several lines, a custom well attested in several provincial laws. This way of attesting one's property was also used when a *konungsefni*, a claimant to the crown, tried to get hold of the royal power; the longer and more glorious the pedigree, the greater the authorization for the claimant. This is well known from all royal houses among Germanic and Celtic peoples, where the first ancestor, the *heros eponymos*, normally was a god, preferably *Óðinn* (Hauck 1955; Turville-Petre 1957; Wenskus 1961, 1977; Wolfram 1970; Höfler 1973; Dumville 1977; Sawyer 1978:12 f.; Moisl 1981; Hedeager 1996; cf. Sisam 1953; Dumville 1976).[12]

It is difficult for us nowadays to understand the importance, as well as the intellectual and cultural stimulation, that such 'boring' rattling off of names quite certainly had on the audience at that time, where each name in the long list was some kind of cipher with underlying messages to the listener, as most probably was the case with the abstruse part of the famous Rök rune stone in the province of Östergötland in Sweden, where four kings from Zealand for some reason are listed (*Valkar fim, Raðulfs syniʀ, Hraiðulfaʀ fim, Rugulfs syniʀ, Haislaʀ fim, Haruðs syniʀ, Gunnmundaʀ fim, Biarnaʀ syniʀ...*). As Aron J. Gurevich (1973:76) has written: "Enumeration of genealogies and names is an old culture's formalized language in which every name conceals a complex of stories and events, and every name, by necessity, invokes a series of associations and emotions".

With this background it is interesting to note that on some Swedish rune stones there are enumerations of five ancestors. The best known inscription is probably found on the Malsta stone from the province of Hälsingland.

hrumuntrit ... staina þinaftiʀ hikiulf- • brisa sun • in brisi uas lina sun • in lini uas unaʀ sun • in un ua[s uf]aksun in ufaka þurisun krua uas muþiʀ hikiulf- in þa barlaf in þa kuþ run • hrumunt hikiulfa sun faþi runaʀ þisaʀ • uiʀ sutum stin þina nur i balas[t]in

kiulfiʀ uarþ um lanti þisu in þa nur i uika i þrim bium in þa lanakr in þa fiþrasiu

Romund erected these stones (or this stone) after Hæ-Gylfe, the son of Bræse, and Bræse was the son of Line, and Line was the son of Unn, and Unn was the son of Ofeg, and Ofeg was the son of Tore. Groa was the mother of Hæ-Gylfe. And then **barlaf**, and then Gudrun. Romund, the son of Hæ-Gylfe carved these runes. We took this stone from north at Balsten.

---

[12] Cf. also the entries *Genealogier, Konungatal* and *Langfeðgatal* in *KL*.

Gylfe acquired this land and then land **nur i uika** in three hamlets and then **lanakr** and then Färdsjö.

We have here a legal document over a unique kind of 'estate', including a farm, probably Malsta, then farms or arable land in hamlets to the north, and then the farms **lanakr** (probably Lönånger) and Färdsjö (Brink 1994). The one who owned and claimed the land was *Hæ-Gylfe*, the father of *Romund*. This property is attested on the rune stone with the enumeration of five ancestors: *Bræse*, *Line*, *Unn*, *Ofeg* and *Tore*.

The same inheritance rules appear to be found on the Sandsjö stone (Sm 71) in the province of Småland, Sweden, where a man *Ærinvard* erected a rune stone, probably for attesting his property and *óðal*, and on that listed his five paternal ancestors:

> **erinuorþr let reisa stein þena eftiʀ heka faþur sin auk heru faþur hans auk karl hans faþur...heru hans faþur auk þiagn hans faþur auk eftiʀ þe lagfaþrga fem.**

> Ærnvard erected this stone after Hægge, his father, and after Hæra, his father, and Karl, his father, and Hæra, his father, and Thegn, his father, and after these five forefathers.

It is notable that this legal 'five generation rule' is found also in the early provincial laws regarding inheritance. In the two provincial laws, *Upplandslagen* and *Hälsingelagen*, there is an enactment where how to inherit property is stipulated. After regulating who inherited from whom, the law says: "This is the inheritance procedure until the fifth line or generation".[13]

This 'rule' of inheritance is also found in the poem *Hyndluljóð*, where *Óttar*, a claimant to a royal throne, is given five noble ancestors in a *langfeðgatal*: *Innsteinn*, *Álfr*, *Úlfr*, *Sæfari* and *Svanr rauði*. These were the acquired paternal ancestors qualified by early Norse laws as the *baugamenn* 'those who pay and receive the rings', i.e. the compensation for a murdered kinsman (cf. Phillpotts 1913, Gurevich 1973:76 f.). Furthermore, this observation is illustrated for a Norwegian regal enumeration found in *Huersu Noregr bygðist*, where the eponym was *Nórr* (Hjärne 1979:349).

The Viking Age rule for claiming land (and titles) by enumerating five paternal ancestors, found on rune stones and in *Hyndluljóð* and *Huersu Noregr bygðist*, is also found in the ancient *Law of the Gulathing* in western Norway, in the regulation concerning the possession of land and property and especially the extremely important right to *óðal* (Gtl 266):

> *Nu er þar domr settr. þeir scolo telia til langfeðra sinna. v. er átt hava. en sa hinn sette er bæðe atte at eign oc at óðrle.*

"Now when the doom is set, [the claimant] shall enumerate his ancestors, the five who have owned the land and the sixth who had it both in ownership and in *óðal*."

---

[13] Holmbäck & Wessén (1940:306, 316 f.). I thank Prof. Birgit Sawyer, Trondheim, for drawing my attention to these examples.

From this we can see the obvious resemblance between the Malsta runic inscription and what is regulated in the early *Gulathing Law*. We also learn, that in the *Gulathing Law* area, purchased land and property is not considered to be *óðal*, until it had remained in the family for five generations.[14] To conclude, it seems possible that an old legal custom in Viking Age Scandinavia prevailed that said one had to be able to enumerate five ancestors to attest one's proprietal right to land and *óðal*.[15]

Cultic and legal practices in early Scandinavia

After consulting source materials other than the provincial laws and Old Icelandic sagas, such as runic inscriptions, place-names and a tenth-century treaty from Russia, we may try to give some comments on this evidence. As was assumed to start with, we obviously had laws and legal conduct in our Viking Age society in Scandinavia, something that presumably nobody ever doubted.[16] However, in the Viking Age there probably were no comprehensive laws, direct forebears to the later provincial laws.[17] Instead there probably were legal customs and legal traditions that differed between provinces. Thanks to the runic evidence, we obtain an insight into some of these legal customs: in the province of Hälsingland there is evidence of *liuþrettr* 'the law of the people (the *land*)', probably to be understood as the law of the *hælsing(i)ar*, the people living in the province of Hälsingland, the most likely explanation of this word. This implies that, in the ninth century, the people of Hälsingland thought that they had a corpus of legal rules and customs that could be looked upon as a *liuþrettr*, 'law of the people'. One of these rules is mentioned on the Forsa rune ring, namely most probably the maintenance of the *vi*, the pagan cult site, but, in my opinion, also the assembly place for several communal matters. And in a society where it was practically impossible to distinguish legal and cultic matters, the *vi* obviously had both legal and cultic

---

[14] Notably, in the *Frostathing Law* (XII:4) one was only required to be able to name three generations of kinsmen for calling it *óðal* (Gurevich 1973:77).

[15] Also other legal matters of inheritance are found in Scandinavian, especially Swedish, runic inscriptions, see Fenger 1983:54 f.; Sawyer 1988; Stein-Wilkeshuis 1993; Engman 1996.

[16] In my opinion, for accurate views regarding *þing* and law in early Scandinavia, see Foote & Wilson 1980:90–92, 370–386; Steinsland & Meulengracht Sørensen 1998:134–137.

[17] Another aspect is that Scandinavia in the Viking Age probably was not at all homogeneous regarding law and legal practice. Iceland, especially, with its unique societal and legal system, with no king (or kings) but with several *goðar*, probably diverges in a fundamental way from the rest of Scandinavia. As Jesse Byock (1993:205) has written: "The Icelandic state did not even pretend to have the means or the mandate to enforce its authority. Instead, tenth-century Icelanders created a complex court apparatus to endorse resolutions arrived at by private parties". There is always the risk that Icelandic legal practices and traditions are superimposed on eastern Scandinavian ones, due to the impact of the great Old Icelandic literary production and the attention paid to it by scholars.

prerogatives, something that is so remarkably attested in the Oklunda runic inscription.

The word OSw *vi*, ODa *væ*, OWN *vé* is found in many place-names in Scandinavia (Andersson 1992:77 f.; Strid 1993:103; Brink 1996a:261; Andersen 1998), however in Norway never as the principal or second (generic) element (*NSL*, p. 336 f.). Since many of these place-names have the name of a pagan god or goddess as a first element, as in *Frösvi*, *Odense* (< *Óðinsvæ*), *Torsvi* and *Frövi*, this had led philologists and toponymists to translate the word and place-name element with 'pagan cult site'. This interpretation is strengthened by the comparison with the occurrence of, e.g., German *Weihnachten*, 'the Holy Nights, and OSax. *wîh*, OEng. *wêoh*, *wig* 'idol'. The word goes back to a proto-Germanic adjective **wīha-*, as in Gothic *weihs*, 'holy'. However, we have to admit that we don't know the exact semantic content the word had one thousand years ago.

One must remember that the strings or ropes that enclosed the *þing* at, e.g., *Gulathing* were called *vébǫnd*, and that both the Forsa rune ring (probably) and the Oklunda inscription talk about a *vi* in connection with legal matters. This indicates that *vi* had some judicial semantic content in Viking Age Scandinavia. The fact that Lat. *victima*, 'sacrificial animal', is formed on the same root makes an old custom mentioned in the sagas interesting to note. In *Egil's Saga* (chap. 65), Egill is again at the *Gulathing* for a case, and the explanation is: *þat voro ok lǫg, er Egill mælti ok forn siðuenja, at huerjom manni var rétt at skora á annan til hólmgaungu, huárt er hann skylldi verja sakir firi sik eða sækja*.[18] *Hólmganga* and *einvígi* seem to be old and accepted ways of regulating a quarrel between two litigants; they are mentioned in several sagas (Bø 1969:132 ff.; Byock 1993:107), and in the odd Old Swedish *Hednalagen*, the pagan law (Nelson 1944:57; Wessén 1968:49 ff.). The saga continues with the episode of Egil's *hólmgang*:

> At that Atli and Egil struck their hands together and confirmed between them that they should go on the *hólm*, and he who won the victory should have the estates they contended for before. After that they made ready for *hólmgang*. Egil walked out and had helmet on head and shield before him, and a halberd in hand; but the sword Dragvandil he secured to his right hand. It was the practice of *holmgang*-men, so as not to need to draw their sword on the *holm*, rather to let sword keep with hand, so that the sword might be ready the instant he wished. Atli had the same equipment as Egil, and was well used to *holmgangs*. He was a strong and dauntless man.
>
> A big bull was led forward there, which was called the beast of sacrifice. He should slaughter him who won the victory. Sometimes it was the one beast, sometimes each one who went on the *holm* had his own led forth.[19]

---

[18] "That too was a law that Egil pronounced, and the custom of old, that it was every man's right to challenge another to *holmgang*, whether he would defend or prosecute a suit".

[19] *Síðan taka þeir Atli ok Egill hondum saman, ok festa þat með sér, at þeir skolu á hólm ganga, ok sá er sigr fær skal eiga jarðer þær, er þeir deilldu áðr vm. Epter þat búaz veir til hólmgaungu. Geck Egill framm, ok hafði hjálm á hofði ok skjolld firi sér ok kesje í hendi, en suerðit Draguandil festi hann við hægri hond sér. þat var siðr hólmgaungumanna, at þurfa ecki at bregða suerði sínu á*

This custom of sacrificing one or several animals after a *hólmgang* or a settled case at a *þing* is mentioned in several occasions in the sagas. The combination of Latin *victima* and OSc. *vi* with the slaughtering of animals at a *þing* assembly site after a lawsuit was settled is striking.

The information presented above makes it plausible, at least for me, to interpret Scandinavian *vi* as a prehistoric assembly place for legal, cultic and probably also other communal matters. The position of the *vi* for communal matters and as an asylum site was later taken over by the church (see below).

As discussed above there are several place-names *Vi* or compounded with *-vi* in Scandinavia. In general, the places whose names include this element have a central position in their settlement districts, very often the church has been erected on the *vi* or is close to a farm or hamlet with a name containing the root *vi*. In one province, Gästrikland in northern Sweden, we find a coherent structure, so that in the centre of every old parish (= prehistoric settlement district) there is a hamlet *Vi* which, during the Middle Ages, for some reason was in royal hands (Brink 1996a:261). Therefore, it seems obvious that the place-name *Vi/-vi* denoted 'the assembly place for the people living in a settlement district'. This also seems to be the case for the *vi*-sites in Medelpad, Hälsingland and Gästrikland, and, even if not so clearly, in other parts of Sweden. In some cases a *vi* may have been established by a single individual, a couple of important men or a family, similar to that of the Bällsta rune-stone monument; in some other cases the *vi* may have been excluded for a certain category of people, which may be the case for *Karlavi* 'the *vi* of the *karlar* (retainers, military escort)' on Öland.

The Oklunda text and context take us a step further. It seems obvious that the *vi* implied by the runic inscription should be connected to the *lund* '(sanctified) grove' that the three neighbouring hamlets bear witness to, namely *Lundby*, *Oklunda* and *Lunda*. Thus, on this site we have had a *lund*, a grove with some special function for society, a grove and site that it was possible to call a *vi* (Nordén 1930:260; 1931:346 ff.; Lönnqvist & Widmark 1997:158).

Analysing in the same way the settlement districts of northern Sweden, it becomes obvious that the *vi*-sites we find in Gästrikland, Hälsingland and Medelpad have a direct counterpart in *hov* sites especially in the province of Jämtland, but also in Ångermanland and Hälsingland (Brink 1990b; 1996a). In these cases *hov* and *vi* must be understood as similar phenomena. This is also the case with the *hof*-names in Norway.

We may thus conclude that in Scandinavia we are still able to a great extent to reconstruct the centripetal societal arena of a settlement district, the assembly place for most probably legal, cultic and trading matters as well as feasting and playing games in general (Brink 1997). The indicators are particularly the place-

---

hólmi, láta helldr suerðit hendi fylgja, suá at þegar veri suerðit tiltækt, er hann villdi. Atli hafði enn
sama búnað sem Egill. Hann var vanr hólmgaungum. Han var sterkr maðr ok enn mesti fullhugi. Þar
var leiddr fram graðungr mikill ok gamall. Var þat kallat blótnaut. Þat skylldi sá hauggua, er sigr
hefði. Var þat stundum eitt naut, stundum lét sitt huárr framm leiða, sá er á hólm geck (emphasis
mine).

name elements *vi*, *hov* and *lund* (cf. Andersson 1992; Brink 1996a). Regarding the latter word, it is perhaps safe to add that not all place-names containing the element *lund* have had this origin. It is extremely difficult to separate these 'special groves', from profane groves.

Conclusion

From these scattered sources presented above, we get some fragments of legal practice in Viking Age Scandinavia. The evidence is very fragmentary and the content in the different sources is also often more or less difficult to interpret. However, we may pile up something like a dozen judicial practices, rules and traditions, that may mirror the legal society of that period. Hopefully legal historians will again analyse them, and discuss their juridical value and status.

1) Perhaps the most important evidence is the occurrence of the word *liuþrettr* on the Forsa rune ring, (probably) dating from the ninth century. This must mean, as far as I can see, that in the early Viking Age there was a law, or at least legal customs and rules within a legal procedure, that could be called *liuþrettr*, i.e. "the 'law' of the people". And since by this time people were identified in provinces (*land*), this notion probably referred to the people of *hælsing(i)ar*, thus the territory of *Hälsingland*.

2) One finds another legal practice on the Oklunda inscription, namely the likely existence of protected places. This inscription suggests that in Viking Age Scandinavia there was a right to asylum in certain places and in given circumstances. A malefactor had the same possibility in Christian times of seeking a church for protection. The (unsolved) question is whether the ecclesiastical law took over this custom from pagan law or if it was an inheritance from Canon Law. All the same, it is interesting that in Scandinavia, during the Viking age, the cult and (probably) *þing* assembly site was the place to seek asylum after having perpetrated a serious crime.

3) In the legal procedure in Viking Age Scandinavia it was important in general to announce not only crimes, but social matters of some importance. This custom has been shown to be typical for an oral society, where everything had to be orally transmitted and remembered. It suffices to mention the *lǫgsǫgumaðr*, whose task was to remember the 'law' and recite it at the *þing*, to grasp the importance memory and the spoken word had in early Scandinavian society. In this connection, Aron J. Gurevich (1973:79) has written the following wise words:

> In the system of proof on the *thing* by the ancient Scandinavians, the parties had to recite the oaths and formulas clearly and distinctly and to possess a certain number of witnesses and oath-helpers. Memory played an immense rôle in a preliterate society. The witnesses had to recite before the law court what they had heard from their fathers and grandfathers.

4) There seems to be an obvious link between law and cult in the pre-Christian period. Several indications show that legal procedure and cultic activities and perceptions where so intimately interwoven that in principle it was impossible to separate the one from the other.

5) The word and place-name element *vi* in Scandinavia, normally translated as 'a pagan cult site', hence something belonging to the religious cultural sphere in society, probably had a wider semantic content. As argued in this paper, a *vi* may be given the meaning 'assembly site', for communal matters, such as cultic, legal and other matters.

6) A vital part of the legal procedure in early Scandinavia must have been oath-taking. Not only the accused, but also other individuals in his social proximity (*eðgærðsmæn*), could be used as oath-takers. The evocation of pagan gods when taking an oath also seems likely.

7) If my interpretation of the Forsa rune ring is correct, we may have had special oath-rings at the *þing*s. This is the old opinion, when we still believed in the historical accuracy of the so called *Ulfljóts Law*, mentioned in *Landnámabók* (*Hauksbók* and *Melabók*, chap. 268), i.e. *The Book of Settlement*:

> ...*baugr tvíeyringr eða meiri skyldi liggja í hverju hofuðhofi á stalla. Þann baug skyldi hverr goði hafa á hendi sér til logþinga allra, þeira er hann skyldi sjálfr heyja, ok rjóða hann þar áðr í roðru nauts blóðs þess, er hann blótaði þar sjálfr. Hverr sá maðr, er þar þurfti logskil af hendi at leysa at dómi skyldi áðr eið vinna at þeim baugi ok nefna sér vátta ij eða fleiri. "Nefni ek í þat vætti", skyldi hann segja, "at ek vinn eið at baugi, logeið, hjálpi mér svá Freyr ok Njorðr ok hinn almáttki oss (áss).*

> ...a ring, weighing two örar or more, should be placed on the altar in each of the main *hof*. This ring should every *goði* have on his hand at all the *logþing* he was going to open, and make it red with the blood from the sacrificial animal, that he himself sacrificed there. Each man proceeding cases at the *thing*, must first take an oath on that ring and name two witnesses or more. "I name you as a witness", he should state, "that I take this oath on the ring, law oath, so help *me Freyr and Njorðr and the almighty áss*".

After Olaf Olsen's (1966:34 ff.) sound analysis of this, *Ulfljóts Law* has been looked upon as a forgery from Christian times, but as I have proposed earlier (Brink 1996b:46), I think it would be interesting to analyse this law once more to see if it is totally useless as a historical source. There are several instances in the text that today may be explained by new, independent source material.

8) In the light of the first observation (above), it is possible to trace *þing* assemblies for large congregations such as whole provinces (*land*), which the inscription on the Forsa ring indicates. Such assembly sites are known from other parts, such as *Þingvellir* in Iceland and Tynwald Hill on Man, but Hög may be more equivalent to, for example, Frosta or Gula in Norway. For *þing*s lower down in the legal hierarchy, we have several examples of *þing* sites, the most famous one being Bällsta in Uppland. In these cases *þing* assembly sites could be established

and owned by a group, a family or a single person, such as Ulvkel, Arnkel and Gye in Bällsta or Jarlabanke single-handedly in Vallentuna, Uppland, Sweden (Brink 1998:300).

9) It seems likely that large mounds have been used as *þing* assembly sites. This too has been an old truth regarding our early society in Scandinavia, but has now and then been questioned as being a purely romantic belief. The discussion above supports the old idea when the available sources are presented.

10) We can just discern the existence of some large or small legal districts, perhaps with some kind of special jurisdiction, as in the case of *Danelaw*, *Bergslag(en)*, *Roslag(en)* and *Luþerlag*. Since some of these (potential ones), *Njǫrðarlǫg*, *Frøyslǫg* and *Tyslǫg*, have a pagan deity as the first element in their names, it is possible to assume that these districts were dedicated in some way to a pagan god.

11) Finally, in Viking Age Scandinavia, there is the legal custom, which seems to have been fairly widespread, of enumerating—on a rune stone or orally with witnesses at a *þing* assembly—one's forefathers who also owned the land and property one was claiming, thus submitting evidence concerning one's inherited property and *óðal* rights. For many regions the enumeration of *five* forefathers was a rule, as can be gathered from rune stones in the provinces of Hälsingland and Småland, and also in western Norway, as stated in an enactment in the early *Gulathing Law*.

References

Textual sources:

[Abbr.: DrB = *Dräpsbalken*; EdsB = *Edsöresbalken*; KL = *Kulturhistorisk lexikon*; NGL = *Norges gamle Love*; NSL = *Norsk stadnamnleksikon*; RGA = *Reallexikon der Germanischen Altertumskunde*; SAOB = *Ordbok över svenska språket utg. av Svenska akademien*; Sdw = K. F. Söderwall].

Egils Saga Skallagrímssonar: see Jónsson (ed.) 1886-88, Jones (trans.) 1960.
Frostatingslova: see Hagland & Sandnes (trans.) 1994.
Gulatingslova: see Eithun, Rindal & Ulset (eds.) 1994, Robberstad (tr.) 1937.
Snorri Sturluson
        Heimskringla: see Jónsson (ed.) 1911; Hollander (trans.) 1964.
Rimbert
        Vita Anskarii: see Odelman (trans.) 1986.
Tacitus
        Germania: see Much (ed. & trans.) 1967; Önnerfors (ed. & trans.) 1969.

Bibliography:

Andersen, H.
    1998   Vier og lunde. *Skalk* 1: 15-27.

Andersson, Th.
1992   Kultplatsbeteckningar i nordiska ortnamn. In *Sakrale navne*. G. Fellows-
            Jensen & B. Holmberg (eds.), pp. 77-105. (NORNA-rapporter 48). Uppsala:
            NORNA förlaget.
Bagge, S.
1989   Review of Elsa Sjöholm 1988. (*Norsk*) *historisk tidsskrift* 69: 500-507.
Barlau, S. B.
1981   Old Icelandic kinship terminology: An anomaly. *Ethnology. An
            International Journal of Cultural and Social Anthropology* 20: 191-202.
Barnes, M.
1974   'Tingsted'. *Kulturhistoriskt lexikon för nordisk medeltid* 18. Cols. 382-387.
            Malmö: Allhems.
Breisch, A.
1994   *Frid och fredlöshet. Sociala band och utanförskap på Island under äldre
            medeltid.* (Studia historica Upsaliensia 174). Stockholm: Almqvist &
            Wiksell International.
Brink, S.
1990a   *Sockenbildning och sockennamn. Studier i äldre territoriell indelning i
            Norden.* (Acta Academiae Regiae Gustavi Adolphi 57). Stockholm:
            Almqvist & Wiksell International.
1990b   Cult sites in northern Sweden. In *Old Norse and Finnish Religions and
            Cultic Place-names.* O. Ahlbäck (ed)., pp. 458-489. (Scripta instituti
            Donneriani Aboensis XIII). Stockholm: Almqvist & Wiksell International.
1991   Sockenbildningen i Sverige. In *Kyrka och socken i medeltidens Sverige.*
            O. Ferm (ed.), pp. 113-142. (Studier till Det medeltida Sverige 5).
            Stockholm: Riksantikvarieämbetet.
1994   En vikingatida storbonde i södra Norrland. *Tor. Journal of Archaeology* 26:
            145-162.
1996a   Political and social structures in early Scandinavia. A settlement-historical
            pre-study of the central place. *Tor. Journal of Archaeology* 28: 235-281.
1996b   Forsaringen – Nordens äldsta lagbud. In *Femtende tværfaglige
            Vikingesymposium. Århus Universitet 1996.* E. Roesdahl & P. Meulengracht
            Sørensen (eds.), pp. 27-55. Århus: Forlaget Hikuin og Afdeling for
            Middelalder-arkæologi.
1997   Political and social structures in early Scandinavia 2. Aspects on space and
            territoriality – the settlement district. *Tor. Journal of Archaeology* 29: 389-437.
1998   Land, bygd, distrikt och centralort i Sydsverige. Några bebyggelsehistoriska
            nedslag. In *Centrala platser - Centrala frågor. Samhällsstrukturen under
            järnålder. En vänbok till Berta Stjernquist.* L. Larsson & B. Hårdh (eds.),
            pp. 297-326. (Uppåkrastudier 1; Acta Archaeologica Lundensia. Ser. in 8°
            28). Stockholm: Almqvist & Wiksell International.
n.d.   Tanumsbygdens bosättningshistoria med särskilt utgångspunkt från
            bebyggelsenamnen. [Manuscript.]
Bugge, S.
1877   Rune-indskriften paa Ringen i Forsa kirke i nordre Helsingland. In
            *Christiania universitets festskrift i anledning af Upsala universitets
            jubilæum.* Pp. 3-60. Christiania: H. J. Jensens Bogtrykkeri.
Buti, G. G.
1987   The Eggja inscription: A functionalistic approach. *Runor och runinskrifter.*
            Pp. 47-53. (KVHAA. Konferenser 15). Stockholm: Almqvist & Wiksell
            International.

Bø, O.
1969　　Hólmganga and einvígi. Scandinavian forms of the duel. *Medieval Scandinavia* 2: 132-148.

Bøe, A.
1965　　Lagting. *Kulturhistoriskt lexikon för nordisk medeltid* 10. Cols. 178-183. Malmö: Allhems.

Dumville, D.
1976　　The Anglian collection of royal genealogies and regnal lists. *Anglo-Saxon England* 5: 23-50.
1977　　Kingship, genealogies and regnal lists. In *Early medieval kingship*. P. Sawyer & I. Wood (eds.), pp. 72-104. Leeds: School of History, University of Leeds.

Eithun, B., M. Rindal & T. Ulset (eds.)
1994　　*Den eldre Gulatingslova*. (Norrøne tekster 6). Oslo: Riksarkivet.

Engman, F.
1996　　*Arv och gender under yngre järnålder och tidig medeltid*. D-uppsats i arkeologi vid Stockholms universitet. Stockholm: Department of Archaeology, University of Stockholm.

Fellows-Jensen, G.
1993　　Tingwall, Dingwall and Thingwall. *Twenty-Eight Papers Presented to Hans Bekker-Nielsen on the Occasion of his Sixtieth Birthday*. Pp. 53-67. Odense: Odense University Press.

Fenger, O.
1971　　*Fejde og mandebod. Studier over slægtsansvaret i germansk og gammeldansk ret*. Copenhagen: Juristforbundets forlag.
1983　　*Gammeldansk ret. Dansk rets historie i oldtid og middelalder*. (Ny indsigt). Viby: Centrum.
1987　　Om kildeværdien af normative tekster. In *Tradition og historieskrivning. Kilderne til Nordens ældste historie*. K. Hastrup & P. Meulengracht Sørensen (eds.), pp. 39-51. (Acta Jutlandica 63:2. Hum. Serie 61). Århus: Århus universitetsforlag.
1991　　Germansk retsorden med særligt henblik på det 7. århundrede. In *Høvdingesamfund og kongemagt. Fra stamme til stat i Danmark* 2. P. Mortensen & B. Rasmusen (eds.), pp. 155-164. (Jysk Arkæologisk Selskabs Skrifter 22:2). Århus: Jysk Arkæologisk Selskab.

Foote, P.
1987　　Reflections on *Landabrigðisþáttr* and *Rekaþáttr* in *Grágás*. In *Tradition og historieskrivning. Kilderne til Nordens ældste historie*. K. Hastrup & P. Meulengracht Sørensen. (Acta Jutlandica 63:2. Hum. Serie 61). Århus: Århus universitetsforlag.

Foote, P. G., & D. M. Wilson
1980　　*The Viking Achievement, The Society and Culture of Early Medieval Scandinavia*. (Great Civilizations Series). London: Sidgwick & Jackson.

Friesen, O. von
1933　　De svenska runinskrifterna. In *Runorna*. O. von Friesen (ed.), pp. 145-248. (Nordisk kultur 6). Stockholm: Bonniers.

Grønvik, O.
1985　　*Runene på Eggjastenen. En hedensk gravinnskrift fra slutten av 600-tallet*. Oslo: Universitetsforlaget.

Gurevich, A. Y.
1973　　Edda and Law. Commentary upon *Hyndlolióð*. *Arkiv för nordisk filologi* 88: 72-84.

Hafström G.
1949   Sockenindelningens ursprung. *Historiska studier tillägnade Nils Ahnlund 23/8/49.* Pp. 51-67. Stockholm: Norstedt.
1964   Från kultsocken till storkommun. *Från bygd och vildmark. Luleå stifts årsbok* 51: 29-47.

Hagland, J. R., & J. Sandnes
1994   Om lova og lagdømmet. *Frostatingslova.* (Norrøne bokverk). Oslo: Det norske samlaget.

Hauck, K.
1955   Lebensnormen und Kultmythen in germanischen Stammes- und Herrschergenealogien. *Saeculum* 6: 186-223.

Hedeager, L.
1996   Myter og materiell kultur: Den nordiske oprindelsesmyte i det tidlige kristne Europa. *Tor. Journal of Archaeology* 28: 217-234.

Hertzberg, E.
1905   Vore ældste Lovtexters oprindelige Nedskrivelsestid. In *Historiske Afhandlinger. Tilegnet Professor Dr. J. E. Sars.* Pp. 92-117. Christiania: Aschehong.

Hjärne, E.
1947   Rod och runor. *Kungl. Humanistiska Vetenskaps-Samfundets i Uppsala årsbok* [1946]: 21-126.
1979   *Land och ledung* 1. Ur Erland Hjärnes historiska författarskap utg. av G. Åqvist. (Rättshistoriskt bibliotek 31). Stockholm: Nordiska Bokhandeln.

Höfler, O.
1973   Abstammungstraditionen. *Reallexikon der germanischen Altertumskunde* 1. 2d ed. Berlin: de Gruyter.

Hollander, L. M.
1964   *Heimskringla. History of the Kings of Norway.* Transl. with Introd. and Notes by Lee M. Hollander. Austin, TX: University of Texas Press.

Holmbäck, Å., & E. Wessén
1940   *Södermannalagen och Hälsingelagen.* (Svenska landskapslagar 3). Stockholm: Geber.

Ingvarsson, L.
1970   *Refsingar á Íslandi á Þjóðveldistímanum.* Reykjavík: Bókaútgáfa Menningarsjóðs.

Jacobsen, L.
1931   *Eggjum-stenen.* Copenhagen: Levin & Munledgaard.

Jansson, S. B. F.
1977   *Runinskrifter i Sverige.* Stockholm: AWE/Geber.

Jesch, J.
1998   Murder and treachery in the Viking Age. In *Crime and Punishment in the Middle Ages.* T. Haskett (ed.), pp. 63-85. Victoria: Humanities Centre, University of Victoria.

Jones, G.
1960   *Egil's Saga.* Transl. from the Old Icelandic, with Introduction and Notes by Gwyn Jones. New York: Syracuse University Press.

Jónsson, F. (ed.)
1886-88   *Egils Saga Skallagrímssonar.* Copenhagen: S. L. Möller.
1911   *Heimskringla. Nóregs konunga sǫgur,* udg. ved Finnur Jónsson. Copenhagen: Gad.

Kisbye, T.
1988   *Vikingerne i England – sproglige spor.* Copenhagen: Akademisk forlag.

Knudsen, T.
1960   Gulatingsloven. *Kulturhistoriskt lexikon för nordisk medeltid* 5, cols. 559-565. Malmö: Allhems.

Kroman, E.
1975   Vederloven. *Kulturhistoriskt lexikon för nordisk medeltid* 19, cols. 612-614. Malmö: Allhems.

Kulturhistoriskt lexikon
1956-78 *Kulturhistoriskt lexikon för nordisk medeltid från vikingatid till reformationstid.* 1–22. Malmö: Allhems.

Larson, L. M.
1935   *The Earliest Norwegian Laws. Being the Gulathing Law and the Frostathing Law.* Translated from the Old Norwegian. (Records of Civilization. Sources and studies 20). New York: Columbia University Press.

Lindqvist, S.
1925   Inglingehögen och Tynwald Hill. *Rig* 8: 113-121.

Lönnqvist, O., & G. Widmark
1997   Den fredlöse och Oklunda-ristningens band. *Saga och sed* [1996–97]: 145-149.

Meulengracht Sørensen, P.
1992   *Fortælling og ære. Studier i islændingesagaerne.* Århus: Århus University Press.

Moisl, H.
1981   Anglo-Saxon royal genealogies and Germanic oral tradition. *Journal of Medieval History* 7: 215-248.

Much, R.
1967   *Die Germania des Tacitus.* 3rd ed. (Germanische Bibliothek 5 Reihe). Heidelberg: Carl Winter Universitätsverlag.

Nelson, A.
1944   Envig och ära. *Saga och sed* [1944]: 57-95.

Nilsson, B.
1991   Frids- och asylföreskrifter rörande den medeltida sockenkyrkan. *Kyrka och socken i medeltidens Sverige.* O. Ferm (ed.), pp. 4473-4504. (Studier till Det medeltida Sverige 5). Stockholm: Riksantikvarieämbetet.

Nordén, A.
1930   Baldershagen och tempeldagen. Oklunda-inskriften, en rättsurkund från en fornöstgötsk blotlund. *Ord och bild* 39: 255-261.
1931   Ett rättsdokument från en fornsvensk offerlund. Oklundaristningen, en nyupptäckt östgötsk rökrune-inskrift. *Fornvännen* 26: 330-351.

Norges gamle Love. 1:1–5 Christiania 1846–95. 2:1–2 Oslo 1912–1934.

Norsk stadnamnleksikon
1990   *Norsk stadnamnleksikon.* J. Sandnes & O. Stemshaug (eds.). 3rd ed. Oslo: Det norske Samlaget.

Odelman, E. (trans.), A. Ekenberg *et al.* (comm.s)
1986   *Boken om Ansgar.* (Skrifter utg. av Samfundet Pro fide et christianismo 10). Stockholm: Proprius.

Ólafsson, G.
1987   Þingnes by Elliðavatn: The first local assembly in Iceland? In *Proceedings of the Tenth Viking Congress, Larkollen, Norway, 1985.* J. Knirk (ed.), pp. 343-349. (Universitetets Oldsaksamlings skrifter. Ny rekke 9). Oslo: Unversitetets Oldsaksamling.

Olsen, M.
1905   *Det gamle norske Ønavn Njardarlog.* (Christiania Videnskabs-Selskabs Forhandlinger 1905:5). Christiania.
1919   *Eggjum-stenens indskrift med de ældre runer.* Christiania.
Olsen, O.
1966   *Hørg, hov og kirke. Historiske og arkeologiske vikingetidsstudier.* Copenhagen: Gad.
Olson, E.
1916   *De appellativa substantivens bildning i fornsvenska. Bidrag till den fornsvenska ordbildningsläran.* Lund: Gleerups.
Önnerfors, A. (ed. & trans.)
1969   Tacitus, *Germania.* 3 ed. Stockholm: Natur och Kultur.
Ordbok över svenska språket utg. av Svenska akademien. 1–.
1898 ff. Lund: Gleerup.
Peterson, L.
1993   Namnformen *uifin* på Oklundahällen – nominativ eller ackusativ? *Studia anthroponymica Scandinavica* 11: 33-40.
Phillpotts, B. S.
1913   *Kindred and Clan in the Middle Ages and After. A Study in the Sociology of the Teutonic Races.* Cambridge: Cambridge University Press.
Rehfeldt, B.
1954   Recht, Religion und moral bei den frühen Germanen. *Zeitschrift für Rechtsgeschichte. Germ. Abt.* 71: 1-22.
Reallexikon der Germanischen Altertumskunde
1973 ff. *Reallexikon der Germanischen Altertumskunde* 1–. 2 Aufl. Berlin/New York: de Gruyter.
Rindal, M.
1994   Innleiing. In *Den eldre Gulatingslova.* B. Eithun, M. Rindal & T. Ulset (eds.), pp. 7-30. (Norrøne tekster 6). Oslo: Riksarkivet.
Robberstad, K.
1937   *Gulatingslovi.* (Norrøne bokverk 33). Oslo: Det norske samlaget.
Ruthström, B.
1988   Oklunda-ristningen i rättslig belysning. *Arkiv för nordisk filologi* 103: 64-75.
1990   Forsa-ristningen – vikingatida vi-rätt? *Arkiv för nordisk filologi* 105: 41-56.
Salberger, E.
1980   *Östgötska runstudier.* Göteborg: Scripta runica.
Sawyer, B.
1988   *Property and Inheritance in Viking Scandinavia: The Runic Evidence.* (Occasional papers on medieval topics 2). Alingsås: Victoria Förlag.
Sawyer, P.
1978   *From Roman Britain to Norman England.* London: Methuen.
1982   *Kings and Vikings. Scandinavia and Europe AD 700-1100.* London: Methuen.
1987   The bloodfeud in fact and fiction. *Tradition og historieskrivning. Kilderne til Nordens ældste historie.* K. Hastrup & P. Meulengracht Sørensen (eds.), pp. 27-38. (Acta Jutlandica 63:2. Hum. Serie 61). Århus: Århus Universitetsforlag.
Schledermann, H.
1974   Tingsted. *Kulturhistoriskt lexikon för nordisk medeltid* 18. Cols. 373-376. Malmö: Allhems.

See, K. von
1964   *Altnordische Rechtswörter. Philologische Studien zur Rechtsauffassung und Rechtsgesinnung der Germanen.* (Hermaea. Germanische Forschungen. Neue Folge 16). Tübingen: Max Niemeyer.

Sisam, K.
1953   Anglo-Saxon royal genealogies. *Proceedings of the British Academy* 39: 287-348.

Sjöholm, E.
1988   *Sveriges medeltidslagar. Europeisk rättstradition i politisk omvandling.* (Rättshistoriskt bibliotek 41). Stockholm: Nordiska bokhandeln.

Söderwall, K. F.
1884–1918 *Ordbok öfver svenska medeltids-språket* 1–2. Lund: Svenska fornskrifts-sällskaper.

Springer, O.
1970   Inscriptional evidence of early north Germanic legal terminology. In *Indo-European and Indo-Europeans. Papers Presented at the Third Indo-European Conference at the University of Pennsylvania.* G. Cardona *et al.* (eds.), pp. 35-48. (Haney Foundation Series 9). Philadelphia: University of Pennsylvania Press.

Stein-Wilkeshuis, M.
1982   The right to social welfare in early medieval Iceland. *Journal of Medieval History* 8: 343-352.
1986   Laws in medieval Iceland. *Journal of Medieval History* 12: 37-53.
1991   A Viking-age treaty between Constantinople and northern merchants, with its provision on theft and robbery. *Scando-Slavica* 37: 35-47.
1993   Runestones and the law of inheritance in medieval Scandinavia. *Actes à cause de Mort (Acts of last will).* Pp. 21-34. (Recueils de la Société Jean Bodin 60). Bruxelles: De Boeck Université.
1994   Legal prescriptions on manslaughter and injury in a Viking Age treaty between Constantinople and northern merchants. *Scandinavian Journal of History* 19: 1-16.
1998   Scandinavian Law in a tenth-century Rus'–Greek commercial treaty? In *The Community, the Family and the Saint. Patterns of Power in Early Medieval Europe.* J. Hill & M. Swan (eds.), pp. 311-322. (International Medieval Research 4). Turnhout: Brepols.

Steinsland, G., & P. Meulengracht-Sørensen
1998   *Människor och makter i vikingarnas värld.* Stockholm: Ordfront.

Stjernquist, B.
1987   Spring cults in Scandinavian prehistory. *Gifts to the Gods.* T. Linders & G. Nordquist (eds.), pp. 149-157. (Boreas 15). Stockholm: Almqvist & Wiksell International.
1998   The basic perception of the religious activities at cult-sites such as springs, lakes and rivers. In *The World-View of Prehistoric Man.* L. Larsson & B. Stjernquist (eds.), pp. 158-178. (KVHAA Konferenser 40). Stockholm: KVHAA.

Strid, J.-P.
1993   *Kulturlandskapets språkliga dimension. Ortnamnen.* Stockholm: Riksantikvarieämbetet.

Ståhle, C. I.
1954   Den första utgåvan av Upplandslagen och dess förlaga. *Arkiv för nordisk filologi* 69: 91-143.

Sveaas Andersen, P.
  1974   Ting. *Kulturhistoriskt lexikon för nordisk medeltid* 18. Cols. 346-359.
             Malmö: Allhems.
Turville-Petre, J.
  1957   Hengest and Horsa. *Saga-book of the Viking Society* 14: 273-290.
  1977   Outlawry. *Sjötíu ritgerðir, helgaðar Jakobi Benediktssyni 20. Júli 1977.*
             Reykjavík: Stofnun Árna Magnússonar á Íslandi.
Vries, J. de
  1961   *Altnordisches etymologisches Wörterbuch*. Leiden: Brill.
Wenskus, R.
  1961   *Stammesbildung und Verfassung*. Cologne: Böhlau Verlag.
Wessén, E.
  1968   *Svenskt lagspråk*. Lund: Gleerup.
Wolfram, H.
  1970   The shaping of the early medieval kingdom. *Viator* 1: 1-20.
  1977   Theogonie, Ethnogenese und ein kompromittierter Grossvater im
             Stammbaum Theoderichs des Grossen. In *Festschrift für Helmut Beumann*.
             K. Jäschke & R. Wenskus (eds.), pp. 80-97. Sigmaringen: Thorbecke Verlag.

Discussion

AUSENDA: Is the Scandinavian *þing* the same as the Langobardic *gairethinx*?

GREEN: Yes. Well, the second element is.

AUSENDA: And what does the first one mean?

GREEN: Spear.

AUSENDA: So, it is a warrior assembly.

GREEN: No, a legal gathering to which men come armed with their weapons.

AUSENDA: I agree with you that the present fashion is to trace all Germanic laws to Roman provincial law (page 88), neglecting the fact that even if there may be some late Roman intrusions, such as laws referring to the position of the Church or to the safety of the king, there are many which can only be traced to customary law. These are: the list of compensations for injuries which are found in most early Germanic legislation, the procedure for oath-taking listing the number and status of oath helpers according to the importance of the crime, the procedure concerning engagement and *morgengabe*, and the procedure concerning transfer of *mund* and the payment thereof. It is quite possible that inheritance and succession were considerably affected by Roman law, but not the above listed procedures which are common to most barbarian legislation.

MEULENGRACHT: You use two different types of sources, or sources on two different levels. On the one hand you use what we would call authentic sources, runic inscriptions, on the other hand you make use of what I would call interpretations of authentic sources: that is *Egil's Saga* and *Heimskringla* (page 89). This other level is also in fact the level where you are in the same box as Snorri [laughter], interpreter of sources. Some scholars want to use the sagas as sources, but they are of course fiction, literary constructions. I quite agree, as you know, with your point that it is possible to use them as sources, but I think it is necessary to qualify these words, 'fiction' and 'literary constructions'. We would always have to take into account that Snorri also had some of these sources. Maybe he didn't read runic inscriptions but he heard about things and he was a learned man.

BRINK: I would like to be more accurate on this point and, as I have written elsewhere, I believe that we can use the Icelandic sagas and skaldic verses in discussing legal matters. That is my opinion. I left it out this time because if I was going to discuss it I would have had to be much more qualified in the discussion if I had time to do it. So instead I thought, let's concentrate on these other facts.

MEULENGRACHT: But don't you think that, say, *Heimskringla* could add anything to your evidence here?

BRINK: Yes I think it is open. I think several other sagas as well, may have, even *Hávamál* also has, pieces of gold regarding legal customs in Scandinavia. It is a vast, vast project to work on.

AUSENDA: Do you mean to say that there are legal codes written in Latin in the eleventh or twelfth century for Scandinavians?

JESCH: They are written in the vernacular.

AUSENDA: In the vernacular, OK. Do these legal codes have some relation to preceding customary law?

BRINK: Well, that is what I was trying to formulate in the first paragraphs.... We have a situation in Scandinavia, especially in Sweden, where we have a legal scholar called Elsa Sjöholm who has written two important books in the 1980s where she totally dismissed the provincial laws as having anything to say about Scandinavian society before the time they were written down. After she had written that, nobody, except a Danish legal historian called Ole Fenger, has questioned her. They haven't dared to take up this subject again.

AUSENDA: No, but this was one of the places to question it.

BRINK: The background is probably that there are so few scholars in legal history, and after her fierce statements no one dared to take up this kind of research again. Then there have been some scholars who have challenged her view and she has 'slaughtered' them. So, the situation of legal history in Scandinavia was very bad for two decades. And for myself, I have been tossing around this subject for fifteen years, starting with the Forsa rune ring and then I studied one of the peripheral provincial laws, the northern law in Sweden, the law of the Hälsingar. Elsa Sjöholm studied the southernmost law, the Scanian law, the law which is most heavily influenced by Continental law, Canon law and Roman law, and she made that 'The law of Scandinavia' more or less. So, when I studied the Hälsinge law, I could see that she must be wrong again and again. Some philologists and legal historians continued—Peter Foote in England, for example—to dissect the laws and found old reminiscences in them. Ole Fenger as well as the legal philologist Bo Ruthström have also continued on a small scale discovering very ancient pieces in the laws and now it is probably time to go out again in the air and declare there are older structures also in the provincial laws. Now is the time because we have the Forsa rune ring which has been pre-dated by two hundred years. We have the

Oklunda inscription with resemblances to the Guta Law and the Östgöta Law and we have this treaty between Rus and Scandinavians, and Greeks in Russia during the tenth century which a legal historian from Holland, Martina Stein-Wilkeshuis has brought to light. Here we have reminiscences of what is found in the Scandinavian provincial laws in the tenth century. So, because we have several cases to put forward, it is time to highlight once more customary law in Scandinavia, and also to dissect provincial laws for older structures. Indeed it goes back to the discussion we had before lunch, when we were talking about things that were formerly believed to be old strata in the provincial laws going back to mnemotechnical formulas, which were more or less wiped out of discussions during the seventies and eighties because some scholars could see resemblance with Continental law. Now we have to look at these matters again. So, hopefully, we can have a new departure in Scandinavia looking into the old provincial laws which have been mostly neglected.

GREEN: A point about one word, but a word which opens up a wide field: you say "and appealed to the congregation, the people made noise with their weapons". Then you are more explicit when you say that "the people could collectively make their opinion heard by rattling with their weapons" and then come two words "*vápnabrak* and *vápnatak*". Now here, if anywhere, we can lay our hands, linguistically at any rate, on a legal practice which we can call Common Germanic, or to be more precise, North Germanic and West Germanic, because there is no evidence from East Germanic, but at least that is wider that just Scandinavian evidence. We cannot establish that the word *vápnatak* is Common Germanic by appealing to Old English *wæpengetæc* because that is clearly a loanword from Old Norse. We can, however, establish that the legal practice was common Germanic, if we take account of two words which seem to be wide apart, English 'to play' and German 'pflegen', 'to take care of something', 'to take responsibility for something', 'to take over something'. Now if one goes back to the earliest forms of these words, Old English *plegan* means, above all, 'to make violent movements' especially with weapons. So, 'to play', 'to make violent movement' and 'to play with your spear, to play with your sword', 'battle play' as well. And the same is true on the Continental side, in Old High German, Old Saxon, with the word *spilôn* used with the same distribution of meanings as *plegan* in OE. But to go back to the first word, in Old Saxon and in Old High German the word *plegan* or *pflegan* has the quite different meaning 'to accept responsibility for a legal decision'. I won't go into the evidence for that, but it is quite clearly established on the Continent in several works and also in separate glossaries, which gloss particularly Latin legal terms. We can link these two words with their disparate meanings, however, if we turn to Tacitus, and here I agree with your reservations about Sjöholm's dismissal of the relevance of Tacitus. If we turn to Tacitus (*Germania* XI) where, talking about the legal assembly, he says that if a proposal did not please them, they roared their disagreement, but if they approved, they clashed their spears and, in the same context, in his *Historiae*, the phrase he uses is "*armis laudare*", "to praise with weapons", "to approve with weapons". And lastly, in that same context you say that the congregation must have been allowed to have their weapons at the *þing*. Certainly they must: Tacitus says explicitly that those attending the assembly came armed, because without having their arms they couldn't give approval.

BRINK: That's excellent, thank you very much.

HERSCHEND: In the *Finnsburh* fragment there is a description of the arrows coming like birds and the wolves in the attack. And, as soon as there came the attack, there was the answer on the shield. So, when the attack came, the defenders answered, agreeing in standing up to it. It was a way of showing communal consent. It was a link to the actual fighting situation. But then, I think that this behaviour was surely the root of the approving behaviour during a *þing*.

GREEN: I am not suggesting the idea of armed conflict.

HERSCHEND: No, no. It's just a precedent to a legal procedure which may be born from armed conflict in that there had to be agreement before the battle that everyone was going to engage in.

JESCH: The problem with the laws is a problem of reconstruction. You have a whole series of medieval Scandinavian sources, where I think it is possible to argue that they have traces of earlier things in them and the key to this is a word which has already come up today, and that is 'orality'. To simply say "we are going to ignore what went on before literacy and to concentrate on our literate sources, which obviously will be medieval Christian", that has been the trend in the 70s and 80s, and I think you are quite right that there is now an acceptance that the situation is much more complicated than that. The reconstruction problem, I think, is very similar in the case of the laws, as it is in skaldic poetry. I don't think Snorri made up thousands of stanzas of skaldic poetry, I think they were his sources. There I think we can actually compare Snorri's sources with what he writes. Of course they were transmitted to us by Snorri. That's the problem. You say that in your "opinion cultic and legal (as well as probably also skaldic) matters were intimately connected", and I was wondering if you could say a bit more about this.

BRINK: The one who has written most eloquently on this subject — and I have nothing more to add to that — is Gurevich, who has written about how skaldic and cultic are so interrelated that you cannot separate them from each other. You have the quotation there as well. He is arguing very well for this thesis.

JESCH: The other thing I wanted to include in this, is the treaty in the Nestor chronicle. My Old Church Slavonic not being what it ought to be, I have an English translation which says that in the treaty they made an agreement both in writing and in words. So presumably, they are drawing a parallel between the oral and the literate situation.

GREEN: Could I just hang on a point to what you just said about hearing and reading.

JESCH: No, I said in writing and in words.

GREEN: Yes, but by word you mean word that you hear. That reminds me of a common medieval phrase both in medieval Latin and in various vernaculars, the texts were meant to be both heard and read. In other words, the two are in parallel but not in conflict with each other.

JESCH: Well, I don't actually know what the original said—I only had the translation to go on—but I thought it was very relevant. [Reads part of the translation] "...amicable relations between Christians and Russians, has also deemed it proper to publish and confirm this amity, not merely in words, but also in writing and under a firm oath sworn upon our weapons, according to our religion and our laws".

AUSENDA: Could you please define your term 'provincial law'? In fact, in English historiography this term refers to late Roman law issued by provincial administrations.

BRINK: Provincial laws in Scandinavia go back to the provinces. Again we have the problem of finding the proper translation of the Swedish word, *landskap* or *land* into English. It is normally translated as 'province', and most of these early *land* had their laws written in the vernacular language. Therefore, they are called 'provincial laws'.

AUSENDA: However, 'provincial' is a Latin term, so it is confusing.

BRINK: These are the terms used in scholarly texts.

HERSCHEND: And it is better than 'landscape laws' [laughter].

LUND: I would like to supplement the previous discussion with a reference to Per Norseng, the Norwegian historian, on the sources of medieval Scandinavian history, who summarized the discussion about the Norwegian laws and the possibility of taking them much before the time they were written down and concluded that it is very difficult—most scholars would agree—to take it back more than a hundred years before such time, assuming the contents are more than a hundred years older than the time they were written down. But few people are happy with this, he admitted. So he quoted a Norwegian poet who had stated that it was impossible and we will never give in [laughter].

GREEN: You have Gothic *sakjo* (page 95) and then you say 'fight', 'dispute'. You probably got that from a Gothic dictionary. In point of fact, the context in which the word is used is more 'dispute' than an actual 'fight', and that also on the legal side. Secondly I'd like to suggest quoting a cognate word, which strengthens your case, OHG *sahha* which means a 'legal procedure', a 'legal case', so that both the Gothic and the OHG underline your legal argument at this point.

BRINK: Thank you very much. Most certainly I have translated from Feist (1939).

GREEN: And, of course, the word he uses for 'fight' is ambiguous, it could mean a physical fight, or a legal dispute. And in fact it is a legal dispute here.

GREEN: With reference to the "connection between law and cult" (page 95), I would like to give another parallel to that in West Germanic shared by OHG, OS and OE. I give the OHG word, *êwa*, also with related forms in other languages, meaning both 'law' and 'religion'. And then this old problem in the Housesteads inscriptions, where *Thingsus*, allied to the Langobardic *thinx* or *gairethinx*, the *þing*, is connected with a Germanic deity. I say Germanic deity, although the inscription is in Latin, it was put up by a Frisian cohort.

JESCH: Have you any idea of why there comes a sudden outburst of literacy at this period when we assume that if everything you say is correct, the legal system was oral and didn't really feel the need of fixing things in writing?

BRINK: It is around 800 and later that we start to use the runic alphabet for some kind of literary writing. And then for some reason they have written down two legal statements of some kind in Östergötland and in Hälsingland, fragments of laws that are very difficult to understand, as to what they actually stand for, what they meant or what was their purpose. It is very complicated material. But the consensus is that they are legal texts to be dated to the ninth century.

JESCH: Don't you think that it is very interesting that the impulse to literacy doesn't come in the form of codification, but in the form of recording specific events?

BRINK: Absolutely, this goes entirely against the traditional view of the first laws in Scandinavia. Several other legal historians have recently stated that there were no law codes whatsoever at the time.

GREEN: You talk about "a certain kind of law, identified as Danish law and rules, was used in these parts of England" (page 99). These parts refer to Wessex, Essex, Mercia, as well of course, Danelaw. I am not quite sure about this because, apart from Danelaw itself, this doesn't necessarily follow, because the OE word *lagu* is an independent loan word from Old Norse, and because of that *Essexenalagu* and the other terms could be an OE formation modelled on the word 'Danelaw' but not necessarily implying the practice of Danish law.

BRINK: So, it could actually mean the territory?

GREEN: Yes, that too. And below you talk about *Gulathingslag* referring to an area. May I come back here to *wæpengetæc* in Old English, which means in fact, not the clashing of weapons as it does in Old Norse, but the area where that kind of legal practice was in sway, mainly the counties north of Northamptonshire, where Danish law holds.

DUMVILLE: Doesn't it refer to any particular area within which that would be true, a small area, not the whole thing?

GREEN: Not the whole thing. It is true of any small area north of Northamptonshire, in Danelaw.

DUMVILLE: Could I take it that a little confusion arises from all this. There is a long history in English writing on the business of listing areas by laws, as it were, after the Conquest. It is a historiographical tradition which I think is here coming into the legal context. And it has been very problematic over the years for people who wanted to try to define what the Danelaw was in the late Anglo-Saxon period. I assume that this list that you've got here, which is coming from the legal context, rests on an error, and the three meant are precisely Wessex, Mercia, and Danelaw, which give you a totality, whereas with Essex, Mercia and Danelaw you don't have totality. So that makes sense.

BRINK: Is it a kind of compound for which we don't know the actual meaning?

DUMVILLE: A meaning becomes a sort of formula. But I think the formula begins in historical writing not in legal usage.

"All this most probably must be looked upon as a literary construction by Snorri but...mounds could have had this usage in Scandinavia in the ninth century" (page 102). Presumably mounds which are used in this context attract legends, people ask, "why is that mound there"? So, I assume that at the very least Snorri would have had access, had he sought it, to legendary comments about why they had this name.

BRINK: If you look away from the literary sources and look at mounds in Scandinavia, it seems fairly obvious that many of these mounds, especially those which are at the most central sites in many provinces, can have grown from farms, hamlets or *þing* locations for that province. This makes it possible to assume that actually the very large mounds were, more or less, originally used for some kind of legal practice. And then, when we go back to the literary tradition, i.e. sagas, we have it again there. In my opinion this strengthens the words of Snorri and others regarding these mounds as having something to do with legal practice.

DUMVILLE: In your section on pedigrees, I really found myself in disagreement and worried about where many of your basic assumptions seem to be coming from, regarding genealogies and knowledge of one's forefathers in early Scandinavian society. What I would like you to do is to separate out two things. On the one hand the legal necessity and social necessity to be able to demonstrate who one was in relation to one's society and to property within it. On the other hand, a list among pedigrees, a retrograde patriline which might evoke stories from the names, would be appropriate to demonstrate it to the highest level of society. And where, when we can see pedigrees being augmented, in written usage, we can often find in current situations in England, in Ireland, I suspect too in Scandinavia, though I stand to be corrected there, that names can be added to pedigrees for the sake of producing length and for the sake of producing particular links, but may not carry story with them. They may be artificially constructed names, they may be names which did carry the story.... So, what I suggest, you are talking about two really different things. One has very clear functions in a society, you demonstrate that very sharply, but the other has a learned element to it, which may not be a learned element which is a function purely of a written culture, but may have a longer history than that.

BRINK: In my opinion they are somewhat interrelated.

DUMVILLE: Oh, there has to be some ultimate relationship between them, but this may be a long train ride. And it seems to me that one part of your argument was utterly clear and utterly convincing, the other part is riddled with assumptions, which could be argued about from here to eternity. Here you are quoting Gurevich "Enumeration of genealogies and names is a...formalized language in which every name conceals...stories and events...every name, by necessity, invokes a series of associations and emotions". This is a very primitive and old-fashioned way of looking at genealogies, which has gone a long way since that kind of approach.

HERSCHEND: These catalogues of names are like hoards. They are ordered according to some sort of chronological sequence that have some very old ones that may be at the end of the line. The point is that, by enumerating them, we can take a name and jump out and make a story out of it. So I think that is also why they might be three or even six generations back. It doesn't matter, it is the same as looking at the names in your own culture as some sort of a treasure hoard which can be used for many different purposes. And whether it is scholarly or legal matters that is a minor point, as it is a matter of having a name hoard.

DUMVILLE: It may be a minor point in itself, it is not a minor one within this context. And where you are being so concerned to be so precise in laying out your legal demonstrations, given the controversial scholarly context you have sketched for us, you produce exceedingly controversial, if I may say so, I think very old-fashioned arguments about what genealogy is for, is about.

BRINK: We have these very numerous reminiscences obviously of something which says we have to enumerate our ancestors. There is a link for me, to go to the next step into the pedigrees which we see in description of the Rök stone. Every name mentioned here obviously puts people in some kind of state of emotion or every name had a connotation that we don't know about.

DUMVILLE: It seems to me that that point has been argued through for a number of other cultures, and at the very least, if you are going to use that kind of opinion as a basis, you are going to have to bring in some comparative material. Let me just give you one example. In medieval Irish and Welsh law there are certain requirements in relation to claiming property, where you have to be able to show something for seven or eight generations. That's the most extreme length you can go to. But in Irish pedigree, Irish genealogy that we have in great quantity from the eighth, ninth, tenth, eleventh and twelfth centuries, we have pedigrees which may run to twenty, thirty, forty generations. And we can see that they are stuffed over time. We can see that in a smaller way in the Old English context, as Ken Sisam demostrated thirty or forty years ago, where certain names are being chosen or created in the ornamentation of pedigrees. And we can see ornamentation going on. That is a another quite different statement of what genealogy is about, from what you are requiring in your legal context. And it seems to me, if even what you are arguing in this paper, you are trying to do, your legal material may give, in some sense, a wonderful demonstration, but it is clouded by this other stuff, which relates to other levels.

AUSENDA: If *jarl* is the equivalent of the English 'earl', what would be the equivalent of the English *ceorl*?

VOICES: Karl.

BRINK: It is a matter of dispute regarding *karl* and *ceorl*. There are obvious links between Anglo-Saxon England and Scandinavia. Regarding the *jarl* and the 'earl' I am not that convinced about their relation. I would like to ask Dennis [Green]'s opinion on that.

GREEN: I think the two would actually be independent parallels, rather than a case of a loanword. But, even if they are independent words, that is not to say that they could not have been a semantic influence of the Old Norse word on the already existing English word. This makes it more complicated, but more interesting.

JESCH: *Karl* appears in this inscription from Sandsjö (page 104) in Småland and it struck me, that most runic inscriptions don't go very far back, grandparents at the most, these generational ones are very uncommon. You don't necessarily have to have a learned context to invent a pedigree, and I would like to float the idea, because if you look at this inscription, the last name, the most distant ancestor, is called "Thegn", and if you look at the inscription, his name is placed in the middle, and so given prominence. So here is a family saying, it is a family of *thegns*.

BRINK: That is quite possible, as you are aware that both 'Karl' and 'Thane' are personal names.

JESCH: All the more reason then why you can get away with making up a pedigree.

BRINK: Yes, of course: a good point.

AUSENDA: Ownership of land by individuals is a rather recent phenomenon as land in ancient times was mostly the joint property of clans. It is therefore fitting that it coincides with the introduction of writing and that there are special formulas to confirm it. Is there any trace of a previous ownership by clans?

BRINK: Not that we know of.

GREEN: You talk about German Weihnachten, for Christmas (page 106). What you are doing here is comparing a modern German form with a historical form in Old Saxon, OE, Old Norse and Gothic. Why don't you quote instead OHG *wih* for 'holy'. In addition, when you quote the Old Saxon form, it would help your cāse if you would say that it is a noun and that as a noun it means a temple (admittedly a Jewish temple). Lastly, just after that you say, "We don't know the exact semantic content of this word one thousand years ago", but we know considerably more since 1942 when W. Baetke published a massive survey of the complete evidence for "Das Heilige in Germanischen". So, I don't think your last point really stands unassailably.

BRINK: But still, when we are now trying to look into other sources, especially place-names, there is a new dimension that I tried to illustrate here, a new dimension which gives new material leading to an understanding of what a *vi*, *vé* was in Scandinavia. Obviously this is some kind of area which we still don't know exactly what it was. We have to work on this further.

GREEN: Yes, but then that needs correlation with Baetke's findings.

MAGNUS: May I comment on that? I once excavated a female grave from the early sixth century, with a small square-headed relief brooch with a runic inscription saying, "I Wir wrote runes for Wiwia". Here we have two names, one female and one male, both beginning with *wi*. Those two could be connected with the word *vi* being a cultic place, and they could in some way have been connected with recurrent rituals.

BRINK: For cultic locations we have also place-names in *vi*, obviously going back to some kind of prehistoric cult, or something like that.

GREEN: You say that it is "extremely difficult to separate these special *lund* 'groves' from profane 'groves'" (page 107). I agree, but I would like to ask how different really is the position with a word like *hov* because the Germanic etymology means an enclosure, a yard which is fenced off and from that it branches out into the religious context of a temple enclosure. The only one of these words which seems to me to be unambiguously religious is *vi*, the others, I think, are open to that doubt.

BRINK: Again, behind these words there is a vast literature and scholarly discussion. For example *hov*, we have in Old Norwegian dialects the word *hof* meaning hillock. As you know, it goes back to a proto-Germanic **huða* where one semantic component is 'hill'. So there was a discussion during recent years on the fact that the original meaning in Scandinavian was actually 'small hill' and from that we got this secondary meaning of 'cult site' or whatever. I am not convinced of that even though there is consensus about this in Scandinavia. In 1966 Olaf Olsen dealt with the *hov* problem in Scandinavia and one of his ideas was that *hov* was a borrowing from the German word which you have referred to. I think that is much more likely because *hov* might be some kind of hall building, of communal house, or some kind of building, as Olsen argued, where other cultic activities took place. *Vi* is the most secure word we have for a pagan cult site. As I was trying to show in my paper, maybe it is not so easy even here: it probably has some broader semantic meaning.

DUMVILLE: With reference to the Gurevich comment, how wise is it to describe pre-Christian Scandinavia as a pre-literate society, which is what you appear to be doing here.

BRINK: It was an oral society, thereby I have not made any qualifications.

DUMVILLE: So you say, but I mean runes. What do you mean then by literacy?

BRINK: In a different society you have the written texts as some kind of codifiers while runic inscriptions are not used as literary evidence. However, in early Scandinavian society, we have two legal inscriptions and we have thousands of runic inscriptions all with the same kind of content: "So and so erected this". But that is in some way on the threshold to literate society, but could Preben [Meulengracht] comment on this?

MEULENGRACHT: That is what my paper is about [laughter].

ARRHENIUS: I wanted to comment on this. In the settlement layers we almost never find any pieces of runic inscriptions.

DUMVILLE: Dangerous material.

VESTERGAARD: I think we have got to limit the discussion and define what you understand by 'oral society'. Oral society is an ordered and structured society just as much as a literate society.

DUMVILLE: There are now immense texts on literacy and pre-literacy.

References in the discussion

Textual sources:

Egil's Saga: see References at end of paper.
Finnsburh: see Fry 1974.
Heimskringla: see *Textual sources* (Snorri Sturluson) at end of paper.
Tacitus
> *Germania*: see Anderson (ed.) 1938.
> *Historiae*: see Heubner (ed.) 1978.

Bibliography:

Anderson, J. G. C. (ed.)
1938   *Tacitus, Germania.* Oxford: Clarendon Press.
Baetke, W.
1942   *Das Heilige in Germanischen.* Tübingen: Mohr.
Fenger, O.
1991   See References at end of paper.
Feist, S.
1939   *Vergleichende Wörterbuch der Gotischen Sprache...*3. [Neubearbeitung und Vermehrte Auflaghen.] Leiden: Brill.
Fry, D. K.
1974   *Finnsburh. Fragment and Episode.* London: Methuen.
Heubner, H. (ed.)
1978   *Tacitus, Historiae.* Stuttgart: Teubner.
Norseng, P.
1987   Lovmaterialet som kilde til tidlig middelalder. In *Kilderne til den tidlige middelalders historie. Rapporter til den XX nordiske historikerkongres, Reykjavik 1987*, 1. G. Karlsson (ed.), pp. 48-77. Reykjavik: Sagnfræðistofnun Háskola Islands.
Ruthström, B.
1988   See References at end of paper.
Sjöholm, E.
1988   See References at end of paper.
Sisam, K.
1953   See References at end of paper.
Stein-Wilkeshuis, M.
1998   See References at end of paper.

RURAL ECONOMY: ECOLOGY, HUNTING, PASTORALISM, AGRICULTURAL AND NUTRITIONAL ASPECTS

LISE BENDER JØRGENSEN

Institute of Archaeology, Museum of Natural History and Archaeology, Norwegian University of Science and Technology, Erling Skakkes gt. 47b, N-7491 Trondheim

Introduction

Rural economy is one of those fundamental aspects of early societies that tends to fall between the stools of several specialists. The work of botanists, zoologists, geologists, geographers and various others are all central to the understanding of how ecology and biology interacted with human know-how and technology to serve the needs for food, clothing, housing and other necessities. In recent years, research has been done by many Scandinavian scholars on this subject, enlarging our empirical base for the understanding of Vendel and Viking Age economy. This multiplicity is important, supplying us with a depth of knowledge that we would not be able to reach in any other way. There are, however, disadvantages, creating a number of highly specialized research fields or subdisciplines that tend to be difficult to penetrate for the general archaeologist. For that reason, overviews are quite rare. They do, however, exist. For Norway, Ingvild Øye's 1976 MA dissertation is still the main work (Øye Sølvberg 1976). A 'History of Norwegian Agriculture' is in preparation, and will include much recent work. The equivalent 'History of Danish Agriculture' published in 1988 includes a substantial section on the relevant period by Lotte Hedeager. For Sweden, the recent *Det svenska jordbrukets historia* supplies useful surveys by Mats Widgren & Ellen Anne Pedersen (1998), and Janken Myrdal (1998, 1999).

The rural economy of Vendel and Viking Age Scandinavia was based on a kaleidoscope of interlinking occupations. Agriculture was only a part of it. Fishing, forestry, iron production and quarrying were emerging industries that contributed substantially to the tissue of late Iron Age society, as did crafts such as textile production, carpentry, bone- and hornworking, and various types of smithing. Understanding how all these functioned and interlinked is a challenge, and also fundamental for understanding the structure of society. To highlight this, I have elected to focus on the variety of resources of Scandinavia and how they were used.

Ecology

Before addressing the subject of rural economy it is important to state that Scandinavia is by no means homogeneous. On the contrary: the present-day

129

countries of Norway, Sweden and Denmark cover an enormous area: from north to south well over 2,000 km, across from Bergen to Stockholm some 800 km. Accordingly a wide range of ecological units are represented. Norway is, as the name says, the way to the north: a long coast with some of the best fishing in the world and high mountains with potential for hunting and pastoralism, while only a few areas are well suited for agriculture. Sweden has massive forests, interspersed with good agricultural land, but also a long tradition for exploiting metal ore. Lowland Denmark offers good conditions for agriculture, and fishing too. The ecology of Scandinavia—in the sixth to tenth centuries as well as today— embraces arctic, sub-arctic and temperate climate zones, coasts and inland, highland and lowland, arable land, forests, moors and wetlands. Some areas are densely populated, others thinly, and some are almost uninhabitable (NUB 1977).

Climate is a variable factor. Recent research has shown cyclic changes, normally lasting some 260 years. One change took place *ca* 500 AD, cooling the temperature by *ca* 0.5° C and increasing rainfall. In Denmark, this meant better grazing and a regeneration of forests, beech becoming the main tree. On the sandy soils of Jutland, heathland was spreading, securing winter fodder. The next climate change, in the tenth century AD, meant lower rainfall, warmer summers and colder winters (Aaby 1985; Lamb 1982:162 ff.). In Norway, the Viking Age and early Middle Ages saw settlements spreading to grounds hitherto unfarmed (Lamb 1982:168).

Rural economy of the Vendel and Viking periods

In most of Europe, agriculture and pastoralism were introduced during the Stone Age, with the transition from hunter/gatherer to farming societies. In Scandinavia, things did not quite happen this way, although the Neolithic did reach Southern Scandinavia around 4000 BC. In the North, people stuck to the Mesolithic way of life much longer, well into the first millennium BC. In some ways, it has never been quite abandoned—in northern Norway, for example, fish is a much more reliable food source than grain. In consequence, the rural economy of Vendel and Viking period Scandinavia was much more varied than on the Continent or the British Isles.

Pastoralism

Cattle, pigs, sheep and goats were the main domestic animals, all of them introduced in Scandinavia with the arrival of agriculture. They supplied meat, fat, tallow, hides and horn. Oxen were used as draught animals and sheep procured wool. Hens and geese were added to the stock during the Iron Age, as were cats. Dogs were used for shepherding, hunting and as watchdogs. Horses served for warfare, riding and other transport purposes, but also for their meat. Osteological investigations show that horseflesh was an important part of the diet throughout the first millennium AD (Pedersen & Widgren 1998:364ff).

One native Scandinavian animal was domesticated too, the reindeer. Tame reindeer are mentioned by Ohthere (Lund 1984:20), but scholars have interpreted this evidence in different ways, and several regard the domestication of reindeer as of much later date. Kjell-Åke Aronsson has argued that evidence for the herding of forest reindeer dates as early as to the beginnings of the first millennium; Inger Storli has argued for reindeer pastoralism before or during the Viking Age (Aronsson 1991, Storli 1991:85 ff.). Reindeer pastoralism is a feature of the Saami people, supplying them with meat, milk, and transport, as well as fur and antlers. Reindeer demand huge tracts of lands such as are available in the tundras and forests of northern Scandinavia.

Cattle were the most important type of livestock. Evidence for this is found in investigations of osteological finds and settlement remains. Excavated Iron Age houses frequently include traces of stall partitions, indicating how many animals were kept. Counting them suggests that early Iron Age farms in Denmark had 10-15 head of cattle. During the Roman and Migration periods numbers went up to 15-30, in Viking Age farms, byres with room for 80-100 animals have been found (Hedeager 1988). In Sweden, similar calculations suggest that the average Migration period farm had a stock of about 15. During the Vendel and Viking periods, cattle remained the dominant form of livestock (Pedersen & Widgren 1998:364 ff).

Further evidence is supplied by archaeozoology, giving details of how the cattle where kept and used. In Denmark, about one half of the animals were slaughtered before the age of 3.5 years. Thus most cows had at least one calf, and could serve for multiple purposes: milk, meat, manure, and also renewal and securing of the breeding stock. A number of cows lived around ten years. They formed the staple of dairy cattle, highly treasured by the farmer.

In later times, oxen were a major export from several parts of Scandinavia, such as Western Jutland (Frandsen 1994). These animals were raised on individual farms, but were later sold to a larger estate. When they were 4-5 years old, they were walked down the peninsula and sold. This walk took about 14 days, and the oxen had to be re-fattened for 3 weeks on the marshes before they were slaughtered. The Jutland oxen were renowned for their high-quality meat, but the real reason for this trade was the demand posed by the growing number of towns with non-food producing inhabitants, combined with the fact that meat is best transported on the hoof.

When did this ox-trade begin? Large amounts of undecomposed cattle manure found in the early layers of Ribe (*ca* 720 AD) have been interpreted as possible evidence of an eighth century ox-trade, perhaps stemming from the large byres found at contemporary Jutland settlements such as Vorbasse and Omgaard (Bencard & Bender Jørgensen 1990:145; Bender Jørgensen & Eriksen 1995:70). Demands for leather may also have added to the production of cattle.

Milk is a staple commodity in modern Scandinavia. Most people drink milk regularly, even as adults, and milk products such as butter and cheese are important parts of the diet. In her study of diet and stockraising in Medieval Sweden, Maria Vretemark has studied the history of Swedish food consumption and finds that milk and animal products played an even greater role in earlier times. She argues that, during the Middle Ages, bread and other cereal food types slowly replaced milk products as the staple food of the general population. The reasons for this were partly economic, in that cereals gave a better overall yield than animal production, and partly ideological, bread holding an important place in Christian culture. Still, in many places milk products held the role as basic food and were only replaced by potatoes and cereals as late as in the nineteenth century. Fresh milk was seen primarily as a raw material that had to be treated, coagulated into junket (*skyr*) or fresh cheese. Junket could keep for months, and the waste product, whey (*valle*) could be used as a preservative for butter and meat (Vretemark 1997:166 f.).

Meat was a seasonal product, as slaughtering was mainly done at the end of the grazing season: cattle and sheep in October, pig in November-December. Preservation was vital, and was done in a multitude of ways: drying, smoking, salting, fermentation, or, as mentioned above, in whey. In northern Scandinavia, freezing was commonly used, too. Drying was perhaps the most common method: dried meat could keep for years. Dried meat (*pinnekjött*) is an important ingredient in traditional Norwegian cooking. Fermentation is even easier: the unopened animal is covered, often in a pit, and left to ferment. It is important to keep out air; salt is necessary too, but is sufficiently present in the animal's blood and entrails. Today, this method sounds revolting to most people; it is, however, still used, e.g. in the sour herring, 'surströmning', a delicacy of northern Sweden (Vretemark 1997:166 f., Israelsson 1990:22 f.).

Pigs were kept for meat, and were usually sent off into the forest to feed on mast. In south Scandinavia, they could often do that all year round, utilizing an ecological niche. In hard winters, they were taken into the village. As pigs eat almost everything, they had a useful function removing waste. Pigs can even be kept in dense settlements and towns, quickly turning household waste and grain into meat. In the late Iron Age, increased cultivation and fencing reduced grazing areas. This turned pigs into the most important form of livestock. Starting on the Continent, this development reached Scandinavia in the Viking Age, particularly in the south, and at magnate farms and in early towns (Pedersen & Widgren 1998:369).

Sheep are less prestigious than cattle, but are hardy and sustain far harsher climatic conditions. They offer a meat source in many areas where other types of livestock cannot be kept. In addition to meat, they supply milk, tallow, horn, skin and bone, and also our most important textile fibre, wool. Sheep have been an important part of animal husbandry in Scandinavia ever since their introduction. The Swedish Migration period farm mentioned above is supposed to have had a flock of 30 sheep. It was situated on the island of Öland, one of the Baltic islands that show a marked, increasing predominance of sheep in the Iron Age. Reasons for this have been discussed, such as an increased demand for wool, or that the hardy sheep gave better returns on meagre soils (Pedersen & Widgren 1998:368).

In the Norse world of the North Atlantic, sheep farming is a basic element of the rural economy even today. The sheep graze all year round, growing wool with qualities that traditionally have been exploited in minute detail. This particularly applies to textiles to be used at sea. Wool for fishermen's mittens is different from that for their sweaters. For the former, promising white ewe lambs are put on certain pastures, and mating and wool harvest are postponed until the animal is three years old. Earlier mating and succeeding pregnancies result in poorer wool quality. Sweater wool is selected from two-year old wethers. Sails, too, were made of wool. Experimental archaeology has shown that to produce a wool sail for a viking ship, access to wool from large flocks of sheep is neccessary. For 100 square metres of sailcloth, 100 km warp yarns and 80 km weft must be spun, and woven into 15-16 lengths of cloth before the sailmaker can start his work. The introduction of sails, which happened around 700, thus meant a major increase in demand for wool— and for (wo)manpower to work it (Lightfoot 1996, 1997; Bender Jørgensen 1999, in press; Cooke & Christiansen 2000; Christiansen 2001).

Analyses demonstrated that fleece types from Scandinavia became more and more specialized during the first millennium AD in Scandinavia (Bender Jørgensen & Walton 1986; Walton 1988). This indicates that wool was important and was produced for a range of different purposes. A survey of textile remains from Scandinavia and Northern Europe has established signs of organized textile production since the early Iron Age, adding a range of 'brand cloth' to homespuns (Bender Jørgensen 1986, 1992).

Agriculture

Around 200-300 AD the 'Celtic fields' of the early Iron Age were replaced by an infield-outfield system. The areas close to the settlement (infields) consisted of enclosed meadows, intended for hay production, and constantly cultivated fields. The outfields, further away from the settlement, were used for grazing. Stone walls were constructed to form cattle paths to the outfields. This way, the cattle could be kept close to the settlement at night, without risk of the animals devouring or trampling the crops. In Sweden, Mats Widgren has investigated fossil agrarian landscapes in Östergötland, and found that the basic unit of this system was the '*hägnadslag*' (enclosure society), a village-like organization consisting of 4-5 farms and covering an area of generally 4+ square kilometres of land. After the introduction of this system, a period of expansion followed, creating a very open landscape. Around 400 AD a peak was reached, and the Migration period saw a decline, perhaps due to over-exploitation of arable land compared to pastures, followed by a lack of manure. In the seventh and eighth centuries, both arable and pasture recovered, without any apparent changes in the layout of the land until after AD 1000 when the cultivation of cereals expanded (Widgren 1983). Recently, Widgren has reinterpreted the development in the Vendel and Viking Periods in the light of recent research (Widgren 1998). He argues that the *hägnadslag* should be seen as Iron Age estates, and that after *ca* 500 AD these were split and restructured into what became the territories of the medieval villages. This must reflect a major reorganization of society, touching most *hägnadslag* — but not all. Some retained their territories unchanged, turning into manors that are recognizable in historical times. Widgren sees this as a development of a hierarchy of estates that made it possible for leading families to exploit the work of others to create a surplus of food, clothing and other necessities and thus construct the foundation for their power.

In Denmark and southwestern Norway, similar changes in settlement layout and organization have been observed. One is dated *ca* AD 200, another sometime in the sixth century, a third around 1000 AD, indicating a homogeneous development of agricultural systems and technology in southern Scandinavia (Hedeager & Kristiansen 1988, 1990, Hvass 1988, Myhre 1979, 1985, Nissen Jaubert 1996).

The most important crop of the infield-outfield system was hay, winter fodder for the animals. Hay was cut during the summer, to be dried and stored. In the early Iron Age, harvesting was done with an iron sickle, and from the first century AD with a short scythe. The rake appeared around this time, too. About 200-300 AD the long scythe was added to the harvesting tools, accompanied by a better rake. Both facilitated the hay harvest, approximately doubling the efficiency (Myrdal 1988). The hay was transported by a horse-drawn wagon, the Tranbær-type, also thought to have appeared *ca* 200 AD, replacing the earlier ox-drawn cart (Schovsboe 1987). Finally, a barn section was added to the typical Iron Age long-house, completing the 'hay package' of the late Roman Iron Age. Later, around 7-800 AD, a more efficient carriage was introduced. The yoke of earlier wagons was replaced by the harness, better enabling the transfering of power from the horses and permitting a larger and stronger carriage construction (Schovsboe 1987).

Cereals. Part of the infield was used for cereal production. Hulled barley (*hordeum vulgare*) was the main crop, along with wheat, millet, oats, and from about 2-300 AD rye. Corn spurrey also seems to have been cultivated. Flax was grown for its fibre and especially its oil, as were other plants with a high oil content such as Gold-of-pleasure (*camelina sativa*).

Hulled barley had replaced naked barley and speltoid and naked wheat as the main cereal all over Scandinavia around 1000 BC. Karin Viklund suggests that this, too, was part of a 'package', consisting of a permanent field system, three-aisled longhouses with cattle stalls that made it possible to collect manure, and the iron sickle (Viklund 1998). The sickle meant that the cereal could be cut closer to the ground so that straw became available for fodder, enhancing the production of manure. Hulled barley is the cereal most responsive to manuring, and the 'package' proved very stable. It even made it possible to introduce farming permanently to northern Scandinavia, except for the northernmost parts of Norway, the counties of north Troms and Finnmark where summers are definitely too short for cereals (Jørgensen 1988). Hulled barley remained the predominant cereal in Scandinavia until *ca* 800 AD, although other crops such as rye, oats and flax grew in importance.

At the beginning of the Viking Age, evidence of autumn-sown rye signals that crop rotation systems were introduced in southern Scandinavia. These made it possible to keep the same number of livestock even though new fields were brought under the plough (Viklund 1998). A typical crop succession would be rye-barley-fallow. The fallow year was neccessary to allow the time to work and manure the fields before sowing rye in the autumn. With a fallow year, and a summer and a winter crop in rotation, manuring could be minimized: only one third of the fields, the fallow before rye sowing, was manured each year. Rye does well with fresh dung, while barley favours decomposed manure. The three-field rotation system produces about the same yield of the two cereals (Engelmark 1992:372 ff.).

The hulled barley was used for thin, flat bread, baked on an open fire. This type of bread is still typical of northern Sweden and of Norway. Oats seem to have been preferred for bread and porridge in parts of western Sweden—a tradition that also lived on until close to our times (Viklund 1998:141 f.). In Denmark, Bent Aaby considers that barley was primarily used for porridge and beer, while oats were fodder for the animals (Aaby 1995). During the Viking Age, rye presumably became the main bread cereal in southern Scandinavia. It took another half millennium for rye bread to reach Central Sweden, and it never replaced barley bread in the north. Karin Viklund argues that this was not due to climatic or other environmental changes, as both rye and oats give satisfactory yields in northern Sweden. Farms there, however, were small, and based on stock-rearing and milk products rather than cereals. Instead, Viklund views the barley as a symbolic crop, establishing the farmer's identity in contrast to other groups such as hunters, fishers and Saami (Viklund 1998:174).

Bread has been found at several sites, especially in Sweden but also some in Denmark (Hansson 1996:68). Sweden has almost 100 finds of charred bread, mostly dating to the Iron Age. Birka and Helgö in Central Sweden are the best sources. These breads are small, thin and biscuit-like; some have holes in the centre, allowing them to be hung on wires of iron or bronze (Viklund 1998:143). They are generally made from at least two different cereals, one of them almost always barley. The proportion of cereals used for the breads corresponds roughly to the proportion in which they were cultivated. Ann-Marie Hansson defines bread as being baked, in contrast to grain-paste and porridge (1994), and argues that the Birka loaves may well have been baked on a baking slab or an iron pan (1996:70). Viklund also does not consider these breads to have been baked in ovens; indeed, she states, there are few signs of such structures, and she views leavened, oven-baked bread as an effect of the increasing cultivation of rye in southern Scandinavia (Viklund 1998:143 f.).

Fishing

In Scandinavia, fishing has always had an important role in the rural economy.
Two fish species in particular are important, herring and cod. On my native island,
Bornholm, people talk of *sild* (herring), and fish (other fish species). Similar
expressions are used in Norway, along with a third phenomenon, *ufisk,* meaning
'non-fish', uncommon species such as cuttlefish and shellfish that are considered
to be of no value.

During the Middle Ages, herring fishing was very important in Denmark and
western Sweden. The Scanian market at Skanör, where the herring was landed,
salted and sold, was renowned all over Europe and gave huge income to the
Danish king, but there was abundant herring fishing at numerous other sites.
Herring move in huge shoals, tending to appear seasonally at certain places, and
this made fishing it so lucrative. Routes do, however, change, leaving the
fishermen and merchants suddenly empty-handed. This is well known from
historical sources, archaeological evidence is as yet scarce. Fish bones are only
recovered when the soil is sieved, and that is a fairly recent technique. A recent
find from Roskilde Fjord, however, indicates that herring was a main fish of the
Viking Age, together with cod and flatfish (Bødker Enghoff 1996). There is an
interesting difference between herring remains of the tenth century, where all types
of bone were found, and those of the eleventh that only contain gill bones. This
indicates that 'industrial' herring fishing only started in the eleventh century,
probably triggered by increased access to salt (Bødker Enghoff 1996).

North of the 62°, great numbers of Atlantic cod, *skrei,* appear every year in late
winter to spawn, creating an important economic resource. Preservation is easy, the
fish is dried on racks. There is plenty of wind and, as the fishing season is early in
the year, the dried fish is ready to pack and store when summer warmth brings
flies. Dried fish, stockfish, was Norway's prime export during the Middle Ages,
feeding people all over Europe and securing cheap, plentiful food for the meagre
spring season and during Lent. It is still a major export, especially to Catholic
countries like Italy. A number of small, seasonal fishing settlements have been
found along the Norwegian coast. One of these, at Hjartøy west of Bergen, was
founded in the Migration period. It seems to have suffered a setback in the sixth
century, only to recover and flourish in the Vendel and Viking periods. At
Allmenningværet in Trøndelag, a similar settlement was dated to *ca* 900-1200, and
several other sites, yet undated, are also expected to belong to the Vendel-Viking
periods (Alsaker 1989, 1995; Magnus 1974). The most important cod fishing,
today as well as in the Middle Ages, is at Lofoten. The beginnings of major,
organized fishing at Lofoten are disputed: at the end of the eleventh century, there
is plenty of evidence of its existence, but arguments have been presented for an
earlier, Viking Age beginning (Bertelsen 1994).

Sea mammals such as whales, seals and walrus were important maritime
resources. They supplied a lot of meat, but also blubber (e.g. for lamps), and their
bones were used for various tools such as weaving swords and ironing boards

(Sjøvold 1974:248 f.). The famous Lewis chessmen were carved from walrus ivory, presumably in Trondheim during the twelfth century. Other examples of walrus ivory derive from, e.g., the court of Charles the Bald, *ca* 870-880 (Roesdahl & Wilson 1992:384 f.). Ropes made of walrus hides were famed for their strength.

Down was another important resource of the Norwegian coast. Eiderdowns were collected and exported. They were used for bedding, but also quilted clothing (Blindheim 1979). *Fugela feðrum* (feathers) were among the merchandise that Ohthere received from the Saami (Lund 1984:20). The nesting cliffs also offered possibilities for fowling and egg gathering. Later sources inform us that fowling was done with a small stick with a fish hook at the end. The birds were pulled out from the rocks with this stick, then their neck was wrung, and they were thrown into the sea for later collecting. The fowler then proceeded to gather eggs. Two men could gather more than a barrel of eggs in 1-2 hours. Fowling was dangerous work and many were killed (Berglund 1994:77 f.).

Hunting

Hunting as a source of meat, antler, and furs was important during the Vendel and Viking periods. Reindeer and elk were the prime targets. This has left a number of traces, particularly in the mountains of the Scandinavian peninsula. Constructions such as pit traps and bowmen's positions have been recorded, along with various types of fencing intended to lead the animals towards the traps. Remains of hunting weapons have also been recovered, especially arrows that missed their goal and ended up in a snowdrift (Farbregd 1972; Barth 1996). Egil Mikkelsen has excavated a hunting installation in Grimsdalen, Dovre. It proved to be a 3 km long, funnel-shaped reindeer trapping system, constructed from *ca* 1700 pine trunks. In connection with this, three shacks for the trappers were built. The hunting installation was used from the fifth century and into the fourteenth, with a peak around 900-1250 AD when large-scale trapping of reindeer took place. Excavations have revealed about 56,000 bone fragments, 83% of which are reindeer. Fox is the most common fur animal, and ptarmigan represents the mountain fowl. Some 10% of the bones, however, derive from domestic animals such as horse, cattle, pigs and sheep. These, and some cod and herring bones, probably represent the travelling food of the trappers. Meat, fur and antlers were the main products of this type of hunt. They were intended partly for local consumption, partly for long-distance trade. Reindeer antler has been found in small quantities in Haithabu, Lund and Aarhus as part of comb-makers' raw materials and forms the main basis for this artisan's craft in early medieval towns in Norway (Mikkelsen 1994).

Hunting also began to become a sport of the upper classes in Vendel and Viking period Scandinavia. Falconry was introduced to western Europe about the beginning of the Migration period. In the tenth century, there is evidence that Norway was providing hunting birds for the European aristocracy, and this type of hunting also became popular among the Scandinavian nobility. Maria Vretemark has found bones of hunting birds in a number of graves from the fifth century onwards, e.g. in the boat graves of Vendel and Valsgärde and in many cremation graves. The goshawk is the most common, but the sparrow-hawk and peregrine falcon have also been found. Owls often accompany the falcons and hawks; they were presumably used as decoys during hunting (Vretemark 1984).

Forestry

The forests of Vendel and Viking period Scandinavia held other resources than game. For those travelling in present-day Norway or Sweden, the massive forests are conspicuous and seem an inexhaustible resource, but it was not always so. Over-exploitation of the forest, e.g. through charcoal production for the copper or iron industry, has happened several times.

The forests have served many purposes, in the past as in the present. They supply timber for building material, but also firewood and charcoal, and tar. Shipwrights and cartwrights required certain types and shapes of timber (Christensen 1995, Schovsboe 1987). Other specific woods were needed for bows, that are preferably made of yew, and for various tool shafts. Troughs and vessels, and items of furniture each have specific properties demanding meticulously selected woods.

Timber is conspicuous as a commodity, and one that has had great economic significance for centuries, perhaps millennia. It is, however, also something that is difficult to pinpoint archaeologically. Much timber has been preserved, particularly in early towns, and it is used eagerly by archaeologists for dendrochronology. As yet, only a few have ventured to ask where it came from, how it was produced and transported, and what kind of organization was behind this. In 1939-1940, Sigurd Grieg excavated the largest mound in Scandinavia, Raknehaugen in Norway. His aim was to find the burial of the fabled King Rakne, but instead he found 75,000 pine trunks (Hagen 1997:194 f.). The forest historian Asbjørn Ording studied this enormous—and unique—evidence, and found that they represented a cultivated forest, felled sometime during the sixth century. None of the trees was over 60 years old, they were very homogeneous, and had grown in an open forest, probably used for pasture. Almost all the timber (97%) had been felled during a single winter. Calculations suggest that a work-force of 160-200 men had worked some 150 days to fell 30,000 trees, to trim and divide them, and to transport the timber from the clearing to the construction site—catering for the lumberjacks not to be forgotten (Hagen 1997). This is the first evidence of large-scale Iron Age forestry in Scandinavia.

A recent investigation of timber samples from medieval Trondheim by Harald Bentz Høgseth reveals sophisticated craftsmanship. Sills, beams and planks each demand different wood properties. To obtain these (particularly for sills and planks), the timber had been artificially aged. One method is to cut off the top of the pine tree and trim 70% of the branches. The tree then needs less water, and the wood turns into pith (*kjerneved*) within 4-6 years. Another method is to bleed the tree by cutting off patches of bark. This takes 3-4 years (Høgseth 1998). The work of Ording and Høgseth gives us tantalizing glimpses of the potential of knowledge lodged in archaeological wood.

Tar was used to impregnate wood, such as boats, bulwarks, houses, wagons, and sleighs, and other organic materials like rope, sails and fishing-nets. Excavations in Ribe, Denmark, revealed that shortly after 700 AD, a market-place had been constructed. Plots for craftsmen were laid out along the bank of the Ribe river, a couple of wells securing the water supply. One of the wells was made from a barrel; the wood was felled in Lower Saxony. Remains of tar suggest that it derived from the Harz in Lower Saxony. The barrel of tar had probably arrived in Ribe via the Elbe, indicating that tar was an important commodity in the early eighth century (Bencard & Bender Jørgensen 1990:145).

Tar is made from pine roots that contain a high percentage of resin. The roots are heated in order to turn the resin liquid, it then flows out as tar. The art of tarmaking consists in heating the roots sufficiently for this to happen, without making the tar catch fire. Hot tar evaporates into highly inflammable gases, and a tar kiln easily turns into a bonfire. In the Scandinavian peninsula, tar was often made in the *utmark*, the wilderness of forests, moors and mountains. Most excavated tar kilns date to the sixteenth to seventeenth centuries. The earliest site yet excavated is dated around 1000 AD (Farbregd 1977, 1989).

Iron production and quarrying

Iron production and quarrying also formed an important part of the rural economy in Scandinavia throughout the first millennium AD. Evidence of major iron production has been found in all three Scandinavian countries. In the county of North Trøndelag in Norway, about 300 iron production sites have been found, dating to *ca* 350 BC to 600 AD. Calculations indicate that each has produced about 50 tons of crude iron. After 700, production changed and moved to the neighbouring county of South Trøndelag (Stenvik 1996; Prestvold 1996). In southern Norway, Telemark developed a large iron production in the Viking Age and into the Middle Ages (Martens 1988). Similar large-scale production followed by changes of location has been observed in Sweden (Magnusson 1986). In Denmark, major iron production took place in western Jutland during the Roman and Migration periods. Very few traces have as yet been found of that of the Vendel and Viking periods (Voss 1993; Juottijärvi 1995).

Soapstone and hones were major export merchandise of the Viking Age. Both were quarried in Scandinavia, particularly Norway. Many soapstone quarries have been recorded (Skjølsvold 1961, Resi 1979, Berg 1999, Østerås 1999 and forthcoming). Difficulties of dating such constructions has made research problematic; recent excavations are, however, starting to establish a framework (Østerås forthcoming).

Heid Gjøstein Resi has studied the remains of soapstone vessels from Hedeby. She found that trade in these items started *ca* 850, and continued into the Middle Ages. Hones have been the object of studies by Resi and Siri Myrvoll (Resi 1990; Myrvoll 1991:115-141; 1992). A grey schist found around Eidsborg in Telemark was the starting point for an organized production of hones in standard sizes starting *ca* 800 AD and continuing into the Middle Ages. The Eidsborg hones replaced an earlier type of purple hones. The provenance of the purple hones is as yet unknown, but they probably derive from Scandinavia.

Economics

The economics of the sixth to tenth centuries have been discussed by many scholars, and a range of explanations have been offered. Earlier perceptions of trade, modelled on the modern market economy, have been revised several times. The period in question is a transition phase between an earlier economic system based on gift exchange and redistribution, to a market economy and monetarization. Central questions in this debate are whether the transition happened for economic or political reasons (e.g. Hodges 1982; Andrén 1989; Christophersen 1989; Carver 1993; Christophersen 1994; Hedeager 1994; Saunders 1995; Anderton 1999). Still, we have much work in front of us. Mats Widgren has recently asked for an integration of the archaeology of the chiefs and the human geography of the peasants (1998). The rich evidence of emerging industries in late Iron Age Scandinavia opens up great potential for investigating craftsmanship and work organization. Here, perhaps, new ways may be found towards answering Widgren's plea.

References

Aaby, B.
    1985   'Klima'. In *Arkæologi leksikon*, pp. 148-150. Copenhagen: Politiken.
Andrén, A.
    1989   State and towns in the Middle Ages. The Scandinavian experience. *Theory and Society* 18: 585-609.
Anderton, M. (ed.)
    1999   *Anglo-Saxon Trading Centres. Beyond the Emporia.* Glasgow: Cruithne Press.
Alsaker, S.
    1989   Fra sild til olje. Et fiskevær fra jernalderen. *Arkeo* [1989] 1: 4-11.
    1995   Fiskevær gjennom 1500 år. *Spor* [1995] 1: 40-43.
Aronsson, K-Å
    1991   *Forest Reindeer Herding AD 1-1800.* (Archaeology and Environment 10). Umeå: Umeå Universitet.

Barth, E. K.
1996   *Fangstanlegg for rein, gammel virksomhet og tradisjon i Rondane.*
          Trondheim: NINA-NIKU.
Bencard, M., & L. Bender Jørgensen
1990   *Ribe Excavations 1970-76,* vol. 4, *Excavation and Stratigraphy.* Esbjerg:
          Sydjysk Universitetsforlag.
Bender Jørgensen, L.
1986   *Forhistoriske textiler i Skandinavien - Prehistoric Scandinavian Textiles.*
          (Nordiske Fortidsminder, Ser. B, vol. 9). Copenhagen: Det Kgl. Nordiske
          Oldskriftselskab.
1992   *North European Textiles until AD 1000.* Aarhus: Aarhus University Press.
1999   Seilet som kvinnene spant. *Spor* [1999] 1: 32-33.
n.d.   Textiles of Seafaring. In *Report of the 7th NESAT Symposium.* F. Pritchard
          & J. P. Wild (eds.). Edinburgh: National Museums of Scotland.
Bender Jørgensen, L., & P. Eriksen
1995   *Trabjerg - En vestjysk landsby fra vikingetiden.* (Jysk Arkæologisk Selskabs
          Skrifter XXXI:1). Højbjerg: Jysk Arkeologisk Selskav.
Bender Jørgensen, L., & P. Walton
1986   Dyes and fleece types in prehistoric textiles from Scandinavia and Germany.
          Journal of Danish Archaeology 5: 177-88.
Berg, A.
1999   Ny aktivitet i gammelt stenbrudd. *Spor* [1999] 2: 20-22.
Berglund, B. (ed.)
1994   *Helgelands Historie,* bd. 2. Mosjøen: Helgelands Historielag.
Bertelsen, R.
1994   Helgelendingene og Vågan i Lofoten. In *Helgelands historie,* bd. 2.
          B. Berglund (ed.), pp. 113-132. Mosjøen: Helgelands Historielag.
Björn, C. (ed.)
1988   *Det danske landbrugs historie I. Oldtid og middelalder.* Odense:
          Landbohistorisk selskab.
Blindheim, C.
1979   Til vikingetidens drakt- og handelshistorie. Gammelt funn i nytt lys.
          Universitetets Oldsakssamlings Årbok [1979]: 136-144.
Bødker Enghoff, I.
1996   Danmarks første sildeindustri? *Marinarkæologisk nyhedsbrev fra Roskilde,*
          Nr. 6.
Carver, M.
1993   *Arguments in Stone. Archaeological Research and the European Town in the
          First Millennium.* (Oxbow Monographs 29). Oxford: Oxbow.
Christensen, A. E.
1995   Båtbygging, naturgitt desentralisering av et viktig håndverk? *Varia* 30: 123-130.
Christiansen, C.
2001   Primitive woolworking and sheep farming in Shetland. Unpublished Ph.D.
          thesis, University of Manchester.
Christophersen, A.
1989   Kjøpe, selge, bytte, gi. Vareutvikling og byoppkomst i Norge ca. 800-1100:
          en modell. *Medeltidens Födelse.* Pp. 109-145. Lund: Gyllenstiernska
          Krapperupsstiftelsen.
1994   Power and impotence: political background of urbanisation in Trøndelag
          900-1100 AD. *Archaeologia Polona* 32: 95-108.
Cooke, B., & C. Christiansen
2000   Hva gjør ullduk til seilduk? *Spor* [2000] 1: 24-26.

Engelmark, R.
1992   A review of the farming economy in South Scania based on botanical
            evidence. In *The Archaeology of the Cultural Landscape.* I. Larsson,
            J. Callmer & B. Stjernqvist (eds.), pp. 369-375. Lund: Almquist & Wiksell
            International.
Farbregd, O.
1972   *Pilefunn frå Oppdalsfjella.* Trondheim: Miscellanea.
1977   Miletufter og reiskaper frå tjørebrenning i myr. *Årbok for Norsk Skogbruk-
            museum* 8: 171-188.
1989   Tjørebrenning – en enkel, men spennende kunst. *Spor* [1989] 1: 10-14.
Frandsen, K.-E.
1994   *Okser på vandring. Produktion og eksport af stude fra Danmark i midten af
            1600-tallet.* Skive: Skippershoved.
Hagen, A.
1997   *Gåten om kong Raknes grav. Hovedtrekk i norsk arkeologi.* Oslo: Cappelen.
Hansson, A.-M.
1994   Grain-paste, porridge and bread. Ancient cereal-based food. *Laborativ
            Arkeologi.* (Journal of Nordic Archaeological Science) 7: 5-20.
1996   Bread in Birka and on Björkö. *Laborativ Arkeologi* (Journal of Nordic
            Archaeological Science) 9: 61-78.
1997   *On Plant Food in the Scandinavian Peninsula in Early Medieval Times.*
            (Theses and Papers in Archaeology, B:5). Stockholm: Stockholm University.
Hedeager, L.
1988   Jernalderen. In *Det danske landbrugs historie I. Oldtid og middelalder.*
            Landbohistorisk selskab. C. Bjørn (ed.), pp. 109-203. Odense:
            Landbohistorisk selskab.
1990   *Danmarks jernalder - mellem stamme og stat.* Aarhus: Aarhus
            Universitetsforlag.
1994   Warrior economy and trading economy in Viking-age Scandinavia. *Journal
            of European Archaeology* 2 (1): 130-148.
Helles Olesen, L.
1982   Ældre jernalders bebyggelse i Vestjylland. Unpublished M. Phil. dissertation
            from the University of Aarhus.
Hodges, R.
1982   *Dark Age Economics. The Origins of Towns and Trade AD 600-1000.*
            London: Duckworth.
Høgseth, H. B.
1998   Middelalderske bygningslevninger som kunskapsformidler. Tømmerhus i
            Nidaros som material- og kulturhistoriske dokument i tiden ca. 1025 til 1475
            e. Kr. Unpubl. M.Phil. thesis, Dept.of Archaeology, University of Trondheim.
Israelsson, I.
1990   Forntida mat. *Forntida teknik* 2/89 and 1/90: 3-37.
Juottijärvi, A.
1995   Slagger og ovnanlæg. In *Trabjerg. En vestjysk landsby fra vikingetiden.*
            L. Bender Jørgensen & P. Eriksen (eds.), pp. 73-78. Højbjerg: Jysk
            Arkæologisk Selskabs Skrifter.
Jørgensen, R.
1988   Utviklingstendenser i nord-norsk bosetning ved overgangen fra eldre til
            yngre jernalder. In *Folkevandringstiden i Norden.* U. Näsman & J. Lund
            (eds.), pp. 67-74. Aarhus: Aarhus Universitetsforlag.
Lamb, H. H.
1982   *Climate History and the Modern World.* London-New York: Methuen.

Lightfoot, A.
1996   *Ullarbeid på Shetland*, Video. Lillehammer: Håndverksregisteret, Maihaugen.
1997   Ullseil i tusen år. *Spor* [1997] 2: 10-15.
Lund, N. (ed.)
1984   *Two Voyagers at the Court of King Alfred.* York: Sessions.
Magnus, B.
1974   Fisker eller bonde? Undersøkelser av hustufter på ytterkysten. *Viking* 1974: 68-107.
Magnusson, G.
1986   *Lågteknisk järnhantering i Jämtlands län.* Stockholm: Jernkontoret.
Martens, I.
1988   *Jernvinna på Mosstrand i Telemark.* (Norske Oldfunn XIII). Oslo: Universitetets Oldsaksamling.
Mikkelsen, E.
1994   *Fangstprodukter i vikingetidens og middelalderens økonomi.* (Universitetets Oldsakssamlings Skrifter, Ny rekke nr. 18). Oslo: Universitetets Oldsaksamling.
Myhre, B.
1979   Agrarian development, settlement history, and social organisation in Southwest Norway in the Iron Age. In *New Directions in Scandinavian Prehistory and Early History.* K. Kristiansen & C. Paludan-Müller (eds.), pp. 224-271. Copenhagen: The National Museum of Denmark.
Myrdal, J.
1985   *Medeltidens åkerbruk. Agrarteknik i Sverige ca. 1000 till 1520.* (Nordiska Museets handlingar 105). Borås: Nordiska Museet.
1988   Agrarteknik och samhälle under två tusin år. In *Folkevandringstiden i Norden.* U. Näsman & J. Lund (eds.), pp. 187-226. Aarhus: Aarhus Universitetsforlag.
1998   *Det svenska jordbrukets historia I: Jordbrukets första femtusen år.* Borås: Natur och Kultur/LTs Förlag.
1999   *Det svenska jordbrukets historia II: Jordbruket under feodalismen 1000-1700.* Borås: Natur och Kultur/LTs Förlag.
Myrvoll, S.
1991   Hones. In *Ribe Excavations 1970-76*, vol. 3., pp. 115-141. Esbjerg: Sydjysk Universitetsforlag.
1992   *Handelstorget i Skien - a study of activity on an early medieval site.* NUB nr. 2. Bergen: Riksantikvaren Utgravningskontoret for Bergen.
Nissen Jaubert, A.
1996   Peuplement et structures d'habitat au Danemark durant les IIIe-XIIe siècles dans leur contexte nord-ouest europeen. Thèse de doctorat (nouveau régime), École des Hautes Études en Sciences Sociales, Histoire et Civilisation, Paris
NUB
1977   *Naturgeografisk regionindeling av Norden.* Stockholm: Nordic Council of Ministers.
Prestvold, K.
1996   Iron production and society. power, ideology and social structure in Inntrøndelag during the Early Iron Age: Stability and social change. *Norwegian Archaeological Review* 29: 41-62.
Resi, H. G.
1979   *Die Specksteinfunde aus Haithabu.* (Berichte über die Ausgrabungen in Haithabu, Ber. 14). Neumünster: Karl Wachholz Verlag.

Resi, H. G. (cont.)
1990   Die Wetz- und Schleifsteine aus Haithabu. (Berichte über die Ausgrabungen in Haithabu, Ber. 28). Neumünster: Karl Wachholz Verlag.

Roesdahl, E., & D. Wilson
1992   From Viking to Crusader. Scandinavia and Europe 800-1200. Uddevalla: Nordic Council of Ministers.

Saunders, T.
1995   Trade, towns and states: a reconsideration of early medieval economics. Norwegian Archaeological Review 28: 31-53.

Schovsboe, P. O.
1987   Oldtidens vogne i Norden. Frederikshavn: Bangsbomuseet.

Sjøvold, T.
1974   The Iron Age Settlement of Arctic Norway. Tromsø/Oslo/Bergen: Universitetsforlaget.

Stenvik, L. F. (ed.)
1996   Undersøkelser i forbindelse med kraftutbygging i Meråker, Nord-Trøndelag. (Rapport Arkeologisk Serie 1996:1). Trondheim: NTNU Vitenskapsmuseet.

Viklund, K.
1998   Cereals, Weeds and Crop Processing in Iron Age Sweden. Methodological and Interpretive Aspects of Archaeobotanical Evidence. (Archaeology and Environment 14). Umeå: Umeå Universitet.

Voss, O.
1993   Jernudvinding. In Da klinger i muld...25 års arkæologi i Danmark. S. Hvass & B. Storgaard (eds), pp. 206-209. Copenhagen/Århus: Det Kgl. Nordiske Oldskriftselskab & Jysk Arkæologisk Selskab.

Vretemark, M.
1984   Prehistoric falconry in Sweden. Sachsen Symposium Skara 1983. U. E. Hagberg, L. Jacobson & C. Ask (eds.), pp. 46-52. Skara: Skara Länsmuseum.
1997   Från ben till boskap. Kosthåll och djurhållning med utgångspunkt i medeltida benmaterial from Skara. (Skrifter från Länsmuseet i Skara 25). Skara: Skara Länsmuseum.

Walton, P.
1988   Dyes and wools in Iron Age textiles from Norway and Denmark. Journal of Danish Archaeology 7: 144-158.

Widgren, M.
1983   Settlement and Farming Systems in the Early Iron Age. (Stockholm Studies in Human Geography). Stockholm: Almquist & Wiksell International.
1988   Kulturgeografernas bönder och arkeologernas guld - finns det någon väg till en syntes? In Centrala Platser - Centrala Frågor. L. Larsson & B. Hårdh (eds.), 281-296. Lund: Almqvist & Wiksell International.

Widgren, M., & E. A. Pedersen
1998   Järnålder 500 f.Kr.-1000 e.Kr. In Det svenska jordbrukets historia I. Jordbrukets första femtusen år. J. Myrdal (ed.), pp. 237-482. Borås: Natur och Kultur/LTs Förlag.

Østerås, B.
1999   Eit klebersteinsbrot fortel si historie. Spor [1999] 2: 23-25.
n.d.   Slipsteinsberget. Cand. philol. thesis, Norwegian University of Science & Technology, Trondheim.

Øye Sølvberg, I.
1976   Driftsmåter i vestnorsk jordbruk ca. 600-1350. Bergen/Oslo/Tromsø: Universitetsforlaget.

Discussion

AUSENDA: You say (page 131) that 50% of the animals were slaughtered at age 3.5 years; were they male calves which would not be kept because useless without milk? Why were they kept that long?

BENDER: I got these numbers from Lotte Hedeager's work on Danish agriculture.

AUSENDA: In general female calves are kept because they become cows and give milk, whereas among populations which do not eat meat, male calves are useless because they do not give milk and so are slaughtered. When there is a market, they are sold for meat, but when there is no market, they are slaughtered very early.

BENDER: What you say is that they were slaughtered before the age of 3.5 years, which also included those slaughtered typically in November, at the end of the first year. The point Hedeager makes is that most of the females were allowed to have at least one calf. That way the farmers had the widest base to pick the calves that were suitable to let live and become part of the breeding stock.

AUSENDA: Normally, only 3% of male calves are kept for breeding purposes. In fact, to draw carts they would have to be spayed, which is a fairly difficult operation. One has to be quite competent to perform it. So it would be interesting to know how this structure worked.

BENDER: I was going to say that the numbers include those slaughtered; they are rough figures.

HERSCHEND: Because Öland is such a good place for preserving bones, there are tons of bones from Iron Age settlements. The point is meat production, dairy products are not so essential. It is clearly an agriculture aimed at meat production.

AUSENDA: Do you mean that before the advent of cereal consumption the greater part of the caloric intake was supplied by meat and milk products?

BENDER: Yes, according to specialists' reports it seems a feature of Scandinavia that milk products had an important position as the food that common people had when everything else was lacking. Milk products had the position that today are taken up by foods like potatoes, rice, etc.

AUSENDA: Is there some kind of a diagram showing the proportion of cereal intake and meat and other intakes?

ARRHENIUS: In Scandinavia there is a gene that many people have which makes it so that they can tolerate milk much better. They have this gene for milk, which obviously was an extremely important food not only for children but also for older people, as in Scandinavia people seem to be drinking milk at all ages.

AUSENDA: It would be interesting to have some kind of table.

ARRHENIUS: Yes this was made for the Stone Age, I don't know about the Iron Age, but for the Stone Age there are such lists.

BENDER: It is the work of Andrew Sherratt (1983).

ARRHENIUS: I was thinking of studies analysing isotopes and trace elements in skeletons which give close information on what people used to actually eat.

HERSCHEND: Some farms are preserved, where to this very day you can see the fields and you can see that the Iron Age field and the infield system is 15 to 20 metres. And it is over-manured. There are some very good Norwegian examples. So the Iron Age field is very small, more like a garden, very, very manured. Actually they grow the thing in manure, and when you go in and look at the farm and the byres, you can see that in the average farm there are some 16 to 20 cows, some 30 to 35 sheep, and 5 or 6 pigs. So, if you add up the calories from these, you can see that something like 76 to 80% of the intake was actually from animal products. The whole point is, they were like Americans from the Midwest, they ate beef all the time.

AUSENDA: Among all the populations of East Africa, the only ones studied who used to have a greater caloric intake from animal food, were the Masai. All the others obtain about 70% of their caloric intake from cereal foods. Because for them livestock are units of account. It would be interesting to see a study of this.

HERSCHEND: That was made from the seventeenth century and it can be shown that it was fifty-fifty in seventeenth-century Sweden.

AUSENDA: Then you would say that meat consumption would be in a higher proportion.

HERSCHEND: At least you can count the number of byres in a settlement. There are two cows in each compartment. So, if you have a very large bone material, the relative numbers of bones, given the absolute number of byres, would give you the proportions.

AUSENDA: This makes sense. But it would be quite interesting to quantify it more accurately.

BRINK: There must be regional differences in Scandinavia.

BENDER: I was wondering whether blood was used the same way the Masai do.

ARRHENIUS: I am sure it was.

AUSENDA: You say you found traces of blood in food remains?

ARRHENIUS: Yes, I found blood residues on ceramics which appear to be a mixture of organic material, consisting of blood and different kinds of seeds.

AUSENDA: Bread is a relatively late and sophisticated food as it is used with sauces and pot roasts. In general agricultural societies consume cereal gruels as staple foods and bread only once in a while. Ovens are rarely used. What was the situation in Sweden?

BENDER: I suppose Prof. Arrhenius can explain it in greater detail. One of her students has been doing the work that I am quoting. It seems that there were all kinds of products made out of cereals, like gruel, paste and both unleavened and leavened bread. There seem to be differences between various periods and regions in Scandinavia. Barley was the most common cereal during most of the Iron Age but, towards the end, rye started coming in from the South. There are indications of ovens and the use of leavened bread in the eighth, ninth and tenth centuries.

AUSENDA: What kind of ovens did they have?

ARRHENIUS: There were different kinds: they could have a heated flat stone on which they baked pancakes, and then they had small round ovens, made of ceramics, similar to ovens found all around the Mediterranean nowadays.

AUSENDA: At what time approximately were they used?

ARRHENIUS: The modern ones are still in use. The round ovens in Scandinavia are found from the Stone Age to medieval times. In medieval times they began to build them with bricks.

GREEN: What are these round ovens made of?

ARRHENIUS: Clay. They were made from the Stone Age in this way. In the Iron Age settlements they are a very common find as a collapsed heap. Probably it was a local production in every household. You had your own production, and you also had your own place to keep your seed in stock. And what is important is the practice of mixing different seeds and also peas in the flour. Peas were a very important crop.

BENDER: Viklund says explicitly that there is little evidence for ovens before the end of the Iron Age; you are saying the opposite.

ARRHENIUS: Klindt-Jensen (1957) has published such an oven from the Roman Iron Age in Bornholm and in Helgö. They were found as far back as the Migration period.

BENDER: Viklund says that bread was flat bread, unleavened, baked on iron pans, and that leavened bread came very late.

ARRHENIUS: But the bread found in Helgö was dated to 380 and 450.

BENDER: Well, my sources say something else. Lotte Headeager (1988) has a picture of Swedish Iron-Age loaves, but the reference only says they are from the Historical Museum in Stockholm; it doesn't say which site they come from. I wasn't able to check it there.

ARRIIENIUS: Hansson published a book on their distribution and different shapes. But there obviously also was trade in bread.

BENDER: As a Dane living in Sweden and Norway, it is interesting to note how much modern bread differs in the three countries. Where Denmark has leavened bread of rye and wheat, Sweden has 'knäckebröd' (crisp bread), Norway flat bread. They are quite different traditions based on the species of cereals commonly grown in the different climates.

AUSENDA: Were grucls also eaten?

VOICE: Porridge.

BENDER: I suppose so.

AUSENDA: One should be able to see from the the bowls used to cook gruels that are found.

ARRHENIUS: They are used to boil gruel but also some sorts of polenta that could be cut into pieces.

AUSENDA: You say that pigs were kept especially for meat. They could also be kept for fat in countries where there is no olive oil. Were pigs bred for a long time or were they imported from the South? Did pigs come north from the Mediterranean or were they native to Scandinavia?

ARRHENIUS: It is quite sure that pigs were used for fat. They used tar, and they also mixed tar and fat and tallow. We find pieces of tallow in the settlements mixed with resin.

HERSCHEND: Whales, seals, pigs, geese are the fat suppliers in Scandinavia.

AUSENDA: In that order? [Laughter].

DUMVILLE: You mention the ox trade. Did this go as far as parchment production in non-Christian contexts for export into the Christian world?

BENDER: This is a theory drawing on evidence from a later time. It's well known that ox trade was an important economic feature in the Middle Ages, going South from Jutland. Parchment is one more possibility for the utilization of the animals. Meat and leather are what you normally think of, but parchment has got to come from somewhere.

DUMVILLE: Well, it could of course come from sheep as well. What is strange about the evidence from Norway and Sweden—I don't know much about the Danish situation—is that the level of imported books continues to be extremely high until quite a late date. The evidence from Sweden is very much the best because of the centralized remains in the royal archives in Stockholm, and some specialist work on parchments. What we see is that well into the thirteenth century, the bulk of ecclesiastical books being used were imports from England and Germany: the implication of that would be that there would be much less demand for parchment production, unless of course, we are missing a vast area of manuscript material.

LUND: But the point is that it was exported, and then re-imported, perhaps in the form of books.

DUMVILLE: This may be a *reductio ad absurdum*. It is intriguing, the idea that in the eighth century you make parchment and send it off to the Christians.

LUND: No, they made hides.

ARRHENIUS: Yes, hides of cows and also of sheep. And then it is very probable that also the hides could be exported. It is said that in Scandinavia, the hard winters favoured cattle and sheep breeding, because insects cannot stand the winter. This means that the hides are undisturbed as we find no holes in them which makes them particularly good for parchment production.

HOLMQUIST: You wrote about wool production (page 133). What about other textiles?

BENDER: Vegetable fibres are a bit difficult to pinpoint because little work has been done to date. Flax is the most important, but flax is used for more than one purpose. Oil flax and fibre flax are different species, and most of the prehistoric flax seeds found belong to the oil type. Textile finds show that linens were common south of the Elbe, but strangely rare in Scandinavia before the Vendel period. Scandinavians must have known linen textiles virtually for millennia (flax is an older textile fibre than wool), but they do not seem to have been a common part of their clothing before the Vendel period, at least according to what we find in the graves.

AUSENDA: When you write about an organized textile production, do you mean that there were markets?

BENDER: In my opinion, there is evidence of an organized textile production in central Europe from the early Iron Age (*ca* 800 BC). Products of that textile production appeared in Scandinavia first in the late Bronze Age (*ca* 600 BC), but particularly in the Roman period. In the Migration period these products seem to disappear from Scandinavia, to reappear in the Vendel period and Viking periods. It's not a static thing, but something that is developed increasingly with better technology and organization, and linked with economic, social and political demand.

AUSENDA: If textiles are sold, production must be organized and also places where production can be concentrated and stocked.

BENDER: In the Roman period the main market for standardized textiles was within the Roman empire. I see the needs of the army as the main moving principle for large-scale production, and I have argued that some of the textiles we find in Roman-period Scandinavia are products of the same system that supplied the Roman army. Scandinavians wearing such fabrics probably saw them as Roman imports, just like Roman bronzes or glass, although cut according to Germanic fashion (Bender Jørgensen 1992).

AUSENDA: There must have been ports where large markets took place. In the last century in East Africa there were ports on the Red Sea where goods were concentrated even from nomadic populations. There were also markets and the goods were sold to merchants who came by ship bringing in turn goods that could be exchanged at those ports. If textiles were sold to the Roman army by the thousands there must have been places like these.

BENDER: Oh, yes. Within the Roman empire there is no doubt that there was an economy like the one you described. There were centres where standardized textiles were produced and shipped, transported all the way into the Empire and some of them ended up in Scandinavia. In Scandinavia I don't see that as a mass import, I see that as a prestige goods import. It should be seen as aligned with prestige goods.

HERSCHEND: It is an import into Scandinavia. The export out of Scandinavia of any clothes whatsoever is balanced with exports from the Romans to the Scandinavians.

ARRHENIUS: What is 'felt'?

BENDER: It is very conspicuous and that among the thousands of textile finds I have recorded from all over Scandinavia, only one or two were of felt. These were found with Roman Hemmoor bronze buckets and, I suppose, came to Scandinavia with these.

AUSENDA: What were the felts used for?

BENDER: I think felt was part of the range of textiles produced for the Roman army. I am working on the textiles from a Roman quarry in the Egyptian desert, the Mons Claudianus. Here some 50,000 to 100,000 textiles have been found, all dated within the first half of the second century (see Bingen *et al*. 1992, 1997; Peacock & Maxfield 1997, Maxfield & Peacock 2001). The textiles comprise much felt, always uniform in quality, 3 mm thick, sometimes dyed , e.g. green, occasionally with elaborate applique decoration in several colours. Some of the felts were used for padded clothes, others probably served as saddle blankets for horses or donkeys. Felt may be used for a lot of purposes, but for some reason, very little of it seems to have reached Scandinavia.

ARRHENIUS: But if you are looking at the Viking Age, there is a lot of felt.

BENDER: No, you are thinking of fulled cloth, and that is something quite different. Fulled cloth gets a felt-like appearance, but cannot be termed felt. Felt has no woven structure.

ARRHENIUS: No, but wasn't it fulled cloth that was produced in Scandinavia?

BENDER: Perhaps. That's something that my colleague Inga Hägg is working on. I haven't found that kind of cloth in the past of Scandinavia. She's got a lot of it in Hedeby. I would like to find it more widespread, to say that it was produced in Scandinavia.

AUSENDA: Yesterday's remark that fishing was practised in the winter months while livestock breeding was the main activity during the rest of the year seems to be confirmed by your statement about the fishing season in winter.

BENDER: That's a matter of biology. Cod fishing in northern Norway starts towards the end of the winter, at different dates according to what part of the coast it concerns. It starts towards the end of January. Perhaps Bente [Magnus], being a native of Norway, knows better than I.

MAGNUS: Cod is fished in late winter and there is also fresh water fishing.

BENDER: In Central Norway the 24th of February traditionally marked the beginning of cod fishing; but the late winter fishing at Lofoten—still the largest in the world—is primarily linked with the spawning of the Atlantic cod. Serious fishing begins when the cod arrive, often in late January but sometimes later. Still, there is always fish in the Norwegian seas, and during spring and summer there were several seasons. The *fiskerbonde*, fisher-farmer, was an important effect of this. The farming was done by the fisherman's wife as women were in charge of the farms when the men were out fishing.

AUSENDA: But there are certain kinds of work that only men normally do such as pulling a plough or heavy work like that.

ARRHENIUS: Women do that work too.

HERSCHEND: When do you think that you can see that there is a social difference of what people eat in Scandinavia? I think that that is an important question we have in the sixth to tenth centuries.

BENDER: I don't think I am qualified to answer that question. I suppose there are people there who could.

HERSCHEND: Deer and pig seem to be the preferred food for the incipient upper classes. That is essential because they are very easy to trace archaeologically.

BRINK: There has been a study of social differences based on excavations conducted in Gästrikland compared with the farmer or a wealthy owner in the nothern part Uppland and it is interesting to compare what they had to eat. They found that the wealthy ate swan.

HOLMQUIST: That is touched upon in a forthcoming dissertation, and there is also a question concerning the different food habits between genders.

AUSENDA: On gender difference in food habits, there is a parallel from East Africa where, when livestock is sacrificed and eaten at ceremonies, men slaughter the animals and keep for themselves the limbs and muscles and send the entrails to their wives in the tents, as women are very keen especially of liver. This might be a clue to explain the difference in bone deposits between centre and periphery in Scandinavian sacrifices.

DUMVILLE: Could you please explain to the town-dweller exactly what is the danger in fowling (page 137).

BENDER: For fowling you have to be a good climber. In later times it was customary that if somebody was killed during fowling, he was not allowed to be buried in the churchyard, unless somebody else was willing to go the same route and came back. If the other person also fell, neither were allowed to be buried in the churchyard [laughter].

AUSENDA: On trees being felled in great numbers and placed in a mound (page 138), why would they be piled up in a mound if not for ceremonial purposes?

BENDER: The timber in question was found to have been cut from a total 30,000 trees. No one has been able yet to find a sensible explanation.

HERSCHEND: Perhaps there is an essential thing that is always the problem with surplus, that is surplus of men. If you have nothing to do, that is the only thing, producing men. The great problem in Scandinavian prehistory is that there is too much surplus of men.

ARRHENIUS: It could be a trading station. The timber is all of fine quality and then it must be kept wet to use it for ship building. In fact one had very bad experiences when some of the oak wood wasn't kept wet enough with the consequence that the boards have to be made thinner and not too broad. So perhaps it was a rather clever man, who knew that he must keep his wood wet. I have excavated another big mound which contained charcoal. They has used more than a hectare of forest to make that charcoal. Yes, charcoal, and it was in a grave from the end of the eighth century AD.

AUSENDA: So timber could be gathered in a mound either to keep it wet or to make charcoal.

BENDER: I don't think that the mound was built to keep timber wet. In that case they would have succeeded very well, because it was still wet after 1500 years.

MAGNUS: I only want to say that you give the references on tar making (page 139), you say here that most charcoal is dated to the sixteenth century, it is the only sign of trading from 1000 AD we are given.

BENDER: That was Oddmunn Farbregd's paper in *Spor* (1989).

ARRHENIUS: No, but even in the settlements, when we look at what is loosely called charcoal, it consists of a lot of pieces of tar. I think there are other settlements with lots of pieces of tar.

BENDER: Tar and pitch were produced ever since the Neolithic. I searched for evidence for tar making in Scandinavia. At Ribe we could prove that tar was imported from Germany.

ARRHENIUS: Yes, but in Sweden we have tar made from pine and some made from birch from early on.

References in the discussion

[Abbr.: DFIFAO = Documents de Fouille de l'Institut Français d'Archéologie Orientale; O. Claud. = *Ostraka* from *Mons Claudianus*].

Bender Jørgensen, L.
    1992   See References at end of paper.
Bingen, J., *et al.*
    1992   *Mons Claudianus. Ostraka Graeca et Latina.* (O. Claud. 1 à 190), (DFIFAO
                29). Cairo: I.F.A.O.
    1997   *Mons Claudianus. Ostraka Graeca et Latina.* (O. Claud. 191 à 416),
                DFIFAO 32 [see above]. Cairo: I.F.A.O.
Farbregd, O.
    1989   See References at end of paper.
Hansson, A.-M.
    1997   See References at end of paper.
Hedeager, L.
    1988   See References at end of paper.
Klindt-Jensen, O.
    1957   Bornholm i folkevandringstiden. Copenhagen: Nationalmuseet.
Maxfield, V. A., & D. P. S. Peacock
    2001   *Survey and Excavations. Mons Claudianus II. Excavations Part I.* (FIFAO
                43). Cairo: I.F.A.O.
Peacock, D. P. S., & V. L. Maxfield
    1997   *Survey and Excavations. Mons Claudianus I. Topography and Quarries.*
                (FIFAO 37). Cairo: I.F.A.O.
Sherratt, A.
    1983   The secondary exploitation of animals in the old world. *World Archaeology*
                15 (1): 90-104.
Viklund, K.
    1998   See References at end of paper.

PATTERNS OF SETTLEMENT AND DEFENCE AT THE PROTO-TOWN OF BIRKA,
LAKE MÄLAR, EASTERN SWEDEN

LENA HOLMQUIST OLAUSSON

Archaeological Research Laboratory, Stockholm University, Greenska Villan,
S-106 91 Stockholm

Introduction

The Viking Age in Scandinavia was a dynamic transitional period which witnessed much political, social and economic change. One of the phenomena which manifested itself in a major way in northern Europe and around the Baltic Sea at this time, was the emergence of specialized central places directed to trade (Fig. 7-1).

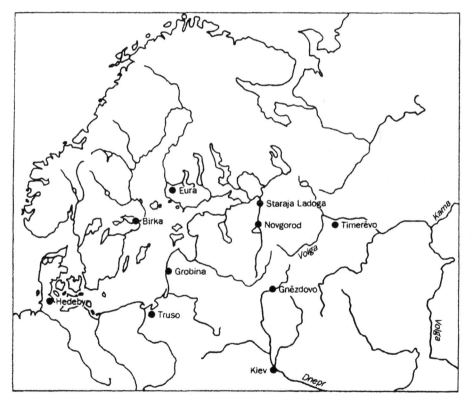

Fig. 7-1: Map of proto-towns in NE Europe and around the Baltic in the Viking Age (after Jansson 2000:110).

153

These places accumulated a range of specific functions, including the pursuit of craftwork. They stand apart from the surrounding rural settlements which were almost entirely agrarian-based and whose economy had until now stood for the population's main livelihood. These multifunctional trading places had a vital role to play in the incipient urbanization process. This saw a transition from small loosely-connected kingdoms to a unified realm where the king's sway manifested itself in the wielding of power over the people, but only to a lesser extent over land. In Sweden, the unification of the realm was an extended process which took many centuries. Within the Baltic Sea region, these early urban formations included Hedeby in present-day Germany, Ribe in Denmark, and Staraja Ladoga in Russia (cf. e.g. Clarke & Ambrosiani 1991 and literature cited therein). In central Sweden, the equivalent for the Viking Age Svea kingdom—called in contemporary written sources, such as Rimbert and Adam of Bremen, "the land of the *Sueones"*—is Birka, situated on the island of Björkö in Lake Mälar. A much-discussed question concerns whether these specialized trading places, though so clearly different from the settlements of the rural hinterland, can be considered fully-developed towns. The historian has a relatively clear definition of the term 'town' (cf. e.g. Andersson 1979), but it is difficult to apply such a teminology to archaeological material, and north-European archaeology lacks an operational definition. Worth noting is the fact that towns proper do not appear in Sweden before the thirteenth century, i.e. several centuries later than the places here being discussed. For this reason, I here employ the term proto-town. For many centuries, researchers have discussed the driving forces behind these early proto-towns. One cardinal issue concerns how they relate to the towns of classical antiquity and whether they represent continuity or a broken tradition (Schück 1926, Clarke & Simms 1985).

Landscape and settlement population in the Mälar valley

During the Viking Age, Lake Mälar constituted an inlet of the Baltic Sea and its water was brackish. Today, the Mälar is a fresh-water lake, surrounded by the provinces of Uppland, Södermanland and Västmanland. The Mälar Basin's fissure-valley landscape is characterized by clay soil and forested plateaux. The Mälar Islands (which include Björkö, Birka's island) exhibit some of the most fertile agricultural land in Sweden, second only to the province of Scania in southern Sweden. These islands belong to a warmer climatic zone than does the adjacent coastal area. Geologically the Mälar basin forms part of the sub-Cambrian peneplain, with its wealth of fissures and faults (Sporrong 1985:40). This comprises the environmental background to the successive and even distribution of settlement units which characterize the area from the Bronze Age onwards (Hyenstrand 1979). A further important factor for our understanding of the prerequisites for settlement and cultivation in the Mälar valley, is the land-rise with its annual increase of 0.5 cm. This provides a continuous supplement of new grazing-land along the shore meadows, of great significance to animal husbandry.

The Mälar constituted the heart of the surrounding countryside, and was of vital importance for communication. The waterways provided the most important transport routes during prehistoric times. Today Lake Mälar is covered by ice on average one third of the year. During the Viking Age, the climate was a few degrees warmer, but even so, the winter routes over the Mälar would have been important. It was considerably more difficult to travel by land owing to the absence of developed road systems. From the Middle Ages and onwards, it is documented that markets were held on the ice of Lake Mälar and it is highly likely that these already took place during the Viking Age (Arrhenius 1993). In the case of Birka, winter would have been the period when trade flourished in furs from the north (Norrland) and iron from the area north of the Mälar valley known as Bergslagen.

A conservative estimate reckons that there would have been 4,000 farms and villages in the Mälar valley in the later Iron Age, and that each farm would have held *ca* 10-12 persons (Hyenstrand 1974:88, 1982:164ff). The dominant occupation on these farms would have been animal husbandry, while some farms would have pursued minor trade and craftwork.

Birka was a solitary settlement but was in no way isolated. It could not have existed without provisions of food and fuel from the surrounding hinterland. Björkö is a small island with only a limited extent of arable land. For the Viking Age, it has been estimated that Birka would have held between 500 and 1000 inhabitants (Gräslund 1980:83), though a more conservative estimate of 500 is probably more accurate. For the Middle Ages, it has been estimated that the farmers of Uppland could have produced a surplus of at least 10% (Broberg 1990:114-115). Working with the same estimates for the Viking Age, this would mean that every fourth farm in the Mälar valley would have needed to contribute provisions for Birka (Holmquist Olausson 1993:19). During the post-Birka period on Björkö, that is in historic times, there existed at most five farms at any one period. These farms are today grouped in a closely knit hamlet of old-fashioned character, whose structure has its origins in the early Middle Ages. The earliest written documentation for this hamlet dates from 1322 (Holmquist Olausson 1982, *SD* III:562). As early as during the Viking Age there may have existed an agrarian settlement on this site or in its vicinity, as indicated by the nearby cemetery of later Iron Age character.

Birka's archaeological remains

The archaeological remains at Birka consist principally of the town-area proper, located within the town rampart (today covering an area of *ca* 13 hectares, allowing for the land-rise), with up to 2 m-thick cultural layers. The area is called the Black Earth on account of the high quantities of soot and carbon in the soil. The area is encompassed by a semicircular embankment which originally ran for a length of *ca* 700 m, today *ca* 450 m, of stone and earth construction. The embankment stops abruptly to the south, but would have originally connected up with the hill-fort

(Fig. 7-2). To the north, it meets the shoreline where a defensive pilework stretches out to secure the town's seaward entrance. The town was further defended by a hill-fort with a military station (the Garrison), and a possible quay berth. Just outside the town area lies a large cemetery containing several thousand graves which is one of the largest in Scandinavia. In addition, there are a number of smaller isolated cemeteries which probably belonged to a population living outside the town walls. That which is now to be seen of visible remains at Birka, echoes the final phase of the town's existence. It is generally considered that the town was abandoned fairly suddenly between the years 965 and 990.[1]

Fig. 7-2: Aerial view of Birka. The open field contains the site of the town. In the foreground, the town wall and the largest cemetery; in the background, the hill-fort (Photo: Jan Norrman).

The majority of the archaeological excavations that have been conducted at Birka have concentrated on the cemeteries and the Black Earth. Birka has a long research tradition. The earliest known excavations took place already in the seventeenth century and the most extensive excavations were conducted in the nineteenth century by Hjalmar Stolpe (E. Hyenstrand 1992; Holmquist Olausson

---

[1] This observation is supported by the latest coin find in Birka (cf. Jansson 1985:183, 228).

1993). The largest twentieth-century excavation campaign took place between 1990 and 1995, when 350 m^2 of the harbour area were investigated, enabling the reconstruction of a small 4 m x 5 m rectangular wooden house. The site contained the remains of a bronze-casting workshop (Ambrosiani 1996). The Archaeological Research Laboratory at the University of Stockholm has conducted excavations in two stages on Björkö, concentrating on the town periphery, in 1975-1989 and 1995-2000.

Birka's preserved archaeological remains appear to form a unit resulting from a deliberate plan, but the question is if, at any one stage during Birka's existence, the site ever looked like it does today or if its fortification systems changed over time. The question that presented itself at the beginning of the present investigations concerned whether it was possible to distinguish archaeologically the strategic stages in the planning and building of these fortifications. Important in that respect was also establishing how these related to the settlements on Björkö. This embraced also the question of Birka's emergence, and if any settlement existed prior to the town.

Birka before Birka

My working hypothesis has been that, in contrast to earlier research which considered Birka to have been established on an uninhabited island, there was an earlier settlement which played an important role in the emergence of the proto-town.

Examination of previous excavation results and older maps of Birka (from the seventeenth century onwards) combined with prospecting methods, especially a phosphate survey, indicated that there might have been such an early settlement, at the northern section of Birka's town rampart (Holmquist Olausson 1993). Excavation of that rampart confirmed this by the discovery of an early occupation layer beneath it. This layer proved to be several centuries earlier than the town of Birka (dated especially by radiocarbon ^{14}C). Within the town rampart structure itself, several building phases could be recognized which indicated that the rampart had been repeatedly rebuilt and re-fortified. Up against the town rampart lie about fifteen artificial earthen terraces of varying size, on which houses once stood. These terraces are visible on the ground, in contrast to the buildings of the Black Earth which have not left any traces behind, owing to land cultivation of the area after the town was abandoned.

Our excavation of the town rampart was extended to include one of these terraces. In this way, the various constructional stages of the town rampart and terrace could be correlated. It became apparent that the rampart's design had been adapted in accordance with the different activities on the terrace. This was the only terrace of those still remaining along the town rampart to have been fully excavated. Three different building phases with differentiated foci were found:

*ca 400-700. Traces of the earliest occupation consisted of isolated postholes from the roof-bearing posts of a house, and the remains of hearths. The occupation layer produced a sherd of imported glass which dated to the seventh century and belonged to a vessel manufactured in the *reticella* technique. Such sherds have previously been found only at two other locations in Sweden: the workshop site on nearby Helgö, and one of the rich boat graves at Valsgärde. All three sherds are remarkably similar and have most probably come from the one Frankish glass workshop (Henricson 1993:143).[2]

ca 750-800. At the transition between the Vendel and Viking periods, a terrace was built above the remains of the older house. Excavations showed that a three-aisled longhouse, *ca* 20 m long and 5-6 m wide, had stood on this terrace. The walls were of wattle and daub construction. This house differs markedly from the houses previously excavated in the Black Earth and shows considerable similarity with the more everyday settlement buildings of the surrounding countryside. The floor layer of the longhouse also produced glass sherds, but of a later type, together with many rich finds including pottery sherds of a highly characteristic type termed 'relief-band amphorae'. Other finds which could be connected with a trading activity were also found. These included about fifty silver Islamic coins (dated between 700 and 900), and several different types of metal weights indicative of an intricate weight system. The considerable size of the house, its siting on a highly prominent ridge and its rich finds, all indicate inhabitants holding high social status within society. Similar high status is witnessed by the double grave which lay beneath the western long wall of the house. This grave contained the burial of a fully armed warrior and above him, a 'sacrificed' youth who had been decapitated. Besides a complete set of weapons, a whole elk antler was deposited against the warrior, for which practice there is no known parallel among Viking Age burials. This symbolic manifestation reminds one of the well-known 'dancing warrior' (god)-motif (Holmqvist 1960). This motif, of a man with lance in hand and animal-figured headdress, is to be found on a specific range of objects from the later Iron Age, including the helmets from Vendel and Valsgärde. The warrior's equipment can possibly be interpreted as a rank marker, or of symbolical ritual significance (Holmquist Olausson 1990).

ca 800. In the ninth century, the town rampart was considerably refortified and thereby achieved its final form. The underlying causes can only be speculated about, but probably concerned a sovereign political decision steered possibly by increasing threats from the Mälar valley and Baltic Sea area.

The longhouse was deserted/laid waste after a fire during this period and the area at the terrace became subsequently a craft working site that was integrated with the town of Birka. The workshops which were erected on the terraces specialized in iron smithing, bronze casting and the manufacture of glass beads. The houses were of the semi-subterranean pit-house type ('Grubenhaus'), and perhaps simple shelters were also erected.

---

[2] The manufacture of glass did not exist in Scandinavia during the later Iron Age, except in the form of bead-making from imported glass.

In my opinion, the origin of Birka is to be sought in this area at the town rampart. The site shows indications of far-ranging trading contacts long before the Viking town of Birka was founded. The re-use of the deserted longhouse terrace shows the dynamic development of Birka, a fact mostly unobserved in previous research.

Birka's fortification

The area around the northern section of Birka's town rampart thus proved in many respects to be a perfect choice for examining the genesis of Birka and the growth of its fortifications. A further strategic site at Birka is its hill-fort, known as 'Borg' or 'Borgen' (lit. 'the fort') (Fig. 7-3). This fort with its massive ramparts, is one of the few monumental constructions known from the Viking Age in Sweden. Unlike the town rampart, the hill-fort rampart had not previously been examined archaeologically. All former archaeological investigations, as already mentioned, have concentrated on the cemeteries and the town area inside the rampart.

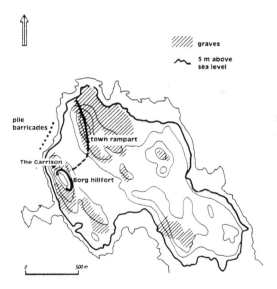

Fig. 7-3: The fortifications of Birka (drawing by Franciska Sieurin-Lönnqvist).

Thus Birka's defences have until now been an unknown research entity. Yet an understanding of these defensive systems is central to our understanding of the 'Birka construct' and is vital to any discussion of any military-political function and the town's role in a north-European perspective. The present study of Birka's fortifications forms part of a larger research project termed 'Hill-forts and fortifications in Central Sweden 400-1100 AD'. Excavation of the hill-fort forms an integral part of that research project.

The term 'hill-fort' (Sw *fornborg*) in Sweden is applied collectively to large-scale enclosures dating from the Bronze Age until the Viking Age. The Mälar valley has *ca* 500 hill-forts registered, with a chronological weighting towards the Migration period (fifth – sixth centuries). These are considered to have had mainly a defensive function, since the period is generally considered to be one of major unrest. These forts are usually situated on high ground and where evidence is visible, are constructed in a dry-stone walling technique.

The hill-fort at Birka differs from a classic hill-fort by its proximity to a town settlement and surrounding site-complexes. It has been claimed that the fort either was in existence before the town was founded or came into being late in the tenth century (Arbman 1939). This stems from the theory, prevalent among early researchers, that such proto-towns were defended at a late stage. The only written source to mention the fort is Archbishop Rimbert's narrative about Ansgar the missionary, written at the end of the ninth century, wherein he refers to 'when the merchants and the people who remained behind take refuge in the fort (*ad civitatem*) which lay nearby' (Rimbert, *Vita Anskarii* , 19; my trans.).

Birka's hill-fort is unique in the Mälar valley also on account of its dating. Those hill-forts in that area that have been so far investigated all fall into a pre-Viking period (Olausson 1995). Birka's fort could be seen as a link between these prehistoric defensive structures and the earliest medieval examples which comprise circular stone towers, donjon, (Sw. 'kastal') dating to the twelfth century (Olausson 2000).[3] These towers are considered to be modelled on Continental stone-building traditions, but the hill-fort at Birka provides clear evidence that knowledge of stone building already existed in the Mälar area over a century before. In my opinion, Birka's fort draws on the native hill-fort tradition, suplemented by certain imported traits such as the wooden superstructure with its presumed parapet and battlements. These were probably modelled on Slavic wooden forts or Saxon ring forts (Tuulse 1952). But it must be remembered that the Vikings were long-distance travellers and many of them must have been familiar with the fortification at Constantinople.

Today the hill-fort consists of a *ca* 350 m long, 2-3 m high and 7-8 m wide rampart with three entrances. The western section terminates in a cliff face which falls sharply down to Lake Mälar.

In 1996, a 3 m-wide and 16 m-long cutting was excavated through the hill-fort rampart within the scope of our project with the purpose of acquiring dating evidence and information on its construction technique and any rebuilding phases. The excavation showed the rampart to be robust and well-planned, made up of a dry stone shell filled with earth, and crowned by a wooden parapet or battlement-like superstructure which showed evidence of repeated burning. Dating evidence indicated that the rampart had been constructed at the same time as the town was founded, and had continued in use throughout the whole Birka period (Holmquist Olausson 1997). The rampart exhibited two main phases, here termed the earlier

---

[3] In Sweden, the Middle Ages are considered to begin around the year 1050.

and later rampart. According to values obtained by radiocarbon (^{14}C) and thermoluminensence (TL) analyses, the earlier rampart was burned down at the beginning of the ninth century. The later rampart showed evidence of repeated burning towards the end of the tenth century and beginning of the eleventh. A burial mound was incorporated into the older rampart: finds of iron cramps and fastenings for restraining timber suggest that the parapet of the older rampart was affixed to the large stone block that stood raised above the burial mound.

A shaft grave was found under this mound, dug into the compact till.[4] On investigation it proved to contain a middle-aged man who had been buried with a horse. Amongst the large stones that formed the superstructure of the grave lay the partial remains of a second human skeleton, which had been placed there in association with, but distinct from, the grave proper. This grave is unique for several reasons. Both its impressive size and early dating (it is assigned to the first half of the 8th century) are unusual for Birka, as also is the inclusion of a horse in the burial (horses have been found in 20 out of the 1100 graves excavated at Birka). The grave must have been clearly visible for quite a distance from the town below. It was probably of great symbolical significance at the time the rampart was erected. Possibly it belonged to a member of one of the founding families at Birka, who might have occupied one of the high status longhouses on the terraces close to the town rampart. On either side of the town, the longhouse with its earthen terraces and the shaft grave together comprise clear symbolic markers directed out at the waterway.

Birka's defences also include the area known as 'the Garrison' (Sw *Garnisonen*), situated just north-west of 'Borg' where the ground slopes down to the lake. The site comprises the weakest part in Birka's defences, where without protection it would have been easy for attacking troops from the shore to gain access to the town. The Garrison lies on sharply sloped land between two rock outcrops, which was extensively utilized and where the soil now comprises extremely artefact-rich cultural deposits. The terraces which were erected to compensate for the ground-slope, carried houses that were surrounded by a wooden palisade. The place received its name, 'Garrison', in the 1930s from Holger Arbman who had found artefacts of special character there.[5] These strongly differentiated this settlement from one of a more everyday kind and included a remarkably high number of weapons, lending a decisively military stamp which is strengthened by the absence of artefacts normally associated with female activity. The weapons included arrowheads, spearheads, axes, fragmentary swords and shields. Even indications of armour were found in the form of chain mail and armour-plate. Iron plate-armour is otherwise unknown from Viking Age Scandinavia (Thordeman 1939, Jansson 1988:619). Also of interest are the large number of keys and lock fittings.

---

[4] Unsorted agglomerate of clay, boulders and gravel.

[5] The site was first investigated in the 1870s by Hjalmar Stolpe. He excavated, according to his notes, seven holes. These are not documented, but the finds are preserved.

An excavation of the largest terrace was begun in 1998 and completed in the summer of 2000. Here there had stood a hall-like building of considerable size: 19 m long and 9.5 m wide (Fig. 7-4). The house had bowed walls which were doubled, and thus well insulated. The outer walls were in timber-framed technique and the inner walls of wattle and daub. The building was three-aisled and the post-holes indicate that the interior formed two extensive rooms with a hearth in each. The building is almost unique in its construction. The only possible parallel known at present is the 40 m-long and 10 m-wide hall recently excavated at Gamla Uppsala (Old Uppsala) next to the famous mounds (Duczko 1990:184).

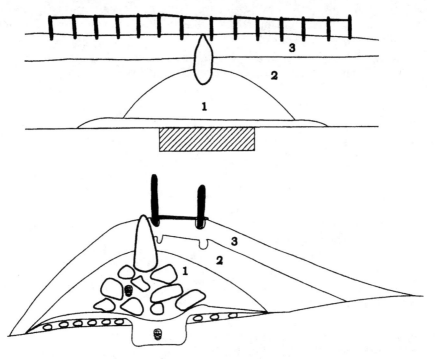

Fig. 7-4: Section of the hill-fort rampart. 1) Shaft-grave with mound and standing stone built into the rampart structure 2) the earliest rampart 3) the second rampart with its wooden superstructure. Drawing by Franciska Sieurin-Lönnqvist (from Risberg *et al.*).

Along the inside walls of the building there had clearly once hung, or stood, spears and shields. Finds of locks, keys, and chest fittings lay concentrated along the outline of the building, indicating that chests must also have lined the walls. Noteworthy too, was the finding here of some 60 Arabic coins and two, for Sweden rare, Byzantine copper coins of Emperor Theophilus minted *ca* 830.[6] These coins seem not to have been intended for use as payment but obtained for

---

[6] On Birka, a total of five Byzantine copper coins have been found, of which three come from the Garrison (one was found in 1934, one in 1997 and one in 2000). For the rest of Sweden the total is two.

some other reason. A further highly remarkable find was the sacrificial deposit in one of the post-holes, of hundreds of fragments of comb cases,[7] a chape, two spears, a large whetstone, and objects in bone and antler including an ornamented Thor's hammer. The belt mounts usually termed 'Oriental', with elements from steppe-nomad, Kazar and Sassanian dress, should also be considered as warrior equipment, belonging to the belts strongly associated with cavalry costume (Jansson 1988:607-614; Minaeva 1996).

The warriors who lived here were well-equipped and well-trained and it is probable that even a small number of horses were kept. Presumably this was a small permanent force which could be extensively augmented in times of need.[8]

Preparation for a coming major publication of the finds is in progress, but even now, from the distribution of the finds, one can maintain that the building's western section (Fig. 7-5), contained the most exclusive and high quality finds such as sherds of glass beakers, a dragon-head of bronze, gilt-bronze mounts, etc. There is every reason to speculate that it was at this end of the building that the high-seat was positioned. The house had royal status and would have been visited by the king on certain occasions.

Fig. 7-5: The 'Warriors hall', 19 m long and 9 m wide, when fully excavated. The main post-holes are marked by children standing in the only remains left - the post-holes.

---

[7] The warrior's belt was equipped with a comb in its pendant comb-case. Combs are mainly found in men's graves at Birka.

[8] The osteological analysis shows that the animals were slaughtered throughout the year and thus that the site must have been inhabited all year round. The bone material indicates that meat was a major item of consumption.

Concluding remarks

In short, one can summarize that these recent investigations show that Birka's fortifications are a demonstration of strength and a clear expression of power. They compose an advanced military construction which was utilized on a permanent basis and constituted an important part of the Birka constructions. Naturally the defences were constructed to meet the needs of contemporary warfare which concentrated on tactics of siege, threat and routing by fire (cf., e.g. Nørgård Jørgensen 1997). Armed conflicts were a recurring and drastic element in society during the later Iron Age and early Middle Ages in Scandinavia. Within historical research particularly on the Continent, this has been a dominant and generally accepted concept (Hindess & Hirst 1975; Runiciman 1989; Halsall 1998; Olausson 2000). Within Swedish archeological research it is fair to say that this has been a poorly represented and underrated field.

By means of this example from Birka, I have attempted to throw light on an inherently dynamic settlement which research has hitherto only marginally observed. The potential of similar dynamics should be kept in mind when studying other proto-towns around the Baltic Sea. In Birka, we can see this taking the form of changes over time and space in the economical and social focus of the settlement. We can now distinguish at least three different types of settlement at Birka: a high status occupation at the town rampart, a craft-oriented occupation in the harbour area of the Black Earth, and a military station up against the hill-fort. All exhibit differing house constructions and differing functions. Quite possibly other types of settlements will be identified in future archaeological excavations. We still lack knowledge of how the central parts of the town looked.

The dating evidence produced by our project shows that Birka's existence must now be extended in time, both backwards and forwards. Contrary to the findings of earlier research, I believe that it is now established that there was a settlement at Birka prior to the year 750. This observation has now found further support in the recent important scientific investigations carried out by quaternary geologists and archeobotanists from the University of Stockholm. Pollen analyses of the sediment of the Björkö Strait and cores taken at Birka show that the cultivation of cereals, field clearance, an opening up of the landscape and other pastureland indicators occur before the town came into existence. (Karlsson 1997:243; Risberg *et al.* 2001).

Closely connected with the settlement structure of Birka is its defensive system. Here too my view differs from that of previous researchers. I consider that the defensive structures constitutes a collective construction due to a conscious plan of advanced military prowess, established in a single stage. Alternative ideas have been presented of a staged process of development: first the pile barrier out in the water, then the fort, then finally the town rampart (cf Jansson 2000:113-114). But a pile barrier laid out in a restricted section of water can hardly have filled any function if at the same time it was possible to reach the land around it. The same can be said for the fort: without a continuous rampart, the town would have lain wide open to attack.

With regard to Birka's final use, there are signs that the latest wooden construction in the hill-fort rampart burned down at a late stage, towards the end of the tenth century/early eleventh century. It is thus possible that the fort continued to be used even though the town had been abandoned. The military station held a permanent trained armed force which possibly had a separate existence from that of the town. Such could have been of importance for the defence of the Mälar in a wider perspective. It can be noted therefore that the town of Sigtuna, which replaced Birka chronologically, does not have any known town defences and must therefore have been dependent on a defensive system further out in the Mälar. With the discovery of the special hall-building in the Garrison, our view of Birka's settlers has changed and especially our knowledge of warriors and defensive systems in Scandinavia in the important transition between the later Iron Age and Middle Ages, has greatly increased. What we meet here is the first stage away from the warrior towards the professional soldier. The Garrison seems to have formed a separate social unit or society in Birka's town structure. Thus the next step in our research should be to discover how the Garrison worked, by examining the buildings which existed around the hall-building and establishing their function.

References

Textual sources:
[Abb.: *SD = Svenskt Diplomatarium*].

Rimbert
    Vita Anskarii: see Odelman (trans.) 1986.

Bibliography:

Ambrosiani, B., & B. G. Eriksson
  1996   *Birka-Vikingastaden*. Vol. 5. Stockholm: Radios förlag.
Andersson, H.
  1979   Urbaniseringsprocessen i det medeltida Sverige. *Medeltidsstaden*, 7. Stockholm: Riksantikvarieämbetet och Statens Historiska museum.
Arbman, H.
  1939   *Birka-Sveriges äldsta handelsstad*. Från forntid och medeltid 1. Stockholm: Thule.
Arrhenius, B.
  1993   Aspects on [*sic*] barter trade exemplified at Helgö and Birka. In *The Archaeology of Gudme and Svendborg: Papers Presented at a Conference at Svendborg October 1997*. P. O. Nielsen, K. Randsborg & H. Thrane (eds.), pp. 189-194. (Arkæologiske Studier, 10). Copenhagen: Akademisk forlag.
Broberg, A.
  1990   Bönder och samhälle i statsbildningstid. En bebyggelsearkeologisk studie av agrarsamhället i Norra Roden 700-1350. Rapporter från Barknåre-projektet III. *Upplands fornminnesförenings tidskrift* 52.
Clarke, H., & B. Ambrosiani
  1991   *Towns in the Viking Age*. Leicester: Leicester University Press.

Clarke, H. B., & A. Simms
1985   The Comparative History of Urban Origins in Non-Roman Europe: Ireland,
          Wales, Denmark, Germany, Poland and Russia from the Ninth to the
          Thirteenth Century. (British Archaeological Reports, International Series
          255, i-ii). Oxford: B.A.R.
Gräslund, A.-S.
1980   Birka IV. The Burial Customs. A Study of the Graves on Björkö. (Kungl.
          Vitterhets-, historie- och antikvitets-akademien). Stockholm: Almqvist &
          Wiksell International.
Halsall, G. (ed.)
1998   Violence and Society in the Early Medieval West. Woodbridge: The Boydell
          Press.
Henricson, L. G.
1993   Glass vessels and waste from bead production. Appendix 4. In Aspects on
          Birka. Investigations and surveys 1976-1989. Pp. 143-147. (Theses and
          papers in Archaeology, B:3). Stockholm: Stockholm University.
Hindess,B., & P. Q. Hirst
1975   The Pre-capitalist Modes of Production. London: Routledge & Kegan Paul.
Holmquist (Olausson), L.
1982   Markutnyttjandet på Björkö. En förberedande studie. In Vikingatidsstudier.
          B. Arrhenius (ed.), pp. 3-22. (Rapport från Stockholms Univ. Arkeologiska
          forsknings-laboratorium, 1). Stockholm: Stockholm University.
1990   'Älgmannen från Birka'. Presentation av en nyligen undersökt krigargrav
          med männoskooffer. Fornvännen 85: 175-182.
1993   Aspects on [sic] Birka. Investigations and surveys 1976-1989. (Theses and
          papers in Archaeology B:3). Stockholm: Stockholm University.
Holmquist, W.
1960   The dancing gods. Acta Archaeologica 31: 101-127.
Hyenstrand, E.
1992   Early discoveries in the Black Earth. In Investigations in the Black Earth.
          Birka Studies. Volume 1. B. Ambrosiani & H. Clarke (eds.), pp. 23-51.
          Stockholm: Riksantikvarieämbetet och Statens Historiska museer.
Hyenstrand, Å.
1974   Centralbygd-randbygd. (Studies in North-European Archaeology, 5).
          Stockholm university dissertation.
1984   Fasta fornlämningar och arkeologiska regioner. (Riksantikvarieämbetet och
          Statens Historiska Museum, 7). Stockholm: Riksantikvarieämbetet och
          Statens Historiska Museum.
Jansson, I.
1985   Ovala spännbucklor. En studie av vikingatida standardsmycken med
          utgångspunkt från Björköfynden. (Oval brooches. A study of Viking period
          Standard jewellery based on the finds from Björkö (Birka), Sweden. Aun 7.
          Uppsala: Uppsala University.
1988   Wikingerzeitlicher orientalischer Import in Skandinavien. In Oldenburg-
          Staraja Ladoga-Novgorod-Kiev. Handel und Handelsverbindungen im
          südlichen und östlichen Ostseeraum während des frühen Mittelalters.
          Pp. 564-647. (Bericht der Römisch-Germanischen Kommission 69, 1988).
          Frankfurt am Main: Verlag Philipp von Zabern.
2000   Östersjöländerna och vikingatiden. In Att förstå det mänskliga. Humanistisk
          forskning vid Stockholms universitet. K. Dahlbäck (ed.), pp. 109-137.
          Stockholm: Natur och Kultur.

Jankuhn, H.
1986   *Haithabu. Ein Handelsplatz der Wikingerzeit.* 8. [Neubearbeitete und stark erweiterte Auflage]. Neumünster: Wachholtz.

Minaeva, O.
1996   *From Paganism to Christianity. Formation of Medieval Bulgarian Art (681-972).* Frankfurt am Main: Lang.

Nordahl, E.
1993   Södra Kungsgårdsplåtan. Utgrävningar 1988-1991. In *Arkeologi och miljögeologi i Gamla Uppsala.* W. Duczko (ed.), pp. 59-63. (Occasional Papers in Archaeology, 7). Uppsala: Societas Archaeologica Uppsaliensis.

Nørgård Jørgensen, A. (ed.)
1997   *Military Aspects of Scandinavian Society AD 1 to 1300.* (Publications from the National Museum. Studies in Archaeology & History, Vol 2). Copenhagen: National Museum.

Odelman, E. (trans.)
1986   Rimbert : Ansgars liv 1986. *Boken om Ansgar.* Översättning (translation) Eva Odelman. Stockholm: Proprius förlag.

Olausson, M.
1995   *Det inneslutna rummet.* Studier från UV Stockholm. (Arkeologiska undersökningar. Skrifter nr 9). Stockholm: Riksantikvarieämbetet.
2000   Husabyar, krig och krigare. In *En bok om Husbyar.* (Avdelningen för arkeologiska undersökningar. Skrifter nr 33). M. Olausson (ed.), pp. 125-150. Stockholm: Riksantikvarieämbetet.

Risberg, J., & J. Björk
1997   Lithostratigraphy in the Björkö Strait. In *Environment and Vikings.* U. Miller & H. Clarke (eds.), pp. 249-260. (Birka Studies 4). Stockholm/Rixenart: Riksantikvarieämbetet och Statens Historiska Museer.

Risberg, J, A. Henderström, J. Heimdahl, A.-M. Hanson, C. Tingvall & U. Miller
n.d.   Environmental changes and human impact as recorded in a sediment sequence off-shore the Viking Age town. *The Holocene* 12 (4): 445-458.

Runciman, W. G.
1989   *A Treatise on Social Theory.* Vol 2. *Substantive Theory.* Cambridge: Cambridge University Press.

Schück, A.
1926   *Studier rörande det svenska stadsväsendets uppkomst.* Uppsala: Uppsala universitet.

Sporrong, U.
1985   Mälarbygd. *Agrar bebyggelse och odling ur ett historiskt-geografiskt perspektiv.* (Meddelanden från kulturgeografiska institutionen, Stockholms universitet serie B 61). Stockholm: Stockholm universitet.

Svenskt Diplomatarium
1842-1850 Vol III. Utgivet av Bror Emil Hildebrand. Stockholm: Nordstedt & Filii.

Thordeman, B.
1939   *Armour from the Battle of Visby 1361,* Vol. 1-2. Stockholm: Kungl. Vitterhets-, historie- och antikvitets-akademien.

Tuulse, A.
1952   *Borgar i Västerlandet.* Stockholm: Nordisk Rotogravyr.

Discussion

HERSCHEND: You said proto-town, I wonder if you could expand on what is meant by proto-town. I suppose you mean an informal town.

HOLMQUIST: Yes, the first stage in the development of a town.

HERSCHEND: When they built this proto-town what were their ideas? Did they know it was going to be a town, or did they just do something else?

HOLMQUIST: What I wanted to mention is the definition of a town. It is not possible to distinguish if Birka had all the functions that historians use to define towns. We don't know if Birka was an administrative centre and even not if it was populated the whole year round. And I am trying to avoid this discussion by calling it a 'proto-town' because I cannot prove all the functions that historians use for a definition of a town. In this discussion it is important to remember that Sweden had real towns in the legal formal sense first in the thirteenth century.

ARRHENIUS: I would like to know what is the distinction between a trading post and a proto-town.

HOLMQUIST: It is hard to distinguish between them, but perhaps trading posts have just trading without administration, religious or other functions.

ARRHENIUS: So Birka is a place where you have more functions.

HOLMQUIST: Yes, we know from the *Vita Anskarii* that some of these aspects are mentioned in Birka, but we don't know to what extent or how often they took place.

ARRHENIUS: But then I would like to know, did you find the previous settlement, was that a trading post or was it just a common settlement?

HOLMQUIST: I think it was a farm with high social status which existed long before Birka was founded.

ARRHENIUS: With no trading?

HOLMQUIST: Yes, with long-distance trading contacts, as can be inferred from the rich find material.

ARRHENIUS: But if you compare Birka to Lundeborg, is this the same kind as Lundeborg and Gudme, or is it different?

HOLMQUIST: I think it is perhaps a bit too early to construct a typology, but it could also be a chronological question.

ARRHENIUS: Yes, well I think it was good that you clarified that there are three different kinds of trading levels. You have trading in a trading post, such as Lundeborg, you could have an important or a high-status farm which would obviously have trading connections, and you could have a proto-town and later a real town.

HOLMQUIST: And also farms where trading was done for friendship, and you could see that in the same line.

GREEN: You mention Hedeby and Ribe as well as Birka. First, is there any common typology to these, and, if so or even if not, would you also include Dorestad in this typology or does that lie too far south?

HOLMQUIST: Perhaps Dorestad is a bit too far south, I think, for the point you brought up. Perhaps it is not possible to build a functional typology as there are too may functional variations, but it is obvious that you have differential stages in development.

GREEN: And has any comparative work been done on these towns that you mentioned (including Ladoga) which brings out a common typology?

HOLMQUIST: Yes, an important book is Clarke & Simms (1991). Another more popular work is Clarke & Ambrosiani (1993).

GREEN: You seem to express hesitation about the historians' definition of a town or the applicability of their definition to archaeological purposes. Now, does this hesitation result from methodological caution, namely that you hesitate to take over findings of one discipline and apply it to your own, or do you have doubts about the historians' conclusions?

HOLMQUIST: I don't have any doubt about historians. It is a question about different source material. In fact, we have mostly source material in the archaeological record and they have the written sources, and sometimes it is difficult to compare the two. I think the historians' definition suits the historical material which applies to medieval towns, but I think that the archaeologists have to propose their own definition.

HERSCHEND: Isn't that exactly the problem? They were actually started a good many years before they actually became towns, and they were not intended to be towns when they started, when they were invented. They became towns later on by definition. They are not towns.

ARRHENIUS: There, you must be careful because when Clarke and Ambrosiani talk about the "town planning layout", it is not convincing that it always was a planned layout.

HERSCHEND: But the end of the Migration period there is a plan down to ten cm. into position and it is not a town. So planning is not sufficient to define a town, certainly not even a peasants' town.

HOLMQUIST: I don't agree that Birka is a "real town" in line with the definition of the historians. As I said before, we have the first real towns, medieval towns, some hundred years later.

NIELSEN: I have written about this in my paper too and I only say that I have tried to define towns throughout prehistory for twenty years and also in history, but I have not succeeded. I don't know what a town is, and I would never use that term in a prehistoric context. I gave up. I talk about *urban* sites and *rural* sites, and then you can get a relative relationship.

GREEN: If you talk about urban sites people ask you to define what you mean by urban.

NIELSEN: A modern word [laughter]. If you find, for instance, something indicating more than a domestic mode of production, this is also a very important point to consider. But I agree it is really quite complicated.

AUSENDA: In essence what you are saying is that there is a continuum in which it is very difficult to put a critical limit also because it is not a linear continuum but one over several possible lines of development. You can have administration earlier or later. Indeed, it is very difficult to define.

HOLMQUIST: One can define what a fully developed town is like only when it is fully developed.

HERSCHEND: A town is a definition in retrospect. There is no town until you know they are there; you do it looking back in history. It is a historical idea, it is neither a project nor a development idea.

LUND: I would like to throw in that just as when I listen to a symphony or a piece of music, I don't care much whether it is a symphony or a rhapsody or whether it is in C major as long as it works. And I think we are too obsessed with definitions and the only thing we can study is, does it match our preconceived notions which is just our attempt to systematize what we know, in a sometimes very different context. Why don't we just get on and find out what was actually going on there and don't care too much about labels. We can put them on later when we know some more.

DUMVILLE: In Scandinavian studies it seems that the word 'state' is very prevalent. If I were writing about German history nowadays, I would still be speaking in the twelfth century of a pre-state society. How is it then that one can try to speak of a state in the Iron Age in Scandinavia before the early Middle Ages?

BRINK: In Scandinavia we have the *rike*, the early 'state' which is not possible to translate into English. People write 'state' inaccurately but we had a 'state' in Scandinavia during the seventeenth century and later, normally scholars write 'state' and they mean *rike*.

AUSENDA: Is it the same as Gothic *reik*?

LUND: It is the same word but with an entirely different meaning.

BRINK: There are several extremely important words that we use in Scandinavian which are impossible to translate. Instead it is absolutely essential to understand Scandinavian society. Normally we translate the term inaccurately to 'settlement'.

AUSENDA: You used the term 'kingdom'. Would it not be more appropriate to call them 'chiefdoms'?

HOLMQUIST: A *rike* would be the most correct. It is a question about the translation of the term *rike* into English. I think you could call it a sort of kingdom.

DUMVILLE: That implies somebody on top.

AUSENDA: Someone on top with some kind of executive power. A chief generally starts without enforcing power. They rule by consensus, there is a big difference. I have seen some in the field.

ARRHENIUS: These are called petty kings. I know it is not the same in English.

DUMVILLE: This is for example prevalent where you have a multi-layered kingship system, and where you have written texts which show you where it is in use and also where it could be translated as 'king'.

ARRHENIUS: But in Birka it is said that there were two kings or several at the same time.

HOLMQUIST: In the *Vita Anskarii* four kings are mentioned in the vicinity of Birka during Ansgar's lifetime.

AUSENDA: How do these kings rule? That is important.

LUND: That is different from what we see in Ireland because what we have in early Scandinavia is multiple kingship, not a stratified organization.

GREEN: And in English it is the common equivalent for what the Germans call 'Kleinkönige'. Well that is a recognized phenomenon and one has to have a label for it; and a petty kingdom, petty kingship has established itself.

LUND: We would have in Denmark four kings sharing power. It didn't mean that they had their own petty kingdoms, but simply that they were all kings.

HERSCHEND: I think it comes down to a family. The collective approving a king can be a very small body of people and maybe just a family. I mean, there was a king in Ireland and that is just why they didn't bother to make them. Otherwise you can come down to perhaps a kingdom of some 10 by 15 km and 2,000 people. In that terminology you could.

AUSENDA: It is not a question of territory but a question of power. Could he enforce his decisions or could he not enforce them and had to depend on consensus?

HERSCHEND: That is the great problem. That is a matter of charisma. If the condition of being charismatic is not met, he just goes down and will not be a king any more.

AUSENDA: He may have charisma and still he might have to rule by consensus.

HERSCHEND: I think that the Scandinavian kings at least in the Iron Age would have to rule by a good deal of consensus from different layers of society.

GREEN: And this is why this distinction between kingship with real power and petty kingship with undefined power, became relevant to Frankish kingship from Clovis onwards. In looking back to the prehistory of the Franks it disturbed Gregory of Tours in his Latin sources to find only reference to petty kings. So there was a dislocation between early Frankish history with petty kings and the Frankish history which he knew with kingship on a larger scale.

DUMVILLE: It would be helpful (page 155) for the record if a periodization could be offered for Scandinavia at large which would relate the terminology of periodization to broad absolute dates. So, for example, when you say, Vendel time, when do you start?

HOLMQUIST: Yes, the Viking Age is from 750 to 1050, and then our medieval period starts. The Iron Age in Sweden is from 500 BC to 1050 AD: the early Iron Age from 500 BC to 500 AD, the late Iron Age from 500 AD to 1050; the Vendel period goes from *ca* 550 AD to 750 AD, and the Viking Age covers the period from 750 AD to 1050 AD.

NIELSEN: I think there is a very serious methodological problem when defining the Viking Age, because it must be made on the basis of archaeological distinctions; those normally used are historically based, of course, and I cannot use them to excavate; I want potsherds, and I want people to define the archaeological material, we have not succeeded in doing that in Denmark.

BENDER: I think maybe it would be useful to point out that in Scandinavia, terminology is not consistent, particularly for what you call the Vendel period. In Norway this is called the Merovingian period, and in Denmark the late Germanic Iron Age. Then where there is the question where you separate early Iron Age from the late Iron Age. In Denmark we do it after the Roman period, but in Sweden and Norway the separation comes between the Migration and the Vendel/Merovingian period. So there is ample ground for misunderstandings.

HERSCHEND: Yes, but couldn't we just wash them out for this specific purpose and say that somewhere between 375 and 400 a new period starts, which we may call Migration period, Merovingian period or Völkerwanderungszeit or whatever, and sometime about the middle of the eighth century a new period starts which we may call the Viking Age. And historical times, we know when they start [laughter].

It is interesting how many people there actually were in Scandinavia. I think they were very few in the Mälar area, just some 40,000. I made a calculation myself, for the Migration period based on ruined farms; between a colleague and myself we came to about 6,000 and 9,000, but then we didn't bring those in Lingfors which would be around 9,000 on 52,000 ha of agricultural land. And when you mentioned going to Birka and starting a medieval town against historical medieval times, and you find five farms on about 5 km^2 in the island, I think that this is a very small population, so it is also your argument. You argued that Birka must be the central place of a large area. Do you believe in your own calculations on the number of people here which should be very small?

HOLMQUIST: It is not my own calculation. I have quoted Åke Hyenstrand (1974) who wrote that there were 4000 farms in the Mälar basin during the late Iron Age.

HERSCHEND: He made the calculation in Åland on the graves too and he came out with 39 persons and that is very few. So there is a problem with the math behind this, based on graves. I think you should rather go into the agricultural area and take a reasonable farm size. It leads astray, I think, when you count farms.

VESTERGAARD: Why was Birka abandoned so quickly?

HOLMQUIST: There have been several explanations for this. It is a question of what is moving: is it the people actually living there, is it the functions, is it the power? One explanation is based on the land upheaval and the increasing difficulty to get on the shore. However, I think it has to be investigated in political terms. It is a political change that takes place.

GREEN: Could I ask what kind of Roman ware was found in Birka and in particular what kind of glass?

HOLMQUIST: I can't remember just now which Roman glass. I can look it up. And there are some additional remains. Professor Arrhenius has written an article about those finds.

MAGNUS: Where did you locate the Roman find?

HOLMQUIST: At the town rampart of Birka a longhouse was excavated. Beneath the longhouse there were traces of a cultural layer older than the Birka settlement. The post-holes in particular are more ancient than the Viking Age. Below this settlement a grave from the Roman period was found.

MAGNUS: Was the fence of Roman age?

HOLMQUIST: Corresponding to the settlement wall terraces were built; one of them was excavated.

LUND: ^{14}C dating has such a wide margin that it must be narrowed down to tell anything significant.

HOLMQUIST: You can't rely on only one ^{14}C dating: we have ten of them.

LUND: But do they come from different locations, not from the same fire and the same wood?

HOLMQUIST: We also have datings from TL (Thermoluminescence) and artefacts.

ARRHENIUS: All dates are before the Viking Age.

GREEN: About the sacrifice of a young man, was that a slave?

HOLMQUIST: The word should be used with a quotation mark. 'Sacrifice' is a question of definition. Historians of religion called it a sacrifice to the gods. Part of the equipment was found on top of a young man with his head lying beside him. My interpretation is that the 'sacrificed' young man belonged to the grave finds of the buried warrior. However, the question must be studied further.

GREEN: Could it apply to a slave?

HOLMQUIST: He could also have had a different status.

AUSENDA: Were the beads of amber or glass?

HOLMQUIST: Some beads were made of amber, but mostly of glass. We found the waste from bead production.

MAGNUS: Concerning forts and hill-forts. The problem is that of describing something unique.

HOLMQUIST: The hill-fort of Birka had a wooden construction on top, a parapet.

ARRHENIUS: What kind of wooden construction?

HOLMQUIST: I have suggested that a boat-building technique was used in the construction. The same technique of applying rivets used in boat building during the Viking Age.

MAGNUS: The 'Borg' at Birka was deliberately burnt on more that one occasion.

HOLMQUIST: The hill-fort at Birka was built in two stages. First, an early earth/stone wall with a wooden palisade. When it burnt down the wall was built up again, stronger and higher, and with a new palisade. According to the ^{14}C dating, this palisade was burnt down between the end of the tenth century and the beginning of the eleventh.

MAGNUS: Dating to the eleventh century?

DUMVILLE: How can you distinguish between intentional and accidental burning? Buildings burn all the time. Only because it was a fort does not mean that it was deliberately burnt.

HOLMQUIST: There was evidence of further attacks.

ARRHENIUS: Arrowheads found there are an indication of an attack.

HOLMQUIST: In the Garrison there are many finds of arrowheads lying just beneath the grass surface, a sure indication of a sudden abandonment.

VESTERGAARD: I would like to know about garrison places in Sweden. How do they differ from similar constructions in Denmark?

HOLMQUIST: The Garrison differs quite a lot from the so-called 'Trelleborgs' in Denmark. Our Garrison is located on a rocky slope with three or four stone-set terraces.

VESTERGAARD: Are there similar ones all over Sweden?

HOLMQUIST: The Garrison is a unique site so far.

JESCH: You say "absence of feminine artefacts" (page 161), I thought a lot of archaeologists actually linked locks and keys particularly with women.

HOLMQUIST: Yes, perhaps it's time for a new interpretation.

ARRHENIUS: These padlocks are smaller than the ordinary keys carried by women hanging from their waist. The padlocks may have been locks for chests or boxes containing weapons used by the garrison.

HERSCHEND: My questions are: why did they leave, why did they come, why is Birka what it is, why was it located where it is located?

HOLMQUIST: There were several high-status farms, and in this area perhaps Birka was one of the leading ones, which eventually won a competitive position in long-distance trade.

VESTERGAARD: It was because farmsteads and trading places were located in the same place and time.

ARRHENIUS: The difference between for example Helgö and other high status farms where there was trading, is that we know that at Birka from the very beginning there was an enclosure, a wall. This kind of enclosure is not known from the other farms. A few years ago it was said that the enclosure was a late construction, but now through Lena [Holmquist]'s work we know that the wall was there from the very beginning. It was a well enclosed area used for a trading place.

BENDER: Have you ever thought about how this lay-out at Birka compares with that of Ribe that also had a trading area and a fortress?

HOLMQUIST: It may be.

BENDER: Well it is not much published yet but the location of a fort was found a few years ago east of the ditch.

HOLMQUIST: You could compare it with Hedeby and the *Hochburg* hill-fort located nearby. Anyhow their reciprocal relation is not well understood. The *Hochburg* was destroyed during the war and never dated.

DUMVILLE: I had a question on the king's relationship. Do you have a sense at this point of what the area of control and jurisdiction you are envisaging? How far was this king's rule or reign? Are you sure there was a king?

HOLMQUIST: Are we now back to the question of definition? I think it is essential to understand the proto-towns that they were a relatively strong power that could give protection to the merchants.

MAGNUS: There is a highly coloured description in *Vita Anskarii*.

JESCH: When we say 'king' do we mean a military leader of some sort?

HOLMQUIST: Yes, there is also an ongoing discussion about the possible existence of a military king.

MEULENGRACHT: You may add to the definition of a king, that the king had to be a royal king.

DUMVILLE: What does that mean?

MEULENGRACHT: It means that there is a lineage back to some ancient kings. The person who became a king constructed a line showing that he was of royal kin whatever the meaning of the expression.

References in the discussion

Textual sources:

Vita Anskarii: see References at end of paper.

Bibliography:

Clarke, H., & B. Ambrosiani
    1991   See References at end of paper.
Clarke, H. B., & A. Simms
    1985   See References at end of paper.
Hyenstrand, Å.
    1974   See References at end of paper.

URBAN ECONOMY IN SOUTHERN SCANDINAVIA
IN THE SECOND HALF OF THE FIRST MILLENNIUM AD

SVEND NIELSEN

The National Cultural Heritage Agency, Slotsholmsgade 1, DK-1216 Copenhagen

Introduction

The topic under consideration can certainly be approached in many different ways, including the traditional one, the detailed review of relevant, well known urban sites and their settings: Dankirke, Helgö, Ribe, Birka, Kaupang, Hedeby, etc.—a long, boring affair, at least if I had to do it. Besides, such a presentation could not be satisfactorily undertaken in a short paper like this. Furthermore, up-to-date information about these and other sites can easily be found in recent papers and textbooks. Another possible approach is the purely theoretical one, in the present case reflections on the concept of *urbanism*. However, this solution does not seem adequate either, partly for the reasons outlined above.

Hence, I shall do nothing of the kind. Instead I will deal only with certain selected aspects that I consider relevant, not least when we are discussing urbanism and the economy; above all the concept of *mode of production* and the *rural/urban* dichotomy. While these as well as other theoretical positions presented certainly have general applicability, the case histories must concentrate, not least for the sake of brevity, on southern Scandinavia, in particular Denmark, although there will also be a few points relating to Norway and Sweden. I apologize for this 'centrism'.

Something that should constantly be kept in mind in discussions of the period from the sixth to the tenth century AD in Scandinavia is the fact that this was the threshold of 'historical' times. At our disposal we have certain written sources that can supplement the archaeological record. Moreover, a wide range of phenomena in Scandinavia, including the genesis of urban conditions, should be seen in a Continental, not least Frankish perspective. And in this respect the recently published exhibition catalogue *Die Franken* (A. Wieczorek *et al.* 1997) incidentally offers a wealth of useful information. Thus the centre/periphery paradigm used in discussing the Roman period (Heimburg 1998:19 ff.) remains a very useful analytical tool for dealing with the relationship between the Frankish kingdom and Scandinavia. Centre/periphery phenomena appear to be a universal category, as discussed for instance by Sahlins (1988:1 ff., fig. 1), who presents an interesting example from ancient China, recalling the situation in the Europe of the first millennium AD.

At this juncture it may also be appropriate to present a few points of current interest in field archaeology, in particular the enormous increase in the

177

archaeological source material. Thus in Denmark an average of more than 500 excavations are now conducted annually, the great bulk of these are rescue excavations. Accordingly, the financial resources spent, especially in the 1990s, have increased dramatically. The number of excavated sites that belong to the late Iron Age and the Viking Age has admittedly been relatively modest so far. Still, in 1996 around 50 sites from these periods were excavated, and this is by no means an unusual number, as will be evident from the annual journal *Arkæologiske Udgravninger i Danmark (AUD)*. How these steadily accumulating archaeological data are to be used remains to be seen. Finally, it should be noted that a good number of the settlement sites excavated over the last few decades are also relevant to the discussion of urbanism. This is especially true of certain coastal sites. Looking at settlement sites, including the urban ones, it can thus safely be stated that the situation today is completely different from the situation a generation ago.

The domestic mode of production—and beyond

In the discussion of production and economics it is of vital importance to distinguish between domestic production for one's *own* use, and production also intended for exchange/sale, since each type is associated with several important peculiarities, as discussed in detail by Sahlins (1976:41 ff., 84 f.).

The mode of production on the Continent in the Carolingian age and even some time before is an aspect that has been discussed by Hodges (1988:157 ff., quoting Hart). Thus larger-scale production with a view to the sale of commodities like textiles, metals, glass, pottery and stone (soapstone vessels, hone stones and quern stones) can be seen. At various stages this development is also reflected in increased trade and urbanization, as well as the emergence of emporia and use of coins (*sceattas*), not least around the shores of the North Sea. Thus a new economic order was at last emerging after the fall of Rome and the turbulent Migration period.

Christophersen (1982:105 f.), dealing with Scandinavia, also distinguishes between two modes of production which he terms *cottage industry* and *commodity production*. The latter in particular becomes visible in urban surroundings in the course of the Viking Age, and perhaps also embraces itinerant specialists.

As for production, the household, so to speak, constitutes the basic unit and provides a yardstick for following further trends away from a domestic mode of production. Archaeologically this may seem insignificant, but that is not so. For instance, certain objects found during an excavation immediately signal that one has to do with the activities of one or more specialists, i.e. individuals operating beyond a purely domestic sphere. Thus even on a Scandinavian Iron Age farm—in particular a wealthy one with a large household—a certain specialization could exist, for instance in terms of trade and metalworking.

At various kinds of sites, whether of a temporary or more permanent nature, where people gathered to engage in trade or exchange, the first steps were taken towards what might ultimately become a true urban site. Thus what I want to underline is this: the emergence of the historically known town in Scandinavia is certainly *not* simply the product of this or that process in the Viking Age, as some historians and medieval archaeologists seem to think—a point to which I shall revert later. Rather, the genesis of the town should be understood as the result of long-term demographic and urban trends going far back in prehistory. Moreover, this kind of urbanism must not be associated with a demand for permanence and site continuity, as is the case with the historically known town. Finally, it is hardly necessary to underline that prehistoric urbanism and Viking Age town formation were *also* the results of Continental impacts and "royal power".

Specialized crafts

Among specialized crafts it may at first be appropriate to mention the extraction and working of bog iron, inasmuch as iron continued to be of fundamental importance. True, the presence of an expert was not an essential prerequisite to these industries, as evidenced by the case of Iceland, where bog iron in particular was exploited during the early Middle Ages, as long as charcoal could be procured from the tiny forested areas; and a smithy is often found in excavations of farm complexes (Capelle 1980:429ff). Hence, ironworking was done by the individual farmer, and this was probably often the case too in southern Scandinavia during the Iron Age.

However, thanks in particular to extensive digs in south-west Jutland in recent years, it has become apparent that large-scale extraction and smelting of bog iron did eventually develop. Thus at Snorup it is estimated that there are around 2,000 slag-pits, 1,400 of which have been excavated or mapped. The pits in question have been dated to 100-700 AD. It has been suggested that around 50 or more smelting areas like the one at Snorup once existed elsewhere in Jutland. This means a total of 100,000 furnaces and an iron production of 4,000-5,000 tons - and the procurement of large amounts of charcoal (Voss 1993:97 ff.). Generally, then, such enterprises would certainly represent the fulfilment of something beyond local demand, an industry engaged in by small teams of experts who probably also dealt with the further distribution of some of the iron.

Interestingly, an extensive industry where the blooms were obtained elsewhere for further refinement by expert smiths has recently been documented in Ribe. Various traces of this industry—such as objects and structures associated with ironworking, including slags, waste, smiths' hearths and huts—have been analysed. The final product consisted of pieces of iron welded together in bars, ready for further distribution to other smiths. It has been argued that the refining of iron was an industry of considerable economic significance. It was also the oldest craft represented in Ribe, in that it was initiated around 710 AD, and was still plied during the ninth century AD (Madsen 1997:3, 101 ff. & personal communication).

Another early craft plied in Ribe and at a few other Scandinavian sites was that of the bead maker (Jensen 1991:14 ff.), whose products were spread all over the Nordic countries. Probably a few other simple glass objects were also produced, as well as enamel, but not vessels. The raw material was no doubt imported waste glass, or glass from broken vessels, as indicated by accumulations of bits of glass. Some light can be shed on the technology employed to make glass beads by looking at present-day bead makers in Turkey, the only ones left who employ a technique that has survived since antiquity (Sode 1996, *passim* and personal communication). Actually, these beads may be almost identical in shape and colour to Scandinavian ones from the Vendel period and the Viking Age.

Another decisive step away from the domestic mode of production was the mass production of jewellery, a phenomenon intimately connected with an urban economy, since many potential customers lived in or visited urban sites. In the case of Ribe this is especially evident from the large-scale production of oval brooches from the eighth century AD, including the so-called *Berdal* brooches, which were to gain wide distribution (Madsen 1984: fig. 141). Thus the jeweller's art which up to this time had mostly been the work of individuals was now to a considerable extent engaged in by anonymous artisans. We find even more pronounced mass production of very varied quality at the close of the Viking Age in the form of Urnes-style brooches, no doubt also a product of the ever-increasing urbanism (Bertelsen 1992:345 ff.).

Another item of evidence showing that the eighth century AD saw new departures in technology and the economy has to do with the introduction of wheel-made pottery in southern Scandinavia. Recently a greyish-black type of wheel-made ware was found in the Ribe region, no doubt locally produced (personal communication, Claus Feveile and Stig Jensen, Den Antikvariske Samling, Ribe). The lower part of the vessel could be built up by hand, whereas the upper part and the rim were turned on a slow wheel. Since wheel-made pottery and urbanism are found side by side almost everywhere in the Old World, these new pottery finds from Ribe are certainly very interesting. But this kind of pottery is also important because it constituted the potter's first steps into true mass production.

However, the urban economy from the eighth to the tenth century AD also depended on several other crafts, whether in Ribe or elsewhere. There is no reason to go into detail about this well-known phenomenon, but weavers, smiths, carpenters, leather workers and artisans working with antler and bone, especially comb-makers, should at least be mentioned, since they were present at several of the emerging urban sites, especially coastal ones (Ulriksen 1998:132 ff.).

Although sites where such crafts were plied mainly belong to the late Iron Age, there are a few that date back to the early Roman Iron Age, such as the newly discovered Hørup site from B 2 in northern Zealand, which is still under excavation. Here people engaged in crafts like ironworking, bronze casting and comb production with bone and antler (*AUD* 1994:17; 1995:9; 1996:17). This is a rich site with thick cultural layers and was still in use during the Migration period.

Economy: theoretical issues

Prior to a discussion of trade it may be worth presenting certain theoretical positions. The idea that the prehistoric economy constitutes something different from and should thus not be compared to its modern counterpart—the old dispute between formalists and substantivists—is a relatively recent one among Scandinavian scholars. Actually, it was probably not until the XVth Nordic Congress in Visby in 1978 that the theories of Polanyi, for instance, were introduced to a wider audience (Cullberg, Jensen & Mikkelsen 1978, 1:1-17). Thus after a delay of several decades the assembled archaeologists were able to make the acquaintance of such notions as *reciprocity* and *redistribution*, as well as the more familiar *market economy*, each of which was claimed to be characteristic of a certain level of sociopolitical evolution.

At the congress, this paper was severely criticized by Professor Becker, but in the years to come Polanyi's thinking was widely accepted, even in the Nordic countries. Yet Professor Mats P. Malmer (1992:386), discussing weight systems in the Bronze Age, remains sceptical for instance about the extensive gift-giving economy which is claimed to have existed during this era; he argues that what we see here is certainly a kind of *trade*.

Abroad, there have been discussions in recent years of how Polanyi's conception of a 'primitive' economy should be understood or modified (e.g. Service 1985:220 ff.), or whether the conception itself should even be rejected. Thus Kemp (1994:232 ff., 251) questions the applicability of certain theories of an economic-anthropological nature to the case of ancient Egypt. At the general level he is particularly critical of the way "the present" is equated with a "market economy", inasmuch as no economic system has ever existed that was based entirely on market forces. Even today it is naive and illusory to talk about the market economy, since it is subject to all kinds of regulations, and always will be, and he continues:

> How values are formed is ultimately a psychological question outside the scope of economics altogether, which exists as a modern rigorous discipline only because, given sufficient examples of any phenomenon, statistical regularities are bound to occur.

Hence, given that the level of trading and speed of communication were far lower than today, statistical regularities, i.e. the existence of a 'market price', do not provide a realistic approach to ancient economies.

Sjoberg (1960:204 ff.) was already arguing to some extent along the same lines in the 1960s. Since no true market price could exist within the (pre-industrial) societies under consideration, haggling would be the result. Thus he thought that there would inevitably be long disputes about the price when people were trading, and that the final price/result would depend greatly on the skill of the participants.

Recently, weighty arguments about the nature of primitive and archaic economies have also been presented by Bourdieu (1995:177, 192), who warned against naive conceptions of precapitalist societies as far as economics are concerned: "Gentle, hidden exploitation is the form taken by man's exploitation of man whenever overt, brutal exploitation is impossible".

Given the above background, I will argue among other things that the establishment of rigorous schemes to explain economic phenomena is a futile exercise. No doubt gift-giving, reciprocity, redistribution and haggling are timeless phenomena we can encounter in any era from the Stone Age to the present day. At best one could try to consider the *ratios* of these phenomena to one another in the individual cases.

The era which is our concern at this symposium is one when decisive political and economic events are supposed to have taken place: accelerating urbanization, the coming of petty kingdoms/states in certain regions at the expense of chiefdoms, and the establishment of a 'market economy'—a concept, as we can see, which should be used critically.

Unfortunately the concept of market economy is not the only problem among the phenomena mentioned above. Thus in recent years the question of the position of *chiefdoms* has also been raised. It has been stated that these do not constitute a link in an evolutionary chain leading to the emergence of the state (Yoffee 1993:60 ff.); or that societies studied by anthropologists, including chiefdoms, may be an outgrowth of European expansion (Wolf 1990:76 quoting Fried).

Given the role that the concept of chiefdom has played among Scandinavian prehistorians, including the economic position of the chief in his capacity as distributor, not least of luxury goods and imports, this new situation is worth considering. Yoffee (1993) suggests, for instance, that a council of elders may have been at the head of society. However, simply to have to dismiss our Viking chief, the central character in Norse literature, would be unbearable. Thus, in attempting to grasp the position of this figure, we should perhaps not only consult the more traditional type of anthropological literature. Instead, the chief could also be seen as a Scandinavian reflection of what leaders and princes were like farther south in Europe. After all, written sources do exist which can help to illuminate this point. This would be more in accordance with the ideas presented by certain contemporary anthropologists and archaeologists. Thus Näsman (1991:174), quoting Vierck, uses the expression "*imitatio regni Francorum*".

Finally, as regards theoretical issues, unlike certain other archaeologists today, I see no reason to apply the 'world system paradigm' to prehistory, among other reasons because it was intended for use within a 'capitalist mode of production', as originally stated by Wallerstein (1974:347 ff.)

Trade

In several respects we may be justified in talking about a 'Dark Age' in the wake of the collapse of imperial Rome. At least, as far as Denmark is concerned, the graves of the Roman Iron Age, which were often furnished with costly imports testifying to trade and international contacts, almost cease during phase C 3 (Hansen 1987:214). In the subsequent centuries imports became rare in graves, as did other grave goods; and accordingly the role of graves as an archaeological source becomes a modest one for these periods (Näsman 1991:168 f.). Thus as a general rule in the late Iron Age, graves are found particularly in Fenno-Scandia, whereas settlement sites prevail in Denmark.

However, on the island of Bornholm there are in fact many rich graves from the late Iron Age, and here we can immediately see that there were close contacts with the Continent, not least with the Frankish kingdom. This is particularly true of weapons—foreign changes and improvements are immediately reflected in the finds from this island (Jørgensen & al. 1997:104 ff.). The 'Frankish connection' as well as other connections with the Continent should thus not be neglected, and such connections very probably also existed elsewhere in southern Scandinavia, although the archaeological evidence is so far scanty.

In the late Iron Age trade in particular can be illuminated by finds from a variety of sites other than graves. Especially in the last few decades, a large number of sites have been recognized where weights, coins, metal, imported glass and several other imports have been found, as well as traces of specialized crafts. These sites can be arranged hierarchically; for instance from a rich peasant's farm where trade took place, through a natural haven to a regional/supraregional centre or an emporium characterized by international mercantile enterprise. Overviews of the sites in question have recently been published by among others Jørgensen (1994:57 ff.) and Ulriksen (1998:143 ff., 196 ff.). The timespan within which these sites operated is from the late Roman Iron Age to the early Middle Ages.

A good example of a rich peasant's farm with foreign contacts is Dankirke in southwestern Jutland, where a considerable stock of Frankish glass, coins, weights and silver was excavated in the 1960s (see for instance Jensen 1991:11), testifying to early North Sea trade and links with the Merovingian kingdom. The reason I mention this well-known site, often considered a predecessor to Ribe, is that yet another farm site has recently been excavated where a good deal of Frankish glass turned up. This new site is situated at Dejbjerg, somewhat farther north in Jutland and also close to the sea (*AUD* 1993:380; 1995:389). Thus Dankirke may not be as unique a site as has hitherto been thought, and we are probably looking at an era prior to the foundation of Ribe and at a centralization of trade where several leading figures in society could engage in foreign trade.

We also find some trade and foreign connections during the Vendel period and the Viking Age at the large centre at Gudme on Funen. Thus there are some finds that come from the Merovingian/Carolingian area as well as Permian silver rings and Arab coins (Jørgensen 1994:55). It would take us much too far here to discuss this point and the trading that took place at smaller centres and at natural havens which were often of a temporary/seasonal nature. Suffice it to say that at these sites too various kinds of imports may turn up, although the domestic trade and production were certainly the most important aspect. Here as well as elsewhere, then, it is important *not* to exaggerate the economic role of certain aspects of international 'trade', such as the emergence of luxury objects, the circulation of prestige goods and the like. It is often the exotic things that tend to fascinate the archaeologist to a disproportionate degree. Of course, these kinds of objects and others can tell us something about foreign connections and exchanges among the élite; but we should always remember that society was completely addicted to an agrarian subsistence economy, and that only a small fraction of the population engaged in mercantile enterprise in urban surroundings.

Turning to the case of Ribe, it is certainly not without interest to look at the foreign trade there. On the basis of earlier excavations as well as preliminary reports from the recent 'Posthus excavation', the following imports can be mentioned (Jensen 1991:13 ff.):

From Scandinavia: whalebone, elk antler, whetstones and soapstone.
From France and Germany: quernstones, glass and pottery (for wine?).
From southeastern Europe and Constantinople: silver, brass, precious
stones and a lead seal.
From Italy (ultimately): gems and Roman coins.

The presence of such goods testifies to wide-ranging connections where Scandinavians and Frisians to some extent would have acted as middlemen.

The question of exports is a complex one. Of course there are always slaves and amber: unworked amber is in fact found in large quantities in Ribe. Furthermore, various goods made from organic materials may have been shipped, but such substances leave no archaeological traces. Still, the extensive occurrence of cow dung indicates that many cattle were gathered at the site, and it has been proposed that these animals were exported. In this connection it is worth remembering that in the surroundings of Ribe, in the marsh, there were extensive areas where cattle could graze (Jensen 1991:21). At the other end of the geographical area, in Russia, where Scandinavians operated from the eighth century onwards, a tenth-century Muslim geographer informs us that the following goods were sold to Muslim merchants:

Fur, skins, amber, wax, honey, falcons and walrus tusks

Actually, as Sawyer (1992:126) states, this list probably also gives us a good idea of what Scandinavians exported to western Europe.

However, grain, food, timber and iron may also have been traded in Scandinavia during the Viking Age. At least written sources inform us that grain and flour were shipped to Iceland in early times, and the saga of St Olaf tells us that the timber for the church at the Althing, as well as a large bell, were donations from this king.

Coins and precious metals

Given the crucial economic importance of gold, silver and bronze in Scandinavian society, and the fact that all such metals had to be 'imported', there are good reasons to consider these aspects, if only briefly. Furthermore, over the last few decades or so, the use of metal detectors has greatly increased the number of coins, as well as the many kinds of metal finds. As a result these finds have in several cases led to new suggestions about the nature of trade and the economy.

First we have the Roman *denarii* which were acquired in large quantities until the debasement of Septimius Severus. As far as Denmark is concerned at least, we can document on the basis of safely dated *denarii* in graves and in the Illerup bog find that such coins were much in circulation during the third and fourth centuries AD (Nielsen 1987/88:154 f., fig. 2). In Sweden, on the basis of the strikingly similar composition of most large hoards outside the *limes*, Lind (1988:210) argues that the *denarii* travelled north as a result of the payment of tribute to barbarians from the 240s on, and that a good deal of this money ended up in Gotland in particular.

However, the *denarii* remained in circulation to a limited extent throughout the first millennium AD in Denmark (Nielsen 1987/88:165 with further references) and we find the same situation in Sweden (Lind 1988:150 f.). This means that during the period under consideration here, too, some *denarii* were available, but would eventually be melted down and the silver used for jewellery. The *denarii* may have been used as a medium of exchange to some extent, since they turn up at sites where there is supposed to have been trading.

If one wants to understand economic conditions in the past it is worth referring to a most interesting publication by Sarvas (1967:143 ff.) regrettably little known among archaeologists — Malmer (1973:132 ff.) is an exception. Sarvas was particularly interested in the occurrence of hoarded coins and attempted to show how coins were treated in a peasant society — in this case eighteenth-century Finland, for which we have many historical sources. Briefly, Sarvas rejected Bolin's old idea that hoarding was particularly associated with war and unrest, since it could be shown that more money was hoarded in periods of peace than during wars in the century he was discussing.

Among the reasons for hoarding, war does of course play a role, as do inflation and speculation, and for instance the exchange of paper money for copperplate money. Our concern here, however, is Sarvas' Group II hoards, which include the peacetime savings of peasants in the countryside, hidden or buried on their farms (Sarvas 1967:67). This custom prevailed because in a subsistence economy coins were rarely used in accordance with their purpose as a *medium of exchange*. Instead, they were kept simply as capital with metal value, and this no doubt also explains the existence of many late Iron Age coin hoards found in rural surroundings — for instance, on Gotland and Bornholm.

Gold in particular was imported as *solidi* during the Migration period. It has even been possible to demonstrate that a weight system was developed in

Denmark, based on a *solidus* of 4.548 grams (Fonnesbech-Sandberg 1991:240 f.). However, it would take us much too far to go into further detail about such phenomena, and the general area of Roman coins in Denmark. So I will only refer to the important bibliography on Roman coins in Denmark edited by Jensen (1996). This paper includes all the publications by the late Anne Kromann Balling on this topic.

During the Vendel period, not to speak of the Viking Age, the role of Roman coins was much reduced; imports had ceased and most coins had eventually been melted down. However, during the Vendel period at least, a considerable amount of the gold and silver in circulation in society would ultimately have been derived from Roman coins. Other kinds of metal supply may have come from scrap silver, lead and bronze, similarly a legacy of the Imperial period. Thus Steuer (1994:134 ff.) says of south-western Germany in the fourth and fifth centuries AD "dass immer wieder römisches Altmetall in den Höhensiedlungen gefunden wird...Recycling reichte aus". Old metal was also used this way to some extent at Gudme for example. However, looking at the many new sites where metal finds have turned up thanks to the use of metal detectors, we can see that gold and silver objects that can be dated to the Vendel period are rare.

It appears that the early eighth century AD saw a decisive break with previous periods as far as coins are concerned. Up to this time what I have termed a *secondary coin economy* operated (Nielsen 1989:33), the main characteristics of which were that the coins were foreign, and that they were not used in the way intended in their country of origin. However, it has been claimed that from around 721/722 AD, according to dendrochronology, indigenous coins, the so-called Woden/monster sceattas, were struck by a central authority in Ribe, apparently in considerable numbers (Feveile *et al.* 1992:33 ff.). This, then, was a *primary coin economy*, i.e. it used domestic coins intended as a medium of exchange, and of taxation. Thus foreign coins or other valuables would have to be changed to *sceattas* when people visited the recently-founded Ribe market place (Feveile 1996:98). No doubt this was a most important development in the urban economy, as subsequently also manifested in the coming of Hedeby coins. This distinction between a secondary and a primary coin economy is admittedly a very simple one, but as will be understood, its implications are far-reaching.

It can come as no surprise that this introduction of our own coins should be seen against a Frankish background; in the Frankish area silver coins were struck from around 670 AD (Hodges 1988:162 ff.; Henning 1997:797). This topic, 'Nordic *sceattas* and their European context' was recently considered by Pedersen (1997:61 ff.) in a comprehensive study. One of her main points is that *sceattas* in particular should be seen as proofs of long-distance trade, and that they are mainly found at sites where there was commercial activity.

The presence of *sceattas* and Hedeby coins in the eighth and ninth centuries AD respectively should be seen as representing an increase in economic transactions which took place to a considerable degree at various urban sites. Still, the importance of such coins and certain later domestic ones remained limited, and they thus signal the relatively weak position of the central power, at least as far as administration was concerned. The idea of *monopoly coins*, on the other hand, and the coming of a new and efficient monetary system introduced from England, did not penetrate until the reigns of Canute and Hardicanute, when coins were struck in particular at Lund in Scania (Becker 1981:119 ff., 148 ff.).

As we know, until around this time hacksilver and foreign coins still played an important role. For a survey of these means of payment and the history of the research see, for instance, Hårdh (1989:43 ff.), who emphasizes that the material in question must be studied with due consideration for regional peculiarities.

Brita Malmer (1991:209 ff.) has also recently discussed means of payment in the Viking Age. From this paper, only two important aspects need to be repeated. First, the difference between the nominal value of a coin and its metal value could be very substantial. Thus in Viking Age England it could be as much as 33%, and it goes without saying that economic manipulation of this order was not voluntarily accepted. Actually, this state of affairs can only be understood against the background of a strong central power that enforced the use of coins. Secondly, as is well known, anything can theoretically be used as money, i.e. as a means of exchange and a standard of value. In medieval Iceland, for instance, the cow and *vaðmál* (homespun cloth) were widely used, and had equivalent silver values (*Grágás* IV, 191 ff.). However, very little silver and coins were in fact in circulation on the island, and the coins were exclusively foreign ones. Similarly, in Scandinavia during the periods under consideration, economic transactions must to a considerable extent have taken place without the use of coins or silver, as often happened elsewhere well into historical times.

If the medieval written sources at our disposal from Iceland dealing with trade and economy of an apparently 'archaic' nature are treated sensibly, for example with due respect for modern source criticism, they hold a wealth of information which also sheds light on various aspects of late Iron Age and Viking Age Scandinavia. However, strict 'Weibullian' source criticism will not do here; it is also necessary to consider the *ideology* behind a text, as repeatedly stressed by Sørensen (see for instance Sørensen 1989:144).

Finally, the economic importance of Islamic silver is certainly worth remembering. Thus Noonan (1990:255-6) estimates that between 50,000,000 and 100,000,000 whole *dirhams* were imported into the Baltic area during the Viking Age. With an average weight of 2.9 g per coin this means that 1450-2900 kg of silver reached this area, in particular Sweden, during a period of around 170 years.

Transport

When discussing urban economy in a pre-industrial context it is essential to understand the deficiencies of land transport. As repeatedly underlined by several distinguished economists and historians, long-distance transport with bulk goods was very rare, because of the poorly developed transport technology (Boserup

1981:67 ff.; Braudel 1990-386; Finley 1992:126). Accordingly, urban sites had to rely on food supplies from a short distance away.

Unfortunately, these transport and communications aspects have often been ignored by archaeologists, or little attention has been paid to all the obstacles one had to face, for instance, when travelling overland in Scandinavia. In some areas there are mountains and deep fjords, or huge stretches of forest, and in southern Scandinavia one encountered an undrained moraine landscape with many wetlands. In the period up to the Viking Age constructed roads hardly existed, only paths or tracks, apart from some simple roads in connection with fords. It is only when one consults certain medieval written sources that one realizes what ancient transport and communications were actually like. Thus on 'shank's mare' it would take many days to walk a distance which is travelled today in a few hours with modern transport. Certainly horses were used, but even then travel was troublesome. For instance, to take an extreme example, it took 17 days for the people coming from the easternmost part of Iceland to ride to the annual meeting at the Althing at Þingvellir, and it is estimated that one could advance an average of only 37 kilometres in a day's journey (Njarðvik 1974:31-2; Kålund 1913:100).

As far as vehicles are concerned, these had of course existed since the Neolithic, but they were hardly employed beyond the local level. If necessary the horse could be used as a pack animal, and sledges may have been employed during the winter. On the other hand, it is difficult to see what bulk goods could be transported over long distances among self-sufficient communities.

With the coming of the Viking Age, however, there were considerable improvements in land transport. The stirrup and efficient harnessing for the horse were introduced, the latter making it possible to use the horse as a draught animal (Lyngstrøm 1993:150 ff.; White 1981:151). And this was probably also when simple earth roads came into being, radiating at least some distance out from the urban sites and with vehicle traffic, although this remains only a suggestion. At all events some transport with vehicles loaded with heavy goods is to be expected in these urban surroundings. The Viking Age, moreover, was also the period that saw the construction of bridges, some of which were of an imposing size (Jørgensen 1993:228 ff.).

Still, it is *maritime* travel that is really important when we are discussing the improved transport technology of the late Iron Age; and here I am certainly thinking of the introduction of the sail. Thus, as pointed out by among others Carver (1990, fig. 15.3), it is only possible to row 41 miles a day, whereas using the new device, the sail, one could advance twice that distance, 82 miles a day, and double the speed. To this I should add that ships grew larger in the Viking Age, and that they could have considerable cargo capacity (Crumlin-Pedersen 1991: fig. 10). Now bulk goods such as grain, timber, quern stones, metals, etc. could be transported by sea, and over long distances. However, an oceangoing vessel was a costly affair, in itself and because it only had a lifetime of around 30 years. In Iceland it was said that such a vessel cost the price of a good farm (Gelsinger 1981:223-4).

The emergence of urban sites by the sea, such as Ribe, Hedeby, Kaupang, Birka and several others, should, therefore, be seen against the background of the existence of large oceangoing sailing ships engaged in mercantile enterprises. However, even the small local and regional natural havens that began to operate in the course of the late Iron Age, whether on Gotland (Carlsson 1987:6 ff.), in Denmark or elsewhere (Ulriksen 1998, *passim*), certainly owe their existence above all to the sailing ship.

Urbanism

I shall now turn to what I consider my main concern in this context, a discussion of the nature of urbanism and its emergence in Scandinavia. As a point of departure it will be appropriate to look at some current, common definitions of the town as presented by a couple of Danish scholars.

Randsborg (1980:75) states that "town centres are, normally, geographical focal points of a population and production area; they have a surrounding territory which they serve in various ways and which serves and supplies them". Roesdahl (1992:119) informs us that

> ...towns are often defined as fairly large, quite densely populated, permanent settlements with some centralized functions, such as markets, serving the surrounding area. A town might also be a religious centre, a Thing-place, an administrative centre, or a mint. The inhabitants made their living from trade and crafts rather than agriculture, fishing or hunting.

As will be understood, however, vague definitions like these, which we find with some variations over and over again in the literature, are of little help to the prehistoric archaeologist. In addition, it is worth remembering that in English "there is no clear-cut distinction between *village, town* and *city*" (see, e.g., Bradley 1985:418). This is one of the reasons why I would never dream of employing the ideas of town and city in a prehistoric context. Instead, I operate with *urban sites*. *How* 'urban' such sites may be can easily be found out by using a scoring system, as originally done by Butzer (Nielsen 1991:175 ff. with further references). Similarly, in Scandinavia the sites could be classified according to a variety of factors, for instance whether they were temporary or seasonal or had fortifications, and the number of specialized crafts recorded.

A widespread and apparently ineradicable conception among archaeologists is that in a town the urbanites in principle earn their living from trade, crafts and other non-agrarian activities. There is nothing to support such an idea. On the contrary, it remains a fact that one of the main structural differences between a pre-industrial and an industrial town/city is that in the former kind of site a substantial number of the inhabitants remained peasants, or part-time peasants. Even today in the Third World peasants may constitute a large part of the total population of a town, and this point has to be kept in mind whenever one is dealing with the pre-industrial town or city. This is why Kemp (1977:196), on the basis of evidence from Egypt in the 1940s, operates with the idea of the *agricultural town*, even when dealing with Pharaonic Egypt.

In view of this, archaeologists discussing urbanism in first millennium AD Scandinavia will be wise to remember that, at any urban site, a considerable number of the inhabitants, probably the majority, were peasants. If we remember this we avoid chronocentrism and comparisons with later kinds of towns. And furthermore, if we keep this in mind, we do not neglect a most important economic aspect of ancient urbanism.

It is also tacitly assumed by most scholars that the earliest 'towns' in Scandinavia suddenly emerged in, or just prior to, the Viking Age, Ribe being the oldest. This position, however, is hardly well-considered. What ought to interest scholars is what can be termed urban phenomena, in particular the presence of various kinds of experts at a site, such as artisans and tradesmen and production/activities over and above the domestic ones, as already indicated. Thus Gudme and Lundeborg (Thomsen *et al.* 1993) as well as a good many other sites discussed by Jørgensen (1994:57 ff.) and Ulriksen (1998:143 ff.) certainly deserve the designation urban site.

As far as Denmark is concerned, then, urban sites existed far back in the Iron Age, and such sites remain a prerequisite for the understanding of the emergence of urban sites in the Viking Age too. The 'towns' of the latter period, then, were a result of long-term trends involving complex demographic, social, political and economic processes as well as foreign stimuli. Thus the sites in question did not suddenly emerge out of nowhere. After all, the difference between, say, third-century AD Lundeborg and eighth-century AD Ribe is not particular striking; they were both links in a chain.

It may be argued that these urban sites of the Iron Age were not permanent, and that an urban site/town must be a permanent one. This, however, is hardly reasonable in the case of societies where neither the farmsteads nor the villages were permanent sites. Moreover, what is meant by permanence? Kaupang, Birka and Hedeby had a shorter lifetime than several centres and other urban sites that existed in southern Scandinavia during the first millennium AD.

A couple of papers offer good up-to-date surveys of urban formation in Norway and Sweden, including the history of the research, and these should be briefly mentioned here. Thus Solveig Nielsen (1997:179 ff.), quoting several scholars, operates with two angles of inquiry:

1) An *evolutionist* approach which explains the coming of towns in particular as a result of trade.
2) A *genetic* approach which sees the emerging towns as functions of royal power. These sites were regional administrative centres of authority during an era characterized by certain structural changes with the initiation of feudalism.

These ideas may be helpful to historians and medieval archaeologists, but to a prehistorian who sees urban development as a result of long-term trends, they are disputable. For the sake of fairness it should be noted, however, that Christophersen (1989:91 ff.) is well aware of the many dimensions of urbanism, even as far as prehistory is concerned. This is also true of the survey by Helliksen (1994:71 ff.) which discusses town formation and exchanges in late Iron Age Scandinavia.

As already mentioned in the introduction, it is not possible to deal in detail with the comprehensive Scandinavian evidence of urbanism. This is especially true as far as Sweden is concerned. Here I will only refer to the extensive investigations conducted at Birka in recent years, the results of which are now being published (Ambrosiani *et al.* 1995).

As for written evidence of the foundation of towns, Nilsen (1976) went through the available sources for Norway, and it appears that the role of various kings in this respect was important. Thus, if we believe Snorri, Trondheim, Sarpsborg, Oslo and Bergen were all founded by kings. Nilsen (1976:362 ff.) is rather sceptical of this view, and so is the present author, although kings could of course found towns, as the case of Hedeby shows. However, it would take us too far to go into a discussion of this point; suffice it to say that kings, gods and mythical forefathers are often considered to be founders of towns in ancient texts, whether Egyptian, Mesopotamian, Greek or Roman.

Turning to the urban economy, I have already said something about the important role of tradesmen as well as specialists and their products in an urban context. Still, there is yet another economic aspect that is rarely considered specifically, and that is subsistence of the urbanites. This may be exemplified by the case of Hedeby.

At this urban site it has been estimated, with some reservations, on the basis of the associated graves that there would have been around 1,500 individuals (Clarke *et al.* 1991:156 ff.). If we take a more conservative figure, 1,000 people, what does this imply in terms of subsistence and consumption? With our point of departure in the case of a pre-industrial European city presented by van der Woude *et al.* (1995:8) the following can be said.

Each dweller in Hedeby would consume between 1.0 and 1.6 tons of firewood annually, or the equivalent in peat, that is three to five cartfuls of one ton of fuel would be needed each day. The daily bread grain requirement was one kilogram per head, and thus one cart loaded with a ton of grain had to be procured. To this we must add a substantial number of various domestic animals for consumption at the site, as well as certain other kinds of food. The transport of raw materials and building materials to the site is also worth remembering. Thus land transport was a resource-intensive, important aspect of daily life, although food and various goods may also have arrived by ship.

It could tentatively be suggested that half the population of Hedeby were peasants/part-time peasants, which is not an unreasonable estimate (given the 'agricultural town' situation). Then the above-mentioned figures should be reduced by 50%. Still, when we estimate that only a 10% agrarian surplus could be produced in this kind of ancient peasant society (Boserup 1981:63 ff.), a relatively dense agrarian population in the surroundings of Hedeby would be essential to the production of half the food needed at this site.

This leads us to some demographic considerations of the correlation between urbanization and population density. According to Boserup (1981:68 ff.) a population density of 64 persons per square kilometre was needed before urbanization could take place in the ancient world. This figure, however, is not a realistic one, as pointed out by Ambrosiani (1984:131-2), since such a population density hardly existed anywhere in Scandinavia during the periods under consideration here.

Jensen (1982:204) very cautiously suggested a population of 700,000 in Viking Age Denmark, corresponding to a population density of 16 persons per square kilometre. However, in the fertile Hedeby region the figure may easily have been considerably higher, and this would help to explain the early urban development in this case. Anyhow, I firmly believe that there is such a correlation between urbanization and population density as suggested by Boserup, and that this phenomenon constitutes the most important aspect when we are to discuss pre-industrial urbanization.

At the close of the period under consideration, the tenth century, Scandinavian urban sites/towns had been founded in many geographical regions where they operated as 'agents of civilization', perhaps even with an episcopal seat at the head of the ecclesiastical hierarchy. From now on crafts and trade were plied in urban surroundings where the Church and feudalism eventually came to play an important role. The number of urbanites in these sites was very modest, and very few sites would have counted one thousand souls, as was the case in Hedeby. I should finally note that the further development of the medieval town in Denmark has been discussed by Andrén (1985) in an interesting dissertation.

Conclusion

To summarize briefly some of the main theoretical points presented above, it was claimed that the central position of the mode of production concept should be kept in mind; similarly, the importance of the urban/rural dichotomy was stressed, since this makes it possible to deal with urbanism as a relative phenomenon; as for trade and exchange, it was argued that the people involved certainly acted in economically 'sensible' ways, with gain in mind.

The second half of the first millennium saw various technological improvements in transport, such as the building of bridges and probably some local roads used by vehicles that carried various goods to and from urban sites. However, the coming of the oceangoing sailing ship was of paramount importance, making long-distance trade possible. As for crafts, mass production, whether in metalworking, the making of beads or the first experiments with the potter's wheel, signals a new economic order, and this is particularly true of the introduction of coins. It is an important point, moreover, that the inferences to be drawn from these phenomena can be made simply, on the basis of the excavated objects themselves. The developments described above should of course be viewed diachronically, in the sense that a decidedly rural society came increasingly to include urban sites, some of which ultimately became the predecessors of medieval towns.

Acknowledgements—I should like to thank James Manley for having improved my English.

References

Bibliography: ·

Ambrosiani, B.
  1984   Review of E. Boserup 1981. *Fornvännen* 79: 131-132.
Ambrosiani, B., *et al.* (eds.)
  1995   *Excavations in the Black Earth 1990.* (Birka Studies 2). Stockholm: Riksantikvarieämbetet and Statens Historiska Museer.
Andrén, A.
  1985   *Den urbana scenen. Städer och samhälle i det medeltida Danmark.* (Acta Archaeologica Lundensia, Series in 8⁰. Nr. 13). Malmö: CWK Gleerup.
AUD
  1985 & ff.   (Arkæologiske udgravninger i Danmark). Copenhagen. [With English versions/summaries].
Becker, C. J.
  1981   The coinages of Harthacnut and Magnus the Good at Lund c. 1040 - c. 1046. In *Studies in Northern Coinages of the Eleventh Century.* C. J. Becker (ed.), pp. 119-174. (Det Kongelige Danske Videnskabernes Selskab. Historisk-filosofiske Skrifter 9:4). Copenhagen: Munksgaard.
Bertelsen, L. G.
  1992   Urnesfibler i Danmark. *Aarbøger for Nordisk Oldkyndighed og Historie* 1994: 345-370. [English summary: Urnes brooches found at sites in Denmark].
Boserup, E.
  1981   *Population and Technological Change. A Study of Long-Term Trends.* Chicago: The University of Chicago Press.
Bourdieu, P.
  1995   *Outline of a Theory of Practice.* Cambridge: Cambridge University Press.
Bradley, J.
  1985   Planned Anglo-Norman Towns in Ireland. In *The Comparative History of Urban Origins in non-Roman Europe: Ireland, Wales, Denmark, Germany, Poland and Russia from the Ninth to the Thirteenth Century.* H. B. Clarke *et al.* (eds.), pp. 411-467. (BAR, International Series 255, 2). Oxford: B.A.R.
Braudel, F.
  1990   *The Mediterranean and the Mediterranean World in the Age of Philip II*, vol 1. London: Fontana Press.
Capelle, T.
  1980   Bemerkungen zum isländischen Handwerk in der Wikingerzeit und im Mittelalter. *Frühmittelalterliche Studien* 14: 423-436.
Carlsson, D.
  1987   Äldre hamnar- et hotat kulturarv. *Fornvännen* 82: 6-18. [English summary: Old harbours - a threatened heritage].

Carver, M. O.
1990   Pre-viking traffic in the North Sea. In *Maritime Celts, Frisians and Saxons.*
          Papers presented to a conference at Oxford in November 1988. S. McGrail
          (ed.), pp. 117-125. (CBA Research Report 71). London: Council for British
          Archaeology.

Christophersen, A.
1982   Den urbane vareproduksjonens oppkomst og betydning for den
          tidigmiddelalderske byutviklingen. In *Den medeltida staden.* Pp. 104-122.
          (Bebyggelseshistorisk tidskrift 3). [English summary: The emergence of
          urban commodity-production and its significance for early medieval town
          development].
1989   Royal authority and early urbanization in Trondheim during the transition to
          the historical period. (Archaeology and the urban economy. Festschrift to
          Asbjørn E. Herteig). *Arkeologiske Skrifter. Historisk Museum* (Bergen)
          5: 91-135.

Clarke, H., *et al.*
1991   *Towns in the Viking Age.* Leicester: Leicester University Press.

Crumlin-Pedersen, O.
1991   Ship types and sizes AD 800-1400. In *Aspects of Maritime Scandinavia AD
          200-1200.* O. Crumlin-Pedersen (ed.), pp. 69-82. Roskilde: The Viking Ship
          Museum.

Cullberg, C., J. Jensen & E. Mikkelsen
1978   Udvekslingssystemer i Nordens forhistorie. In *Förtryck av mötesföredrag.
          XV nordiska arkeologmötet 1978* Pp. 1: 1-17. Visby (stencil).

Feveile, C.
1996   Sceattas fra Ribe. In *Frisere, Saksere og Danere. Kulturer ved Nordsøen,
          400-1000 e.Kr.* E. Kramer (ed.), pp. 96. Leeuuarden: Van Wijnen-Franeker.

Feveile, C., *et al.*
1992   Sceattasfundene fra Ribe - nogle arkæologiske kendsgerninger. *By, marsk og
          geest* 5: 33-39. (Årsberetning 1992. Den antikvariske Samling i Ribe)
          (1993). [English summary: The sceatta finds from Ribe - some
          archaeological conclusions].

Finley, M. I.
1992   *The Ancient Economy.* [2nd ed]. London. Penguin Books.

Fonnesbech-Sandberg, E.
1991   Centralmagt, centre og periferi i Danmarks folkevandringstid. In *Sentrum -
          Periferi. Sentra og sentrumsdannelser gjennom førhistorisk og historisk tid.*
          Den 18. nordiske arkeologkongress, Trondheim 1989. B. Wiik (ed.), pp.
          233-247. (Gunneria 64, 1), Trondheim. [Abstract: Centralized power, centre
          and periphery in Denmark during the Migration Period].

Gelsinger, B. E.
1981   *Icelandic Enterprise. Commerce and Economy in the Middle Ages.*
          Columbia, SC: University of South Carolina Press.

Grágás
1870   Islændernes Lovbog i Fristatens Tid. Fjerde Del. Oversættelse II (Vilhjálmur
          Finsen). Copenhagen. Brødrene Berlings Bogtrykkeri.

Hansen, U. L.
1987   *Römischer Import im Norden. Warenaustausch zwischen dem Römischen
          Reich und dem freien Germanien während der Kaiserzeit unter besonderer
          Berücksichtigung Nordeuropas.* (Nordiske Fortidsminder. Serie B. Bind 10).
          Copenhagen: Det Kongelige Nordiske Oldskriftselskab.

Hårdh, B.
1989   The function of silver in the Viking Age. In *Coins and Archaeology*. (Medieval Archaeology Research Group). H. Clarke *et al.* (eds.), pp. 43-51. (BAR, International Series 556). Oxford: B.A.R.

Heimburg, U.
1998   Was bedeutet "Romanisierung"? Das Beispiel Niedergermanien. *Antike Welt* 1: 19-40.

Helliksen, W.
1994   Byutvikling og vareutveksling i yngre jernalder i Norden. Teorier og kildemateriale. *Viking* 47: 71-86. [English summary: Commodity exchange and the emergence of towns in the Late Iron Age in the Nordic countries. Theories and data].

Henning, J.
1997   Handel, Verkehrswege und Beförderungsmittel im Merowingerreich. In *Die Franken*, 2. A. Wieczorek *et al.* (eds.), pp. 789- 801. Mainz: Philipp von Zabern.

Hodges, R.
1988   Charlemagne's elephant and the beginnings of commoditisation in Europe. *Acta Archaeologica* 59 (1989): 155-168.

Jensen, J. (ed.)
1996   *Anne Kromann Balling. 5. august 1935−7. marts 1996. Til Minde.* Copenhagen: Nationalmuseet.

Jensen, J. S.
1982   *The Prehistory of Denmark.* London: Methuen. [Reprinted 1995].

Jensen, S.
1991   *Ribes vikinger.* Ribe: Den antikvariske Samling. [Available in English & German versions).

Jørgensen, L.
1994   The find material from the settlement of Gudme II - Composition and interpretation. In *The Archaeology of Gudme and Lundeborg*. Papers presented at a Conference at Svendborg, October 1991. (Arkæologiske Studier X). P. O. Nielsen *et al.* (eds.), pp. 53-63. Copenhagen: Akademisk Forlag.

Jørgensen, L., *et al.*
1997   *Nørre Sandegård Vest. A Cemetery from the 6th-8th Centuries on Bornholm.* (Nordiske Fortidsminder. Serie B. Volume 14). Copenhagen: Det Kongelige Nordiske Oldskriftselskab.

Jørgensen, M. S.
1993   Land transport. In *Digging into the Past. 25 years of Archaeology in Denmark*. S. Hvass *et al.* (eds.), pp. 228-230. Copenhagen/Højbjerg: The Royal Society of Northern Antiquaries & Jutland Archaeological Society.

Kålund, K.
1913   En islandsk Vejviser for Pilgrimme fra 12. Aarhundrede. *Aarbøger for Nordisk Oldkyndighed og Historie.* [1913]: 51-105.

Kemp, B. J.
1977   The early development of towns in Egypt. *Antiquity* 51: 185-200.
1994   *Ancient Egypt. Anatomy of a Civilization.* London/New York: Routledge.

Lind, L.
1988   *Romerska denarer funna i Sverige.* Stockholm: Rubicon. [English summary].

Lyngstrøm, H.
1993   Ketting - en vikingetidsgravplads med ryttergrave. *Aarbøger for Nordisk Oldkyndighed og Historie* 1995: 143-179. [English summary: Ketting - a Viking- Age cemetery with equestrian graves].
Madsen, H. B.
1984   Metal-casting. Techniques, production and workshops. In *Ribe Excavations 1970-76*, 2. M. Bencard (ed.), pp. 15-189. Esbjerg: Sydjysk Universitetsforlag.
1997   Smedens affald. In *Ribe Excavations 1970-76*, 5. Pp. 1-102. (Ms).
Malmer, B.
1991   Om vikingatidens betalningsmedel. In *Fra Stamme til Stat i Danmark* 2. *Høvdingesamfund og Kongemagt*. P. Mortensen *et al.* (eds.), pp. 209-215. (Jysk Arkæologisk Selskabs Skrifter XXII:2). Højbjerg: Jysk Arkæologisk Selskab. [English summary].
Malmer, M. P.
1973   En korologisk aspekt på tolkningen av den gotländska järnålderns myntfynd. In Honos Ella Kivikoski. P. Sarvas *et al.* (eds.), pp. 132-136. *Suomen muinaismuistoyhdistyksen aikakauskirja* 75.
1992   Weight systems in the Scandinavian Bronze Age. *Antiquity* 66/251: 377-388.
Näsman, U.
1991   Det syvende århundrede - et mørkt tidsrum i ny belysning. In *Fra Stamme til Stat i Danmark* 2. *Høvdingesamfund og Kongemagt*. P. Mortensen *et al.* (eds.), pp. 165-178. (Jysk Arkæologisk Selskabs Skrifter XXII:2). Højbjerg: Jysk Arkæologisk Selskab. [English summary: The seventh century - a dark age in a new light].
Nielsen, Solveig
1997   Byudviklingen i Skandinavien i perioden 700-1100 e.Kr. *LAG* 6: 179-227.
Nielsen, Svend
1987-88   Roman denarii in Denmark - an archaeological approach. *Nordisk Numismatisk Årsskrift* [1987-88]: 147-169. [Dansk resumé: Romerske denarer i Danmark - en arkæologisk tolkning].
1989   Roman Denarii and Iron-Age Denmark. In *Coins and Archaeology*. Medieval Archaeology Research Group. Proceedings of the first meeting at Isegran, Norway 1988. H. Clarke *et al.* eds., pp, 29-36. (BAR, International Series, 556). Oxford: B.A.R.
1991   Urbanisering: aktuel forskning og nogle teoretiske betragtninger. In *Norsk byarkeologi inn i 1990-årene*. Seminar i Bergen 13.-14. december 1989. S. Myrvoll *et al.* (eds.), pp. 175-183. *N.U.B.* 1.
Nilsen, H.
1976   *Norrøne historieskriveres syn på de eldste norske byenes oppkomst og tidlige utvikling* (rev. utg.). Bergen. Private edition.
Njarðvik, N.
1974   *Islands ældste historie. Fra landnam til fristatens fald*. Copenhagen: Gyldendal.
Noonan, T. S.
1990   Dirham exports to the Baltic in the Viking Age: some preliminary observations. In *Sigtuna Papers. Proceedings of the Sigtuna Symposium on Viking-Age Coinage 1-4 June 1989*. K. Jonsson *et al.* (eds.), pp. 251-257. (Commentationes de nummis saeculorum IX-XI in Suecia repertis. Nova series 6). London/Stockholm: Spink & Son/Kungl. Vitterhets Historie och Antikvitets Akademien.

Pedersen, A.
1997   En undersøgelse af de nordiske sceattas og deres europæiske kontekst. *LAG*
            6: 61-178.
Randsborg, K.
1980   *The Viking Age in Denmark. The Formation of a State.* London: Duckworth.
Roesdahl, E.
1992   *The Vikings.* Harmondsworth: Penguin Books.
Sahlins, M.
1976   *Stone Age Economics.* London: Tavistock Publications.
1988   Cosmologies of capitalism: The trans-Pacific sector of the "world system".
            (Radcliffe-Brown Lecture in Social Anthropology). *Proceedings of the
            British Academy* 74: 1-51.
Sarvas, P.
1967   De finska myntskatterna från 1700- talet. *Nordisk Numismatisk Årsskrift*
            [1967]: 23-146. [English summary].
Sawyer, P.
1992   Resources and settlements. In *From Viking to Crusader. The Scandinavians
            and Europe 800-1200.* E. Roesdahl *et al.* (eds.), pp. 126-135. (Exhibition
            Catalogue). Uddevalla.
Service, E. R.
1985   *A Century of Controversy. Ethnological Issues from 1860-1960.* (Studies in
            Anthropology). London: Academic Press.
Sjoberg, G.
1960   *The Preindustrial City. Past and Present.* Glencoe, IL: The Free Press.
Sode, T.
1996   *Anatolske glasperler.* Copenhagen: Forlaget Thot. [English Summary].
Steuer, H.
1994   Handwerk auf spätantiken Höhensiedlungen des 4./5. Jahrhunderts in
            Südwestdeutschland. In *The Archaeology of Gudme and Lundeborg.* Papers
            presented at a Conference at Svendborg, October 1991. P. O. Nielsen *et al.*
            (eds.), pp. 128-144. (Arkæologiske Studier X). Copenhagen: Akademisk Forlag.
Sørensen, P. M.
1989   Den norrøne litteratur og virkeligheden. *Collegium Medievale* 2 (1989/2):
            135-146. [English summary: The Norse literature and reality].
Thomsen, P., *et al.*
1993   *Lundeborg - en anløbsplads fra jernalderen.* (Skrifter fra Svendborg &
            Omegns Museum, 32). Svendborg: Svendborg & Omegns Museum.
Ulriksen, J.
1998   *Anløbspladser. Besejling og bebyggelse i Danmark mellem 200 og 1100 e.
            Kr.* Roskilde: Vikingeskibshallen. [English summary].
Voss, O.
1993   Snorup. Et jernudvindingsområde i Sydvestjylland. *Nationalmuseets
            Arbejdsmark* [1993]: 97-111. [Summary: Snorup - an iron smelting area in
            south-west Jutland].
Wallerstein, I.
1974   *The Modern World-System I. Capitalist Agriculture and the Origins of the
            European World-Economy in the Sixteenth Century.* New York/San
            Francisco/London: Academic Press.
White, L., Jr.
1981   The expansion of technology 500-1500. In *The Fontana Economic History
            of Europe. The Middle Ages.* C. M. Cipolla (ed.), pp. 143-174. Glasgow:
            Collins/Fontana Books.

Wolf, E. R.
   1990   *Europe and the People Without History.* Berkeley/Los Angeles/ London:
               University of California Press.
van der Woude, A., *et al.*
   1995   Introduction: The hierarchies, provisioning, and demographic patterns of
               cities. In *Urbanization in History. A Process of Dynamic Interactions.*
               A. van der Woude *et al.* (eds.), pp. 1-19. Oxford: Clarendon Press.
Yoffee, N.
   1993   Too many chiefs? (or, Safe texts for the '90s). In *Archaeological Theory:
               Who Sets the Agenda?* N. Yoffee *et al.* (eds.), pp. 60-78. Cambridge:
               Cambridge University Press.

Discussion

GREEN: You talk about being at the threshold to historical times (page 177) and that is in connection with written sources. My question is, if you are defining here the threshold between prehistory and history by reference to written records: do you see this criterion as being written records about the culture from outside, or written records from within the culture or both? Because if it is both, then the dating may be different.

NIELSEN: I am in particular thinking about Frankish records and the like which can be used as far as Scandinavia is concerned.

AUSENDA: Why do you say of urbanism "at last emerging after the fall of Rome"; do you mean that urbanism outside the *limes* was impossible in Roman times?

NIELSEN: No, I am talking about the Migration period when there was a general collapse as far as urbanism, trade and so on are concerned. So there is a problem with the Migration period and economy. Its expansion started again with the coming of the earliest Frankish kings.

MAGNUS: You say (page 179) "Hence ironworking was done by individual farmers", do you mean both iron extraction and smithing?

NIELSEN: Yes, both. Yes it could be undertaken by individual farmers.

ARRHENIUS: This was not only in Jutland. In other places as well they have a larger extraction, in northern Scania, in Möre, Småland and in northern Sweden. But we now begin to realize that the mountain ore was also extracted especially for steel production. The extraction was not carried out as a proper mining operation as only the iron found on the surface of the ore was collected. This is a technique which is more specialized, perhaps only used on some bigger estates. We are just beginning to develop these ideas. The old thought that the extraction was done in the periphery and coming down to the central area is perhaps not quite right. It was perhaps more useful to alloy different kinds of metals when one wants to produce more complicated items such as weapons.

HERSCHEND: Why did it take such a long time before there were urban sites in Scandinavia; there were also special jobs like iron production, house building, ship building, before urban settlement.

NIELSEN: As far as the sailing ship was concerned, I also think it is very strange that they did not use the sail until the sixth/seventh century or so, because we know that sails were used by the Romans when they crossed the Channel, and between the Rhine estuary and the river they must have used sailing ships. And then it took half a millennium before the sailing ship was introduced to Scandinavia—I cannot explain it.

ARRHENIUS: It is not on a proper farm site that you will find bead production. It is on estates which were also specialized in the production of iron, and so on. We have very clear examples of productions on what I believe to have been larger estates.

NIELSEN: That is not a farm site.

ARRHENIUS: Well it is not an urban site either.

NIELSEN: It is, of course it is [laughter].

ARRHENIUS: On a real urban site we have a heavy phosphate-rich layer of black soil. And we have no black soil on those estates.

NIELSEN: I distinguish two kinds of sites, urban sites and rural sites. And, if it is not a rural site, it is, therefore, an urban site. They did more than *domestic* production and that is important and you can see that archaeologically. They do make brooches and they make specialized crafts, so that is why it is urban, it is very urban.

ARRHENIUS: No, then we get lots of urban sites, if they only make brooches.

HOLMQUIST: Is smithing done on an urban site? Iron smithing and things like that? I think perhaps, you must have more than one function: administration, religion or something.

NIELSEN: Well, of course, Ribe is much more than urban, but it started at the bottom and it is absolutely impossible to say when you go from a farm site to a *villa* to a town or a city. You will never be able to distinguish this archaeologically, because there are no definitions. That is my central point and I have tried for several years to explain it in Denmark, but they go on in the traditional way, I do not.

AUSENDA: I would like to give you a perspective on incipient urbanization from eastern Sudan where I did fieldwork. As soon as there is a concentration of lines of communications, e.g. at wellheads, huts are built where common goods, such as matches, shatta (red pepper), cigarettes, salt, onions, etc., are sold to the herders who bring their livestock to be watered at the wells. That is the embryo of a town. The village of Waggar which now has about 10,000 inhabitants, a market, an administration, several mosques, started in the 1930s as a group of such huts around a group of wells. Indeed, in eastern Sudan and many areas in the Middle East, a town is called primarily a 'souq'. When people in the bush go to town, they say they are going to the 'souq'. The town's main function is considered that of a trading centre. If concentration of trade supports an increasing number of traders who begin to settle and live there to look after their goods, the settlement gradually becomes permanent and grows into a town. It is very difficult to set a borderline signalling when all the combined functions of the settlement are such that it may be classified as a town.

BRINK: Yes, the problem of how to define urban sites is quite difficult.

HERSCHEND: I think this is one of the key problems and with archaeological material it is very difficult to distinguish between production and trade. I think there is a point in Dr. Ausenda's mentioning that the amount of trade is actually essential to the idea of an urban settlement. And it is not equally essential to the episcopal palace, and certainly not to the manorial economy, which is a centre from which you go on to the trade centre. I think there should be a phase between the rural and the town.

HOLMQUIST: Perhaps 'proto-town'.

GREEN: On page 182, you stick your neck out in my direction saying that "simply to dismiss our Viking chieftain, the central character in Norse literature, would be unbearable". It would help those like myself working in a word discipline as opposed to archaeologists to know what you mean by chieftain and what Latin or vernacular equivalent you have in mind in talking about him in connection with Nordic literature.

NIELSEN: I am afraid that the kind of chieftain I am thinking of is defined as such in anthropological terms. This may create some difficulty, so I would like to use the word 'leader' instead, to avoid the problem.

GREEN: Well, that avoids most of the problems, but there are still some.

BRINK: There are huge problems regarding the terminology for leaders in our pre-Christian society in Scandinavia.

NIELSEN: For instance, it is too difficult to go into greater detail, suffice it to say that the socio-political system envisaged by anthropologists is being criticized by themselves, as they say, as I was right here, that those political structures may be the result of European expansion. So, maybe there is no such system as we thought was the case.

GREEN: The trouble with drawing up a hierarchy for one discipline and then for written literature, is: how do you make your equations between your hierarchy in one discipline and your terminology in your written literary tradition?

BRINK: This is especially problematic when we take anthropological definitions which were set down in Christian and Western cultures and then try to apply it to a totally different pre-Christian culture. What was a *þulr*? Well, he obviously had to talk, but he was also a kind of leader. Obviously the term has Anglo-Saxon connections, but we don't know what it was. From its etymology we can tell that he had some speaking, talking function: a spokesman. Hence I would categorize such a person as a lesser chief.

NIELSEN: I was also thinking that we could call him a *goði*, but that may cause new problems.

BRINK: We have *goði* in early Iceland, however, also *guþe*, the eastern equivalent found on rune stones and place-names. So, we had the same function in eastern Scandinavia. Obviously there was some religious dimension to a *goði* but for Iceland he was a secular man. So, there are huge problems.

HERSCHEND: It doesn't matter if you don't know what the word means as long as it is there. And you may call this *þulr* a 'spokesman', and it is quite a major function. One need not know what the word means [laughter]. It is all right as long as you don't provide a definition. There is hardly any other way to start figuring it out. They are good terms, they shouldn't be thrown away just because we don't know what they mean exactly. I think, the *þing* is a very good one and we just don't know what it means, but it is good for our many observations.

AUSENDA: When you discussed market prices, you said that they do not exist in non-urban contexts. I disagree with you, I believe that 'market-price' levels exist even in very primitive economies. For instance, Jean Louis Burckhardt, a Swiss from Geneva, who visited in the mid 1810s the general area where I did my field-work, found that several equal bowls of 'dhurra' (sorghum) were exchanged for one bowl of milk, which basically amounted to a market price. I have witnessed several instances of 'market'-influenced price levels, e.g. once when a quantity of Western-made sardine cans distributed to refugees in Kassala were all sold at once to the local market, and this made the price plummet. Furthermore all kinds of livestock were auctioned daily at a 'market' and the final prices offered depended entirely on supply and demand: they fell during times of drought and came back up when water was plentiful, because in times of drought they could not keep the animals and had to sell them off to make some money out of them before they would die. Even gold in those remote hamlets was priced just about at the international market price. Furthermore, I have never seen haggling in 'primitive' markets: the mechanism is much simpler, if the purchaser thinks the price is too high he will not buy. People who live in a subsistence economy do not need to haggle because their basic needs are supplied by their own cultivation and livestock and when they do not have enough they obtain them on loan from relatives or starve. It seems to me that the archaeologist who wrote this was never in the field, but dug close to Egyptian cities. He probably inferred the reaction of a primitive market from the Khan el Khalili discussions by Western tourists and local merchants who might have wished to profit from the lack of knowledge of the going prices on the part of 'foreigners' by starting with high prices on the basis that 'sometimes it works'. In primitive economies would-be purchasers are not 'foreigners' and the price is logically set by their priorities rather than by psychological and pleonastic needs of someone belonging to a consumerist economy who only wants something he doesn't really need. I believe that haggling is a modern phenomonon, not a 'primitive' one. That was my first comment.

I agree that chiefdoms are usually responses to outside pressures (page 182), and councils of elders are diffuse in egalitarian societies. Chiefs tend to appear in special situations, whether for raids or war or the necessity to negotiate with important 'foreign' structures; if these phenomena become frequent the institution becomes permanent and tends to elicit surplus for its own support and for the activities, truly needed or imagined, that it is supposed to perform. This is more or less how chiefdoms come about.

HERSCHEND: I will come on to silver rings. If you analyse payment rings, you see that instead of having an even weight of half a mark, they have eleven of the lower parts, when twelve are needed to make half a mark. And it is very typical that in this silver-rich island (Gotland) the payment rings are below what would be the natural price. And I think that is, even if a technical one, an indication that there is a market price, at least in Gotland in the Viking Age, since there is a margin between the natural price and the weight of the silver rings. So there is no trouble in getting silver, there is a lot perhaps. So there are technical examples of market prices.

NIELSEN: I want to stress one point from Kemp's book. He says that the present is made synonymous with the market economy. This is the writer's point because everyone here probably thinks that today we have a market economy, but the point is that we have not, there are all kinds of regulations. For instance, if we did not belong to the European Union, we could buy very cheap grain from the United States. You can buy a lot from abroad very cheaply and some must be more expensive. But that is no market economy.

AUSENDA: I agree, we have institutionally conditioned economies (in which, however, goods are generally priced according to a market influenced level, even if some are priced according to political constraints) whereas the primitive ones are much freer and therefore closer to market economies.

NIELSEN: So, that's what I think we should talk about.

AUSENDA: Even the price of gold in Sudan responded instantly to international pricing.

NIELSEN: Well, I admit it is very difficult and maybe it is also so that certain goods were influenced by the market and perhaps others were not.

GREEN: You talk about *imitatio regni Francorum* (page 182). Do you imply by that petty kingship on the one hand or what the Germans call 'Grosskönigtum' on the other?

NIELSEN: I don't know. If I can avoid it, I would not like to call those individuals by any special term, such as 'king', 'chief', and the like, because their attributes and functions were certainly quite different from what those terms imply in modern situations.

GREEN: What are the grounds in using this phrase, *imitatio regni Francorum* at this point?

NIELSEN: That is easy to answer. There are apparently close connections between the Frankish realm and Scandinavia.

GREEN: In regard to kingship in particular?

NIELSEN: No, at both the material and the cultural level. Then it would make sense to believe that Scandinavians would imitate the princes and kings in the Merovingian realm. That's what Näsman thinks, too.

GREEN: You mention glass and pottery and wine (page 184). What earliest evidence have we in the North for wine being known there or imported there and what is the nature of that evidence?

NIELSEN: Well, I have written a paper once, it is in the reference list.

ARRHENIUS: I could say that we have analysed bottle ware and that some ware had contained wine. The so-called Badorfer ware had contained wine or something else with oxalic acid, most probably wine, dated to the ninth century. And maybe this wine import existed already in the late eighth century and early ninth century.

GREEN: But not before?

ARRHENIUS: In the analyses of earlier ceramics there are no examples. These are the only examples we have for imported ceramics containing wine. Homemade ceramics show only traces of other kinds of food.

NIELSEN: As far as the earlier period is concerned, I don't know of any evidence of wine in Scandinavia, but I think it must have been there. My point, when I wrote this paper, was that those amphorae contained the wine from provincial Romans, they never turn up in Scandinavia. We do not have amphorae, not yet.

GREEN: And further south, even in Germany, these amphorae are very close to the *limes*, not far inland from the *limes*.

NIELSEN: Yes, and in Britain too there is a book on the subject by Peacock and Williams (1986). I think wine was imported beginning in the Roman Iron Age, but neither I nor anyone else can prove it.

ARRHENIUS: I can also say that in some of the Roman vessels that are found they do not contain wine but beer or, rather, mead. Although these vessels in their home country apparently were used for wine.

GREEN: There is evidence that the Goths, while still in northern Poland, were acquainted with wine at that stage, before they moved further south, and I raise this question, just wondering whether there were any offshoots of that in southern Scandinavia as early as that.

ARRHENIUS: No, I only know of mead.

GREEN: The word and also not merely amphorae, but Roman wine sets in Gothic chiefs' graves.

ARRHENIUS: Yes, but that was what I talked about, that we have such wine sets, also in Scandinavia and in Denmark, but we found that it was not wine, it was mead or perhaps beer.

GREEN: There is also linguistic evidence, I am not going into that, that the Latin loanword probably reached the Goths at a time when they were still in northern Poland.

ARRHENIUS: We must look at the ceramics, only ceramics can show whether wine was known in Scandinavia in Roman times.

DUMVILLE: I was interested in your remarks about slaves (page 184), "various groups of organic materials may have been shipped, presumably slaves as well". How would one set about archaeologically finding evidence of whether a slave trade existed? What would you be looking for?

ARRHENIUS: If you go to Scotland and see the brochs where the people were hiding, there must have been a reason why they hid. The existence of the brochs might be evidence of the existence of a slave trade.

BRINK: The only way might be to find the terminology for slaves to indicate whether they are old or young.

DUMVILLE: People talk a lot about slaving, slave taking, slave transporting, and so on. But, of course, it has been argued by people working in the modern period that you have to have a terrific infrastructure in order to be able to seriously conduct slave trading operations....

BRINK: In the Scandinavian language we have two words for slave that have been taken from abroad and brought back home. This means that there must have been some here as well.

HERSCHEND: A good indication of this is that one of those slaves, or the persons who were called such, lived in the byre. There are Iron Age examples of people living in the byres in some 8 m² rooms, with a small mud fireplace and a fire. In the Iron Age, there would be settlements ranging from a byre to a hearth that only gives warmth and is not used for cooking, to a small kitchen, to a larger kitchen, to halls.

ARRHENIUS: Yes, but there is a difference between the existence of slaves here and there. To have a valid advanced slave trade, that's something else.

MEULENGRACHT: The definition of a slave will never be on an economic basis or turn on economic terms of living in caves or in the open air; it is defined in legal terms, and you will not find them in archaeology.

JESCH: Are there any shackles or things like that? I seem to remember that some have been found at Hedeby.

LUND: Well, we do have some evidence of slaves being transported for sale in the Arabic sources. I forget whether it is Ibn Fadlan or another. But he does record the sort of pleasures they had with women before they sold them off. But, generally I think when they rounded up people the intention was to hold them to ransom and get rid of them as quickly as possible rather than to sell them off to third parties.

DUMVILLE: Of course there is the gender question as well, once you get into the Viking Age evidence for women being seized and maybe killed or left. So, that in fact, well I doubt they were purely ransomed.

GREEN: There is, of course, further evidence for slave trade much further south, but that doesn't necessarily apply to Scandinavia.

HERSCHEND: I am not sure that there was anything like having a legal concept of slave; this doesn't mean that there weren't any slaves.

MEULENGRACHT: You can make a difference between slaves and tenants, or labourers in that way.

BRINK: There is a very informative new book on slaves in Scandinavia, written by Tore Iversen (1997) for anyone interested in the problem.

AUSENDA: There is a parallel between the circulation of *denarii* in Scandinavia (page 185) and the circulation of Maria Theresa silver thalers in Ethiopia and East Africa. They were used until recently and can be found in goldsmiths' shops in Kassala, Sudan, and Keren, Eritrea. Women used them as pendants on necklaces as they were at the same time an ornament and a small saving in case of need.

I also agree with the interpretation that coins were only capital in a subsistence economy. Even in the Italian Alps at the turn of the century money was quite seldom necessary as, except for salt, wine and few other items, farmers were self-sufficient. To obtain money, they sold chestnuts or walnuts.

MAGNUS: You say "*sceattas* in particular should be seen as proofs of long-distance trade and that they are mainly found at sites where there was commercial activity" (page 186). But there is one *sceatt* found in Ervik, on the tip of the promontory of Stad in west Norway which hardly could have been a site of long-distance trade. There at the beginning of the nineteenth century in an area of shifting sands one *sceatt* was found together with several Migration period cruciform brooches.

GREEN: Third paragraph (page 187), you talk about the cow being used as money. I would just like to place this in a wider context and remind you of the relationship between German 'Vieh', 'cattle', English 'fee', money or charge of money, and Old Norse *fé*, both meanings, and further of the relationship between Latin *pecus* and *pecunia*, which is a much wider problem.

GREEN: You talk about the horse being used as a pack animal (page 188). I would like to ask what is the earliest evidence in Scandinavia for the ass or donkey or mule being used for this purpose. I ask because coming in from a linguistic point of view, the ass is an import from the south into northern Europe, and the German word 'Esel', for example, with its cognate in English goes back to Latin diminutive *asellus*. So the Old Norse form for this animal, *asni*, is quite definitely not from Latin direct, but from French. So that suggests that the use of this animal as a pack animal was later in the North than it was in Germany or England. Is there any evidence from your field to substantiate that?

NIELSEN: I have never heard about bones from asses or donkeys in Scandinavia in the prehistorical context ever. It must be medieval.

MAGNUS: About pack horses, you are thinking of Denmark. On the Scandinavian peninsula winter is a very good time for travel.

NIELSEN: Yes, of course, I do mention sledges.

MAGNUS: Yes, not only sledges, but you can move freely over frozen lakes. There is one thing more. You don't need sledges for transporting hay, there are much simpler conveyances.

NIELSEN: Yes, I know. It is called a slide-car.

ARRHENIUS: They are used quite a lot. Yes, I was saying the same thing. I should add ice-skating which is very important: one half of the Baltic Sea would also be iced.

NIELSEN: And the Birka trade would have taken place also in winter. The situation is somewhat different in Denmark, because in winter there is mostly just mud. Even in recent times a whole vehicle could disappear in a river.

ARRHENIUS: In Sweden at that time there were no roads, so these winter roads gave the only possibility for transports to the hinterland apart from the waterways.

GREEN: In that connection in the eastern Baltic, right through the Middle Ages, the winter was the time for military campaigns.

MAGNUS: How do you know that "a considerable number of urban inhabitants were peasants" (page 189)?

HOLMQUIST: In Birka, with such little land it was hard to get from the island. So, I think it must have been a sort of system and all the farms around in the Mälar area must be involved, some of them.

NIELSEN: It is possible that Birka represented a particular case. However, generally in pre-industrial towns a large proportion had to get food by agriculture. It is the same in medieval towns in Denmark, that a large proportion were peasants. And if you go to the Third World today it is the same. I drew one example from Egypt where you cannot get food from hundreds of kilometres away. That's why I quoted those historians. It is from within a radius of 20 or 30 km that they get most of their food. It would be different if the town was by the sea or a large river. Still the problem of food supply is always there when you have many people together and no railways. That is what I wanted to underscore.

HOLMQUIST: That is one of the most important questions. But I think of Lund, the early medieval Lund had 1,000 inhabitants, and so many farms within that area would not be possible, they must have had also supplies from the outside.

BRINK: They must have had supplies by boat.

GREEN: I just want to mention that in German there is a specialist term for this 'Ackerbürger', someone who lives in a town and works on the fields outside.

NIELSEN: The problem is also important because ancient societies only produced a 10% food surplus; this is the figure used by historians and economists. So, if there is only a 10% surplus, and there were say 1,000 inhabitants in Hedeby, then there had to be ten times as many people nearby to supply them.

[AUSENDA's afterthought: in calculating the ratio of farm workers required, one should bear in mind that the population also included women and children].

HOLMQUIST: Yes, but to supply them 500 inhabitants.

NIELSEN: But they had to live very close to Hedeby.

ARRHENIUS: There I think we have an initial town. Indeed I always think that there are valid reasons for the accumulation in the area of phosphate-rich heavy black soil, at which point you have a town. Fish is something you can really bring into a town, it is a very important staple when dried. So, I would like to put into the definition of a town also that it must be a black soil area.

BENDER: Amazing things are possible if you want to. Mons Claudianus, a Roman quarry I worked on in Egypt is 120 km from the Nile. It is in the middle of the desert, in the middle of mountains. It is very difficult to obtain any food there and it is even more difficult to get water. Nonetheless, almost 1,000 people lived there for a number of years and they got their supplies all the time from the Nile. It must have cost a lot and we see this quarry as an imperial status symbol. It wouldn't be an everyday thing. My point is, it can be done. We were at the time staggered....

AUSENDA: What did they quarry, gold?

BENDER: Granite. The pillars in front of the Pantheon came from that place. And when we go to Ravenna, in the middle of the piazza del Popolo there is a pillar from that site.

AUSENDA: A density of 64 per km^2 (page 192) is exceedingly high.

NIELSEN: That is what I wrote.

AUSENDA: On the basis of Third World data on the one hand and of cemetery populations on the other, figures of 7 per km^2 and 6 per km^2 were arrived at for Anglo-Saxon England and eastern *Francia* (Ausenda 1997:423; Siegmund 1998:209). Even nowadays, if you make a comparison with Third and Fourth World countries that is the figure you would get.

References in the discusion

Ausenda, G.
   1997   Current issues and future directions in the study of the early Anglo-Saxon Period. In *The Anglo-Saxons from the Migration Period to the Eighth Century: An Ethnographic Perspective.* J. Hines (ed.), pp. 411-450. Woodbridge: The Boydell Press.

Iversen, T.
   1997   *Trelledommen. Norsk slaveri i meddelalderen.* (Historisk institutt. Universitetet i Bergen, Skrifter 1). Bergen: Universitetet i Bergen.

Kemp, B.
   1994   See References at end of paper.

Peacock, D. P. S., & D. F. Williams
   1986   *Amphorae and the Roman Economy: An Introductory Guide.* (Longman archaeological series). London: Longman.

Siegmund, F.
   1998   Social structure and relations. In *Franks and Alamanni from the Merovingian Period to the Eighth Century: An Ethnographic Perspective.* Ian Wood (ed.), pp. 177-212. Woodbridge: The Boydell Press.

VIKINGS IN THE BRITISH ISLES: A QUESTION OF SOURCES

DAVID N. DUMVILLE

Girton College, Cambridge, GB-CB3 OJG

In this paper I shall be concerned largely with what has come to be known, following a famous discussion led by Peter Sawyer (Sawyer *et al.* 1969), as the First Viking Age; in other words I shall not seek to progress beyond the middle years of the tenth century.

This leads me to some necessary definitions of the terminology which I shall use in this paper. 'The British Isles' is the term used since the time of Polybius (second century B.C.) for the sum of the islands of Ireland and Britain and their associated minor islands (Rivet & Smith 1979:39, 282), including Mann (the views of some Irish nationalists notwithstanding, it is not a term reflecting British hegemonistic intents); the 'Western Isles' are the Hebrides, Inner and Outer; the 'Northern Isles' comprise the Orkney and Shetland groups. (Currently fashionable as a replacement for 'the British Isles' is 'the Atlantic archipelago', which I shall not use.)

Looking towards Scandinavia, I shall refer to vikings, not Vikings: in other words, I regard this as a common noun meaning 'pirates' (though no doubt usually pirates having some association with the Scandinavian world) rather than as an ethnic denominator, whether meaning 'inhabitants of the Vik' or simply 'Scandinavians' (Fell 1986; cf. Hødnebø 1987). This deliberate and mediaeval usage will have consequences as the argument of my paper develops. I shall avoid the word 'Norse' except in reference to language and literature, for the simple reason that in English (and American English) usage there is now utter confusion as to whether it means 'Scandinavian' or 'Norwegian'. 'Nordic' I avoid because it has unfortunate connotations for the average English-speaker.

The sources which I shall consider are written texts, now literary, now documentary. I am concerned with historical interpretation arising from those texts. I claim no competence in the interpretation of archaeological data.

Scandinavian interaction with the British Isles in the Viking Age is of course a segment, albeit an important segment, of the whole history of Scandinavian expansionism in the central Middle Ages (for still indispensable surveys see Kendrick 1930; Shetelig 1940; Sawyer 1962; Graham-Campbell & Kidd 1980; see also Graham-Campbell 1994; Haywood 1995; Sawyer 1997). It presents particular problems of interpretation because of the ethnically and politically complex situation within the Insular world and the great variety of types of source-material consequently pertaining to this relatively small area. It also offers the earliest evidence for those Scandinavian military activities abroad which came to define the Viking Age. While the British Isles cannot be considered in isolation from a

209

larger context, they do provide a study-area offering sufficient variety of sources, geography, polities, and social structures to enable the historian to test hypotheses about viking activity in the round (for a useful survey of problems, see Wormald 1982).

The first event of the Viking Age in the British Isles to be recorded in contemporary written sources (above all, the writings of Alcuin; cf. Bullough 1993) was a raid on the church of Lindisfarne (N. Northumbria) in 793. Less precisely dated piratical activities seem to have been taking place in southern England also, not later than the 790s. In the Gaelic world too, the mid-790s saw the beginning of record of similar irruptions. The question has often been asked as to where these vikings came from. Had they indeed sailed from Norway for a summer's adventure? Numismatic evidence suggests that this is possible (Skaare 1976:39-47, 117). Or does their appearance in the southern half of mainland Britain, in Ireland, and in the Western Isles in the 790s presuppose a longer history of Scandinavian activity in parts of northern Britain beyond the reach of surviving written record for the later eighth century? For it is worth remembering that while the occasional piece of information about north British affairs is preserved in sources deriving from records of that period, in general the history of that region at that time is lost (cf. Downham 2000). It is entirely possible, therefore, to imagine Scandinavian settlement of, for example, the Northern Isles in the middle or second half of the eighth century if other evidence suggests that as a possibility. In recent years there have been two contradictory approaches to this issue. On the one hand, an archaeological case has been developed that viking activity in the British Isles (and presumptively in north Britain—most naturally the Northern Isles) began perhaps a generation before the 790s (for example, Myhre 1993; cf. Roesdahl 1994:111-13). On the other hand, it has been argued from *Vita Sancti Findani* (ed. Holder-Egger 1887; cf. Löwe 1986) (the Life of St Findan of Rheinau—an Irishman kidnapped by vikings—written after 878) that Orkney in the 840s, though visited and perhaps controlled by vikings, had an Irish-educated bishop (Thomson & Omand 1986): this view brings difficulties of various sorts (the passage was interpreted quite differently by Löwe 1985:77). Whatever one may make of the archaeological argument for an earlier beginning to the Viking Age in the British Isles (and therefore to the Viking Age as a whole), there is of course no doubt about the comprehensive Scandinavianization of the Northern Isles; the antecedent Pictish culture was superseded (Wainwright 1962 remains the starting point for discussion). When Scandinavian control there was achieved may be a matter for debate, but it is fair to say that comprehension of what happened in Ireland and northern Britain from the mid-790s to the 820s would be easier if that generation were preceded by one in which the Northern Isles had been conquered.

This opening discussion has introduced one theme of my paper, namely, the blanks in the historical record of the Viking Age in the British Isles. The gaps are substantial and sometimes absolute. They can sometimes be waved aside in favour of an archaeological or a linguistic record which only occasionally addresses the same issues as the literary and (where available) documentary sources. The gaps in written sources inhibit sensible historians from attempting to write about areas, periods, and themes for which they have no evidence. All too often, however, historians (and others) find themselves tempted to make arguments from silence. The consequences are writ large across the received history of the Insular Viking Age. Furthermore, in the last generation (since Sawyer 1962 and d'Haenens 1967) there has been a vigorous attempt to write Viking Age history in the teeth of the contemporary written sources. It may be argued, therefore, that historical approaches to this era in Insular history as a whole are in disarray. What is needed is a method which will enable historians to overcome the partial nature both of their sources and of their own approaches.

The general proposition which I offer for consideration is hardly new, but it nonetheless seems constantly to be forgotten, whether by students of viking activity in a particular area or by writers of general books called *The Vikings* or the like. This is that we have allowed the separate national sources to dictate to us our very fragmented views of the Viking Age. It might be said that the way to treat Viking Age history is to range as freely and imaginatively across frontiers as did vikings themselves (cf. Nelson 1978-81). In the Insular context we can in this way build up a picture of viking activities and their consequences, both specific and general, which can then be confronted with, on the one hand, a similarly constructed picture of the Viking Age in (for example) *Francia* and, on the other, the pictures provided by scholars working in other disciplines.

In recent times the only major attempt to consider the (First) Viking Age in the British Isles as a whole has been the trilogy of books published by Alfred Smyth (1977; 1975/9) which was focused particularly on the relationship between Dublin and York but whose exposition and evidence led him to consider the entire region. Although these books received significant criticism in reviews—much of it valid (cf. Ó Corráin 1978/9; Page 1982)—they nevertheless justified themselves as a whole by inviting scholars to consider the geographical range and the appetite for power of viking leaders whose careers ranged across lands and seas with a broader vision than that of many modern scholars. In putting the Dublin Scandinavian dynasty, which Irish-language writers came to call Uí Hímair ('descendants of Ívarr'), at the centre of his story, Smyth followed in the footsteps of two distinguished mid-nineteenth-century students of Ireland's Viking Age, Charles Haliday (*obit* 1866) and James Henthorn Todd (*obit* 1869). One of the complaints against Smyth's work was his 'lack of intellectual generosity' (Wormald & Frank 1980): not generally mentioned in that connection was his debt to those two pioneers, whose work (Todd 1867; Haliday 1881, 1884) is only occasionally cited in his books. Smyth's use of sources was often grotesque: for example, the first eight chapters of his *Scandinavian Kings in the British Isles, 850-880* (1977:1-126) deal with sources and issues which cannot credibly be discussed in relation to the first half of the ninth century (cf. McTurk 1974-7; 1978-81). Nevertheless, Smyth offered in much of the rest of his trilogy significant insights, new and rediscovered, into the history of the British Isles from about 850 to about 950: the early and continuing connection of Dublin and York and the mechanics of that link; the context of the viking assaults on England from 865; the invaders' disdain for international boundaries; the importance of slaving in viking activities; the good quality of vikings' local and strategic intelligence-gathering (cf. Reuter 1990:404); the fundamental importance of taking sources of the widest relevant origin into account; and the apparently large role played by the English Danelaw in the development of legend about ninth-century viking leaders (1977:54-67).

One of the unfortunate absentees from Smyth's work, a problem noted by various reviewers, is any careful assessment of the strengths and weaknesses, merits and demerits, of the various written sources for his subject. The reason for such absence is clear to any of his readers. But combination of such an assessment with Smyth's insistence on drawing on sources of diverse geographlcal origins will provide a means by which common themes and issues can be assessed across the entire study-area. I proceed, therefore, to a region-by-region survey, beginning in Scotland and travelling in an anti-clockwise direction.

Scotland was not a single political entity in the Viking Age or for long after. At the beginning of the Viking Age it was divided between a Pictish area stretching from the Northern Isles to the Firth of Forth (which had, in 741, incorporated by conquest the Gaelic overkingdom of Dál Riata; this led to an increasing gaelicization of Pictland, which seems to have achieved a critical level by about 900 — on all this, cf. Dumville 1997b:33-6), a British area in southwestern Scotland comprising a kingdom of Strathclyde stretching from Loch Lomond to Ayrshire at the beginning of the period, but as far south as the Yorkshire-Westmorland border by 927 (Dumville 1997b:31-2), and another kingdom or kingdoms in what is now called Galloway. What is now southeastern Scotland was part of (English) Northumbria until an uncertain date in the tenth century (Barrow 1966 = 1973:139-61 for discussion). From the Pictish region we have evidence for one or two annalistic chronicles being kept, but we see these only in later redactions, incorporated into different works, whether native or Irish in origin (Bannerman 1974:9-26 and M. O. Anderson 1980:235-60, esp. 249-53). There is also a very small amount of inscriptional evidence (Forsyth 1996). In this region, as in all the other non-English parts of the British Isles, coinage was not produced, but the introduction of coin seems to have constituted an aspect of viking activity (cf. Graham-Campbell et al. 1995). For Strathclyde we have the slender remnants of a chronicle, preserved in Irish and Welsh sources, running down through the ninth century (Hughes 1980:71-2, 95-6, 98-9), and we have some external sources noticing the interaction of Strathclyders with other groups. For Galloway in the Viking Age, we have effectively no written sources before the eleventh century (cf. Oram 1995).

The Isle of Mann requires separate notice. There are only inscriptions by way of native sources (Page 1983); the thirteenth-century 'Chronicle of Mann and the Isles' begins in the eleventh century but there is little to suggest that it preserves contemporary Viking Age testimony. A considerable amount of numismatic testimony is available for Mann, though principally relating to the Second Viking Age. Mann is of considerable interest as a Brittonic polity which succumbed to viking conquest from the Western Isles around 900 (Graham-Campbell 1998 for the date), becoming an island of Norse and Gaelic speech closely linked to other such regions of similar history—Cumbria and Galloway.

From Ireland, with its very strong literary tradition in both Latin and the vernacular, we have a considerable body of evidence for the ninth and tenth centuries. Ecclesiastical chronicles form the backbone of the native record: these, as we have them, are compilations of the second half of the eleventh century and later, but linguistic, stylistic, and text-historical investigations have combined to suggest that annals for the Viking Age have been transmitted with a high degree of accuracy (Ó Máille 1910; Hughes 1972, ch. IV; Mac Niocaill 1975; Dumville 1990, ch. XVII). In the eleventh and twelfth centuries we find a development of the annalistic chronicle embodying saga-material of a kind proper to the imaginative, narrative literature about legendary heroes and events of the distant past (Dumville 1999): the absurdly-titled 'Fragmentary Annals of Ireland' (Radner 1978; formerly called 'The Three Fragments' — O'Donovan 1860) and the 'The Annals of Clonmacnoise' (Murphy 1896) are examples of this new form, and much less credit can be given to their narrative sections. This in turn developed into full-blown narrative history, albeit with a partially visible annalistic base, in *Cocad Gaedel re Gallaib*, 'The War of the Irish with the Foreigners', probably written at the beginning of the twelfth century (edited and translated by Todd 1867; cf. Ní Mhaonaigh 1995 & 1996), a work whose concerns are above all those of Irish dynastic politics in the last years of the Second Viking Age. A wide range of other evidence, including inscriptional and numismatic, is available from Ireland for the study of this period.

For Wales we begin to have a significant body of information only with the onset of the Viking Age. A rather thin Latin chronicle (known to modern scholarship as *Annales Cambriae*) can be traced back with confidence to the mid-tenth century (and with some credibility back to the early ninth) from later manuscripts and derivative texts (Dumville 2002a; 2002b), including late mediaeval Welsh translations known as *Brutiau*. The entries for this period are laconically worded and the record is by no means continuous: the chronicle seems to have been kept at St Davids (in Dyfed, southwestern Wales) but also has notices of events in North Wales (Hughes 1980:67-100). There is inscriptional evidence from the period (Nash-Williams 1950), as too numismatic evidence from imported coinage. Irish sources also take some note of Welsh affairs. The most famous work by a Welsh author of this period is the biography of Alfred, king of Wessex, by Asser, bishop of St Davids (Stevenson 1904, 1959; Keynes & Lapidge 1983). This serves to point up the fact that English influence increased in ninth-century Wales, such that, after the battle of Edington in 878, all Welsh kings had, within the next fifteen years, accepted the overlordship of King Alfred; and his successors as kings of Wessex, and then kings of England, until 1016 generally retained this connection (Dumville 1993, chs. XV-XVI). As a result, English sources contain important evidence for Welsh Viking Age history.

The other Brittonic-speaking region of the British Isles was greatly affected by the events of the First Viking Age. The territory of the rulers of Cornwall suffered progressive loss to West Saxon aggression throughout the eighth century, and in the ninth the Cornish seem to have regarded the arrival of vikings in their region as a heaven-sent opportunity to beat the English back. The failure of a combined Cornish-Scandinavian army at the battle of Hingston Down in 838 probably led to English overlordship and by the late ninth century to complete incorporation of Cornwall into England (Hoskins 1960). We owe such knowledge as we have of Cornish affairs in this era to English and Welsh sources. One or two local inscriptions bear on the history of this period (Macalister 1949:176-87), while Cornish (or Anglo-Cornish) documents of the tenth century help to give a more rounded picture.

Ninth- and tenth-century England has left a wealth of source-material. both literary and documentary, but there remain numerous gaps in our knowledge. of English history of this period. The principal narrative source is 'The Anglo-Saxon Chronicle' (Whitelock 1961, 1979, for explication and translation) which seems to have been compiled in Wessex in 892 (Sawyer 1962:16-19; Dumville 1992, ch. III). The author did not have access to contemporary records for the whole of the ninth century; so its account is very uneven (Sawyer 1962:16-20). For the period from 865 the military interactions of various English and viking armies provide the narrative focus of this chronicle, a feature which remained true of its contemporary continuations to 920. We learn from charter-evidence some significant things about viking activities in Southumbria (see, for example, Sawyer 1968, no. 206, of A.D. 855), while remnants of a Northumbrian chronicle or chronicles of the period survive in eleventh- and twelfth-century sources (Offler 1958; Hunter Blair 1963; Dumville 1993, ch. X). Some localities are well served by written evidence, but large parts of the country have no history in this period. Correspondence, legislation, biography, and hagiography all contribute to the picture, as do foreign sources—Irish, Welsh, Frankish, and papal, in particular. coinage, whether produced by English kings or their opposites in the Danelaw, makes a formidable contribution. Substantial, but still insufficient, progress has been made in eliminating from modern accounts 'information' derived from non-contemporary sources (for an example see Dumville 1992, ch. II).

That problem seems to remain acute in Frankish history too. In spite of the wealth of contemporary record for ninth-century *Francia* and for tenth-century 'France' and 'Germany', the history of the Viking Age in the west of the European continent seems to remain dependent to an alarming degree on eleventh-century and later texts (Vogel 1906 remains the standard account; cf. Zettel 1977). The famous 'Treaty of Saint-Clair-sur-Epte', by which Normandy was supposedly established in 911, rests on no contemporary evidence, for example (for the nearest approximation, see Lauer 1940-9: 209-12, no. 92; for subsequent grants of regions to vikings see Lauer 1905). As in Ireland, so in *Francia*, an image of the viking developed in the eleventh century, which owed a great deal more to the literary and political concerns of that period than to the history of the First Viking Age itself (Dumville n.d.). Frankish sources have also necessarily been used to write the political history of Denmark in the ninth century but, mixed with a dose of Danish nationalism and anachronistic notions of 'state-formation', have produced alarming and (for the historian) incredible accounts of the activities of a Danish monarchy (Randsborg 1980; Roesdahl 1982; Hodges & Whitehouse 1983:102-22; for some mild but pointed comments, Lund 1981b:28-9; for a supposedly moderate statement, see Axboe 1995; for trenchant criticism, Maund 1994).

This brings us last to Scandinavian written sources. Of guaranteedly contemporary written records for the First Viking Age there are only runic inscriptions. The extent to which skaldic poetry transmitted in later manuscripts (and, indeed, in later literary works) can be taken to be faithful to its form in the pre-Christian period remains controversial. It is clear that events and personalities of the Viking Age in the British Isles played large roles in the developing legends which were to be drawn on in the writing of Old Norse saga-literature in the thirteenth century, but there is no known method of drawing from that literature any accurate information about the Viking Age itself. The temptation for modern writers to resort to it when writing ninth- or tenth-century history is well known, but succumbing to such temptation is as unacceptable in this context as it is in the study of other prehistoric or protohistoric Heroic Ages. The narratives of often superb literary artists distant in time and place from the period celebrated are not suitable as fodder for historians of the Viking Age. (For the extraction of a very uncertain sacrificial site practiced by vikings, see Smyth 1977:189-94, 201-23; Frank 1984; Einarsson 1986-9; Frank 1986-9; Einarsson & Frank 1990-3). The same must also hold true for twelfth-century accounts of the settlement of Iceland: that there was an Insular dimension to the settlement-process seems likely, but its extent remains controversial and is difficult to estimate on the basis of such sources (cf., for example, Sigurðsson 1988). In sum, while the prose literature of the Scandinavian world attests to the role of the colonies in developing the legends (and perhaps even antecedent literary texts—although students of Old Norse do not seem very well disposed to the notion of Old Norse first being written in Roman-letter orthography in the Insular colonies), it does not present usable narrative information. But of the deep mutual interpenetration of Scandinavian and Insular cultures as a result of colonization, Old Norse literature leaves us in no doubt; a particularly remarkable example is the Eddic poem *Rígsþula* (Dronke 1997:159-238).

What emerges from a survey of the written sources of information for the Viking Age in the British Isles is their great unevenness in almost every respect. For some areas we have very little information, for others a great deal; but, even in the latter case, there are great discrepancies between the volumes of information pertaining to particular areas or periods or themes. The various 'national' sources are in some respects very different from one another in form or content. They may, for various reasons, have greatly differing value. The texts or information in question may have been transmitted to us in very different ways. Different potential sources may have been investigated or exploited to varying degrees and effect. There may be differing levels of theoretical difficulty in approaching some sources. Historical research has advanced in varying degrees in relation to the particular region or ethnic group. Use of 'foreign' sources by those unfamiliar with their context of production can give rise to misunderstanding. And differing modern historical traditions—notably when affected by nationalism or other ideologies—can give historians varying senses of what constitute the important issues.

I propose, therefore, to pass in review the issues which historians of the various countries—considered in the same geographical order as before—have deemed important in approaching the First Viking Age.

The scantiness of the written sources for Scottish history and the poor quality of some which have consequently been pressed into service have restricted the range of issues which Scottish historians have been able to pursue. Increasingly in recent years it has been archaeology which has been providing the source-material, the theoretical frameworks, and the questions for discussion (B. E. Crawford 1987; cf. Dumville 1986-9). To some extent also, toponymic (and other linguistic) research has been increasing its contribution to historical debate (Nicolaisen 1976 marks a significant moment; see now B. E. Crawford 1995). One of the enduring issues has been whether the Scandinavian take-over of the Northern and Western Isles was peaceful or not. Certainly the results in the two areas were very different from one another. What is most striking in the Northern Isles is the complete Scandinavianization of their local toponymy and the absence of any clear indication that the previous, Pictish, inhabitants had any input into their subsequent history and culture; the same applies to some of the northernmost parts of the mainland. In the Western Isles, on the other hand, the linguistic picture (from toponymy and from modern Scottish Gaelic dialects) is much patchier, seemingly attesting to a varyingly hybrid society across the Hebrides (for a thoughtful discussion see Fellows-Jensen 1984). For this region we also have some exiguous written records. But since we do not know whether the Outer Hebrides had all been subjected to Gaelic settlement in the seventh and eighth centuries (cf. Bannerman 1974), it is difficult to assess the Scandinavian impact in that part of the region.

Two areas of what are now Scotland disappear utterly from the written record of the ninth and tenth centuries. One is the Argyll mainland of whose history we know nothing from about 800 to about 1100 (on place-names, cf. Fellows-Jensen 1984:163-4; on the period from 1100 see McDonald 1997): a wave of the hand has usually allowed it to be attributed to Pictland or Dál Riata or Scandinavians, but I have seen no convincing discussion of its fate. The other area is Galloway, whose very name implies hybrid Gaelic-Scandinavian culture (I am not convinced by the objections raised in recent years by Daphne Brooks 1991; 1994:60-1, 72-6), but whose pre-Viking Age history is sufficiently obscure that it is not possible to say how much was occupied by Britons, English, and Gaels and therefore precisely what vikings' impact may have been. Galwegian history is now being researched and debated (cf. Hill *et al.* 1996) and it is possible that some enlightenment may result, but again the materials are largely archaeological and linguistic.

If both the extent of Scandinavian settlement in northern Britain and its social effects in particular regions still remain undefined, one major political question has repeatedly been asked: what effects did viking behaviour have on political development towards what would eventually be the kingdom of Scots? As the question is framed here it is evident that it has nationalistic, anachronistic, and deterministic aspects to it, none of which is acceptable in the Viking Age context. In detail, the question can be put in different ways. A question asked since the middle ages themselves concerns the extent to which the viking impact on North Britain was responsible for the political 'union' (the favoured word, although 'conquest' is what all the—uniformly non-contemporary—sources offer) of Dál Riata and Pictland by the Gaels. In the last few years, historians resorting exclusively to contemporary sources of information have asked instead about the origins of the kingdoms of Muréb/Muriab (Moray), formerly northern Pictland, and Alba, formerly southern Pictland, and the reasons for the break-up of the long-standing Pictish overkingdom. While it is unlikely that vikings had no part to play, this approach is still too novel for any consensus to have been reached (cf. Dumville 1997b:33-6). Furthermore, the absence of any history for Argyll in this period is a severely limiting factor. Relatively young, too, are questions about the relationship of the kings of Alba to the viking dynasty of Dublin and York, and the ability of the kingdom of Alba to expand southwards into Northumbria because of vikings' seizure of York in 866/7.

The outstanding single event of North-British history in this period was the four-month siege and eventual capture of Dumbarton, the capital of Strathclyde, in 870 by the Dublin-York vikings (Mac Airt & Mac Niocaill 1983:326/7 [870.6]; cf. *ibid.* [871.2]). While there has been a great deal of discussion (largely inconclusive in detail) about the subsequent relationship of Strathclyde and Alba (Mac Airt & Mac Niocaill 1983:328/9 [872.5]) there has been no sustained consideration of the relationship of Strathclyde with viking polities.

Very little effort has been devoted by Scottish historians to charting the course of Church-history in the Viking Age (cf. Dumville 1997b for recent discussion). Not the least reason is the highly fragmentary nature of the evidence. Even for the relatively well documented church of Iona, the history is relatively obscure, even if it is clear that the relics of St Columba were divided between Kells in Ireland and Dunkeld in what would be Alba, and that Iona became an administratively less important part of the widespread Columban group of churches (Herbert 1988; Rollason 1978; Pörnbacher 1997). More churches emerge into the historical record as time passes, but we know very little about the history of any one of them in the Viking Age. For much of Scotland few questions have been asked about the processes by which Scandinavian settlers received Christianity.

The upshot of all this is that historians have asked only the most obvious questions—and not all of those—because they have been led and constrained by the exiguous written evidence, or led by later and inadmissible texts. Only in respect of the activities of the viking dynasty of Dublin and York have questions been asked about intention: securing control of the central Scottish lowlands has been postulated by Alfred Smyth (1975:35-6, 94-6; cf. 1977:143-53) as these vikings' aim because of the need to ensure ready communication between their twin centres of power. There has been little debate about this; and comparable questions of vikings' intent elsewhere in North Britain have hardly been broached.

The questions which can be asked concerning the Isle of Mann in the First Viking Age are largely determined by archaeology (Wilson 1974). The frame, however, is provided by written sources. These make it quite clear that Mann was an island of British speech in the early Middle Ages. A King Merfyn who died in 682 seems to have made a considerable reputation for himself, presumably by projecting his power by sea from this central point in the Irish Sea (Mac Airt & Mac Niocaill 1983:146 [682.2]). The Second Dynasty of Gwynedd (north-west Wales), which took its origin in 826, seems to have been descended from a Manx royal line (for genealogical evidence see Bartrum 1966:10, §4, and 46, §19). An inscribed cross bearing the name *Guriat* (Modern Welsh Gwriad), found on Mann a century ago (Macalister 1949:190, no. 1066), may commemorate the father of Merfyn, king of Gwynedd (826-44). When we next have Manx historical records, the island has become part of a Gaelic and Scandinavian world: a bilingual society whose origins seem to be associated with comparable developments in Galloway and Cumbria, it is strongly affiliated to the Western Isles. The most recent survey of the archaeological evidence has put viking settlement of Mann around 900 (Graham-Campbell 1998), rather later than the previous estimates. What is striking is that, as in the Northern Isles, all traces of the antecedent Brittonic language have vanished, which prompts questions about the fate of the pre-existing population. Although the earliest identifiable viking burials seem clearly pagan, evidence for a Christian element among the settler-population is discoverable in the course of the tenth century. Mann remained within Scandinavian orbit until the thirteenth century, but the Gaelic element of its culture became more marked over time, just as in the Western Isles, and no doubt results from its close links with that region throughout the period. One of the surprises of the study of Manx history, archaeology, language, and numismatics is how few were its demonstrable links with Ireland in the Viking Age. It was the southernmost of the *suðreyjar*: it seems especially to have looked north during this period. Settlement is therefore the principal issue, but also of importance is the reorientation of Mann's previous connections with Wales and Ireland.

In Viking Age Irish history the issues are, in general, much more sharply defined than in Scottish history, and there is (as we have seen) a substantial body of evidence on which to draw. The question which has remained at centre-stage throughout has been vikings' effects on the Church (Hughes 1966:197-237 and 1967). To what extent did they damage religious life and traditions of ecclesiastical art and learning? Did their attacks on ecclesiastical settlements materially impoverish the Church? Did they have unique responsibility for the plundering and burning of churches (Lucas 1967; Hughes 1972:148-59; Etchingham 1996)? Did such humiliation of Ireland's saints lead to widespread disrespect for the Church on the part of the native population? When, if ever, did vikings in Ireland convert to Christianity (Abrams 1997)? Are the visible changes in ecclesiastical settlement patterns between the eighth century and the eleventh the result of Scandinavian intervention? Scholars have more or less abandoned discussion of whether the linguistic changes visible in Irish in the tenth century are to be attributed to social and political upheaval. The view that the extensive Old Irish law tracts contained evidence for significant, even radical, social change in the ninth century (Binchy 1962) has been abandoned as a result of redatings of the relevant texts (cf. Charles-Edwards 1980), and the question whether or not viking activity caused social change has not been revisited. The important role of Scandinavian settlers and traders in the development of Irish urban life and the consequent broadening of the economy is universally acknowledged, but there is dispute as to whether an urban society had been developing at major ecclesiastical settlements prior to and during the Viking Age.

The effects of vikings' intervention on the Irish polity are contested. The mobility of viking warfare may have both inspired Irish kings (probably only overkings) to develop the institutions necessary to respond in kind and invited military commanders to think of effective local countermeasures to reduce vikings' ability to move freely. To what extent did vikings' military activities therefore provide a model for or encouragement to inter-provincial warfare? To what extent did viking behaviour generally increase the level of violence in Irish society? What were the effects of some Irish rulers eventually finding it convenient to make alliances with viking leaders? What was the nature of treaty-making with vikings in Ireland (cf. Lund 1987 and Dumville 1992, ch. I, on treaties)?

A question not often asked nowadays is how near vikings came to dominating Ireland by their military campaigns. This silence results largely from the discrediting of the relevance of the portrayal of viking activities and achievements in *Cocad Gaedel re Gallaib* to the conditions of the First Viking Age. However, there is other evidence for Scandinavian domination of Ireland in the late 840s (Dumville 1997a:56-7) and the question might usefully be debated again. This in turn leads to the question of vikings' intentions in Ireland, a subject which has long since ceased to be a live issue (cf. Smyth 1977:143). However, whether conquest was intended but frustrated or never attempted is an important matter, as is the corollary of intention to colonize. The nature of such Scandinavian rural settlement as can be identified has begun to be discussed again in the last few years (Bradley 1988; Etchingham 1994). Two questions which have received no discussion are the size (and number) of viking armies in Ireland and the extent to which vikings' assaults on secular settlements took place, both of which issues have loomed large in discussions of other countries' history.

In Viking Age Wales one has first to find one's vikings. The most basic question for the First Viking Age is how much contact vikings had with Wales (Loyn 1976 for a survey). That there was significant activity along the north and south coasts seems certain and understandable in view of viking activities in Ireland and England. A little toponymic and growing archaeological evidence may be held to suggest some settlement in north-west and south-west (Redknap 2000). Whether the development of viking power had any effect on the growth of the power of the Second Dynasty of Gwynedd in Wales remains uncertain. Conflict between them can be seen in the reign of Rhodri Mawr (844-78) (Mac Airt & Mac Niocaill 1983:314-15 [856.6]): indeed, towards the end of his reign, Rhodri had to flee from vikings to Ireland; after he returned he was killed in battle with a Mercian (English) army acting as proxies for their viking overlords (Mac Airt & Mac Niocaill 1983:332/3 [877.3, 878.1]). Probably from 878 to the early 890s the Venedotian dynasty was 'allied' with the vikings of York. This looks like determination by the Dublin-York dynasty to control northern Wales. After the (temporary) expulsion of the vikings from Dublin in 902 (Mac Airt & Mac Niocaill 1983:352/3 [902.2]), according to the rather unsatisfactory 'Fragmentary Annals of Ireland' (Radner 1978:166-73, 180-3) Uí Hímair attempted settlement in Anglesey and then in the Wirral, presumably remaining there until they re-established themselves at Dublin in 917 (Mac Airt & Mac Niocaill 1983:366/7 [917.2-4]). On the whole, hostility between Welsh and vikings is apparent, and the extraordinary Anglo-Welsh alliance which was generally maintained from 878/893 to 1016 seems to have been fuelled by a shared hostility towards viking power: it is striking that that alliance ended when a Danish king succeeded to the English throne. It would be generally agreed that the centuries-old hostility of English and Welsh was tamed by the sense of a common threat: by the time when the threat had subsided with the English conquest of the Danelaw, on the one hand the English government was sufficiently strong to keep the Welsh kings in line, and on the other viking raids on Wales resumed after 960. For the next two centuries, Wales, faced with Scandinavian rule in Mann and Irish coastal towns, suffered from repeated viking incursions, on some occasions encouraged by internal Welsh rivalries for power (Maund 1991); it has even been argued that, for a time in the late tenth and early eleventh centuries in Wales, native government wholly broke down (Davies 1990).

In Cornish history, the essential question concerning the First Viking Age is not of settlement or effects on the Church (for lack of evidence as much as anything else) but of the extent to which viking activity provoked the kings of Wessex rapidly to bring Cornwall under their complete domination for fear of leaving themselves exposed to a newly powerful assault from the west. Only in the Second Viking Age do we find clear evidence of Cornwall being exposed to the ravages of Scandinavian forces ('Anglo-Saxon Chronicle', 981C, 997CDE: Whitelock 1961, 1979).

In English Viking Age history the dominant evidential forms have proved to be annalistic and toponymic. In the last generation the questions posed by Peter Sawyer (1957/8; 1962) have driven the scholarly agenda. The principal issues have been five in number. (i) The reliability of even contemporary narrative sources for the First Viking Age has been in question. (ii) The size of viking armies has been much debated. (iii) The nature and extent of Scandinavian settlement in England, formerly determined in large part by toponymic evidence, has been in question, calling into doubt the reliability of such evidence and modes of interpretation (Lund 1981a). While now in most Danelaw-counties there is a very high level of

Scandinavianization of place-names, right down to the level of field-names, it has been disputed whether this can be taken as a manifestation of extensive Scandinavian colonization. Since the Old-English dialects of Danelaw-counties were affected by the Old Norse of the settler-population, that Scandinavian linguistic element of English dialects has had centuries to penetrate the local toponymy: there is no straightforward correlation between extent of Scandinavian toponymy in modern times and extent of Scandinavian settlement in the late ninth and early tenth centuries. This issue problematizes another: (iv) what was the ethnic balance between English and Scandinavians in the areas of colonization and, consequently also, (v) what effect did settlement have on social structure? It has been argued that preconceived and unjustifiable notions of the structure of English society before 850 have caused further misinterpretations of the effects of Scandinavian settlement. Of these issues, those of the nature and social consequences of colonization have emerged as those for which the evidence is most difficult to handle. Nevertheless, scholars have in general concluded that viking armies were much larger than Sawyer sought to suggest (cf. Brooks 1979) and that a larger-scale settlement did take place in the Danelaw once military control had been established. The latter point remains hotly contested, however (cf. Hadley 1996c for recent discussion).

The political dimensions of the subject have not received major reconsideration since 1979, but neither have all of Smyth's conclusions on such matters been fully integrated into received wisdom. 'The Anglo-Saxon Chronicle' still provides the main narrative focus, even though it is clear that much is omitted from its account: the chronicler's concern from 865 with the struggles for control of large kingdoms and with a small number of armies on which a sharp focus is maintained ensures that. This is a (partisan) military and political record. Perhaps as a result, there has been little study of the quantity and effects of destruction caused by viking armies; until very recently (Dumville 1992, ch. II and 1997b; Foot 1991; Hadley 1996a and 1996b) the effects on the Church have been rather glossed over, the economic issues, except the Scandinavian contributions to trade and urban life, have been sidelined. Beyond what is found in 'The Anglo-Saxon Chronicle' little has been said about the intentions of viking armies and, even more surprisingly, little that is new has been written about the reasons for vikings' successes and failures. Their successes seem to have been most spectacular in England: but these had a politically catalytic rather than conclusive character, for within a century the outcome was West Saxon conquest of viking kingdoms.

This quick survey of the countries of the Viking Age British Isles and the issues which have loomed largest in their historiography has provided a very varied set of questions. One is bound to ask at once whether these reflect the different interactions of vikings with the various peoples whom they assaulted or whether they are instead reflections of the different types of source available. It is very clear that lack of appropriate sources is a major problem for the historian in respect of many of the questions which (s)he would ask. In principle, this means that many questions about the history of the Viking Age in the British Isles cannot be answered—at least from the written evidence. One cannot, after all, write history without sources of information—or can one?

A few points about the source-problems will display some of the possibilities. In Ireland the ecclesiastical chronicles have strict criteria of relevance (which viking activities, by their very novelty, force open somewhat; Dumville 1990, ch. XVII) and concentrate very heavily on vikings' interaction with the Church. In England, on the other hand, 'The Anglo-Saxon Chronicle', the central narrative source, is concerned with high politics, strategy, and the clash of major armies. Consequently Irish historians have given no serious consideration to whether secular high-status sites were attacked by vikings or to what vikings' strategic aims might have been in relation to native secular rulers. On the other hand, English historians have concentrated on the role of viking rulers and their armies as conquerors of their native opponents and have given almost no detailed attention to the interaction of vikings and the Church both in what became the Danelaw (for an exception see Morris 1977 and 1981) and in the territories which they failed to conquer, except for the initial raids on either side of 800.

The high level of systematic study and exploitation of toponymic evidence in England has ensured that it has loomed large in discussion of English Viking Age history and that settlement has been high on the list of topics discussed. The lack of comparably systematic work in relation to the Celtic-speaking countries (except Cornwall: Padel 1985) and the always English-speaking parts of southeastern Scotland has ensured that no comparable discussions could take place concerning those areas (but cf. Fellows-Jensen 1983, 1985, 1991).

The complete absence of contemporary written evidence for the Scandinavian take-over of the Northern Isles and the near-complete absence for the Western Isles has allowed arguments to be mounted from highly uncertain interpretations of archaeological evidence that the Scandinavian arrival there was essentially peaceful (see discussion by Ritchie 1974 and I. A. Crawford 1974 and 1981). If that was indeed so, the phenomenon was unique among all the regions of the British Isles.

In sum, the possibility opens before us that a composite picture of viking activity across the British Isles might be created by aggregating the experiences of the various parts of the Insular world—by creating a comprehensive model able to be applied across this region as a basis for discussion and further work which could then modify the general picture in the light of particular local circumstances. Occasionally a preemptive strike has been launched against any such attempt to generalize or create a composite picture (see, for example, Morris 1982:70-1, and Hall 1994:44). However, such is the nature of the source-problem that this approach must, I think, be attempted. What would a composite picture look like?

We do not know how the Viking Age began in the British Isles, unless it began at Lindisfarne in 793, which does not seem very probable. If it began in the Northern Isles at some point in the second half of the eighth century, it seems likely to have done so with great force—on the evidence of effective cultural replacement there (Wainwright 1962; I. A. Crawford 1981)—delivered from

Norway. That would permit the possibility that the earliest recorded phase of viking activity, from 793, originated from the Northern Isles or was mediated thence: evidence for some English and other Insular goods finding their way back to Norway in this period (Skaare 1976:39-47, 117; Wamers 1983; 1985; cf. Blindheim 1978, but the main thrust of her argument is unacceptable) must keep Norway in the picture.

The raids of the first visible generation (790s-820s) could have been carried out by a few ships' crews, but there are sufficient hints that many more were involved, especially when one looks to *Francia* and its relationships with Denmark (Vogel 1906; cf. Keary 1891 for the only full-length treatment in English). The raids which we see were directed towards plunder and profit—towards negotiable commodities. These included 'precious metals and jewels, live human bodies, and (with increasing understanding of the societies attacked) other valuables (especially of a religious character) which might be ransomed. While vikings' involvement in slave trading (as urged by Smyth 1977:154-68; cf. P. Anderson 1974: 173-8) has proved controversial (Lund 1981b:32-3; Holm 1986; Karras 1988), the taking of human prey for personal satisfaction or amusement and for ransom is not to be overlooked. We might remind ourselves of an Irish chronicler's report of an event in 821:

> *Orggan Étir ó genntibh: præd mór di mnáibh do brid ass.*
> Plundering of Howth [Co. Dublin] by heathens; a great booty of women was carried off by them (Mac Airt & Mac Niocaill 1983:276 [821.3]; my trans.).

This is unlikely to have been a unique event.

The softest targets were smallish coastal and island-sites, especially monasteries. Hit-and-run operations were easiest and the element of surprise was very much present. Around the northern and western coasts of Scotland in particular vikings were encountering a hitherto flourishing monastic thalassocracy (Dumville 1997b). Documentary evidence from southern England in the first quarter of the ninth century allows us to measure some of the nervousness which vikings' presence had generated and to understand that even at this stage the invaders had been building forts in the course of their operations, which local rulers were at pains to destroy (Sawyer 1968: nos. 1264, 168, 177, 186). In southern Britain and in Ireland viking activity no doubt had a damaging but not crippling effect on the institutions and places attacked: if matters had not gone further, this would have been a passing episode of no great significance. In northern Britain, however, matters had gone further: not only had the Northern Isles been transformed culturally, but in this next generation conquest had proceeded into the Western Isles and to the very edge of historical record. The process was presumably mixed: in some places the shock of assault was no doubt as great as farther north (I. A. Crawford 1974 on Udal, North Uist; cf. Mac Airt & Mac Niocaill 1983:250/1 [794-7, 795.3], 258/9 [802.9], 262/3 [806.8]) but there is no possibility that it had the same overall effect, for the result of Scandinavian conquest and settlement within the Western Isles was the creation of a culturally hybrid society (which, by the end of the ninth century, was exporting that hybridity elsewhere).

By 812 vikings had reached both southernmost England and Ireland (Mac Airt & Mac Niocaill 1983:268/9 [812.11]). Their fortunes were mixed. Even this phase of uncontrolled raiding and probing, however, contained within itself a conquest— this time of the Western Isles. No generation was to pass without further conquests being added. In other words, there is no phase of simple raiding discoverable when viking activity is looked at as a whole; but some areas did experience that as a preliminary to more vigorous and comprehensive assaults.

In these years down to 830 we must imagine word going round the Scandinavian world about the opportunities to be had among the Christians. The whole of western Europe was no doubt being described as a region ripe for plunder (cf. Lund 1989); what the Franks had been doing to pagans for three centuries was now about to be repaid.

From the 830s onwards we see more sustained attacks being mounted by viking forces in Ireland and southern Britain. In England the attackers are sometimes described as Danes. We find these groups beginning to winter in British (and Continental) estuaries and on Irish lakes. Attacks begin on unfortified coastal urban trading centres in England (for example, Southampton) and in *Francia*. We see the beginnings of establishment of various kinds of permanent settlement— Dublin in 841 is perhaps one of the earliest (Mac Airt & Mac Niocaill 1983:298/9 [841.4]). There were more frequent and more serious raids on ecclesiastical settlements, with the raiders still in search of the same negotiable goods. Tribute-taking begins to be recorded (see especially Joranson 1923). The natives were still often disorganized, but some response is visible in respect of the fortification of church-settlements and secular centres. We find evidence for the sophistication of vikings' exploitation of estate-centres in the course of military campaigns (Brooks & Graham-Campbell 1986).

It has been argued that depopulation of towns in the ninth century was due to viking activities (Wallace-Hadrill 1975:13-18). It is more difficult to measure effects in the countryside. If rural regions also became unsafe, were they increasingly unable to produce surpluses? As attacks on estate- or manorial centres, be these ecclesiastical or secular, became critical, significant disruption of the economy (and perhaps of social relations) would have occurred. We have to consider what happened to the dependent peasantry when a monastery (for example) ceased to exist (Wallace-Hadrill 1975:15-16; Dumvilie 1992, ch. II). A question which Insular sources barely hint at, but which Frankish texts give fuller coverage, is that of refugees—a topic barely studied in the mediaeval context.

In Ireland the principal struggles for control seem to have taken place in the 830s and 840s. If we can credit a report in 'The Annals of Saint-Bertin' for 847, that year seems to have marked the high point of viking successes in Ireland, with widespread tribute-paying by native rulers. But the following year, attested by both the same Frankish chronicle and Irish chronicles, seems to have seen a highly successful fight back by the natives (Dumville 1997a:56-7). When in 849 a rival body of vikings appeared in Ireland with a force of 140 ships (Mac Airt & Mac Niocaill 1983:308/9 [849.6]) and in 851 assaulted Dublin and Annagassan (Linn Duachaill) (Mac Airt & Mac Niocaill 1983:310/11 [851.3]) they were attacking an already weakened force: it is precisely at this time that we first see alliances between vikings and native rulers (Mac Airt & Mac Niocaill 1983:308/9 [850.3], but cf. 1983:310/11 [851.2] for the *dénouement*) and natives beginning to behave *more gentilium* (Mac Airt & Mac Niocaill 1983:306/7 [847.3]). When in 853 the famous Amlaíb (Óláfr) arrived in Ireland, 'the foreigners [that is, Scandinavians] of Ireland submitted to him' and then he took 'tribute from the Irish' (Mac Airt & Mac Niocaill 1983:312/13 [853.2]). Over the next twenty years, Dublin was made the principal locus of Scandinavian activity in Ireland (until Óláfr was killed in Pictland in 872 [Miller 1999]) and Ímar/Ívarr, *rex Nordmannorum totius Hibernie et Brittanie*, died in 873 [Mac Airt & Mac Niocaill 1983:328-9, 873.3]) but from the mid-860s the focus of its rulers' interest had shifted to Britain.

The next generation, then, was to see the intention to conquer shifted to Strathclyde, Pictland, Gwynedd, and the English kingdoms. This is not to say that areas other than Ireland had been ignored in the previous generation—the pattern of raiding is detectable across Britain, and sometimes quite large battles were fought—but (at least within the British Isles) there does seem to be a pattern of new targets in each generation. Through the ninth century, in each of the constituent countries of the British Isles, we see attempts by Scandinavians to take control. In the end the Irish were perhaps saved from domination by this shift in vikings' interest, as much as by fighting among Scandinavians in Ireland and the chaotic quality of Irish native politics, whose military manifestations continued throughout the Viking Age.

We should, I think, consider this intention to take control as the normal development of viking activities. Had the various groups of invaders been uniformly successful, we should have seen a Scandinavian Ireland, Britain, western and northern *Francia*, a sort of Scandinavian 'empire'. And this is to say nothing of settlement, if by that we mean the installation of a Scandinavian peasantry, as well as a military nobility, on the land (Lund 1981a; I. A. Crawford 1981; cf. Musset 1975). In the ninth and earlier tenth centuries this control would typically have meant suppression of native dynasties or, in the first instance, the installation of quisling members of native lines; the suppression of many churches, perhaps especially monasteries, and the division of their lands among the invaders' leaders; at best a very hard time for Christianity (especially if we were to pick up the suggestion that a self-conscious paganism developed in opposition to the Christianity of the native ruling classes—Wallace-Hadrill 1975:12-13; but cf. Coupland 1991). Scandinavian control would have remained essentially military control during this period.

We should expect to see a new pattern of trade links developed by the newly dominant group—this is particularly marked in Ireland—but also the exploitation of existing trade relationships. The range of these networks is displayed by many different wares, but is particularly noticeable in respect of coinage. The arrival of

Arabic coinage in the British Isles is one feature. So too is the appearance of significant quantities of coin (especially English) in the non-monetary economies of the Insular Celts (but cf. Gerriets 1985 on Ireland).

We recognize the development or intensification of some spirit of patriotism—perhaps fuelled too by religion—on the part of peoples attacked, the recognition of a distinction between 'us' and 'them', the familiar and the unfamiliar. We find racial hatred clearly expressed too (Page 1987). But wherever we have records, we also find some natives deeming it to be in their interest to join the invaders, whether temporarily or on a more permanent basis.

In areas where Scandinavians achieved a long-term presence, we see cultural hybridization taking place—in language, less certainly in literature, in art, and in social customs. Except in the Northern Isles, we see the development of bilingualism, although in the case of the bilingual, bicultural *Gallgoídil* of the Western Isles bilingualism was exported at the expense of indigenous languages and cultures in some of the areas to which they spread (notably Mann and Galloway).

Consequent on all the foregoing, we find changes in the polities of the countries attacked—the collapse or near-collapse of kingdoms, followed (where complete collapse was averted) by reorganization and (in varying degrees) by recovery. In other words, vikings brought political change, sometimes straightforwardly decisive and long-term in character, sometimes catalytic and less predictable in its results.

Plainly, the degree to which all these factors eventuated varied with the individual circumstances of the kingdom, region, or country attacked. But it seems sensible to me to deduce that vikings' intentions within a given period were more or less constant and therefore predictable. This is given added point by Alfred Smyth's demonstration that in the British Isles (and to some extent in *Francia*) one small group of leaders was active throughout the area from about 850. The deduction does not rest on this (and these Dublin-based vikings were certainly not the only group active at that time) but to the extent that a single group (and perhaps family) was responsible for such widespread military and political activity we may anticipate a certain homogeneity of intention and action. I argue, therefore, that, where we are considering Scandinavian intentions (and to some extent, accordingly, behaviour) in the British Isles in this period, we find ourselves dealing with a more or less uniform factor—but we must remember that vikings' resources did not always match their intentions. It was rather the response of the natives attacked by vikings which was a variable, yet, where the indigenes were beaten down militarily, again certain predictable results would occur.

Lack of sources, or insufficiently exploited sources, should not then, I think, be a bar to an attempt to understand the Viking Age. While we struggle with artificially fragmented sources, we are fighting with one arm tied behind our backs, and unnecessarily so.

This model will enable us to say, for example, that—in spite of our lack of sources telling us of attacks on English churches after 835—in England vikings were the cause of the monastic (and, in some places, general ecclesiastical) collapse visible by 890. We shall not then be able to be seduced by Peter Sawyer's assertion that monasteries disappeared in a mere half-century because the English lost interest in monasticism.

Likewise, we shall doubt that vikings learned from the Irish the habit of plundering churches (Morris 1978/9:182) but shall rather agree with F. J. Byrne (1973:212) that 'the frequency of lay attacks upon religious houses was a product of the [v]iking wars'. We shall also be unlikely to allow that Irish secular settlements were not normally attacked by vikings, or that there was no attempt to gain military control in Ireland.

We shall find it hard to allow that there was peaceful settlement in the Northern Isles, in the (secondary) settlement in the Western Isles, or (in the third phase of that movement) in Mann, Galloway, and Cumbria (and perhaps, on the Continent, in the Cotentin).

We shall suspect that vikings (and in this case the vikings of Dublin) did indeed attempt to gain control in Gwynedd (and in some measure succeeded) and perhaps more generally in Wales. It is unlikely that they went to the trouble of a four-month siege of Dumbarton in 870, only to leave the kingdom of Strathclyde alone once they had succeeded in taking its capital. And their campaigning in Alba in the same period is unlikely to have been simply a series of booty-seizing expeditions.

How the Churches of the British Isles reacted pastorally to the presence of heathen Scandinavians in their jurisdictions is a question which has been asked, but not insistently enough and never (I think) in relation to the whole area. Conversion of the viking dynasty of Dublin did not apparently begin for a century and was then a result of the activities of Uí Hímair in England (Abrams 1997). How long it took for Dublin and its kingdom, rather than just its ruler, to become Christian remains unknown, as does the progress of conversion in the other, smaller Scandinavian enclaves. In relation to Mann and the Western Isles it has been speculated that conversion was rapid, but the case remains to be made in detail and that will be particularly difficult for some of the Hebridean islands where generalization will be especially dangerous. And the rest of Scotland presents a wide range of problems. In England numismatic evidence begins to provide testimony to the christianization of the Danelaw. But already in the south we find that there must have been uncertainty and debate about whether and how to proceed with missionary endeavour. Somehow the moral strength and energy were found to undertake the task—and just in time, it seems, for a fierce letter from Pope Formosus (datable 891/896) indicated that ignoring the problem would bring sanctions (Dumville 1992, ch. VI). External contact in this case brought endorsement and encouragement. Perhaps the same message was coming from *Francia* (Nelson 1997) where the problem had been addressed, but in not wholly similar circumstances. In any case, we should be most unwise to suppose that the problem had not been discussed across the Channel, both between churchmen and between kings. But should we make the same assumptions about Ireland?

The outstanding problem is settlement (cf. Lund 1981a on numbers and their detection): it has come to seem increasingly unlikely that Scandinavians settled in overwhelming numbers anywhere other than in the Northern Isles, just possibly in parts of the Western Isles and Galloway, and in Mann. Only there was there cultural change on such a scale that that conclusion would be justified. The precise reasons for this variation remain to be discovered.

More generally, we need to know whether there is an identifiable point of transition in the colonies, among the population of Scandinavian origin, from being vikings to being thoroughly settled.

It might be argued that, within the First Viking Age, the settlers within what became the kingdom of England lost their inclination (and perhaps even ability) to conduct viking expeditions once they had been securely incorporated within a fundamentally native political unit. In England, that position had not been achieved until the reign of Edgar (957-75): only with the effective termination of the Dublin Uí Hímair dynasty's attempts to rule in England was that certain (for a useful outline chronology see Smyth 1978; for the last king, see Downham 2003), although whether the Scandinavian population of the Southern Danelaw had been involved in any viking expeditions since 920 must be held to be very doubtful (cf. Lund 1981a:154, 170 n. 45 on an episode of the mid-910s). That the population of Scandinavian origin in the Danelaw was suddenly going to revert to viking behaviour in the context of the Second Viking Age must be held very doubtful: by that stage (and indeed already in the 940s, one might think) it was a question of the giving or withholding of political allegiance which was the crucial issue, rather than reversion to the lifestyle of grandparents (and increasingly distant ancestors, however appealingly heroic).

On the other hand, in what would eventually become the duchy of Normandy, the situation was very different (Bates 1982 for a survey). However gallicized the settler-population might become, the political unit was one ruled by descendants of the original viking settlers. The position was complicated by the existence of more than one settled group: in particular, the settlers in the Cotentin—some at least of whom, on the onomastic evidence, were *Gallgoídil* (Musset 1975:47-9)—had taken control of what had been until the 910s part of the kingdom of Brittany (the county and diocese of Coutances were within *Noua Britannia* which had been taken by the Bretons from the Franks in the time of King Salomon in the ninth century [Smith 1991]) and seem not to have been part of the process by which Hrólfr/Rollo gained his settlement around Rouen; these groups were not easily reconciled to one another and incorporated within a single political unit. Connections with Scandinavia and with other Scandinavian colonies were maintained and support was given to viking groups even in the eleventh century. The transition from patterns of viking behaviour was not, therefore, simply a function of settlement; loss of political independence was also a prerequisite. The history of the Scandinavian colonies in Ireland might equally be interpreted thus.

Some general rules about viking behaviour in the period 790-960 in the British Isles may therefore, I submit, be formulated. What this comparative and combinatory approach tends to do is, among other things, to challenge some of those views first advanced in the decade from 1958 and which have subsequently become dogma. These have relied in part on some rather implausible challenges to primary sources but above all on absence of evidence. What is next needed is to confront my proposed model with the evidence from the Frankish world (and Spain [Sánchez-Albornoz 1968]) and with vikings' eastward activities in the Baltic lands, Russia, and beyond.

When the focus is widened to include *Francia*, further questions come into view. The reactions of ecclesiastical communities to the viking threat might involve flight with the relics of their founders (for recent reconsideration of this in relation to Normandy, see Lifshitz 1992, 1995a, 1995b). Narratives of such translations have a long history on the Continent and there are those which are historically dubious. But the question—once put—whether such relic-flights (or subsequent forcible captures from vikings' territory) occurred in the British Isles must receive an affirmative answer: the issue has not, however, been studied and narratives are few. Churches in areas which might be attacked, but which had not been settled, by vikings might react to the threat by seeking a lay patron (if they did not already have one) or a lay abbot: this phenomenon has attracted much more attention in relation to the Continent (cf. Felten 1979) than to the British Isles; to what extent did Insular churches react thus? In Ireland we can observe a widespread practice of ecclesiastical pluralism in the Viking Age. It is not known, but has sometimes been suspected, to be another type of reaction to newly troubled circumstances.

When the consequences of viking activities for ecclesiastical culture across the Carolingian and sub-Carolingian worlds can be rated severely (see some pointed comments by Wormald 1976, reviewing Löwe 1973; cf. Riché 1968), the conventional interpretation of the phenomenon in England, Scotland, and Ireland (Wales seems to have suffered severely only in the Second Viking Age) does not seem at all threatened or in need of support. The near-collapse of latinate culture in England (cf. Gneuss 1984 and 1986; Lapidge 1996:409-54), Scotland, and perhaps Ireland (but cf. Sharpe 1991) can be seen as a facet of vikings' impact on the whole range of the Church's activities.

Students of viking activity in *Francia* have on the whole been less willing to allow revision of the received image of viking activity (despite an invitation by d'Haenens 1967, 1968, and 1970; cf. Zettel 1977), not least because of the sheer quantity of information available and the fewer gaps in the record by comparison with the Insular situation. Alfred, king of Wessex (see Abels 1998), was to write (in the 890s) of the situation in his kingdom before 871 as 'before everything was ravaged and burned'; so too, Frankish bishops assembled in synod at Pîtres in 862 could say in their first *capitulum* that (summary by Coupland 1991:537; for text see Boretius & Krause 1881-97: II.302-10 [no. 272] at p. 304)

> the land was being laid waste because the people had destroyed the fruits of faith, hope and love; the inhabitants were being killed because they themselves had slain with the sword of sin; churches were being burned because the fires of iniquity were

blazing within; the relics of the saints were being taken away because the Franks had driven out the Holy Spirit, and the servants of God were being forced to flee their monasteries because they had failed to put the evil one to flight.

Both the Frankish bishops in 862 and Alfred a generation later sought to interrogate their own societies' behaviour to discover why God had chosen to scourge his people with vikings. The first principle of such analyses will not appeal to everyone today. But the given, the facts, which encouraged such analysis, were the terror and the destruction which vikings had brought (cf. Wallace-Hadrill 1975; Foot 1991). They affected both laity and ecclesiastics; they were not figments of religious imagination. There were two further causes for grief. We discussed at our first colloquium (*apud* Ausenda 1994:213-15) the kind of 'metaphorical bind' (Ian Wood's words) in which Christians might find themselves when confronted by 'the scourge of God': what could one justifiably do or even hope to do in such a situation? This must have affected attitudes towards evangelizing vikings. Secondly, as Timothy Reuter has put it, with unkind perceptiveness (but also some exaggeration), "we forget that for most of Europe in the eighth and ninth centur[ies] it was the Franks who were the [v]ikings" (1985:91). In other words, the Christian plunderers were now suffering heathen depredations. But this perception will not work in the British Isles. While the role of plunder in Insular socioeconomics was also of great importance, there in the early Middle Ages it was generally Christians (and commonly Christians of the same ethnic group) who were plundering one another. They cannot be said to have provoked Scandinavian retaliation. And viking plundering was of a rather different character from their own local pursuits. There is no justification for saying that "In a brutal age the [v]ikings were brutal, but their brutality was no worse than that of their contemporaries" (D. M. Wilson, *apud* Graham-Campbell & Kidd 1980:7).

Whether at Lindisfarne or at Landévennec (Bardel & Pérennec 1996) churches were being attacked and ecclesiastics were being killed. These basic—if now often questioned—aspects of viking life were the same in England in the 790s or in Brittany in the 910s. Vikings reacted differently to different situations. It was difficult to conquer the Carolingian empire. Some accepted grants of land and office as buffers against other vikings (Goetz 1980, extended by Coupland 1998). But evidently it was possible to keep fleets and armies for long periods in the valleys of the Seine and Loire, to the extent indeed that contemporaries began to speak of 'the Loire vikings' and 'the Seine vikings', and eventually they did secure territory (just at the time when their confrères were losing control in England) (Searle 1985 and 1988:1-58). Here are differences and similarities which we need to study, and the comparisons can be extended farther afield. But there is an argument that vikings defined themselves, that there were certain important givens about their intentions and behaviour, and that we lose sight of these at our peril.

References

Textual sources:

Anglo-Saxon Chronicle: see Whitelock (trans.) 1961 & 1979.
Annales Cambriae: see Dumville (ed.) 2002a; 2002b.
Annals of Saint-Bertin: see Grat *et al.* (ed.) 1964; Nelson (trans.) 1991.
Cocad Gaedel re Gallaib: see Todd (ed. & trans.) 1867.
Council of Pîtres: see Boretius & Krause (eds.) 1890-97: II.302-10 [no. 272], p. 304.
Fragmentary Annals of Ireland: see Radner (ed. & trans.) 1978, O'Donovan (ed. & trans.)
        1860.
Rígspula: see Dronke (ed. & trans.) 1997:159-238.
Vita Sancti Findani: see Holder-Egger (ed.) 1887.

Bibliography:

Abels, R.
    1998   *Alfred the Great. War, Kingship and Culture in Anglo-Saxon England.*
              London: Longman.
Abrams, L.
    1997   The conversion of the Scandinavians of Dublin. *Anglo-Norman Studies* 20: 1-29.
Anderson, M. O.
    1980   *Kings and Kingship in Early Scotland.* Second edition. Edinburgh: Scottish
              Academic Press.
Anderson, P.
    1974   *Passages from Antiquity to Feudalism.* London: NLB.
Ausenda, G. (ed.)
    1994   *After Empire: Towards an Ethnology of Europe's Barbarians.* Woodbridge:
              The Boydell Press.
Axboe, M.
    1995   Danish kings and dendrochronology: archaeological insights into the early
              history of the Danish state. In *After Empire: Towards an Ethnology of
              Europe's Barbarians.* G. Ausenda (ed.), pp. 217-252. Woodbridge: The
              Boydell Press.
Bannerman, J.
    1974   *Studies in the History of Dalriada.* Edinburgh: Scottish Academic Press.
Bardel, A., & R. Pérennec
    1996   Les vikings à Landevennec. Les traces du "passage" des Normands en 913.
              Chronique de Landévennec (nouvelle série) 85: 32-40.
Barrow, G. W. S.
    1966   The Anglo-Scottish border. *Northern History* 1: 21-42.
    1973   *The Kingdom of Scots.* London: Edward Arnold.
Bartrum, P. C. (ed.)
    1966   *Early Welsh Genealogical Tracts.* Cardiff: University of Wales Press.
Bates, D.
    1982   *Normandy before 1066.* London: Longman.
Binchy, D. A.
    1962   The passing of the old order. *Proceedings of the International Congress of
              Celtic Studies held in Dublin, 1959.* B. Ó Cuív (ed.), pp. 119-132. Dublin:
              Dublin Institute for Advanced Studies. [Reissued in 1975: *The Impact of the
              Scandinavian Invasions on the Celtic-speaking Peoples, c. 800-1000 A.D.*,
              ed. B. Ó Cuív.]

Blindheim, C.
1978   Trade problems in the Viking Age. Some reflections on Insular metalwork
            found in Norwegian graves of the Viking Age. In *The Vikings*.
            T. Andersson & K. I. Sandred (eds.), pp. 166-176. Uppsala: Universitas
            Upsaliensis.
Boretius, A., & V. Krause (eds.)
1890-97   *Capitularia Regum Francorum*, 2. *Monumenta Germaniae Historica*.
            Hanover: Hahn.
Bradley, J.
1988   The interpretation of Scandinavian settlement in Ireland. In *Settlement and
            Society in Medieval Ireland. Studies presented to F. X. Martin, O.S.A.*
            J. Bradley (ed.), pp. 49-78. Kilkenny: Boethius Press.
Brooke, D.
1991   Gall-Gaidhil and Galloway. In *Galloway: Land and Lordship*. R. D. Oram
            & G. P. Stell (eds.), pp. 97-116. Edinburgh: Scottish Society for Northern
            Studies.
1994   *Wild Men and Holy Places. St Ninian, Whithorn and the Medieval Realm of
            Galloway*. Edinburgh: Canongate Press.
Brooks, N. P.
1979   England in the ninth century: the crucible of defeat. *Transactions of the
            Royal Historical Society* (5th series) 29: 1-20.
Brooks, N. P., & J. A. Graham-Campbell
1986   Reflections on the Viking-Age silver hoard from Croydon, Surrey. In
            Anglo-Saxon Monetary History. Essays in Memory of Michael Dolley. M. A.
            S. Blackburn (ed.), pp. 91-110. Leicester: Leicester University Press.
Bullough, D. A.
1993   What has Ingeld to do with Lindisfarne? *Anglo-Saxon England* 22: 93-125.
Byrne, F. J.
1973   *Irish Kings and High-kings*. London: Batsford.
Charles-Edwards, T. M.
1980   The *Corpus Iuris Hibernici*. *Studia Hibernica* 20: 141-62.
Coupland, S.
1991   The rod of God's wrath or the people of God's wrath? The carolingian theology
            of the viking invasions. *Journal of Ecclesiastical History* 2: 535-554.
1998   From poachers to gamekeepers: Scandinavian warlords and carolingian
            kings. *Early Medieval Europe* 7: 85-114.
Crawford, B. E.
1987   *Scandinavian Scotland*. Leicester: Leicester University Press.
1995 (ed.) *Scandinavian Settlement in Northern Britain*. London: Leicester University
            Press.
Crawford, I. A.
1974   Scot, Norseman and Gael. *Scottish Archaeological Forum* 6: 1-16.
1981   War or peace—viking colonisation in the Northern and Western Isles of
            Scotland reviewed. In *Proceedings of the Eighth Viking Congress. Århus,
            24-31 August 1977*. H. Bekker-Nielsen *et al.* (eds.), pp. 259-69. Odense:
            Odense University Press.
Davies, W.
1990   *Patterns of Power in Early Wales*. Oxford: Clarendon Press.
d'Haenens, A.
1967   *Les invasions normandes en Belgique au IXe siècle. Le phénomène et sa
            répercussion dans l'historiographie médiévale*. Louvain: Publications
            Universitaires.

1968   Les invasions normandes dans l'empire franc au IXe siècle. Pour une rénovation de la problématique. In *I Normanni e la loro espansione in Europa nell'alto medioevo*. (Atti delle Settimane di studio, XVI). Pp 233-298, 581-588. Spoleto: C.I.S.A.M.

1970   *Les invasions normandes, une catastrophe?* Paris: Flammarion.

Downham, C.

2000   An imaginary viking-raid on Skye in 795? *Scottish Gaelic Studies* 20: 192-196

2003   Eric Bloodaxe axed? The mystery of the last viking-king of York. *Mediaeval Scandinavia* 14: n.a.

Dronke, U. (ed. & trans.)

1997   *The Poetic Edda, II. Mythological Poems*. Oxford: Clarendon Press.

Dumville, D. N.

1986-9   Review of B. E. Crawford 1987. *Saga-book* 22: 463-468.

1990   *Histories and Pseudo-histories of the Insular Middle Ages*. Aldershot: Variorum.

1992   *Wessex and England from Alfred to Edgar*. Woodbridge: Boydell Press.

1993   *Britons and Anglo-Saxons in the Early Middle Ages*. Aldershot: Variorum.

1997a   *The Churches of North Britain in the First Viking-Age*. Whithorn: Friends of the Whithorn Trust.

1997b   *Three Men in a Boat. Scribe, Language and Culture in the Church of Viking-Age Europe*. Cambridge: Cambridge University Press.

1999   A millennium of Gaelic chronicling. In *The Medieval Chronicle*. E. Kooper (ed.), pp. 103-115. Amsterdam: Rodopi.

n.d.   Images of the viking in eleventh-century Latin literature. (Paper presented to the Third International Medieval Latin Congress, Cambridge, September 1998.) [Turnhout: Brepols, in press].

Dumville D. N. (ed. & trans.)

2002a   *Annales Cambriae, A. D. 682-954: Text A and C in Parallel*. Cambridge: Department of Anglo-Saxon, Norse & Celtic, University of Cambridge.

2002b   *Annales Cambriae, A. D. 955-1097: Text B and C in Parallel*. Cambridge: Department of Anglo-Saxon, Norse & Celtic, University of Cambridge.

Einarsson, B.

1986-9   De Normannorum atrocitate, or On the execution of royalty by the aquiline method. *Saga-book* 22: 79-82

Einarsson, B., & R. Frank

1990-3   The blood-eagle once more: two notes. *Saga-book* 23: 80-3.

Etchingham, C.

1994   Evidence of Scandinavian settlement in Wicklow. In *Wicklow—History and Society*. K. Hannigan & W. Nolan (eds.), pp. 113-138. Dublin: Geography Publications.

1996   *Viking Raids on Irish Church Settlements in the Ninth Century: a Reconsideration of the Annals*. Maynooth: St Patrick's College.

Fell, C.

1986   Old English *wicing*: a question of semantics. *Proceedings of the British Academy* 72: 295-316

Fellows-Jensen, G.

1983   Scandinavian settlement in the Isle of Man and north-west England: the place-name evidence. In *The Viking Age in the Isle of Man*. C. Fell *et al.* (eds.), pp. 37-52. London: Viking Society for Northern Research.

1984   Viking settlement in the Northern and Western Isles - the place-name evidence as seen from Denmark and the Danelaw. In *The Northern and Western Isles in the Viking World: Survival, Continuity and Change*. A. Fenton & H. Pálsson (eds.) pp. 148-168. Edinburgh: John Donald.

Fellows-Jensen, G. (*cont.*)
    1985   Scandinavian settlement in Cumbria and Dumfriesshire: the place-name evidence. In *The Scandinavians in Cumbria*. J. R. Baldwin & I. D. Whyte (eds.), pp. 65-82. Edinburgh: Scottish Society for Northern Studies.
    1991   Scandinavians in Dumfriesshire and Galloway: the place-name evidence. In *Galloway: Land and Lordship*. R. D. Oram & G. P. Stell (eds.), pp. 77-95. Edinburgh: Scottish Society for Northern Studies.
Felten, F. J.
    1979   *Äbte und Laienäbte im Frankenreich*. Stuttgart: Anton Hiersemann.
Foot, S.
    1991   Violence against christians? The vikings and the Church in ninth-century England. *Medieval History* 1 (3): 3-12.
Forsyth, K. S.
    1996   *The Ogham Inscriptions of Scotland: an Edited Corpus* (Ph.D. Dissertation, Harvard University). Ann Arbor, MI: UMI Dissertation Services.
Frank, R.
    1984   Viking atrocity and skaldic verse: the rite of the blood-eagle. *English Historical Review* 99: 332-43.
    1986-9   The blood-eagle again. *Saga-book* 22: 287-289.
Gerriets, M.
    1985   Money in early christian Ireland according to the Irish laws. *Comparative Studies in Society and History* 27: 323-339.
Gneuss, H.
    1984   Anglo-Saxon libraries from the Conversion to the Benedictine reform. In *Angli e Sassoni al di qua e al di là del mare*. (Atti delle Settimane di studio, XXXII). Pp. 643-699. Spoleto: C.I.S.A.M.
    1986   King Alfred and the history of Anglo-Saxon libraries. In *Modes of Interpretation of Old English Literature. Essays in Honour of Stanley Greenfield*. P. R. Brown *et al.* (eds.), pp. 29-49. Toronto: University of Toronto Press.
Goetz, H.-W.
    1980   Zur Landnahmepolitik der Normannen im fränkischen Reich. *Annalen des historischen Vereins für den Niederrhein* 183: 9-17.
Graham-Campbell, J.
    1994 (ed.) *Cultural Atlas of the Viking World*. Abingdon: Andromeda Oxford.
    1998   The early Viking Age in the Irish Sea area. In *Ireland and Scandinavia in the Early Viking-Age*. H. B. Clarke *et al.* (eds.), pp. 104-130. Dublin: Four Courts Press.
Graham-Campbell, J., & D. Kidd
    1980   *The Vikings*. London: British Museum Publications.
Graham-Campbell, J., *et al.*
    1995   *The Viking-Age Gold and Silver of Scotland (AD 850-1100)*. Edinburgh: National Museums of Scotland.
Grat, F., *et al.* (eds.)
    1964   *Les Annales de Saint-Bertin*. Paris: Publications de la Société de l'histoire de France
Hadley, D. M.
    1996a   Conquest, colonization and the Church: ecclesiastical organization in the Danelaw. *Historical Research* 69: 109-28.
    1996b   The vikings' relationship with christianity reconsidered. In *Church and People in Britain and Scandinavia*. I. Brohed (ed.), pp. 59-76. Lund: Lund University Press.

1996c   "And they proceeded to plough and support themselves": the Scandinavian settlement of England. *Anglo-Norman Studies* 19: 69-96.

Haliday, C.
1881   *The Scandinavian Kingdom of Dublin.* Dublin: M. H. Gill. (2nd edn, 1884; 3rd edn, Shannon: Irish University Press, 1969.)

Hall, R. A.
1994   Vikings gone west? A summary review. In *The Twelfth Viking Congress.* B. Ambrosiani & H. Clarke (eds.), pp. 32-49. Stockholm: Birka Project.

Haywood, J.
1995   *The Penguin Historical Atlas of the Vikings.* London: Penguin Books.

Herbert, M.
1988   *Iona, Kells, and Derry.* Oxford: Clarendon Press.

Hill, P., *et al.*
1996   *Whithorn and St Ninian. The Excavation of a Monastic Town, 1984-91.* Whithorn: Whithorn Trust.

Hødnebø, F.
1987   Who were the first vikings? In *Proceedings of the Tenth Viking Congress. Larkollen, Norway, 1985.* J. E. Knirk (ed.), pp. 43-54. Oslo: Universitetets Oldsaksamling.

Hodges, R., & D. Whitehouse
1983   *Mohammed, Charlemagne and the Origins of Europe. Archaeology and the Pirenne Thesis.* London: Duckworth.

Holder-Egger, O. (ed.)
1887   Vita Sancti Findani. In *Monumenta Germaniae Historica: Scriptores* [in folio], XV, 1. Georg Waitz *et al.* (eds.), pp. 502-506. Hanover: Hahn. [Repr. Anton Hiersemann, Stuttgart 1963.]

Holm, P.
1986   The slave trade of Dublin, ninth to twelfth centuries. *Peritia* 5: 317-345.

Hoskins, W. G.
1960   *The Westward Expansion of Wessex.* Leicester: Leicester University Press.

Hughes, K.
1966   *The Church in Early Irish Society.* London: Methuen.
1967   Introduction. To *A History of Medieval Ireland.* By A. J. Otway-Ruthven, pp. 1-33. London: Ernest Benn (2nd edn 1980). (Introduction reprinted Hughes 1987.)
1972   *Early Christian Ireland: Introduction to the Sources.* London: The Sources of History.
1980   *Celtic Britain in the Early Middle Ages. Studies in Scottish and Welsh Sources.* Woodbridge: The Boydell Press.
1987   *Church and Society in Ireland, 400-1200.* Northampton: Variorum.

Hunter Blair, P.
1963   Some observations on the *Historia Regum* attributed to Symeon of Durham. In *Celt and Saxon.* N. K. Chadwick (ed.), pp. 63-118. Cambridge: Cambridge University Press. (Rev. imp., 1964). [Paper reprinted Hunter Blair 1984].
1984   *Anglo-Saxon Northumbria.* London: Variorum.

Joranson, E.
1923   *The Danegeld in France.* Rock Island, IL: Augustana Library.

Karras, R. M.
1988   *Slavery and Society in Medieval Scandinavia.* New Haven, CT: Yale University Press.

Keary, C. F.
1891   *The Vikings in Western Christendom A.D. 789 to A.D. 888*. London:
            T. Fisher Unwin.
Kendrick, T. D.
1930   *A History of the Vikings*. London: Methuen.
Keynes, S., & M. Lapidge (trans.)
1983   *Alfred the Great. Asser's Life of King Alfred and Other Contemporary
            Sources*. Harmondsworth: Penguin Books.
Lapidge, M.
1996   *Anglo-Latin Literature 600-899*. London: Hambledon Press.
Lauer, P. (ed.)
1905   *Les Annales de Flodoard*. Paris: Alphonse Picard.
1940-9   *Recueil des actes de Charles III le Simple, roi de France (893-923)*. Paris:
            Imprimerie nationale.
Lifshitz, F.
1992   The 'exodus of holy bodies' reconsidered: the translation of the relics of St.
            Gildard of Rouen to Soissons. *Analecta Bollandiana* 110: 329-340.
1995a   The migration of Neustrian relics in the Viking Age: the myth of voluntary
            exodus, the reality of coercion and theft. *Early Medieval Europe* 4: 175-192.
1995b   *The Norman Conquest of Pious Neustria. Historiographic Discourse and
            Saintly Relics, 684-1090*. Toronto: Pontifical Institute of Mediaeval Studies.
Löwe, H.
1973   *Deutschlands Geschichtsquellen im Mittelalter, V. Die Karolinger vom
            Vertrag von Verdun bis zum Herrschaftsantritt der Herrscher aus dem
            sächsischen Hause: das Westfränkische Reich*. Weimar: Böhlau.
1985   Findan von Rheinau. Eine irische Peregrinatio im 9. Jahrhundert. *Studi
            medievali* (3rd series) 26: 53-100.
1986   Zur Überlieferungsgeschichte der Vita Findani. *Deutsches Archiv für
            Erforschung des Mittelalters* 42: 25-85.
Loyn, H.
1976   *The Vikings in Wales*. London: University College/Viking Society for
            Northern Research.
Lucas, A. T.
1967   The plundering and burning of churches in Ireland, 7th to 16th century. In
            *North Munster Studies—Essays in Commemoration of Monsignor Michael
            Moloney*. E. Rynne (ed.), pp. 172-229. Limerick: Thomond Archaeological
            Society.
Lund, N.
1981a   The settlers: where do we get them from—and do we need them? In
            Proceedings of the Eighth Viking Congress, Århus, 24-31 August 1977.
            H. Bekker-Nielsen *et al.* (eds.), pp. 147-71. Odense: Odense University Press.
1981b   Viking Age society in Denmark—evidence and theories. In *Danish
            Medieval History, New Currents*. N. Skyum-Nielsen & N. Lund (eds.),
            pp. 22-35. Copenhagen: Museum Tusculanum Press.
1987   Peace and non-peace in the Viking Age - Ottar in Biarmaland, the Rus in
            Byzantium, and Danes and Norwegians in England. In *Proceedings of
            the Tenth Viking Congress. Larkollen, Norway, 1985*. J. E. Knirk (ed.),
            pp. 255-269. Oslo: Universitetets Oldsaksamling.
1989   Allies of God or man? The viking expansion in a European perspective.
            Viator 20: 45-59.

Mac Airt, S., & G. Mac Niocaill (eds. & trans.)
 1983 *The Annals of Ulster to A.D. 1131*, I. Dublin: Dublin Institute for Advanced Studies.
Macalister, R. A. S.
 1945/9 *Corpus inscriptionum Insularum Celticarum*, 2 vols. Dublin: Stationery Office.
McDonald, R. A.
 1997 *The Kingdom of the Isles. Scotland's Western Seaboard c. 1100 - c. 1336.* East Linton: Tuckwell Press.
Mac Niocaill, G.
 1975 *The Medieval Irish Annals.* Dublin: Dublin Historical Association.
McTurk, R. W.
 1974-7 Review of Smyth 1975. *Saga-book* 19: 471-476.
 1978-81 Review of Smyth 1977. *Saga-book* 20: 231-234.
Maund, K. L.
 1991 *Ireland, Wales, and England in the Eleventh Century.* Woodbridge: The Boydell Press.
 1994 'A turmoil of warring princes': political leadership in ninth-century Denmark. *The Haskins Society Journal* 6: 29-47.
Miller, M.
 1999 Amlaíb trahens centum. *Scottish Gaelic Studies* 19: 241-245.
Morris, C. D.
 1977 Northumbria and the viking settlement: the evidence for land-holding. *Archaeologia Aeliana* (5th series) 5: 81-103.
 1978/9 The vikings and Irish monasteries. *Durham University Journal* 71: 175-185.
 1981 Viking and native in northern England. A case-study. In *Proceedings of the Eighth Viking Congress, Århus, 24-31 August 1977.* H. Bekker Nielsen *et al.* (eds.), pp. 223-244. Odense: Odense University Press.
 1982 The vikings in the British Isles: some aspects of their settlement and economy. In *The Vikings.* R. T. Farrell (ed.), pp. 70-94. Chichester: Phillimore.
Murphy, D. (ed.)
 1896 *The Annals of Clonmacnoise.* Dublin: Royal Society of Antiquaries of Ireland.
Musset, L.
 1975 Pour l'étude comparative de deux fondations politiques des vikings: le royaume d'York et le duché de Rouen. *Northern History* 10: 40-54.
Myhre, B.
 1993 The beginning of the Viking Age—some current archaeological problems. In *Viking Revaluations.* A. Faulkes & R. Perkins (eds.), pp. 182-216. London: Viking Society for Northern Research.
Nash-Williams, V. E.
 1950 *The Early Christian Monuments of Wales.* Cardiff: University of Wales Press.
Nelson, J. L.
 1978-81 Review of Smyth 1977. *Journal of the Society of Archivists* 6: 230-231.
 1997 '...*sicut olim gens Francorum...nunc gens Anglorum*': Fulk's letter to Alfred revisited. In *Alfred the Wise. Studies in Honour of Janet Bately on the Occasion of her Sixty-fifth Birthday.* J. Roberts *et al.* (eds.), pp. 135-144. Cambridge: D. S. Brewer.
Nelson, J. L. (trans.)
 1991 *The Annals of St Bertin.* Manchester: Manchester University Press.
Nicolaisen, W. F. H.
 1976 *Scottish Place-names.* London: Batsford.

Ní Mhaonaigh, M.
　　1995　　*Cogad Gáedel re Gallaib*: some dating considerations. *Peritia* 9: 354-377.
　　1996　　*Cogad Gáedel re Gallaib* and the annals: a comparison. *Ériu* 47: 101-126.
Ó Corráin, D.
　　1978/9　　High-kings, vikings and other kings. *Irish Historical Studies* 21: 283-323.
O'Donovan, J. (ed. & trans.)
　　1860　　*Annals of Ireland. Three Fragments, copied from Ancient Sources by Dubhaltach Mac Firbisigh*. Dublin: Irish Archaeological and Celtic Society.
Offler, H. S.
　　1958　　*Medieval Historians of Durham*. Durham: University of Durham.
Ó Máille, T.
　　1910　　*The Language of the Annals of Ulster*. Manchester: Manchester Univ. Press.
Oram, R. D.
　　1995　　Scandinavian settlement in south-west Scotland with a special study of Bysbie. In *Scandinavian Settlement in Northern Britain*. B. E. Crawford (ed.), pp. 127-140. London: Leicester University Press.
Padel, O. J.
　　1985　　*Cornish Place-name Elements*. Nottingham: English Place-name Society.
Page, R. I.
　　1982　　A tale of two cities. (Review of Smyth 1975/9.) *Peritia* 1: 335-351.
　　1987　　*'A Most Vile People': Early English Historians on the Vikings*. London: University College/Viking Society for Northern Research.
Pörnbacher, M. (ed. & trans.)
　　1997　　*Walahfrid Strabo, Zwei Legenden: Blathmac, der Martyrer von Iona (Hy); Mammes, der christliche Orpheus*. Sigmaringen: Jan Thorbecke Verlag.
Radner, J. N. (ed. & trans.)
　　1978　　*Fragmentary Annals of Ireland*. Dublin: Dublin Institute for Advanced Studies.
Randsborg, K.
　　1980　　*The Viking Age in Denmark. The Formation of a State*. London: Duckworth.
Redknap, M.
　　2000　　*Vikings in Wales. An Archaeological Quest*. Cardiff: National Museums and Galleries of Wales.
Reuter, T.
　　1985　　Plunder and tribute in the carolingian empire. *Transactions of the Royal Historical Society* (5th series) 35: 75-94.
　　1990　　The end of carolingian military expansion. In *Charlemagne's Heir. New Perspectives on the Reign of Louis the Pious (814-840)*. P. Godman & R. Collins (eds.), pp. 391-405. Oxford: Clarendon Press.
Riché, P.
　　1968　　Conséquences des invasions normandes sur la culture monastique dans l'Occident franc. In *I Normanni e la loro espansione in Europa nell'alto medioevo*. (Atti delle Settimane di studio, XVI). Pp 705-726. Spoleto: C.I.S.A.M.
Ritchie, A.
　　1974　　Pict and Norseman in northern Scotland. *Scottish Archaeological Forum* 6: 23-36.
Rivet, A. L. F., & C. Smith
　　1979　　*The Place-names of Roman Britain*. London: Batsford.
Roesdahl, E.
　　1982　　*Viking Age Denmark*. London: British Museum Publications.

1994   Dendrochronology and viking studies in Denmark, with a note on the beginning of the Viking Age. In *The Twelfth Viking Congress.* B. Ambrosiani & H. Clarke (eds.), pp. 106-116. Stockholm: Birka Project.

Rollason, D. W.
1978   Lists of saints' resting-places in Anglo-Saxon England. *Anglo-Saxon England* 7: 61-93.

Sánchez-Albornoz, C.
1968   Invasiones normandas a la España cristiana durante el siglo IX. In *I Normanni e la loro espansione in Europa nell'Alto Medioevo.* (Atti delle Settimane di studio, XVI). Pp. 367-408. Spoleto: C.I.S.A.M.

Sawyer, P. H.
1957/8   The density of the Danish settlement in England. *University of Birmingham Historical Journal* 6: 1-17.
1962   *The Age of the Vikings.* London: Edward Arnold (2nd edn, 1971).
1968   *Anglo-Saxon Charters. An Annotated List and Bibliography.* London: Royal Historical Society.
1997 (ed.) *The Oxford Illustrated History of the Vikings.* Oxford: Oxford University Press.

Sawyer, P. H., *et al.*
1969   The two Viking Ages of Britain. A discussion. *Mediaeval Scandinavia* 2: 163-207.

Searle, E.
1985   Frankish rivalries and Norse warriors. *Anglo-Norman Studies* 8: 198-213.
1988   *Predatory Kinship and the Creation of Norman Power, 840-1066.* Berkeley, CA: University of California Press.

Sharpe, R.
1991   *Medieval Irish Saints' Lives.* Oxford: Clarendon Press.

Shetelig, H.
1940   *Viking Antiquities in Great Britain and Ireland, I. An Introduction to the Viking History of Western Europe.* Oslo: H. Aschehoug.

Sigurðsson, G.
1988   *Gaelic Influence in Iceland: Historical and Literary Contacts. A Survey of Research.* Reykjavík: Bókaútgáfa Menningarsjóðs.

Skaare, K.
1976   *Coins and Coinage in Viking-Age Norway.* Oslo: Universitetsforlaget.

Smith, J. M. H.
1991   *Province and Empire: Carolingian Brittany.* Cambridge: Cambridge University Press.

Smyth, A. P.
1975/9   *Scandinavian York and Dublin.* 2 vols. Dublin: Templekieran Press.
1977   *Scandinavian Kings in the British Isles, 850-880.* Oxford: Oxford University Press.
1978   The chronology of Northumbrian history in the ninth and tenth centuries. In *Viking Age York and the North.* R. A. Hall (ed.), pp. 8-10. London: Council for British Archaeology.

Stevenson, W. H.
1904   *Asser's Life of King Alfred.* Oxford: Clarendon Press. (Rev. imp., by D. Whitelock, 1959.)

Thomson, W. P. L., & C. J. Omand (trans.)
1986   St Findan and the Pictish-Norse tradition. In *The People of Orkney.* R. J. Berry & H. N. Firth (eds.), pp. 279-287. Kirkwall: Orkney Press.

Todd, J. H. (ed. & trans.)
  1867   *Cogadh Gaedhel re Gallaibh. The War of the Gaedhil with the Gaill.*
            London: Longmans, Green, Reader, and Dyer.
Vogel, W.
  1906   *Die Normannen und das fränkische Reich bis zur Gründung der Normandie
            (799-911).* Heidelberg: Carl Winter Verlag.
Wainwright, F. T. (ed.)
  1962   *The Northern Isles.* Edinburgh: Thomas Nelson.
Waitz, G., & W. Wattenbach *et al.* (eds.)
  1887   [*Supplementa tomorum I-XII, pars III, Supplementum tomi XIII.*]
            Monumenta Germaniae Historica. Scriptores (in Folio), 15, Teil 1. Hanover:
            Hahn. [Repr. 1963 Anton Hiersemann Verlag, Stuttgart).
Wallace-Hadrill, J. M.
  1975   *The Vikings in Francia.* Reading: University of Reading.
Wamers, E.
  1983   Some ecclesiastical and secular Insular metalwork found in Norwegian
            viking graves. *Peritia* 2: 277-306.
  1985   *Insularer Metallschmuck in wikingerzeitlichen Gräbern Nordeuropas.
            Untersuchungen zur skandinavischen Westexpansion.* Neumünster: Karl
            Wachholtz.
Whitelock, D. (trans.)
  1961   *The Anglo-Saxon Chronicle. A Revised Translation.* London: Eyre &
            Spottiswoode. (Rev. imp., 1965.)
  1979   *English Historical Documents, c. 500-1042.* 2nd edition. London: Eyre
            Methuen.
Wilson, D. M.
  1974   *The Viking Age in the Isle of Man. The Archaeological Evidence.* Odense:
            Odense University Press.
Wormald, C. P.
  1976   Review of Löwe 1973. *English Historical Review* 91: 622-3.
  1982   Viking studies: whence and whither? In *The Vikings.* R. T. Farrell (ed.),
            pp. 128-153. Chichester: Phillimore.
Wormald, C. P., & R. Frank
  1980   Communications. *American Historical Review* 85: 268-70. (Further to
            R. Frank, review of Smyth 1977, ibid., 84 [1979] 135-136.)
Zettel, H.
  1977   *Das Bild der Normannen und der Normanneneinfalle in westfränkischen,
            ostfränkischen und angelsächsischen Quellen des 8. bis 11. Jahrhunderts.*
            Munich: Wilhelm Fink.

Discussion

JESCH: In what I define as strictly contemporary Old Norse sources (runic inscriptions and skaldic poems), the word *víkingr* is not at all common (page 209), and it's always used in the plural except when it is used as a personal name. The plural uses in runic inscriptions and skaldic poetry are either neutral—there is not enough context to tell us what they mean—or they are actually pejorative; so even the late eleventh-century people speaking the Scandinavian language used the word 'viking' in a pejorative sense. So that is some support, I think, for your argument.

MEULENGRACHT: I am thinking about *Víkingarvísur*.

JESCH: The problem is that people assume that the word has ethnic reference in these poems. It is not quite clear in *Víkingarvísur* which group the word 'viking' refers to. The pattern I think I have identified (Jesch 2001:44-56) in all the skaldic poems from before 1100 is that, more often than not, it refers to the opponents, and therefore it is pejorative. And they don't have to be Scandinavian, they can be anybody, they can be Wends.

LUND: Could I throw in one more point about the runic inscriptions? They may be uncertain, but I find it unlikely that in the runic inscriptions they should be pejorative about the people...or criticizing the people. The purpose of a runic inscription is to commemorate them and they are normally praising them very much. Therefore, to have a runic inscription commemorating someone who died in a Viking raid, they were probably proud of it.

JESCH: Well, there are two words, and both occur in runic inscriptions, the activity of *víking*, a feminine noun, and the person *víkingr*, a masculine noun. And I was not actually saying that runic inscriptions were pejorative. But the problem there is that they are so few. There are a lot of references to people who went abroad, but only three inscriptions, two from Skåne and one from Västergötland, which use the word *víking*. That's the feminine noun. And only three inscriptions use the masculine noun *víkingr*, one from Gotland, one from Denmark and the Bro inscription (U617) which says of the commemorated that he was *víkinga vörðr*. This can be taken in two ways, as "someone guarding Vikings" or "guarding the country against the Vikings". I am not suggesting that any has a pejorative sense, actually I think they are not clear.

MEULENGRACHT: You avoid the term 'Norse' "except in reference to language and literature", but isn't that due to Icelandic and American propaganda?

DUMVILLE: Possibly, but I started out two or three years ago to compile lists from secondary literature, to see who used 'Norse' to mean what. And there are many authors who use 'Norse' to mean Norwegian, and they oppose it explicitly to Danish. And there are authors who use it to mean Scandinavian. There is utter confusion.

MEULENGRACHT: Oh, I am glad that I can still use it as reference to language and literature [laughter].

JESCH: I think this is a problem that actually arises mainly in the British Isles context where we like to distiguish between the Danish kind of settlers in the East and the settlers in the Northwest, whom we don't quite like to call Norwegians, because they have a Celtic tinge.

MEULENGRACHT: You are using "written texts, now literary now documentary". I put that question earlier in this symposium still I think: what does 'literary' mean?

DUMVILLE: What I mean is in opposition to documentary, and I put this in in anticipation of a group of archaeologists gathered. The problem that I see over and over again in scholarly literature is people referring to any written sources as documentary. The distinction I am making here is between texts which are documentary in the sense that they have a legal function or a pragmatic function, and a text which is in some sense literature. That is the distinction in my paper.

LUND: The *Anglo-Saxon Chronicle* is literary.

DUMVILLE: Yes.

BRINK: From recent excavations in Scandinavia there are reasons to believe that Scandinavians were Christian already in the tenth century.

DUMVILLE: You mean there were Scandinavian Christians.

BRINK: There have been two projects in Scandinavia, in Norway and Sweden, on the problem of Christianization. And the main conclusion reached by both projects was that "You cannot pinpoint Christianization, it's a long process lasting several hundred years. Therefore, it is very difficult to define this people as Christians in this period".

DUMVILLE: There is that risk of never being quite clear what we mean when we say Christian, or perhaps rather being too clear of what we mean, and not allowing for a great deal of loose practice by a variety of native people.

NIELSEN: There are now graves, probably one of the earliest ones was ^{14}C dated to around 880, and there is high precision on the datings, but of course, as we said, there are some problems with ^{14}C datings on the Vikings. Anyhow, 880 is a high-precision dating substantially earlier than the rune stone at Jelling, and in this cemetery at Sebbersund the graves are all oriented east-west and have no grave-goods, and then in the middle of all this there is a stave church with two or three crosses. So, it is a case of very early Christianity.

ARRHENIUS: Nowadays, the archaeologists don't put the beginning of the Viking Age to 800 (page 210). This dating derives from the oldest layer in Birka and in Ribe and the reason for this dating is a production in these layers of brooches spread all around Scandinavia. But around 750 we have the production that we also find in the other graves.

BENDER: The earlier agreement on the beginning of the Viking Age is breaking up. You put it at 750. I would say with the foundation of Ribe at the beginning of the eighth century. At the moment historians are still fighting on their barricades for the Lindisfarne dating. There is now an open discussion about when the Viking Age began; we'll see what the situation looks like in ten years time. The important thing, in my opinion, is that the barrier of the Lindisfarne raid as the starting point has been lifted.

DUMVILLE: I wouldn't see Lindisfarne as a barrier. It is simply a point at which one can see a phenomenon, which may have a much longer history. So, for me, and I think probably for any historian, there would be no difficulty in supposing that the Viking Age opened at almost any date as long as there is an activity which characterizes the Viking Age, once it becomes a historical phenomenon, i.e. a phenomenon documented by written sources. We can push it back as far as we like on other kinds of evidence. On written evidence we haven't got it attested as a phenomenon from the early eighth century, and that is all historians would want to say. They have no competence in these other matters.

BENDER: The question is whether you see the Vikings from the point of view of the receiver (that would be the historian), or from the point of view of the sender (that is what the Scandinavian archaeologist would do).

LUND: We are approaching the same situation as we had with the towns. It becomes a matter of definition. In fact, as he states in *Kings and Vikings*, Peter Sawyer's point is that the Viking Age began when Scandinavians first attacked western Europe and it ended when those attacks ceased (1982:6). But when we are talking about the beginning of the Viking Age, in about 700 or 704, when the oldest part of Ribe is dated, that's a new periodization of Scandinavian history.

DUMVILLE: But had there been a series of viking attacks through the eighth century on what is now northern Scotland, they wouldn't be documented. So that if you look at the historians' point of view, there is no difficulty with almost any date, because we simply have a phenomenon recorded from a certain point, when this kind of activity impinges on societies which are both producing records and then keeping those records.

HERSCHEND: I think that there was some sort of argument on what the reasons were for writing anything whatsoever about Vikings in England. So I would like to sort out what the sources were written for.

DUMVILLE: The documentary sources provide rather vague dates for Viking activity, whereas the literary sources provide very explicit dates. In other words we see in charters that Vikings have had to be dealt with for some while in the past.

AUSENDA: Out of curiosity: what is the approximate number of surviving Pictish words and place-names (page 212)?

DUMVILLE: Well, you have to distinguish these two things and personal names. And the problem is how many languages we understand under the name Pictish. But, that aside, the number would be, I guess, about 50 personal names. The number of words from inscriptions would perhaps be 10 to 15. And then from place-names it gets much trickier, because place-name studies in Scotland have proceeded less than in many other places. But there is a group of elements which belong to the Brittonic division of Celtic. And I suppose that these would be 6 to 10 in number on which substantial work has been done.

JESCH: Could you say a bit more about "the prose literature of the Scandinavian world attests to the role of the colonies in developing the legends" (page 217).

DUMVILLE: I suppose it was an attempt to provoke those of you who deal with Old Norse literature and with Old Norse language, into telling me that I failed to take note of the large volume of scholarly literature. For various reasons I started looking around in scholarly literature to try and find discussions about the possibility that Old Norse as a written Latin-letter language had originated outside Scandinavia. And I didn't get anywhere on that, and I was wondering whether there had been any discussion.

GREEN: There is a point that can be made on the linguistic side, namely that Old Norse *bókstafr* is almost certainly a loanword from Old English *bocstæf*. Now *bókstafr* stands as opposed to *rúnastafr* and obviously implies differentiation between two forms of writing. Whether the loanword coming from OE implies that the differentiation between two forms of writing was first established for Norse speakers in England or not I don't know. But one might explore that.

DUMVILLE: OK, thank you. One other thing that occurs to me is to raise the Irish experience which seems to have some superficial parallels. Irish became a Latin-letter language having been previously a monumental written language, with cipher rather than an alphabet. In the earliest written Irish one does find traces of two quite distinct orthographies, one of which has a continuity with the monumental inscription form of writing, and another which has to be explained in terms of a new attempt in relation to that, and eventually one becomes dominant. Again, I wonder whether there is something parallel in the Old Norse situation which could be helpful in trying to understand the origins of writing in Latin letters.

JESCH: Talking of the prose literature from the Scandinavian world, you say that "it does not present usable narrative information" (page 217), and, therefore, you seem to dismiss it, but that may just be because no one has yet devised a method of extracting useful information from this. I think sources that don't provide useful narrative information are of all kinds. I don't think inscriptions on coins provide usable narrative information, and yet they can be linked to other sources.

DUMVILLE: What I am thinking of here is that, given where the bulk of narrative literature in Norse comes from chronologically—and then you have to add to that generic considerations—I have no confidence that there will be a manner of extracting suitably usable information about the early Viking Age from such a literature.

BRINK: On this problem Preben [Meulengracht] has written a most important paper a few years ago (1991) in a book called *Høvdingesamfund og kongemagt*. We are discussing a methodological way to approach these materials, as it is important for us to use anything available. For me it is quite important to have a methodological relation to these sources. We should also discuss on an interdiscipinary basis, how the English can relate to these literary sources and whether they have anything to relate to. And thereby maybe we can make our conclusions more probable.

GREEN: About the density of Pictish populations before Scandinavian arrival (page 217). If that density were very low, that might be the explanation, if it is not so low what would be the explanation?

DUMVILLE: Yes, there is a very dense population, argued for on purely archaeological grounds, for the historical Pictish period. Archaeologists have been disputing almost fifteen years, I suppose, the possibility of continuity in material culture in spite of the apparent evidence pointing very strongly in the other direction. But on this there would be an archaeologist vehemently on each side of the issue. So, if there has been a complete cultural change in language, whatever the explanation, it is the same debate always, does it imply an extirpation of the population? Does it imply what the UN would call cultural genocide, or something else?

GREEN: Or change of language by those inhabitants.

DUMVILLE: Yes, sure, that is cultural genocide.

LUND: Well, Lucien Musset drew attention to the extent to which place-names depend on written transmission. If you don't have an administration which records place-names, they can be changed from one generation to the next.

GREEN: Talking about Manx history, you say (page 218) that there were few links with Ireland in the Viking Age. Can you say briefly what the explanation for that would be? If it is so, I would be highly surprised.

DUMVILLE: Yes, it is an argument which has been generated largely on numismatic evidence, but, once formulated, it has explained a lot of problems from the written evidence, which pertain to this question, I suppose, from the middle of the ninth century onwards. When we can begin to make anything of [the Isle of] Mann's history, which is essentially the middle of the twelfth century, Mann is very clearly on a north-south line of communication on which Mann is the southernmost and the Outer Hebrides, I suppose, are the northernmost point, from which you then go towards the Northern Isles and towards Scandinavia. What has been argued by my colleague Mark Blackburn is that it is quite striking how you appear to have two separate economic zones within the Irish Sea part of the Scandinavian world, one of which is Dublin and the other Scandinavian towns, which had economic links with England, and you might therefore think that Mann would probably be in the way; and another zone which is the Western Isles and Mann. What is striking is that we cannot demonstrate any clear historical links until the early 940s between the Dublin Scandinavian kingdom and the other Irish-Scandinavian kingdoms and the Western Isles. And that has always seemed odd. Blackburn's development of the numismatic evidence has solved the problem which was there, but it may turn out, of course, that this construction is wrong. But for the moment it seems that we have two economic zones on numismatic evidence, two political zones on written evidence.

AUSENDA: On the idea that "viking armies were much larger than Sawyer sought to suggest" (page 221), could it be perhaps because they were more mobile, hence produced an impression of greater numbers?

DUMVILLE: Perhaps, but the argument doesn't entirely turn on that. And there is a problem here, in that we stand more or less at the end of the phase in discussion about how large an army might be in the Viking Age; by and large we have forgotten what the starting point of discussion was, because it has been so intense all the time. The starting point of the discussion was in Peter Sawyer's *Age of the Vikings* in 1962—what he pointed out, absolutely correctly, is that whenever we could find evidence from native sources as to the size of armies within those native cultures, the armies were very small. One couldn't speak of an army, for example, referring to a group of less than, say, 20 people. So that the amount of shock an army could produce in the viking context didn't necessarily relate to the ability to convey huge numbers of warriors across the territory. Now, that was then taken up by people of a lesser quality of scholarship and the proposition was advanced that all armies in this period were small, which was not at all what Sawyer had started out by arguing, though it has to be said that Sawyer, having seen everybody running with the proposition so enthusiastically then joined the fun [laughter]. There was then a good deal of investigation on what numbers we could draw directly from contemporary source-material for the size of viking and other (native) armies of the period. And the numbers went back up again, not to the thousands, but to armies of hundreds of people being transported whether overland or by sea. There is another whole discussion which for me is still the natural point of reference, which relates to the question of the extent of settlement, particularly in the English Danelaw. How from the evidence of social history and later records one estimates the extent of Scandinavian settlement, and how one then moves from these centres of Scandinavian settlement to the size of the armies which seized control in the ninth century, that whole matter has been dealt with in exemplary fashion by Niels Lund.

LUND: Perhaps I could add a report of a funny experience I had with this debate when Peter Sawyer and Ken Cameron formed more or less a pair of Kilkenny cats when I was in Leeds for a couple of years. I also went down to Nottingham and discussed these matters with Ken Cameron and studied the field names in the archives in Nottingham. And during a break in the work I asked, "Ken, tell me how many settlers would you settle for, how many do you require to explain the linguistic influence of Old Norse in England?". "Well, what about 5,000?" he said. I went back to Leeds and asked Peter: "How many settlers, in fact, after all this discussion about the size of armies, do you think settled in eastern and northern England?" "Well, shall we come down to 5,000?" [Laughter].

AUSENDA: On the earliest recorded phase of Viking activity at Lindisfarne in 793, most probably because the monastery kept records, and most certainly earlier on a 'non-official' basis, it would seem that a lot depended on the improvements to the navigation technology. It would appear that crossing such a wide stretch of sea was hardly ever attempted in the fifth and sixth centuries, whereas at some later date it became a much easier entreprise. Is it not possible to determine that critical period and the type of improvements which made the longer navigation and ensuing surprise possible?

DUMVILLE: There is a question of what the assumptions are. There are at least two concerning where these Lindisfarne raiders came from: one is that they came from Scandinavia directly by whatever route, the other is that they set out from pre-existing bases within the British Isles, and that would raise very different kinds of questions, I take it, because of the absence of any kind of history of what is now northern Scotland. It is not possible to say that they did not come from there. What has been argued is that because coin material from eighth-century Northumbria had been finding its way back into southwestern Norwegian graves, argued to be dated not long after this there is some direct line of transmission of material. But that doesn't of itself completely answer the question about where these raiders came from.

AUSENDA: On the argument that "depopulation of towns in the ninth century was due to viking activity (Wallace-Hadrill 1975:13-18)" (page 224); it was almost certainly the other way round. In other words that the population of towns had declined due to economic reasons. Isn't there any clue to this opposite explanation?

DUMVILLE: For that to work, a population decrease would have had to have been rapid and disastrous, so that all the goods were left there for someone to loot.

AUSENDA: No, when the population dwindles, the people who remain there still have goods which can be looted easily. It is much easier to raid a small town with few people, than to raid a huge city, for instance.

ARRHENIUS: I am curious about the arrival of Arabic coinage in the British Isles (page 226)?

DUMVILLE: As far as I am aware, Arabic coinage first makes its appearance in the British Isles in the late ninth century.

ARRHENIUS: Yes, so I read. That is because early Arabic coinage begins to come more often to Scandinavia.

DUMVILLE: In any case, Arabic coins were associated with Carolingian coinage as the two came together to the British Isles.

HERSCHEND: I would say that there is a metrological point here. When Arabic coins arrived in Gotland in Scandinavia, they started a slight circulation which came out in such a way that the greater the hoards the heavier the coins. And it so happens that eighth-century Arabic coins are low-weight, so that they tend easily to go out in some sort of semi-market economy and to circulate much more. For that reason, one or two singular Arabic coins do not date very precisely: they are old already when they arrive and for economic reasons they are sorted out of the bulk of coins.

AUSENDA: On the decline of monasteries in the ninth century (page 227), I would discount the religious motive and look for an economic one. Nowadays monasteries are emptying because life has become easier for lay people and life in monasteries is no longer considered attractive. It is probable that during the English 'crisis' the surplus produced by monasteries was no longer saleable, hence there was no longer a standard of living which would attract people. Would you kindly comment?

DUMVILLE: Yes, it is too unidimensional for me. There is also a problem of what you mean by 'monasteries', which is quite acute. Certainly the more disturbed the English countryside became, the more difficult it would have been for English religious communities to maintain themselves. There is the question of direct attacks, there is the question of assaults on what I should call the nerve centres, owned by these ecclesiastical communities. There is the question of whether one's intentions in entering ecclesiastical life can be met in circumstances of having pirates racing around and doing unpleasant things to the members of ecclesiastical communities. And then, leaving aside the vikings altogether, there are the questions, which is what Sawyer was going into, as to whether we see in this period the decline of ecclesiastical communities. But the upshot of the discussion is not sufficient in itself to deal with what we see in terms of ecclesiastical organization, and of the numbers of religious houses in this period. So, certainly there has to be an economic component but I shouldn't think it is the only one.

GREEN: As I said before, I like your comparative approach. What I would like to argue is how far you would concede the point that there might be a possible danger of filling the gaps in one area by information taken from another?

DUMVILLE: It would be possible to come from a whole series of particulars relating to the various countries, to the various categories of source material and so on, to assault this generalizing proposition. That's precisely what I was seeking to provoke.

LUND: Are you then to have the chronological dimension as well?

DUMVILLE: Perhaps I will. Go on and explain it a little more.

LUND: Well, using sources from not only different areas and various kinds, but also from different periods within the Viking Age. I was thinking of eleventh-century sources for the ninth century, for example.

DUMVILLE: Insofar as viking activity was still to be, even if on a lesser scale, a feature of eleventh-century life, then there are possible lines of comparison. To work that out as a systematic method would take a lot of thought; as it is, this is the result of twenty years of very disorderly, very occasional thinking.

JESCH: Again perhaps I haven't quite understood your model, or perhaps you haven't quite wanted to commit yourself when you say "more generally we need to know...whether there is an identifiable point of transition from being vikings to being thoroughly settled" (page 228), and it is that question of settlement which I feel you have avoided. I am just not clear to what extent you think your definition of 'viking', your model of 'vikings', must be considered together with the question of Scandinavian settlement and/or not?

DUMVILLE: Yes, I have avoided the settlement-question to this extent, that I deliberately didn't want to get drawn into that discussion. If we are talking about the English Danelaw, then I take the process of transition to be essentially coincident with the process of seizure of power across England, of the creation of England as a politically unified West Saxony. By way of a radical contrast is the Irish situation, where the written sources make it very clear to us that the Scandinavian kingdoms created in Ireland remained in relationship with piratical political organizations right down to the twelfth century. Although Dublin—and that's where the bulk of the evidence comes from—becomes in the course of the tenth century an economically formatively important place in Ireland more broadly, and therefore attracts the attention of Scandinavian competitors, Irish kings seeking to gain political control all over Ireland came to feel that they had to control Dublin in order to control the rest of Ireland. Nonetheless, the rulers of Dublin down into the twelfth century were still conducting what may be described as viking operations, it seems to me, across the country, in a way quite different from the way that political military forces otherwise operate within the Irish polity. In other words, the kingdom of Dublin is geographically small, and yet its rulers will launch attacks across the length and breadth of the country, still down to the twelfth century. Those kind of attacks and military operations are conducted by natives only when those natives are major overkings. So, in the native part of the polity, power is to be projected across a long distance only by the highest level of overking. But in the Scandinavian part of the polity, such attacks could be conducted within the same geographical area by what, in Irish terms, is a petty kingdom.

AUSENDA: On the "rapid conversion" in Man and the Western Isles, the reason for that probably was that these raiders had settled without many women, hence they had to marry the local ones. Women are always a primary motivation in conversions. Also the basic reason for settlement in large numbers in the Northern Isles could also be women. In fact the Northern Isles were more accessible to a full migration, i.e. with women and children, because they were more peripheral and abandoned, hence the migrants could safely take their women with them.

DUMVILLE: To argue that the Northern Isles were peripheral is one thing, but to argue that they were abandoned would fly in the face of all the archaeological evidence. I do admit that those who would wish to argue that the Scandinavian settlement in the Northern Isles was peaceful would nonetheless argue for a low population-density, small numbers of settlements, in the Northern Isles. They would be relying on their sense of the innate goodness and common sense or whatever the settlers had for those who were on the receiving end of the settlement. But, for the rest of it, I would agree with you wholeheartedly, I take it from the fact that we can see, from the very middle of the ninth century onwards, bilingual, bicultural populations exporting themselves in viking activities from the Western Isles, that this means that a process is taking place in the way you described.

AUSENDA: On "the terror and destruction which vikings had wrought" (page 230), it might easily have been exaggerated, as happens even nowadays to news which is not exactly quantified and qualified. Furthermore the vikings took on the role of the evil doer in fireside lore.

DUMVILLE: Yes, absolutely. But, what is useful about *Francia* is that it gives us a quantity of information about 'viking' activity, which is much richer, and much more varied in its character than we get from England. And what it does is to provide a great deal of difficulty for those who wish to argue that the level of activity was low or did not have a great impact on the civilians.

AUSENDA: I said "exaggerated".

DUMVILLE: Nobody has any problem with the idea that there is exaggeration within the sources, here and there in specific matters, and also on a methodological basis. I don't think that is controversial or difficult. But, again, it has been a habit of the developing discussions to argue that because written sources can be unreliable in this matter and in various other matters, because they can show clear bias, therefore what they say is to be disregarded, and because what they say is disregarded by the modern scholar, therefore, it didn't happen. In other words, a syllogism is being constructed: chroniclers said that vikings raiding burnt down churches, attacked towns with much bloodshed, and so on. These chronicles were written by people on the receiving end and, therefore, they were biased and less than accurate. And because these are the evidence, therefore, there is no evidence.

References in the discussion

Textual sources:

Anglo-Saxon Chronicle: see Dumville & Keynes (eds.) 1983-

Bibliography:

Dumville, D. N., & S. Keynes (eds.)
  1983-   *The Anglo-Saxon Chronicle: A Collaborative Edition* (23 vols.). Cambridge:
           D. S. Brewer.
Jesch, J.
  2001   *Ships and Men in the Late Viking Age: The Vocabulary of Runic Inscriptions
           and Skaldic Verse.* Woodbridge: The Boydell Press.
Meulengracht Sørensen, P.
  1991   Håkon den gode og guderne. In *Høvdingesamfund og kongemagt*.
           P. Mortensen & B. M. Rasmussen (eds.), pp. 235-244. Århus: Århus
           Universitetsforlag.
Musset, L.
  1955   Les destins de la propriété monastique durant les invasions normandes (ix-xi
           siècles). L'exemple de Jumièges. *Jumièges. Congrès scientifique du xiii
           centenaire*. Pp. 49-55. Rouen: Lecerf. [Re-published in *Nordica et
           Normannica*, Paris, Société des études nordiques (Studia nordica, I), 1997:
           351-359].
Sawyer, P. H.
  1962   *The Age of the Vikings.* London: Edward Arnold.
  1982   *Kings and Vikings. Scandinavia and Europe AD 700-1100*. London:
           Methuen.

EAGLES, RAVENS AND WOLVES: BEASTS OF BATTLE, SYMBOLS OF VICTORY AND DEATH

JUDITH JESCH

School of English Studies, The University of Nottingham, University Park, Nottingham GB-NG7 2RD

Introduction

The 'beasts of battle' are traditionally associated with descriptions of warfare throughout early Germanic and other literature. These consumers of corpses on the battlefield symbolize primarily the grim finality of human death, yet also the triumph of the victors, whose achievement is measured in the number of bodies they supply to the carrion-eaters. The underlying symbolism is constant enough and of some antiquity (see e.g. Psalms LXXIX,1-3). Yet it is possible to identify a variety of specific symbolic uses to which carrion-eaters are put in the different Germanic literary traditions. In this paper, I aim to delineate the specifically Scandinavian symbolic uses of this motif and to demonstrate what these reveal about the ideologies of early Scandinavian society.

My focus is largely on early Scandinavian poetry, both skaldic and Eddic. As most of this poetry is recorded in Icelandic manuscripts of the thirteenth century or later, its use as evidence for the Viking Age will always be problematic, especially for the period before AD 1000. Yet there is no doubt that much of both Eddic and skaldic poetry represents in some way, though probably in different ways, an oral tradition that predates the written record. The written texts of skaldic praise poetry are very likely to be relatively accurate representations of their oral predecessors by reason of their literary form, their original historical function, and their association with named (and therefore datable) individuals, both poets and their patrons (Jesch 2001:15-33). Eddic poetry, on the other hand, with its looser forms and less clear functions, and the anonymity of its authors, is more difficult to place in any particular historical or chronological contexts. Its mythological and legendary subject-matter, as well as analogies with other early Germanic poetry (especially Old English) suggest its antiquity as a genre, but the dating of individual poems is fraught with uncertainty and the cause of much scholarly disagreement (summarized in Jónas Kristjánsson 1990 and Fidjestøl 1999). It may be necessary to distinguish between the underlying structures of meaning in the Eddic poems, and their surviving versions which are very much a product of the literate period (Meulengracht Sørensen 1991). Even so, the Eddic poems also have a contribution to make in any search for the symbolic universe of the Viking Age.

Conventionally, the 'beasts of battle' present at the fall of warriors are two birds, the eagle and the raven, and one mammal, the wolf. I propose to look at some of

251

the ways in which these animals are used in Scandinavian poetry, concentrating on their links with battle and warriors in poetry of the tenth century, but drawing out the discussion towards other texts and other meanings, and making some comparisons with material from other early medieval cultures.

A major event marking the end of the period under discussion in this volume is the great sea-battle of *ca* 1000 at Svǫlðr,[1] in which the Norwegian king Óláfr Tryggvason was defeated by a coalition of the king of the Danes, the king of the Swedes, and Eiríkr Hákonarson, scion of the Norwegian jarls of Hlaðir. Halldórr ókristni's poem in praise of the latter (*Eiríksflokkr*) marks the moment of Eiríkr's triumph over Óláfr thus, in st. 7:[2]

Gnýr varð á sjá sverða.	There was crash of swords on the sea.
Sleit ǫrn gera beitu.	The eagle tore at wolf's food. The
Dýrr vá drengja stjóri.	excellent leader of warriors fought.
Drótt kom mǫrg á flótta.	Many a troop fled.

Here we have the classic Viking Age battle in a nutshell: the noise, the carrion bird tearing at the corpses, the leader in the midst of his men, the fleeing enemy. A result of the battle (noted in the following stanza) is that Óláfr's ship, *Ormr inn langi*, which brought him to the battle, is taken over by the victorious jarl as war-booty.

There is a similar conjunction of warriors, carrion birds and a ship in a memorial context on a picture stone from Lärbro (Tängelgårda I) in Gotland (Lindqvist 1941-1942: II, fig. 86). The uppermost panel of this stone is largely taken up with a battle scene: in all, there are one falling and two fallen warriors, three standing figures with their arms raised (at least two of these holding a sword), three birds and one horse. The interpretation of the iconography on this stone is a complex matter, but it is worth noting the presence of three birds (all with the hooked beak of the bird of prey) in the battle scene, at least one of them clearly attacking a fallen warrior. While the usual dating of the group to which this stone belongs (group C) to the (early) eighth century (Lindqvist 1941-1942:I,117-118) would link the monument to the beginning of the period under discussion in this volume, this is probably too early. Lindqvist's dating of the Gotland picture stones to the period 400-1100 has a rather unlikely gap between 800-1000. It is now recognized that his chronology is unsatisfactory (Varenius 1992:80-83; Wilson 1998), but there has as yet been no wholesale redating of the corpus, which is now also larger by some 70 stones since Lindqvist surveyed it. Lärbro Tängelgårda I could well belong to the ninth or even the tenth century (cf. the discussion of the Tjängvide stone in Wilson 1998:49-51).

---

[1] The date of the battle is uncertain and the location of Svǫlðr is not known. Although Icelandic saga-tradition places it in the south Baltic (e.g. *Heimskringla*, see Bjarni Aðalbjarnarson 1979:I,351), it is more likely that Adam of Bremen (*Gesta* II,40), writing less than a century after the battle, is correct to place it in the Øresund (Trillmich & Buchner 1978:276).

[2] Where I use published translations, these are listed in 'References', below. Otherwise, translations from Old Norse are my own.

Both Halldórr ókristni's stanza and the scenes on the Lärbro Tängelgårda I stone emanate from a Scandinavian tradition of commemoration of male achievement, usually, though not necessarily, posthumous. This tradition also includes the commemorative rune stones of the late Viking Age. The separate media of picture stone, rune stone and skaldic eulogy all use varying degrees of, or combinations of, factual statement and symbolic or mythological language or iconography in their commemorative function. While these three forms of commemoration are generally distinct, especially in their geographical distribution, there is enough overlap between them to suggest their common origins in a typically Scandinavian mode of celebrating the dead. Thus, some Gotland picture stones have commemorative runic inscriptions on them (e.g. the Tjängvide stone discussed in Wilson 1998, and depicted on the dust jacket of this volume). Many rune stones have commemorative verse on them (although only the Karlevi stone from Öland has a skaldic stanza, see Jesch 2001:1-6) and others make use of both symbolic and mythological iconography (for some examples see Jansson 1987:144-152). And both skaldic verse and Gotland picture stones allude to well-known mythological stories. It is primarily in this commemorative mode that the Viking Age Scandinavian uses of the beasts of battle are to be seen.

The beasts of battle in Old English and Old Norse poetry

The three beasts of battle, eagle, raven and wolf, are a feature of both Old English and Old Norse poetry. In Old English, this constellation of fauna occurs in a 'typescene', i.e. a number of motifs associated with a particular narrative event, in this case battle. This typescene has been analysed by Griffith, who notes that it always occurs in narrative poetry when battle really takes place and is narrated, but is generally absent when battle is referred to rather than narrated, and is also absent from scenes of single combat. Thus 'the poets felt the beasts to be a compulsory element of battle narration. They do not advance the action, but they are symbolically essential to it, and cannot be eliminated without destroying its poetic coherence' (Griffith 1993:184). Griffith goes on to analyse the component motifs of the typescene: 'in the wake of an army, the dark raven, the dewy-plumaged eagle and the wolf of the forest, eager for slaughter and carrion/food, give voice to their joy' (1993:184). No single motif, however, occurs in all instances of the scene. The formulaic nature of the typescene is shown by the thematic possibilities that are ignored. Thus there is an 'almost total absence of description of the beasts actually eating the slain' (1993:186) at least in part because, in about half of the occurrences, the beasts actually occur 'in anticipation of conflict, before the battle actually begins' (1993:187). Also the language is quite uniform, with relatively little lexical variation in the elaboration of the motifs. The regular use of the typescene before a battle can be extended to conjure up the unpleasantness of hypothetical battles. Thus, in *Beowulf* (ll. 3021b-3027) the scene is used symbolically in the catalogue of miseries which will befall the Geats with the death of Beowulf (Griffith 1993:196).

There has been no rigorous and systematic analysis of the beasts of battle in Old Norse poetry, even though (or perhaps because) the material is much more extensive than in Old English, yet such an analysis is clearly needed. Scholars have long wanted to link the beasts of battle in Old English and Old Norse poetry in some way. R. Frank notes that "It is traditional...to see the wolf, raven, and eagle that together dine off the slain in eight Old English poems and hundreds of skaldic stanzas as relics of a distant Germanic past" but would herself prefer to see the link as an instance of Old Norse influence on Old English (Frank 1987:348-352).[3] It seems to me that, although there clearly is some kind of a link, the two poetic traditions make very different use of the convention. While a full analysis cannot be undertaken here, I would like to draw attention to some of the ways in which Norse poetry differs from Old English in its use of the beasts of battle, using examples from tenth-century skaldic poetry.[4]

In Old English poetry the beasts evoke the grim expectation of slaughter, sometimes from the point of view of the eventual losers of the battle, while the Norse poets use them to glorify the victorious warrior who causes the slaughter. This tendency is obviously strongest in skaldic poetry, which has as its function the praise of warriors and chieftains. The element of anticipation identified by M. S. Griffith in about half of the Old English examples is very rare in the skaldic examples, and the skaldic use of the beasts of battle does not fulfil the requirements of a 'typescene' as in the Old English texts: often it is simply a motif more or less closely linked to the warrior who is being praised. The Norse poetry hardly ever uses the beasts to create an atmosphere, a sense of impending doom, or the elegiac mood that we so often find in the Old English examples. If anything, the tone is quite the opposite: upbeat and positive. The Old Norse convention can be summarized as 'the warrior feeds the beasts of battle, the beasts of battle enjoy their food'. The usage can either be specific, describing the warrior's actions in a particular battle, or general, praising the warrior for his prowess in a campaign or in the whole of his career.

The most characteristic aspect of the beasts of battle in the Norse material, one which is largely absent from the Old English poetry, is this fairly narrow focus on the warrior as the provider of a meal for the beasts. Halldórr ókristni's stanza quoted above has already illustrated an aspect of the motif that Griffith has demonstrated to be absent from the Old English examples, that in which the beasts

---

[3] Frank implicitly ascribes this 'Germanic' view of the beasts of battle to Jacob Grimm, but does not note that he is referring only to Eddic poetry and not the skaldic poetry that is her concern (Grimm 1840:xxv-xxviii). Scholars continue to concentrate on the Old English instances, without questioning the inherited assumption that the Norse examples somehow represent the 'common Germanic origin' of the motif and without any detailed knowledge of the Norse examples (e.g. Honegger 1998).

[4] For some later examples, mainly from the eleventh century, see Jesch 2001:247-252.

of battle eat the slain, and there are plenty of other instances. Egill Skallagrímsson, praising Eiríkr blóðøx to save his head in York, develops the motif at length, mentioning all three beasts several times in sts 10-12:[5]

Rauð hilmir hjǫr,	The prince reddened the blade.
þar vas hrafna gjǫr,	There was food for the ravens.
fleinn hitti fjǫr,	Arrows took life. Bloody spears
flugu dreyrug spjǫr;	flew. The destroyer of Scots fed the
ól flagðs gota	wolf (horse of the giantess). This
fárbjóðr Skota,	sister of Nar (Hel, or Death,
trað nipt Nara	goddess of the dead), trod supper
náttverð ara.	for the eagles.
Flugu hjaldrs tranar	Eagles (battle-cranes) flew over the
á hræs lanar,	rows of corpses. The beaks of the
órut blóðs vanar	ravens (wound-mews) did not lack
benmǫs granar,	blood. The wolf tore at wounds
sleit und freki,	while blood (the wave from the
en oddbreki	spear-point) splashed up towards
gnúði hrafni	the beaks of the ravens.
á hǫfuðstafni.	
Kom gríðar læ	The end of hunger came for the
at Gjalpar skæ;	wolf (steed of the giantess). Eirik
bauð ulfum hræ	offered corpses to the wolf by the
Eiríkr of sæ.	sea.

We also find a gleeful description of the beasts' feast in a number of poems in praise of Eiríkr Hákonarson. Eyjólfr dáðaskáld's *Bandadrápa* (st. 5) shows him raiding in Wendland, so that *unda mór sleit svǫrð víkinga* 'the seagull of wounds [eagle/raven] tore at the scalps of vikings [his opponents]'. In Halldórr's *Eiríksflokkr* (st. 1), his followers are each a *hrægeitunga feitir* 'fattener of the corpse-bird [eagle/raven]' who ensure that *sára mór fekk sylg* 'the seagull of wounds [eagle/raven] got a drink'. Finally, in Þórðr Kolbeinsson's *Eiríksdrápa*, the warriors provide the wolf with a complete meal, both food and drink (st. 14):

Óð—en ærnu náði	Gialp's stud waded in blood, and
íms sveit Freka hveiti,	the dusky one's troop got plenty of
Gera ǫlðra naut gylðir—	Freki's meal [carrion]. The howler
Gjálpar stóð í blóði.	enjoyed Geri's ales [blood].

Snorri (*Edda. Skaldskaparmál*, LVIII) cites this stanza as an example of different terms for wolf: Freki and Geri are the names of Óðinn's wolves, according to *Grímnismál* (st. 19), but can be taken here as common nouns meaning 'wolf', along with the other wolves in the stanza: 'the dusky one' and 'the howler', and the 'horse' of the giantess Gjálp.

---

[5] The authenticity of *Hǫfuðlausn* has been doubted in the past, but current opinion tends to accept that it was indeed composed in tenth-century York (e.g. Hines 1995).

The beasts of battle in skaldic poetry

As these examples show, the simple idea of the warrior feeding the eagle/raven/wolf can be varied in a number of ways, given the large stock of poetic synonyms (*heiti*) and circumlocutions ('kennings') available to the Old Norse poet. This variation has been analysed by Fidjestøl with particular reference to the kennings used in this motif (1982:200-203). Thus, the whole idea can be collapsed into a kenning for a warrior: he becomes the 'feeder' or 'fattener' or 'hunger-diminisher' or 'reddener' or even 'gladdener' of the carrion bird or wolf. When this happens, we tend to be left with only a fleeting image of the beasts of battle enjoying their meal, with the focus remaining on the warrior who provides it. But the idea can also be turned into an indicative statement: the warrior 'feeds' or 'causes to drink' or 'does away with the hunger of' or 'reddens the claws of' or 'gladdens' the beasts of battle. And when the poets use *heiti* or kennings for eagles, ravens and wolves in these statements about the warriors, the focus broadens to include the beasts. There were both *heiti* and kennings for 'wolf' in Þórðr's stanza discussed above, and Egill's stanzas quoted above vary the terms for all three beasts.

The wolf, as the only mammal among the beasts of battle, is easily identified. The birds, however, are more problematic, since there are two of them. Kennings for both the eagle and the raven usually involve a base-word that is another bird. As Snorri noted in his analysis of poetic language, *Skáldskaparmál* (LX):

> There are two birds that there is no need to refer to in any other way than by calling blood or corpses their drink or food. These are the raven and the eagle. All other masculine birds can be referred to in terms of blood or corpses, and then it means eagle or raven.

Where there are two kennings of this type in a stanza, we tend to assume (as Fell did in her translation of Egill, quoted above, which has both 'battle-cranes' and 'wound-mews') that one must refer to the eagle and one to the raven, though there is nothing intrinsic in the kennings to indicate this, and it is often a moot point which is which, as the birds are to a large extent interchangeable. The meaning of a kenning is only certain when one of the birds appears as a base-word, then we know that the kenning must refer to the other bird, as in *gjóðr geira hríðar* 'sea-eagle of the storm of spears [battle]', which must then be the raven, or when the inclusion of Óðinn in the kenning leads us to assume a raven is meant.

There are further examples of this variation in tenth-century skaldic verse. Kormákr, in a poem in praise of Eiríkr's brother, Sigurðr Hákonarson, calls him *Gríðar glaðfœðandi* 'feeder of the steed of the giantess [wolf]' (st. 4). Einarr skálaglamm calls their father Hákon Sigurðarson *sverða sverrifjarðar svanglýjaði* 'gladdener of the swan [raven or eagle] of the gushing fjord [blood] of the sword' (*Vellekla*, st. 8). The same leader is called by Tindr Hallkelsson *verðbjóðr hugins ferðar* 'meal-giver of the troop of the raven' (*Hákonardrápa*, st. 4) using Huginn, the name of one of Óðinn's ravens, as the noun for the bird, and it is said of him later in the same poem that *jarl saddi hrafna, þars odda oføing gingu saman* 'the jarl sated ravens where strong meetings of points [battle] were held', and that he *vann hungri hanga vals* 'conquered the hunger of Óðinn's falcon [raven]', so that *Mistar mávi varð gott til vista* 'the valkyrie's seagull [eagle/raven] had plenty of food' (st. 7).[6]

The motif has a whiff of paganism about it that seems to make it particularly suited to the jarls of Hlaðir, whose court seems to have been a focus of the late tenth-century renaissance of paganism in Norway. Yet their enemy Óláfr Tryggvason, a Christian king and the Apostle of Iceland, is comprehensively associated with the beasts of battle by Hallfreðr vandræðaskáld in two separate poems. In the *Óláfsdrápa* composed in the king's lifetime, it is summarily stated that *opt kom hrafn at blóði* 'the raven often got blood' (st. 3), and then we get a series of vignettes of Óláfr feeding the beasts in different places and against different enemies: *tyggi lét tíðhǫggvit hræ Saxa fyr styggvan, ljótvaxinn Leiknar hest* 'the leader often caused Saxon corpses to be cut down for the ugly horse of the giantess [wolf]' (st. 6); *vísi gaf víða blǫkku stóði kveldriðu brúnt blóð margra Frísa at drekka* 'the leader gave brown blood of Frisians to drink to the dark steed of the giantess [wolf] far and wide' (st. 6); *herstefnir lét goldit hrǫfnum hold Flæmingja* 'the war-leader gave the flesh of Flemings to the ravens'; *gróðr þvarr gjóði geira hríðar* 'the hunger of the sea-eagle of the storm of spears [raven] diminished' (st. 9; this statement, and the following kenning, occur in the context of Óláfr's wars in the British Isles). Finally, Óláfr is called an *ulfa greddir* 'feeder of wolves' (st. 8). In the posthumous *Erfidrápa*, Hallfreðr calls Óláfr *varghollr* 'gracious to wolves' (st. 7), *Heita dýrbliks dynsæðinga hungrdeyfi* 'destroyer of the hunger of the gull [eagle/raven] of the resounding [battle] of the gleam [shield] of Heiti's animal [ship]' (st. 20), and *þverri[r] ulfa sultar* 'diminisher of wolves' hunger' (st. 27). The different uses of the motif in these two poems by the same poet reflect the difference in their function. *Óláfsdrápa* is predominantly a catalogue of the king's youthful exploits, and therefore has a tendency to the indicative statement of the type 'the warrior fed the beasts of battle'. The *Erfidrápa*, on the other hand, is more concerned with its hero's posthumous reputation, which is summed up in the 'feeder of the beasts' type of kenning. Also, it treats extensively of his defeat at Svǫlðr, where it would inappropriate to show him actually feeding the beasts (a motif normally associated with the victor), so the praise must remain general.

Comparative angles

I noted earlier that R. Frank has seen Norse influence behind the beasts of battle in Old English poetry and, indeed, a number of the poems cited above have an

---

[6] This stanza survives only in a very late manuscript of *Jómsvíkinga saga*, and much of the text is conjectural (as restored in Finnur Jónsson 1912-1915:IB,137). Nevertheless, the general meaning is clear enough.

English connection of some sort, so the link is certainly worth considering. There may well have been some cross-fertilization at the lexical level. In particular, the beasts of battle passage in the Old English *Exodus* (ll. 161-169) seems to Frank (1987:349-350) to allude to skaldic motifs, and the use of a kenning, *guðhafoc* 'battle-hawk', for one of the carrion birds in *The Battle of Brunanburh* (l. 64a) is very like the skaldic usages I have just been describing. But if we move from the level of the lexicon to that of the literary form, then it is apparent that even the *Exodus* passage, with its unusual vocabulary, fits the structural patterns outlined by Griffith: although the battle threatened by the advancing Egyptians and anticipated by the fearful Israelites fails to happen, the beasts of battle passage performs its common Old English function of evoking the grim potential of warfare. We may contrast this with a stanza from Einarr skálaglamm's *Vellekla* where Hákon Sigurðarson consults an oracle before a battle in Götaland: *ok haldboði hildar sá ramma hrægamma* 'the one who offered to hold a battle saw strong corpse-vultures [eagles/ravens]' (st. 30). This is a rare appearance of carrion birds in skaldic poetry before the battle takes place, but unlike in Old English poetry, its purpose is not to evoke an atmosphere of doom for men and exultation for the birds, but to anticipate the warrior's glorious, and foreordained, victory in an image of well-fed ravens (or eagles).

It could be argued that the differences between the Old English and the Old Norse uses of the beasts of battle motif are as much a matter of literary genre as of different cultural traditions. Most of the Old English poetry containing this typescene is narrative, and Griffith has shown how the beasts of battle are integral to the narration of battle, while skaldic praise poetry is not really a narrative genre, though it may have some narrative elements. The *Battle of Brunanburh* can be seen as a kind of Old English praise poem which has occasionally (and rather superficially) been likened to skaldic verse. This poem at least implies, even if it does not quite state, that Athelstan and Edmund fed the beasts of battle, by its sandwiching of the beasts passage (ll. 60-65a) between the statement that the two brothers went home to Wessex (ll. 57-59) and the superlative statement that this battle had been the biggest ever in English history (ll. 65b-73). This makes *Brunanburh*, of all the Old English poems with this typescene, most like the Norse skaldic convention, because of this similarity of function, but the similarity is not great as, apart from its context, the beasts passage in *Brunanburh* is lexically and stylistically like the other Old English examples.[7]

The "companionable triads", as Frank calls them, of eagle, raven and wolf are not restricted to Old English and Old Norse poetry, and Frank notes some parallels in other literatures, though mainly to dismiss them (1987:348). However, I find

---

[7] G. Neckel noted that *Brunanburh* is the only example in Old English of the beasts of battle "geradezu am Werk", while "Bei den nordischen Dichtern dagegen ist dies an ungezählten Stellen der Fall". He would ascribe this difference to the fact that the Old English texts were written by "fast lauter Geistliche", while "an den altnordischen Fürstenhofen...hatte man zu der heidnischen Kampfpoesie der Vorfahren lediglich ein ästhetisches Verhältnis" (1915-1919:27-29).

that the use of this motif in *The Gododdin*, for instance, is more like the Old Norse usage than Frank admits (1987:353n.16). This poem is culturally and chronologically quite distant from the skaldic verse I have been looking at: on their title pages, K. Jackson calls it "the oldest Scottish poem" and A. O. H. Jarman "Britain's oldest heroic poem".[8] It is perhaps more accurately seen as a group of poems, and it is thought to be from the sixth or early seventh century, although preserved only in a thirteenth-century Welsh manuscript.[9] However, it is crucially very similar to skaldic poetry in its social function.[10] *The Gododdin* was composed to commemorate and praise dead warriors, and arose out of a specific historical moment, a battle at Catraeth at some time in the sixth century.[11]

In *The Gododdin*, we find that battle is called a "ravens' feast" (l. 25),[12] "raven's gain" (l. 63) or "wolf-feast" (l. 62).[13] The poem consists mainly of a catalogue of individual heroes and their deeds (Jackson 1969:3), so we are told that "He made food for eagles" (l. 215),[14] "He fed the wolves by his hand" (l. 330), "Through his fury he brought/A feast for the birds/From the uproar of battle" (ll. 571-573), "The beaks of grey eagles esteemed his hand;/In his fury he fed birds of prey" (ll. 630-

---

[8] The text of *The Gododdin* is complex and obscure, especially to one, like me, who cannot read Old (or indeed any) Welsh. I cite Jarman's translation, but give variations, where they seem significant, from both Jackson and Koch (the latter, it should be noted, attempts to reconstruct the seventh-century poem). Since each editor presents the text in a slightly different way, it is not possible to use a uniform mode of citation, and I refer to Jarman's text by line number, and to Jackson and Koch by page number.

[9] There is some early poetry of a similar date and with similar subject matter in another thirteenth-century manuscript, the *Book of Taliesin* (Williams 1972:46,49).

[10] Rowland (1990:36) notes that "a panegyric, like *The Gododdin*...plays a specific role in the life of the community, upholding social values and organization".

[11] For a discussion of the problems of dating both the poem and the events it celebrates, see Dumville 1988.

[12] While Jarman's translation of ll. 23-26 ("Quicker to the field of blood/Than to a wedding,/Quicker to the ravens' feast/Than to a burial") suggests, in two parallel examples, a warrior who is keener on war than on the rituals of normal life, Jackson's interpretation (1969:115), admitted by Jarman (1988:78) to be the most obvious reading of the manuscript, suggests a two-stage process: the warrior who is keen both on going to war and on dying honourably on the battlefield ("He would sooner have gone to the battlefield than to a wedding, he would sooner have been food for ravens than get due burial"). Koch's text (1997:53) suggests a young warrior cut off before his chance to live a normal life: "His blood flowed to the ground/before his wedding rite./His flesh went to crows/rather than to thy burial rite." This example illustrates the difficulty of using *The Gododdin* to explore early heroic concepts in detail. Luckily, the translation problems of most Norse poetry are not so great.

[13] Again (see previous note), Jarman (1988:81) assumes a warrior eager to go to battle, while Jackson (1969:117) interprets the lines as referring to a warrior eager to be food for wolves and ravens. Koch (1997:53) puts the statement into the past tense and gives it quite a different meaning: "Rather than to a wedding rite, his flesh went to wolves,/rather than to the altar, his victory spoils to the crow,/rather than to the altar, his blood flowed to the ground".

[14] Koch (1997:75,195) suggests "it was food for eagles that used to delight him".

631),[15] "He fed black ravens on the rampart of a fortress" (l. 971)[16] and "His hand fed the birds" (l. 975). In one of the *Gorchanau* ('additional lays') associated with the poem, a warrior is described as a "Feeder of birds/On bloody corpses" (ll. 1084-1085). However, unlike the skaldic verses, *The Gododdin* may also present us with warriors who are food, rather than feeders: "He was food for ravens, he was benefit to the crow" (l. 272)[17] and, in an interpolated stanza, "the head of Domnall Brecc, ravens gnawed it" (l. 996).[18] This double focus is in keeping with a poem that is as much elegy as eulogy (Jackson 1969:38; Jarman 1988:xl-xli, xliv-xlv), while the more straightforwardly eulogistic skaldic poems concentrate on those who provide the carrion rather than those who become it.

The Norse material also generally lacks the trope by which warriors are identified with beasts, so important in *The Gododdin*: "The swoop of an eagle" (l. 41), "a wolf in fury" (l. 49), "the eagle of graceful movement" (l. 274),[19] "For his warriors, Gwyddien was an eagle" (l. 440), "A fierce eagle, laughing in battle" (l. 508), "the wolf of the host" (l. 603) and "An invincible eagle" (l. 828).[20] However, Scandinavian naming practices for the last millennium and a half or so show that identification of the male with certain animals is a very basic cultural practice there. There was no shortage of men named Ari/Qrn, Hrafn and Ulfr in the Viking Age and ever since, even if the comparison is not made directly in the Norse poetry, as it is in the Old Welsh.

Despite the chronological and linguistic gulf between *The Gododdin* and skaldic verse, they are, I would suggest, more similar in their uses of the beasts of battle than either is to the same topos in Old English poetry.[21] I take it that this similarity arises from their more immediate origins in a warrior culture (from which the Old English is more distant), and the similarity of their literary functions of praise of individual warriors and expression of their common ideology.[22]

---

[15] Koch (1997:23) suggests "he reckoned [the deeds of] his gauntlet, measuring in grey eagles; [for] in urgency, he made food for scavengers".

[16] Koch (1997:23,148) suggests "used to bring black crows down in front of the wall/of the fortified town".

[17] In a note on this line, Jarman (1988:96) wonders whether in fact another example of "a raven feast", i.e. battle, was intended here. Koch (1997:199) notes that "In the immediate context this is presumably a reference to the warriors slain by the hero, rather than the hero's own death".

[18] Jackson (1969:48) calls this a "fragment of a Strathclyde bardic panegyric on Ywain". It is discussed further by Williams (1972:79-80), who dates it to AD 642. See also Dumville 1988:6-7.

[19] This is the same warrior who "was food for the ravens" in l. 272, but see n. 17, above.

[20] Other animals are also used in this way, see Jackson (1969:41) and Jarman (1988:xli-xlii).

[21] As in skaldic verse, warriors are called "battle-leeks" (l. 174) and 'trees of battle' (l. 613). Just as the Norse verse has its parallels in the iconography of the Gotland stones, so we can see a similarly remote, but perhaps relevant, parallel to *The Gododdin* in Pictish sculpture such as the cross-slab from Aberlemno, with a battle-scene including a fallen warrior whose head is being pecked by a raven (described by Hicks 1993:143; depicted in Foster 1996:104; for further examples see Hicks 1993:183-4).

[22] See Rowland (1990:36-37) on the differences between Welsh panegyrics and "fully narrative Old English poems".

Eagles, ravens and wolves in other Norse poetry

Skaldic praise poetry is by no means the only surviving early Norse poetry, though it is the most obvious genre to start with for any study of pre-manuscript Scandinavia: the historical contexts and contents of the stanzas, the named poets, and the tight metrical structure all contribute to a sense of it as genuine, well-preserved and datable. Eddic poetry, on the other hand, is a different matter. It survives mainly in one manuscript from the late thirteenth century and, while most scholars would agree that at least some of the poems in this collection are ancient, there is very little evidence for dating the individual poems. Scholars who have tried have often come up with very different answers (Jónas Kristjánsson 1990). However, it is possible to argue, as Preben Meulengracht Sørensen has done, that for any Eddic poem the date of the surviving text is of secondary importance, and what is important is the evidence it provides for "an underlying universe of meaning, which could manifest itself in varying versions" ("et bagvedliggende betydningsunivers, der...har kunnet manifesteres i vekslende udforminger", 1991:224). There is sufficient evidence in the material already presented to show that eagles, ravens and wolves did indeed belong to the "underlying universe of meaning" of the Viking Age, and the Eddic poems cannot be ignored in discussing this.

The material is, however, quite various. The Eddic poems in which eagles, ravens and wolves are used in a way comparable to skaldic verse are, not surprisingly, those two great glorifications of the warrior life, *Helgakviða Hundingsbana I-II*.[23] In *Helgakviða Hundingsbana I* the warrior-hero Helgi is described by his captain Sinfjǫtli as *sá er opt hefir ǫrno sadda* 'he who has often sated eagles'(st. 35) and, in the flyting between Sinfjǫtli and Guðmundr (sts 44-45), they both make reference to the heroic convention:[24]

'Fyrr vilda ec	'Rather I should like to make
at Frecasteini	ravens sate themselves on your
hrafna seðia	corpse, at Frekastein, than give
á hræom þínom,	your bitches dog-food to devour
enn tícr yðrar	or be feeding your pigs; may ill-
teygia at solli	luck befall you!'
eða gefa gǫltom;	
deili grǫm við þic!'	
'Væri ycr, Sinfiǫtli,	'It would be much more fitting
sæmra myclo	for you, Sinfiotli,
gunni at heyia	to go to battle and make the
oc glaða ǫrno,	eagle happy,

---

[23] Scholars have often stressed the 'skaldic' qualities of *Helgakviða Hundingsbana I*, in particular, and it is sometimes dated to the eleventh or twelfth centuries on the basis of supposed parallels with some skaldic poems (e.g. Neckel 1908:365, 432-436; Bugge 1914).

[24] St. 45 is very closely paralleled in *Helgakviða Hundingsbana II*, st. 23. Note that the place-name Frekasteinn includes the wolf-name *Freki* (also in *Helgakviða Hundingsbana II*, st. 21, along with Arasteinn, in the prose between sts 13 and 14, including *ari* 'eagle').

enn sé ónýtom	than to be bandying useless
orðom at bregðaz,	words,
þótt hringbrotar	though these generous princes
heiptir deili.	may be bitter enemies.

The heroic context in this poem is however extended beyond the specific deeds and career of the adult hero, creating a heroic universe into which he is born. Helgi's success is foreordained at his birth when *arar gullo* "eagles screamed" (st. 1) and one raven *andvanr áto* "lacking food" (st. 5) can say to another raven of the one day-old child in his mail-coat that *sá er varga vinr/við sculom teitir* 'he is a friend of wolves, we should be cheerful' (st. 6). Although this has the element of anticipation that is rare in the skaldic examples, it is a logical development, even a mythologizing, of the skaldic idea of the warrior as the provider of carrion for the beasts of battle, with all three beasts associated with his birth.

In *Helgakviða Hundingsbana II*, the beasts creep into the dialogues between the hero and his beloved, the valkyrie Sigrún. When they first meet, she asks him *Hvar hefir þú, hilmir,/hildi vacþa/eða gǫgl alin/Gunnar systra* "Where have you, prince,/made war/or fed the geese [eagles/ravens]/of Gunn's sisters [valkyries]?" (st. 7) and he replies that *ec biorno tóc/í Bragalundi/oc ætt ara/oddom saddac* "I captured bears/in Bragalund/and the race of eagles/with points sated" (st. 8). And in an extraordinary variation on the Lenore motif, Sigrún anticipates her final night with the ghost of her dead lover by comparing herself with the beasts of battle rejoicing in carrion (st. 43):

Nú em ec svá fegin	"Now I am so glad, at our
fundi ocrom	meeting,
sem átfrekir	as are the greedy hawks of
Óðins haucar,	Odin
er val vito,	when they know of slaughter,
varmar bráðir,	steaming
eða dǫgglitir	food or, dew-drenched, they
dagsbrún siá.	see the dawn".

This is indeed a society (or at least a literary tradition) which interprets everything in terms of the warrior ideal.

The beasts are not especially common in the other 'heroic' poems of the *Edda*,[25] one exception being *Guðrúnarkviða II*, where Guðrún recalls how she was told of the death of her husband Sigurðr, gloatingly, by her brothers who killed him (st. 8):[26]

Líttu þar Sigurð	Look for Sigurd there
á suðrvega!	on the roads southwards!
Þá heyrir þú	There you'll hear
hrafna gialla,	the ravens shriek,

---

[25] Though see *Reginsmál*, sts 13, 18, 20, 22; *Fáfnismál*, st. 35; both with reference to Sigurðr's deeds.

[26] Compare *Brot*, sts 5, 13.

ǫrno gialla,	the eagles shriek;
æzli fegna,	rejoicing in the carrion,
varga þióta	the wolves are howling
um veri þínom.	over your husband.

Here, we are closer to the Old English examples of the topos, with the emphasis on the beasts' rejoicing and noisemaking, and the creation of an atmosphere of doom. The poem shares the elegiac mood of much Old English poetry, however, scholars agree that it postdates Old English poetry and, indeed, the Viking Age (Jónas Kristjánsson 1990:218).

In the mythological poems of the *Edda*, we meet mythological eagles, ravens and wolves, rather than the beasts of battle as such. *Grímnismál* (st. 19) shows us Óðinn, *gunntamiðr, hróðigr Herjafǫðr* 'used to battle, famous Father of Armies', feeding the wolves Freki and Geri. In the poem's immediate context of Óðinn's domestic arrangements in Valhǫll, he may just be tossing them scraps from the table, but the military implication is strongly present, as signalled by the adjectives and the circumlocutory name for Óðinn. The next stanza (st. 20) shows Óðinn using his two ravens, Huginn and Muninn, to gather intelligence from around the world.

Óðinn eventually dies by being eaten by the greatest wolf of all, the Fenriswolf, and the latter inevitably crops up in a number of mythological poems, especially those most concerned with Ragnarǫk (*Vǫluspá, Vafþrúðnismál* and *Lokasenna*). In this larger, cosmological, context, the beasts are not just the happy bystanders who benefit from the corpses provided by the victorious warrior, they acquire eschatalogical significance for humankind, presaging The End. In *Vǫluspá* the eagle eats corpses and wolves run, marking the start of Ragnarǫk (sts 50-51). Even natural phenomena turn out to be a beast in disguise: in *Vafþrúðnismál*, the wind which "passes over all men" is actually a giant wearing an eagle's skin, whose name is *Hræsvelgr,* "corpse-swallower" (st. 37).

These mythological eagles, ravens and wolves are relatively well represented in the iconography of the Viking Age. For instance, the Ledberg rune stone from Östergötland shows Óðinn being devoured by the Fenriswolf (Brate 1911-1918:174-176,pl.LXI; Jansson 1987:151), as does the Kirk Andreas rune stone from the Isle of Man, where he is additionally identified by the raven on his shoulder (Jansson 1987:152). There is clearly much more that could be said about eagles, ravens and wolves in Old Norse mythology and Viking Age art, but here I restrict myself to exploring the associations between these animals and royal and warrior ideology in the commemorative media of the Viking Age.

The mythological, eschatological mode of the Eddic poems, reflecting the negative aspects, the inevitability, of death as well as the more positive glorification of the victorious warrior who inflicts death, can also be seen in a group of poems usually called 'Eddic praise poems': *Haraldskvæði, Eiríksmál* and *Hákonarmál*. There is not space here to summarize the lengthy discussions there have been about the authenticity and interrelationships between these poems, or to interrogate their texts in detail.[27] However, they are a useful control when considering any sort of difference between Eddic and skaldic verse, since they share characteristics of both genres and, indeed, often cause us to question the very definitions of those genres. Like skaldic praise poetry, they are preserved in the kings' sagas, and associated with particular kings, as their titles indicate. Skaldic praise poems can be either posthumous or contemporaneous with the king being eulogized, and so *Eiríksmál* and *Hákonarmál* are clearly posthumous, while *Haraldskvæði* appears to be contemporaneous. While *Eiríksmál* is anonymous, both *Haraldskvæði* and *Hákonarmál* are attributed to known poets, although the former presents a complicated problem of authorship: a number of stanzas thought by some scholars to belong to a poem in praise of Haraldr hárfagri are attributed to up to three different poets in a number of different sources, none of which contains all of the stanzas (Jón Helgason 1968:10-15). On the other hand, all three poems are Eddic in their metre, and it should be noted that this use of looser metres removes one of the planks of the argument used to assert the authenticity of skaldic praise poems: that their strict skaldic metres helped ensure their correct transmission in the oral, pre-written tradition. These three poems are also more like the Eddic genre in their content. They share with many Eddic poems a dialogic and dramatic structure, in which gods and mythological beings appear as speaking characters.

Both *Eiríksmál* and *Hákonarmál* present a dramatic vision of the entry of the dead and defeated king into Valhǫll direct from his final battle, and his welcome there. Both poems associate the king's presence in Valhǫll with an impending Ragnarǫk. This is explicit in *Eiríksmál*, where the necessity of the hero's defeat is explained by Óðinn himself: *Því at óvíst es at vita...sér úlfr enn hǫsvi á sjǫt goða* "Because things are uncertain...the grey wolf [i.e. the Fenriswolf] is gazing on the home of the gods" (st. 7). The association is more indirect, but nevertheless clear enough, in *Hákonarmál*, which says (st. 20):

Mun óbundinn	The wolf of Fenrir will
áýta sjǫt	be let loose upon the
Fenrisulfr of fara,	homes of men before
áðr jafngóðr	so good a prince shall
á auða trǫð	succeed to his vacant
konungmaðr komi.	place.

Thus, these two poems are analogous to the mythological poems cited above, in which the whole thrust is towards the inevitable Ragnarǫk. The praise of Eiríkr and Hákon is not for their ephemeral victories, their success in battle in this world; rather they are elevated to mythological proportions as defenders of the worlds of the gods and humans against forces of evil and destruction.

Haraldskvæði, on the other hand, is set in this world rather than the next and does not have this strongly pagan world-view (although I will argue below that it has a similar mythical focus). It makes use of the beasts (or rather the birds) of

---

[27] See e.g. von See (1981:295-343). Fidjestøl (1982) excludes them from his corpus of court poetry.

battle in a way that I find is most reminiscent of the Eddic poems about the hero Helgi Hundingsbani.[28] The poet begins by asking his audience to listen to his account of a conversation he overheard between a valkyrie (a 'fair, lighthaired maiden') and a raven, which begins (sts 3-4):

"Hvat es yðr, hrafnar?	"How is it with you, ye ravens?
Hvaðan eruð ér komnir	Whence are ye come with bloody
með dreyrgu nefi	beak at the dawning of day? Torn
at degi ǫndverðum?	flesh is hanging from your talons,
Hold loðir yðr í klóm,	and a reek of carrion comes from
hræs þefr gengr ór munni;	your mouths. I doubt not that ye
nær hygg ek yðr í nótt bjǫggu	have passed the night amid a
því es vissuð nái liggja".	scene of carnage".
Hreyfðisk enn hǫsfjaðri	The sworn brother of the eagle
ok of hyrnu þerrði,	shook his dusky plumage, wiped
arnar eiðbróðir,	his beak, and thought upon his
ok at andsvǫrum hugði:	answer:
"Haraldi vér fylgðum,	"We have followed Harold, the
syni Halfdanar,	son of Halfdan, the youthful scion
ungum Ynglingi,	of Yngvi, ever since we came out
síðan ór eggi kómum".	of the egg".

The raven then goes on to tell the valkyrie about different aspects of Haraldr's life and rule, his abilities in sailing and war, his preference for 'drinking Yule' out at sea rather than indoors in the warmth, his generosity and the entertainments at his court, his berserkers who are called *ulfheðnar* 'wolf-skinned', and so on. The stanzas thought by some to be a separate poem on the battle of Hafrsfjǫrðr describe the king's most famous battle, but without making use of the beasts of battle motif (although we do see the *ulfheðnar* in action).[29]

The opening conversation between the valkyrie and the raven, and the description of the latter, imply the eulogistic convention of the warrior who generously provides carrion for the beasts of battle (here only the raven and the eagle). As in *Helgakviða Hundingsbana I*, the topos is used as a framing device for a comprehensive account of the hero's career. As in both Helgi poems, a valkyrie is implicated. Whatever our views on the authenticity of *Haraldskvæði* as a Viking Age poem (and I have my doubts), we have to recognize that it is not a conventional praise poem for a king or his immediate successor(s), recording his recent achievements. The distancing device of the poet and his overheard conversation between a girl and a bird contributes to our sense that this is a poem intended to raise the king to a mythical level, on a par with legendary, semi-divine heroes like Helgi, to create an image of a king for all time, rather than just our time.

---

[28] There are some similarities between *Haraldskvæði* and *Hákonarmál*, too. In the latter, Hákon has a conversation with the valkyrie sent by Óðinn to fetch him to Valhǫll.

[29] Kershaw (1922:76-91) treats the stanzas on Haraldr hárfagri as two separate poems, *The Hrafnsmál* and *The Battle of Hafsfjord*.

Summary and further discussion

Above I have presented a range of material, arguably from the Viking Age, or representing that age's 'universe of meaning' in some way, and showing the symbolic uses of the three 'beasts of battle', eagles, ravens and wolves.[30] I have tried to show how Norse usage both differs from and is more varied than the usages of cognate and parallel literatures such as Old English and Old Welsh. I have also tried to bring out how much of this symbolic usage is dependent on the literary genre in which it appears, with elegiac, eulogistic and mythologizing texts all making different uses of the beasts, although there will sometimes be reminiscences of one in the other.

But what significance does this aspect of 'symbolic life' have for our study of the development of Scandinavian culture in the last quarter of the first millennium? Writing passionately during the First World War, G. Neckel certainly believed, with J. Grimm, that the beasts of battle were a relic of "der heidnischen Germanen".[31] But as a careful scholar, and as a specialist Nordicist, Neckel was alive to the important differences between the Old English and Old Norse uses of the beasts of battle.[32] For Neckel the skaldic uses of the beasts of battle, although the best reflection of the ancient Germanic beliefs in these creatures, are mainly "malerische Phantasiebilder", since "mehr als die dekorative Wirkung wollte man nicht; das innere Leben der Motive starb ab" (1915-1919:29). He also recognized the ways in which the motif developed in later skaldic usage. Thus, the mid-eleventh-century Arnórr jarlaskáld's image of the wolf who has trouble climbing over the piles of corpses is positively "barock" (Neckel 1915-1919:30). Neckel's approach is a kind of textual archaeology:[33] our surviving poems are very much a part of their place and time, but it is still possible to use them to detect the traces of earlier attitudes and beliefs (in his case, those of "der heidnischen Germanen"). Neckel then goes on to speculate what "jene alte Kampfpoesie, auf die die nordische, angelsächsische und deutsche Dichtung zurückweisen" (1915-1919:30-31) might have been like, but it is not necessary to follow him down this particular path.

Without attempting to return to those old heathen 'Germanen', it is still possible to take the beasts of battle back into the first half of the ninth century in

---

[30] A few zoological notes on the beasts are appropriate. All three are known to eat carrion, and would presumably not distinguish human carrion from other sorts. On ravens and various sorts of eagles, see Campbell 1974:232, 255, 279. Wolves eat carrion as well as killing "[p]robably every kind of backboned animal that lives in the range of the wolf" for their food (Mech 1970:179-180). There is also a close relationship between ravens and wolves, "flocks of ravens routinely follow wolf packs from kill to kill and dine on the leavings of the packs" (Mech 1970:287).

[31] "Die Engländer, die heute erklären, sie seien keine Germanen, haben nicht ganz unrecht...die englische Kultur steht der unsrigen ziemlich fern" (Neckel 1915-1919:43).

[32] See n. 3, above. Neckel recognizes that "Grimm kannte die Skalden noch kaum" (1915-1919:30).

[33] He calls the Old English texts with the beasts of battle motif "Blöcke aus einem alten Kunstbau, die neu behauen und neu vermauert sind" (1915-1919:30).

Scandinavia. The inscription on the great stone at Rök in Östergötland, "the most impressive monument ever raised in Sweden to commemorate a dead kinsman... the great memorial of Swedish literature in antiquity" (Jansson 1987:31), contains an allusion to the wolf on the battlefield (Brate 1911-1918:231-255; Jansson 1987:32-33):

Þat sagum tvalfta, hvar hæstR	That I tell twelfth, where the horse
se GunnaR etu vettvangi an,	of Gunn [i.e. steed of the Valkyrie,
kunungaR tvaiR tigiR svað a	the wolf] sees food on the battle-
liggia.	field, where twenty kings lie.

Many links can be made between this text and Old Norse poetry, both Eddic and skaldic, although there is much obscurity in what the Rök inscription means, and who it is about. Nevertheless, there is here a clear association between one of the beasts of battle, and kings and princes at war.

It is possible to trace the uses of the beasts of battle in the Scandinavian culture of the Viking Age, from at least the ninth century onwards. The parallels in Old Welsh poetry have shown that they are not just icons of a distant Germanic past, but that they have a particular function in eulogistic poetry. In Norse poetry, they are intimately associated with the growing power and developing ideology of war-leaders and, eventually, kings, who achieved their position by their prowess on the battlefield. We see this in the immediate praise of historical kings in skaldic poetry, and in the more mythical structures of Eddic poems such as the Helgi poems, or the Eddic-style praise poems. The Gotland picture stones and the Rök stone provide East Norse examples that are parallel. We can perhaps even see it in the raven symbol used on the coins issued in York *ca* 939-940 by the Hiberno-Norse king Anlaf Guthfrithsson (Roesdahl *et al.* 1981:135,140), showing that this ideology was exported with viking rulers to the British Isles.[34] It may be that archaeologists and art historians can produce further evidence linking these beasts with warrior kings before the literate period. However, it is important to remember that animal imagery could be used with a range of meanings in different contexts and we should beware of reading particular meanings into contexts which do not support those meanings (Hawkes 1997:319-320). Poetry has an advantage over the visual arts in providing a more easily-interpretable context for the relevant motifs.

It is possible to see a religious, i.e. heathen, connection behind all this, and certainly eagles, ravens and wolves are all associated with Óðinn in Old Icelandic texts. Nevertheless, this association must be secondary, arising because Óðinn is the god of war, for the animal symbolism is independent of religious associations. After all, it continued to be used by skalds praising Christian kings and rulers in the eleventh century. The beasts were a symbol that could be creatively adapted, and they were, for different ideological purposes. Ultimately, however, their origins lay in the early Scandinavians' observations of the natural world, and their symbolic interpretation of social phenomena in the context of these observations.

---

[34] Although perhaps the Celtic connection should not be ignored here.

References

Textual sources:

Adam of Bremen
  Gesta Hammaburgensis Ecclesiae Pontificum: see Trillmich & Buchner 1978.
The Battle of Brunanburh: see Dobbie 1942.
Beowulf: see Dobbie 1953.
Brot af Sigurðarkviðu: see Neckel & Kuhn 1983: 198-201; Larrington 1996:174-176.
Egill Skallagrímsson
  Hǫfuðlausn: see Finnur Jónsson 1912-1915:IB,30-33; Nordal 1933:185-192;
  Fell 1975:190-193.
Einarr skálaglamm
  Vellekla: see Finnur Jónsson 1912-1915:IB,117-124; cited from Bjarni
  Aðalbjarnarson 1979:I, 209, 261.
Eiríksmál: see Jón Helgason 1968:21-23; Kershaw 1922:97-99.
Exodus: see Krapp 1931.
Eyjólfr dáðaskáld
  Bandadrápa: see Finnur Jónsson 1912-1915:IB,190-192; cited from Bjarni
  Aðalbjarnarson 1979:I, 338.
Fáfnismál: see Neckel & Kuhn 1983:180-188; Larrington 1996:157-165.
The Gododdin: see Jackson 1969 (trans.); Jarman 1988 (ed. & trans.); Koch 1997 (ed. &
  trans.).
Grímnismál: see Neckel & Kuhn 1983:57-68; Larrington 1996:50-60.
Guðrúnarkviða II: see Neckel & Kuhn 1983:224-231; Larrington 1996:196-202.
Hákonarmál: see Jón Helgason 1968:23-28; Kershaw 1922:105-109.
Halldórr ókristni
  Eiríksflokkr: see Finnur Jónsson 1912-1915:IB,193-195; cited from Bjarni
  Aðalbjarnarson 1979:I, 350, 367.
Hallfreðr vandræðaskáld
  Óláfsdrápa: see Finnur Jónsson 1912-1915:IB,148-150; cited from Bjarni
  Aðalbjarnarson 1979:I,263-265.
  Óláfsdrápa. Erfidrápa: see Finnur Jónsson 1912-1915:IB,150-157; cited
  from Bjarni Aðalbjarnarson 1979:I, 368.
Haraldskæði: see Jón Helgason 1968:10-21; Kershaw 1922:83-87, 91.
Helgakviða Hundingsbana I: see Neckel & Kuhn 1983:130-139; Larrington 1996:114-122.
Helgakviða Hundingsbana II: see Neckel & Kuhn 1983:150-161; Larrington 1996:132-141.
Kormákr Ǫgmundarson
  Sigurðardrápa: see Finnur Jónsson 1912-1915:IB, 69-70; cited from Faulkes
  1998:70.
Lokasenna: see Neckel & Kuhn 1983:96-109; Larrington 1996:84-96.
Reginsmál: see Neckel & Kuhn 1983:173-179; Larrington 1996:151-156.
Snorri Sturluson
  Edda. Skáldskaparmál: see Faulkes 1987 (trans.), 1998 (ed.).
  Heimskringla: see Bjarni Aðalbjarnarson 1979.
Þórðr Kolbeinsson
  Eiríksdrápa: see Finnur Jónsson 1912-1915:IB, 203-206; cited from Faulkes
  1998:88.
Tindr Hallkelsson
  Hákonardrápa: see Finnur Jónsson 1912-1915:IB, 136-138; cited from
  Bjarni Aðalbjarnarson 1979:I, 286.
Vafþrúðnismál: see Neckel & Kuhn 1983:45-55; Larrington 1996:39-49.

Vǫluspá: see Neckel & Kuhn 1983:1-16; Larrington 1996:3-13.

Bibliography:

Bjarni Aðalbjarnarson (ed.)
1979   *Snorri Sturluson. Heimskringla.* (Íslenzk fornrit 26-28). Reykjavík: Hið íslenzka fornritafélag. [first published 1941-51].
Brate, E. (ed.)
1911-1918   *Östergötlands runinskrifter.* (Sveriges runinskrifter 2). Stockholm: Kungl. Vitterhets Historie och Antikvitets Akademien.
Bugge, A.
1914   Arnor jarlaskald og det første kvad om Helge Hundingsbane. *Edda* 1: 350-380.
Campbell, B.
1974   *The Dictionary of Birds in Colour.* London: Joseph.
Dobbie, K. E. van (ed.)
1942   *The Anglo-Saxon Minor Poems.* (The Anglo-Saxon Poetic Records 6). New York: University of Columbia Press.
1953   *Beowulf and Judith.* (The Anglo-Saxon Poetic Records 4). New York: Columbia University Press.
Dumville, D.
1988   Early Welsh poetry: problems of historicity. In *Early Welsh Poetry. Studies in the Book of Aneirin.* B. F. Roberts (ed.), pp. 1-16. Aberystwyth: National Library of Wales.
Faulkes, A. (ed./trans.)
1987   *Snorri Sturluson. Edda.* London: Dent.
1998   *Snorri Sturluson. Edda. Skáldskaparmál.* London: Viking Society for Northern Research.
Fell, C. (trans.)
1975   *Egils saga.* London: Dent.
Fidjestøl, B.
1982   *Det norrøne fyrstediktet.* Øvre Ervik: Alvheim & Eide.
1999   *The Dating of Eddic Poetry. A Historical Survey and Methodological Investigation.* (Bibliotheca Arnamagnæana 41). Copenhagen: C. A. Reitzel.
Finnur Jónsson (ed.)
1912-1915   *Den norsk-islandske skjaldedigtning.* Copenhagen: Villadsen & Christensen.
Foote, P.
1984   Things in early Norse verse. In *Festskrift til Ludvig Holm-Olsen.* B. Fidjestøl *et al.* (eds), pp. 74-83. Øvre Ervik: Alvheim & Eide.
Foster, S. M.
1996   *Picts, Gaels and Scots.* London: Batsford.
Frank, R.
1987   Did Anglo-Saxon audiences have a skaldic tooth? *Scandinavian Studies* 59: 338-355.
Griffith, M. S.
1993   Convention and originality in the Old English 'beasts of battle' typescene. *Anglo-Saxon England* 22: 179-199.
Grimm, J. (ed.)
1840   *Andreas und Elene.* Cassel: Fischer.
Hawkes, J.
1997   Symbolic lives: the visual evidence. In *The Anglo-Saxons from the Migration Period to the Eighth Century: An Ethnographic Perspective.* J. Hines (ed.), pp. 311-344. Woodbridge: Boydell.

Hicks, C.
1993   *Animals in Early Medieval Art*. Edinburgh: Edinburgh University Press.
Hines, J.
1995   Egill's *Hǫfuðlausn* in time and place. *Saga-Book* 24 (2-3): 83-104.
Honegger, T.
1998   Form and function: the beasts of battle revisited. *English Studies* 4: 289-298.
Jackson, K. (trans.)
1969   *The Gododdin: The Oldest Scottish Poem*. Edinburgh: Edinburgh University Press.
Jansson, S. B. F.
1987   *Runes in Sweden*. Stockholm: Gidlunds.
Jarman, A. O. H. (ed. & trans.)
1988   *Aneirin: Y Gododdin. Britain's Oldest Heroic Poem*. Llandysul: Gomer.
Jesch, J.
2001   *Ships and Men in the Late Viking Age. The Vocabulary of Runic Inscriptions and Skaldic Verse*. Woodbridge: Boydell.
Jón Helgason (ed.)
1962   *Skjaldevers*. Copenhagen: Munksgaard.
Jónas Kristjánsson
1990   Stages in the composition of Eddic poetry. In *Poetry in the Scandinavian Middle Ages*. T. Pàroli (ed.), pp. 201-218. Spoleto: Centro Italiano di Studi sull'Alto Medioevo.
Kershaw, N. (ed. & trans.)
1922   *Anglo-Saxon and Norse Poems*. Cambridge: Cambridge University Press.
Koch, J. T. (ed. & trans.)
1997   *The Gododdin of Aneirin. Text and Context from Dark-Age North Britain*. Cardiff: University of Wales Press.
Krapp, G. P. (ed.)
1931   *The Junius Manuscript*. (The Anglo-Saxon Poetic Records 1). New York: Columbia University Press.
Larrington, C. (trans.)
1996   *The Poetic Edda*. Oxford: Oxford University Press.
Lindqvist, S.
1941-2   *Gotlands Bildsteine*. Stockholm: Kungl. Vitterhets Historie och Antikvitets Akademien.
Mech, L. D.
1970   *The Wolf: The Ecology and Behavior of an Endangered Species*. Garden City, NY: American Museum of Natural History.
Meulengracht Sørensen, P.
1991   Om eddadigtenes alder. In *Nordisk hedendom: et symposium*. Gro Steinsland *et al.* (eds), pp. 217-228. Odense: Odense University Press.
Neckel, G.
1908   *Beiträge zur Eddaforschung, mit Exkursen zur Heldensage*. Dortmund: Ruhfus.
1915-19   Die kriegerische Kultur der heidnischen Germanen. *Germanisch-romanische Monatsschrift* 7: 17-44.
Neckel, G., & H. Kuhn (eds.)
1983   *Edda. Die Lieder der Codex Regius nebst verwandenten Denkmälern*. Heidelberg: Winter.
Nordal, S. (ed.)
1933   *Egils saga Skalla-Grímssonar*. (Íslenzk fornrit 2). Reykjavík: Hið íslenzka fornritafélag.

Roesdahl, E., *et al.*
1981   *The Vikings in England.* London: Anglo-Danish Project.
Rowland, J.
1990   *Early Welsh Saga Poetry. A Study and Edition of the Englynion.* Cambridge:
           D. S. Brewer.
See, K. von
1981   *Edda, Saga, Skaldendichtung.* Heidelberg: Winter.
Trillmich, W., & R. Buchner (eds. & trans.)
1978   *Quellen des 9. und 11. Jahrhunderts zur Geschichte der Hamburgischen
           Kirche und des Reiches.* Darmstadt: Wissenschaftliche Buchgesellschaft.
           [first published 1961].
Varenius, B.
1992   *Det nordiska skeppet.* (Stockholm Studies in Archaeology, 10). Stockholm:
           Stockholms Universitet.
Williams, I.
1972   *The Beginnings of Welsh Poetry.* Cardiff: University of Wales Press.
Wilson, D.
1998   The Gotland picture-stones. A chronological re-assessment. In *Studien zur
           Archäologie des Ostseeraumes.* A. Wesse (ed.), pp. 49-52. Neumünster:
           Wachholtz.

Discussion

GREEN: You mention (page 253) the beasts of battle, eagle, raven and wolf, as a feature both of OE and ON poetry. I think you can strengthen your case quite considerably if you extend your coverage of these beasts of battle from poetry to name-giving. To complete that evidence we need, I think, to go beyond the evidence of poetry. For the wolf I am thinking of names, such as OHG Hildulf, 'battle wolf', Gundulf, 'battle wolf', Randulf, 'shield wolf', Ortolf, 'spear wolf', and to take another animal, the wild boar, Eburhard, 'as harsh as a wild boar'. Now, I hesitate to use a technical linguistic term when we move to a slightly different category in name giving: the technical term is to refer to them by a Sanskrit word, a *bahuvrihi* compound, i.e. compounds which imply that the name means not what it says, but someone who possesses what is said. *Bahuvrihi* in Sanskrit means literally 'much rice', but it means someone who is rich because he possesses much rice. As an example in name-giving we have a name like Hrodger, literally 'a famous spear', then someone who wields a famous spear, so a warrior. This is slightly different, but it is still a *bahuvrihi* compound. Or again: Wolfram, literally 'wolf plus raven', not someone who possesses a raven, but someone who summons the raven and the wolf by his deeds on the battlefield, where he slaughters his foes. I think that means we have to differentiate between an animal of the battlefield like a wolf, because he can be equated with the warrior (the warrior fights like a wolf) as distinct from the raven (it cannot be said that the warrior fights like a raven, but that he commands or summons the ravens by his deeds, at the scene of his exploits). Both are beasts of the battlefield but there is this differentiation. And just as a further mention, do you know, on the bibliographical side, the work in German of G. Schramm (1957) and G. Müller (1960) on this? I think it would strengthen your case considerably if you could have a reference to that.

JESCH: I am bit worried about that kind of extension. You move very quickly from a naming that somebody possesses something to some other connection with the object described by the name.

GREEN: Yes, but when you are talking about beasts of battle, eagles, ravens and wolves, you must make a distinction between the first two and the third. And you yourself, when you come to this point, make that distinction, by implication.

JESCH: But what I am also trying to do is to keep boars out of it entirely.

GREEN: Yes, I merely brought that in as a further example.

JESCH: It would be interesting to bring in all these beasts in all the different contexts, but I am actually trying to narrow it down to very a specific context which I think is Scandinavian and not Germanic: this actual mention of the warrior.

GREEN: From my point of view, one cannot ignore this Germanic parallel.

MAGNUS: May I ask a question. In what way does the wolf fight? You [Green] make a distinction between wolves, ravens, eagles.

GREEN: The wolf is regarded as an animal like the marten and others, an animal whose ferocity in fighting not any human beings but any other animal is a source of admiration for any human warrior. They fight, whereas the eagle and the raven to do not fight, they eat only carrion. The wolf does that too, but he fights as well.

AUSENDA: And wolves too go around in packs like a *comitatus* [laughter].

GREEN: You say (page 254) that Frank (1987) would prefer to see the link as an instance of Old Norse influence on Old English rather than as "relics of a distant Germanic past". Well, certainly, that is a possibility, I will not deny that, but the onomastic parallels from OHG, not the poetic ones, suggest the former possibility, namely the distant Germanic past. I know you expressed your distance from that, but I think that cannot be ignored.

JESCH: I think the general idea of beasts of battle is probably even older than Germanic.

GREEN: Yes, certainly.

JESCH: I do not deny that it occurred and that it is important. I disagree with Frank, I don't think she has demonstrated that it is Old Norse influence on Old English I think it is quite the opposite, if anything, but I think probably there is no direct connection between the Old Norse and the Old English.

GREEN: No direct influence of one or the other.

JESCH: What I am trying to pin down, is what I think is a particularly Scandinavian development of the basic idea of the beasts of battle.

GREEN: And the basic idea, would you see that as common Germanic?

JESCH: Yes, I do, I should have made that clear.

MEULENGRACHT: You asked for questions on the dating of skaldic poetry. Gifted skalds were able to make new poetry in the style of the older skalds and they did that. So, we have virtually no method to decide what is original skaldic poetry and what is new skaldic poetry made in the old skalds' style.

JESCH: Is what you are saying, that there are certain types of contents, which you cannot argue are old precisely because they are imitating the older poetry?

MEULENGRACHT: No, I would say if you are a clever skald, then you will be able to make a new stanza imitating the classical skalds.

JESCH: Oh, I certainly accept that point and I agree with you that we don't really have a method of distinguishing one from the other. But I cannot imagine them bothering to make up all these thousands of stanzas about obscure battles in the Baltic.

MEULENGRACHT: Some sagas, *Gísla saga*, for example, contains skaldic poetry attributed to Gísli, apparently around the year 1000. Yet Peter Foote has shown, I think, convincingly that this poetry is from the twelfth century.

JESCH: That's a different kind of poetry from the kind of poetry I am talking about. I think there is a very substantial difference in the content, and I do think that you have to take content into account, even though I take all your caveats on one level.

AUSENDA: With reference to page 254, in 1987, during my fieldwork with the Beni Amer, both in eastern Sudan and later in Eritrea, I came across a minstrel who sang in Tigré, a seldom written language, a poem entitled *The war for cattle*. The minstrel sang an epic poem describing the bloody encounters between Beni Amer 'owners' (of cattle) with bandits, *shiftàh*, coming from Ethiopia (*ca* 1948-51), i.e. approximately fifty years after the events. There too there were vultures 'getting fat' on the corpses of dead warriors belonging to different and named clans, always in numbers of seven for each clan. The presence of the vultures gives an even more tragic background to events during which the 'flower' of those clans was killed. I obtained a version from the singer himself the day after one of his performances in exchange for a set of photographs I took of him and his dancers. To my knowledge, the version changed every time he sang, especially since the glorified clans changed according to the audience. I believe I am the only one to have transcribed the poem and obtained a translation. During his performance, the people belonging to the named clans in the audience, would stand up, draw their swords and shout the equivalent of 'hooray' in Tigré. The dancers there, not only the men but also the female dancers did that backward motion which one can see in Egyptian tomb frescos.

When I was in eastern Sudan in 1987, 88, 89, and in Eritrea in 1992, I heard various versions of stanzas sung by a poet, Idriss-wad-Amir (son of Amir) who had served in the colonial coast guard for a while, and had orally composed in Tigré stanzas about his forlorn love for a girl, a street vendor of drinks he had met in Massawa who had been sent back to her native mountains to marry a close cousin chosen by her family. The author had died in Kuwait shortly after the war and had never 'written down' the stanzas. Most probably he did not know how to write. There was no official written version until after the 'liberation' from the Ethiopians in 1991 when a well known Tigré singer sang several stanzas, according to his recollection, for the Tigré-language radio program, thus giving birth to an 'official version'. On the basis of studies by Milman Parry and A. B. Lord—there is also a good book by Minna Skafte Jensen on *The Homeric Question and the Oral-formulaic Theory*—do you not expect that the poem was not originally written but transcribed at a later date, approximately 50 to 100 years, perhaps when alphabetical writing reached Scandinavia?

JESCH: It depends which poem you are talking about. I have a problem with poetry from the tenth century and earlier, where there is a bigger gap. But when you are talking about the poetry supposedly composed in the middle of the eleventh century, then you are already practically in the literate period and you can imagine quite a small gap between the composition and the writing. In the case of skaldic poetry, the argument usually is, because the metre is so strict, it is actually easier to preserve the text more or less in its original form than the other types of poetry that are usually cited in the discussion of oral-formulaic poetry. It is not formulaic, it is nothing that you can give a rough approximation of every time you recite it, in quite a different way. What interested me in your description of that minstrel's performance, is the tone of what's happening, you are saying the vultures give a tragic background to the fall of the flower of the clan, that's quite the opposite, that sounds like Old English, or *The Gododdin*. Skaldic poetry is quite the opposite, very positive, "hey, we slaughtered lots of people and fed hundreds of vultures on their meat". But I think the general idea crops up in a lot of places. I think the problem of orally composed poetry is a very interesting one, and I personally found R. Finnegan's writing on oral poetry in Africa (1988) quite stimulating because she has a much more nuanced view of the back and forth between oral and written traditions and the different contexts in which this poetry is performed and used. So, I think that we can forget Parry and Lord and move on to other parallels.

GREEN: That's high time we did.

HERSCHEND: I was wondering whether one could see the difference between the earlier tradition in Anglo-Saxon poetry and this Norse poetry as a typical difference between those who take part actively working together with wolves, eagles and others, and those who are just retainers, having part of the retainership to look at these beasts in a symbolic way. The best example of people actively working together with eagles, wolves and ravens, that is the *Finnsburh Fragment* where the Danish king anticipates the eagles coming and the wolves coming before the fighting starts and apparently after the fighting he says that "there comes a raven and there comes a battle light" so that there are two types of light at the beginning of the attack. And after the attack we get the raven to feed on the things and we see that the light is the battle light of Finnsburh. This is a very interactive way of working from these, which is not at all present in Norse poetry where they are just mentioned as remembrance of the happy fight. So that could be a retainer point of view, i.e. from an individual active in the fight. By the way it is an act, the act from the king's point of view, while the Norse would be the retainer's point of view.

JESCH: I am not sure I have a view on that just at the moment. I will just think about that. Thank you.

AUSENDA: Could you explain (page 256) the difference between a 'kenning' and an 'epithet'?

JESCH: A kenning is a device that is found in many languages, but again more frequently in Old Norse that in any other literature, in which one thing or object is described in terms of something that it isn't. A classic example that everyone understands, we call the camel 'the ship of the desert', the camel is obviously not a ship, but in the context of the desert, the camel transports.

AUSENDA: So, it is a metaphor.

JESCH: It is a particular kind of metaphor.

HERSCHEND: There is no such a thing as a ship of the desert, and all camels are characterized by an impossibility.

GREEN: [In the preliminary draft] You write, "Lest we are tempted to think that the motif has a whiff of paganism about it", I should lean a bit more emphatically, as you suspect, in the direction of paganism, and ask if you know in this connection of the deliberate suggestion of paganism advanced in the sixth-century anonymous *Opus imperfectum in Matthaeum*, where it is said of the barbarians, we suspect Germanic barbarians, that "they name their sons in accord with the devastation of wild beasts and birds of prey, and it is a source of pride to rave for blood".

JESCH: Thank you, I would appreciate that.

GREEN: Criticism of this name-giving practice and to link up the name-giving with your poetry, I quoted earlier the names 'Hildulf' in OHG, but in OE 'hildewulf' and 'herewulf' can be used as poetic terms for a warrior. I am trying to breach your concern with poetic terminology alone and open it up a bit more for onomastic practice.

JESCH: I hope you don't think I am dismissing all this. Rather than assuming paganism, I was trying to see where the material led and to see if it did suggest paganism. And certainly the eleventh- and twelfth-century Scandinavians, who were Christians, didn't have any necessary assumptions of paganism in this particular motif. So, I think that the two concepts intersect, I would agree with that. I am trying to get away from the notion of a necessary linkage between them.

DUMVILLE: As you probably know there are more poems that need to be taken into account alongside *The Gododdin*, one is the group of poems attributed to Taliesin. It is a difficult material because it is small: twelve poems, partly because most Welsh scholars accept it as genuine of the sixth century. The other body of poetry is allegedly later, 'triads', and there is one body within that, dealing with some of the same characters, some of the same events as Taliesin poetry, which I think will bring you more material and your approach may actually enable you to see some differences between this material which will be helpful to all scholars. So it will be great if that stuff will go in as well. The point I am unhappy about concerns the dating of events. The dating of *The Gododdin* is a hypothesis put forward by Williams about 60 years ago, which directly and flat out contradicts the one piece of external evidence which we have for dating, and I argued fifteen years ago or so, that it made more sense within this badly attested corpus of material if one took the information of the poem pretty much at face value and which the external evidence took in in the same way, and place the events in the same century. So, if we accept this poetry—and, of course, there are different opinions on that and the opinions are growing—the middle of the sixth century, would be about the right point. As far as I know that use would be accepted by general scholarship, but it hasn't been accepted by John Koch. Koch's work has been partly directed towards trying to sort out some of the layers; that's the strong and very interesting point of Koch's work. In other respects, he is trying to be interpretive. You say (page 260), "despite the chronological and liguistic gulf", yes there is a linguistic gulf, there isn't necessarily a chronological gulf, because there is a body of opinion which regards this material as ninth- or tenth-century literature.

JESCH: Ninth- or tenth-century?

DUMVILLE: Yes, a thirteenth-century manuscript, given that one can see that most of the material is not in the Middle Welsh language of the thirteenth century but in Old Welsh. In principle, the dating range for this poetry is to 1150, and then you start arguing down the linguistic points and the metrical point, the historical point and so on. They could be absolutely contemporary, even if the skaldic poetry, is dated from the twelfth century.

JESCH: Oh, you make skaldic poetry seem very easy to date.

MAGNUS: Among the big relief-brooches of the Migration period (page 261) there are at least some with motives of beasts and birds of prey that most likely have an epic background.

ARRHENIUS: I noticed that you have wolves, but I have never seen a wolf and an eagle together. I think it is very important to take notice of when they are shown together when we talk about the iconographic aspect.

HERSCHEND: Yes, but perhaps the wolves are actually the men fighting the pack attacking. And Odin was on his way to feed himself.

AUSENDA: Concerning mythological eagles, ravens and wolves, and previously also boars (page 263), could you kindly give a short excursus on Scandinavian anthroponymy as compared to Germanic. During the meeting on the Anglo-Saxons the observation was made that Germanic anthroponymy used the same animals (raven, wolf and eagle) present in their mythology in such a way that their anthroponyms were compounds made up of two elements one of which in many cases referred to a mythological animal.

On the same topic: why do accounts of Germanic tribal structures also mention lineages' or clans' names, whilst these are not prominent for Scandinavian populations except perhaps for 'ruling' families, although clans and lineages surely existed among them? Why do Scandinavian names use patronymics whilst Germanic ones do not?

GREEN: Could I come in on the last point? First, a question of terminology. It's a false antithesis to place Scandinavian against Germanic. Scandinavian is

Germanic. You mean, non-Scandinavian. And secondly, I do not think that Germanic names do not use patronymics. I can give you three examples one from the one heroic lay which we do have in OHG. Three generations of warriors are referred to by a combination of allitteration and repetition of the same second element, namely 'Heribrand', 'Hadubrand', 'Hildebrand'. These are linked over three generations. Secondly, patronymics are used frequently in name formation, by means of the suffix *-ing*. I know that suffix has a range of meanings, but one of those is patronymic. And lastly, in German, quite frequently the grandson will be given the same name as his grandfather, by-passing the father, but linking two generations together. And that has one outcome in German vocabulary, the modern German word for 'grandson', 'Enkel', OHG *eninchili*, which is a diminutive of the word *ano*, 'grandfather'.

DUMVILLE: Can I just tack on in OE, in documentary sources rather than literary sources it is quite common to have people referred to by their name and father's name.

BRINK: Did we have patronymics in early Scandinavia? By that I mean Viking Age or the age before that.

GREEN: I cannot answer that one.

BRINK: I don't think so, and there is another question.

GREEN: In any case you agree that the contrast mentioned by [Ausenda] does not hold.

BRINK: No. We have exactly the same variety of genealogical name connections.

BRINK: For example in the North, the famous early rune stones from eastern Sweden where we have several family names. And the last thing is that this formation of, not patronymics, because in Scandinavia we have in -ings, has been used widely for the names of inhabitants. The great difference between the Continent and Anglo-Saxon England and Scandinavia is that on the Continent, in Germany and in England the *-inga* formations are patronymics. In Scandinavia we always have or form a topographical appendix. So there we have a difference and we must debate why, but to my knowledge we don't have any patronymics in Scandinavia. The earliest patronyms belong to the nobility in the Middle Ages.

DUMVILLE: Do you mean by patronyms surnames?

BRINK: I mean names related to the father's name.

DUMVILLE: What then do you call Svenson?

BRINK: They started during the Viking Age or thereabouts.

AUSENDA: Could you give a succint list of differences in meter, content, targeted audience, etc. between skaldic and eddic poems and the etymology of both terms?

JESCH: These have been outlined in a number of recent works, for instance Jónas Kristjansson (1988), or in more detail in Peter Hallberg (1975).

AUSENDA: Referring to *Haraldskvæði*, you say it does not have a strong pagan world view: was it written after the christianization of Scandinavia?

JESCH: Well, it was written *down* after the christianization of Scandinavia.

GREEN: *ulfheðnar* for 'wolf skinned': this term, an adjective, can be linked up with an OHG name, Wulfhetan. Here again we have a link between the poetic term and a name.

VESTERGAARD: With reference to page 266, I thought I would give a small example from the Faeroese classification system. It is not something that one can just take and apply because there are great differences between Faeroese society and the Viking Age. But I thought that it might give a clue. If we look at the three animals you mention, what they have in common is that their nouns are all masculine. Another carrion eater that could be mentioned is the crow, which is grammatically feminine, and in the classification system in a farming society you have masculine animals like raven and eagle, animals with which one can have a fair fight. You hate each other, but you can also respect one another. On the other hand you have the crow, which will not kill young lambs but, nevertheless, it will help in the process of eating them. The crow is grammatically feminine, and you cannot fight it with an honest heart, because you don't know what to expect from a female enemy. In the Faeroe Islands crows were believed to have a meeting once a year when they decided which humans were going to die. They are in many cases also the emblems of sorcerers in various communities. In short, it could be useful to your study to look at animals in Scandinavian classificatory systems. You might find some of the same classifications, for instance the classification of a bird or animal as female would be dangerous to men in the battlefield. You have to find a female beast of battle if you want to make a comparison.

GREEN: You say (page 266) "...without attempting to return to those old heathen 'Germanen'", I think you must return to them if we take account of the name-giving evidence.

MEULENGRACHT: You quote (page 267) this passage from the Rök stone with a kenning "*hestr Gunnar*", you translated it "the horse of Gunn".

JESCH: Foote translated it "the horse of Gunn", not I.

MEULENGRACHT: Isn't it a bit surprising that the valkyrie is arriving on a wolf? We have examples of giantesses riding wolves and also in other contexts wolves and giantesses are connected, and the most important is the mother of the famous wolf Fenrir who was a giantess. And you say that "the beasts of the battle in the Scandinavian culture of the Viking Age from the ninth century onwards". Then you say, "They are intimately associated with the growing power and developing ideology of war leaders and eventually kings". Yes, but at least a wolf is, as you show us, a broader image. It means death, destruction, anything opposite to humanity, anything outside the human world and culture and ultimately the wolf is the symbol of Ragnarǫk. So, isn't that the basis of these images of the wolf and its companions on the battlefield?

JESCH: It may be the basis, but why? If the wolf is death, destruction, disaster, why are all these warriors going out of their way to feed it?

MEULENGRACHT: I can't answer that question but in skaldic poetry battle is connected to this horrible non-humanity that is definitely realized in Ragnarǫk.

This is pre-Christian death thinking in the battle, in the animals of the battlefield. There is this double thinking. I think the best expressions of this are the stanzas of Egill Skallagrímsson after the death of his brother at the battle of Brunanburh. This is not Victorian; they win the battle, they are in hall and celebrate the defeat of the Scots. It is recalling all this darkness and horror of death and destruction, not victory. It's always there.

JESCH: It seems to me that what we might perhaps call an elegiac mood, might be a later view. And that, at least in the praise poetry of the tenth and eleventh centuries, you weren't allowed to think of war and death as a bad thing. It was a good thing as long as you were on the winning side.

DUMVILLE: It is not clear that the battle was won.

MEULENGRACHT: It is not clear at all, of this kenning meaning the animals on the battlefield. You say that they are celebrating their aim: "we have got something to eat". Yes, but there is more to this picture, there is still horror.

HERSCHEND: Yes, in the battles sung in these late poems the warriors are separated from the animals, which are a part of the outer world whether hilarious or horrible. They are the only creatures that are together with them.

MEULENGRACHT: That's why I would like to add the giantess as related to the wolf, because that is a much more meaningful picture, because the role of the giantess is the chaos of war.

References in the discussion

Textual sources:

Egill Skallagrímsson: see References at end of paper.
Gísla saga: see Johnston (trans.) 1963.
The Gododdin: see References at end of paper.
Opus imperfectum in Matthaeum: see Migne 1862: 601-946 (here 626).

Bibliography:

Dumville, D.
    1988   See References at end of paper.
Finnegan, R.
    1988   *Literacy and Orality. Studies in the Technology of Communication*. Oxford: Basil Blackwell.
Frank, R.
    1987   See References at end of paper.
Hallberg, P.
    1975   *Old Icelandic Poetry: Eddic Lay and Skaldic Verse*. Lincoln: University of Nebraska Press.
Johnston, G. (trans.)
    1963   *The Saga of Gisli*. (With Notes and an Essay by P. Foote). London: J. M. Dent.
Koch, J.
    1997   See References at end of paper.

Kristjánsson, J.
    1988   *Eddas and Sagas.* Reykjavík: Hið íslenska bókmenntafélag.
Migne, J.-P.
    1862   *Patrologiae cursus completus, Series Graeca* 56. Paris: Published in rue
                d'Amboise.
Müller, G.
    1970   *Studien zu den theriophoren Personennamen der Germanen.* Cologne:
                Böhlau Verlag.
Schramm, G.
    1957   *Namenschatz und Dichtersprache.* Göttingen: Vandenhoeck und Ruprecht.
Skafte Jensen, M.
    1980   *The Homeric Question and the Oral-formulaic Theory.* Copenhagen:
                Museum Tusculanum Press.
Williams, I.
    1972   See References at end of paper.

THE "LUDWIGSLIED" AND THE BATTLE OF SAUCOURT

DENNIS H. GREEN

Trinity College, Cambridge CB2 1TQ

The Old High German poem I have chosen to discuss celebrates the victory of a West Frankish army under king Ludwig III over Viking raiders at Saucourt, at the mouth of the Somme near Abbeville. It depicts this encounter in the widest historical terms, as no less than part of the history of salvation, although with the benefit of hindsight we know it to have been of no more than fleeting significance.

Even though Scandinavian raids on the continental and English coasts may have occurred before 790 it is from this date and for more than a century that they reach a scale and intensity which culminate in the origin of Normandy under Rollo and the establishment of Danelaw in a large part of England. This period of approximately 120 years is conveniently divided into three waves. The first (790-840) consisted of small-scale raids of a hit-and-run nature, largely confined to the coastal area and concentrated on Frisia, but also further afield on Aquitaine. The second phase (841-875) showed a marked increase in Scandinavian ambitions: their attacks became more frequent and more extensive (so that they penetrated inland along the main waterways), including the tactical novelty of their frequent wintering elsewhere in place of returning to the North. From this change it was but a short step to what we find in the third phase (876-911), with the raiders actually beginning to colonize the areas exposed to their attacks, both in *Francia* and England, exercising now a political control over territory which they had previously subjugated only militarily and producing two new areas of Scandinavian dominance on the map of medieval Europe.

The raiders' long-term success over this period, despite occasional setbacks, must have been due in part to their military intelligence, for it is reported often enough to be more than fortuitous that they were well informed about internal dissension amongst the Franks and capitalized on this by launching attacks at times when their enemies were weakened by division, even joining forces with those opposed to Frankish royal power. Thus, when Ludwig the Pious was deposed by his sons in 833 the Vikings seized this opportunity of political discord to attack the trading centre of Dorestad for the first time in the following year. Something similar is reported explicitly with the deposition of Charles the Fat in 887 {"The Northmen hearing of the dissension amongst the Franks and the casting-down of their emperor laid waste places which they had previously hardly touched" (Nelson 1997:35)}.

The position in *Francia* itself was therefore a decisive factor in the history of Viking attacks on the continent. On the one hand, the wealth and internal peace which Charles the Great had procured for the Frankish empire persisted for some time after his death in 814, so that Frankish wealth and trade still continued to

THE SCANDINAVIANS
FROM THE VENDEL PERIOD TO THE TENTH CENTURY

grow and Ludwig the Pious managed to maintain some measure of peace throughout the empire and *Francia* was spared Viking attacks during most of his reign. This situation changed dramatically for the worse with the outbreak of civil war amongst his sons after Ludwig's death in 840. Frankish wealth remained as an obvious magnet for sea-raiders hungry for booty, but the means of defending it were gravely diminished. Although the civil war ended in 843, this was at the cost of dividing the Empire amongst the three contesting Frankish parties, so that the Vikings were presented with the opportunity of now defeating in detail parts of what had earlier been a unified power. *Francia* in fact became the main target of the Vikings in the second phase of their activity (841-875), encouraged by political difficulties amongst the Franks and the readiness of the East Franks to fish in troubled waters. However, Viking activity on the continent was geographically more widespread than this. It still included Spain and Aquitaine (they now reached as far inland as Toulouse), but also Brittany and Neustria (penetrating far up the Loire), the Seine basin (the heartland of West Frankish power) and the region of the Meuse and Lower Rhine. To this last region, including the Saucourt which concerns us, the Vikings were attracted, according to the *Annales Vedastini*, "hearing of dispute amongst the Franks, the Northmen crossed the sea" (Simson 1909:44). Here as elsewhere the combination of wealth and dynastic dissension was fatal for the Franks even though in the short term they may have won the battle at Saucourt.

The interpretation placed on such disastrous events in contemporary records, written by churchmen in Latin and Christian in their terms of reference, is quite clear. By recalling that Jeremiah had prophesied God's punishment on His chosen people as coming from the north it was possible to place these events in a much wider historical framework, assisted by the view that the Franks were the new chosen people (Nelson 1997:19). Like Israel, however, they had offended God by their sins and merited punishment. The *Sermo in tumulatione S. Quintini* therefore quotes Psalm 78.1 to explain contemporary events ("O God, the heathen are come into thine inheritance; thy holy temple they have defiled") and like the Psalmist sees them as an expression of God's anger with sinners (Psalm 78.5; *Sermo 271*). This punishment calls forth the need for repentance and conversion, for which a biblical precedent likewise lay close to hand (Malachi 3.7: "Return unto me, and I will return unto you"). In 862 Charles the Bald saw the necessary precondition for successful military defence as lying in penitence and almsgiving, and in 881, the year of the battle of Saucourt, Hincmar of Reims stressed the need for *poenitentia* and *satisfactio* if victory against the pagans was to be won (Berg 1964:178 f.).

So much on the general background to the *Ludwigslied*, which has to be distinguished from the more specific one yet to be considered. Turning now to the poem itself we may note that, although it is silent about the time and the place of the battle there is enough evidence to make it highly likely that the encounter in 881 at Saucourt is in fact meant. True to its lack of detail about time and place the poem presents its action in what seems at first to be unpromisingly abstract terms. After a general introductory formula in which the poet claims to know of King

Ludwig (thereby implying the reliability of what he has to say) this king's prehistory is briefly sketched: the loss of his father at an early age, his adoption by God for his upbringing, his enthronement by divine authority as ruler of the Franks, and the sharing of his kingdom with his brother Karlmann. After these succinct eight lines the narrative action starts with God's testing of the young ruler in sending the Northmen across the sea to attack the Franks as a punishment for their sinfulness, who are thereby prompted to mend their ways by due penance. The kingdom is in disarray not merely because of the Viking aggression, but more particularly because of Ludwig's absence, who is accordingly ordered by God to return and do battle. Raising his war-banner Ludwig returns to the Franks, who greet him with acclamation as one for whom they have long been waiting. Ludwig holds a council of war with his battle-companions, the powerful ones in his realm, and with the promise of reward encourages them to follow him into battle. He sets out, discovers the whereabouts of the enemy and, after a Christian battle-song, joins battle, which is described briefly, but in noticeably more stirring terms. Victory is won, not least thanks to Ludwig's inborn bravery. The poem closes with thanks to God and the saints for having granted Ludwig victory in battle, with praise of the king himself and with a prayer for God to preserve him in grace.

For all its stylistic abstraction it is possible to date and locate the poem with a relatively high degree of accuracy. It is preserved in a manuscript from the monastery of St Amand, written towards the end of the ninth century and also including, in the same hand, a Latin legend of St Eulalia together with an Old French hymn on the same saint, one of the very earliest examples of vernacular literature in France. If we are correct in linking the *Ludwigslied* with the battle of Saucourt this permits an even more precise dating: between August 881 (when the battle was fought) and August 882 (when Ludwig, referred to in the poem as still alive, met his end). If the poem was composed some time during the course of this year, conceivably in celebration soon after the event itself, then it must have been written down before the end of the ninth century, but after Ludwig's death, since the Latin superscription of the German text refers to him "of pious memory".

Locating where the poem was written down (if not where it may have been first composed) also permits of greater probability than is generally the case in so early a period. A northern French manuscript, written by a scribe versed not merely in Latin, but also in Old French and Old High German, suggests an area of *Francia* which was still bilingual in these vernaculars, as is also borne out by a Romance feature in the orthography of the German text (inorganic *h*, e.g. *hiu* instead of *iu*). Moreover, other sources (in Latin) for the battle of Saucourt can be grouped in a relatively small area of southern Flanders, not all that far from the battlefield itself, where memory of the event and interest in it were best preserved: the *Annales Vedastini* at St Vaast in Arras, the *Chronicon Sithiense* at Sithiu, near St Omer, the *Sermo in tumulatione S. Quintini* at St Quentin, the *Annales Blandinienses* at Ghent, and Hincmar of Reims from that city (Berg 1964:187, map). This relatively close grouping suggests that the manuscript of the *Ludwigslied*, preserved first at St Amand, may have been written down there or in that region. In place as well as time the German monument stands close to the event it commemorates. This is confirmed from the French side of this still bilingual area, for a French *chanson de geste, Gormont et Isembart,* treats of a conflict between Christians and pagans which is based on the same event at Saucourt. In either vernacular, therefore, this battle was commemorated in verse as a vessel of historical tradition.

So far, however, I have simply accepted the view that the battle celebrated at an unnamed place in the German poem is identical with that referred to explicitly in the Latin sources as Saucourt. To be sure about this equation we need to look more closely at the situation in *Francia* at this time (Berg 1964:180 f.; Ehlert 1981:36 f.; Ehrismann 1932:229 f.; Haubrichs 1995:137 f.). At the death of Ludwig the Stammerer in 879 neither of his sons was of age: Ludwig (the hero celebrated in our poem) was seventeen and Karlmann only thirteen. Their right to succession, decided upon by their father a year before his death, came to be questioned, amongst other things because of their youth (this was the basis, as we shall see, of a criticism made by Hincmar of Reims). If I may cut short the complexities of the political hither and thither which are not reflected in any way in the German poem, it is to pass on to both these sons of the Stammerer receiving unction and being crowned at Ferrières in 879, with the official proclamation of the division of royal authority between them at Amiens in 880. As a result, Ludwig III received *Francia* and *Neustria* (the area of West Frankish territory most at threat from the Vikings), whilst the south (Aquitaine, Gothia and Burgundy) fell to Karlmann.

One of the opponents to this settlement of the succession question was Boso, the brother-in-law of Charles the Bald, who proclaimed himself independently as ruler in Burgundy. Against this usurper Ludwig and Karlmann launched a joint campaign in the summer of 880 and laid siege to Boso in Vienne. During his absence, however, Ludwig's territory in the North was subjected to repeated attacks by Vikings profiting from the political turmoil amongst the West Franks, so that Ludwig was obliged to break off his assistance of Karlmann and hurry back to deal with the Northmen. Even in its abbreviated form this sketch should show that Ludwig had to deal not merely with Viking raiders, but also faced opposition from other Frankish parties, of whom Boso was a by no means unique example.

In the light of this sketch it is already possible to see some reflection of these events in the *Ludwigslied*. That we are dealing with the West Frankish ruler, Ludwig III, to whom the historical sources refer in the context of Saucourt, is made probable by several points. The Latin superscription to the poem in the manuscript refers not just to him as dead (*piae memoriae Hluduico rege*), but adds more explicitly *filio Hluduici,* which agrees with the fact that Ludwig III was the son of Ludwig the Stammerer. The poem also specifies early on that this Ludwig as a young man lost his father (3: *Kind uuarth her faterlôs*), which refers to his age of seventeen at this time. We home in still further on this particular ruler when the brother with whom he shared his kingdom is named as Karlmann (7f.). In the light of this explicit naming a later point, made more abstractly (for reasons of a more symbolic nature, as we shall see), is consonant with the historical situation. If the kingdom is in disarray because of Ludwig's absence and if he has to return to restore order by defeating the Vikings this is a more anonymous, but still recognizable allusion to Ludwig's assistance of his brother Karlmann in dealing with Boso in Burgundy, when he had to return northwards on receiving the alarming news of Viking depredations.

This agreement on minor, factual points encourages us to search for further historical parallels, where history is to be understood not just in the Rankean sense of what actually happened, but also in terms of the contemporary understanding of events, above all with regard to the medieval view of history as part of the history of salvation (*Heilsgeschichte*). Despite the potential distortion which such a view may impose on events this is shared by the *Ludwigslied* and the Latin sources from which we hope to derive our 'historical' information. There is, however, a difference between them which has to be taken into account in placing the German poem in its historical setting: whereas the Latin sources claimed to be historical records (in annalistic or chronicle form), the *Ludwigslied* transmitted historical memory in the form of poetic praise of a ruler's victory, with all the licence (poetic and eulogistic) which this could involve. It therefore incorporates a poetic reduction or compression of events for the benefit of an audience, close in time and space and already acquainted with them (as with the bare reference to Ludwig as *kind...faterlôs*). As a work intended for oral delivery to a listening audience it follows a necessarily simpler narrative line (as we shall see in the detail of Ludwig encouraging his warriors to battle). Above all, as a poem composed in eulogy of a ruler it concentrates on his figure and his claims (as we shall again see, this time in connection with Ludwig's succession to the throne). Factors such as these, predominant in the literary genre to which the poem belongs, may lead us to be much less worried than a historian has a right to be when he complains, for example, that the portrayal of Ludwig returning from afar to deal with the attack is in flat contradiction of the fact that he had been in that area for seven months before the encounter at Saucourt took place (Fouracre 1989:81). Poetic compression of events, also to be found in the heroic lay and unavoidable in a genre for oral recital of restricted length, may still rest on tangible historical events. With these qualifications in mind we now resume our quest for further historical features in the *Ludwigslied*.

We have already seen that the mention of Ludwig as a youthful orphan is in agreement with historical facts, but the poem nonetheless adapts these facts to its own purposes, as a comparison with the *Annales Vedastini* shows (Berg 1964:184, 191). The annalist describes how on the death of Ludwig the Stammerer a murderous dissension broke out amongst the Franks, with one party putting forward his two sons as joint successors, whilst another heightened the conflict by calling on the East Franks in the person of (yet another) Ludwig. According to these annals the action therefore proceeds first from the father, then from the leading figures amongst the Franks, whilst the two sons are mere pawns in their hands. By contrast, the *Ludwigslied* sees things from Ludwig's point of view: he has no father, but God steps in, seeing to his upbringing and granting him kingship over the Franks. Even though the repeated stress on his youth (3, 10) may be historically true, its function is not biographical, but rather to underline that for all his youth God calls him to the throne.

In Ludwig's enthronement (5: "[God] gave him the virtues of a ruler, a lordly following, the throne here in *Francia* - long may he occupy it!") the actual course of events is compressed into a simple straightforward action (Berg 1964:184; Kemper 1989:4). God's intervention leads directly to Ludwig's kingship, the political vicissitudes of the struggle for succession are passed over with no hint of disagreement or possible rivals, unthinkable in one designated by God to be ruler. Yet this idealizing adjustment of historical facts serves a political purpose, for Boso, the rival claimant of the two brothers with his power base in Burgundy, enjoyed the support of Pope John VIII who termed him his "spiritual son". This adoption of Boso by God's representative on earth is surpassed by the claim of the German poem that Ludwig had been adopted by God himself as his *magaczogo* (4), responsible for his upbringing in place of his father. By tacitly trumping this usurper's claims in this way the *Ludwigslied* hints at rivalry without allowing it to cast a shadow on Ludwig's designation.

The poem next refers to the division of the kingdom between Ludwig and Karlmann at Amiens in the year 880, focusing again on Ludwig, from whom the action flows (7: "He divided [his office] then with Karlmann, his brother"; Berg 1964:184 f.). This differs pointedly from the depiction of the same event in the *Annales Vedastini*, where it is said that the two brothers came to Amiens with their followers and that the Franks divided the kingdom between them. As with the proposal that the Stammerer's sons should be joint successors the annalist depicts them here, too, as the objects of Frankish politics: it is the leading Franks who divide the kingdom between them (*inter eos*), not the two sons who divide it between themselves (which would demand *inter se*). In his wish to concentrate on the hero of his poem alone the author of the German poem goes even further: according to him it is not the two brothers who divide *Francia* between themselves, but Ludwig alone who does this.

If God intended the blow against the Franks, as we shall see, as a punishment for their sins, a view fully in accord with the widespread clerical interpretation of the Vikings' attacks at large, it follows that these raiders cannot be seen as acting independently, but only as unwitting instruments working out God's will (Berg 1964:179 f., 185 f.). Their attack on *Francia* is therefore presented metahistorically (11: "He [God] let the heathens come over the sea") and their activity is seen in terms of God's will (12: "to admonish the people of the Franks for their sins"). However conventional this interpretation of events may have been at the time when the poem was composed, it is clearly subordinate to the function attributed to Ludwig. Just as God assumed responsibility for the king's upbringing (4) and decided to test him (9 f.), so is the raid of the Vikings meant as a testing of the Franks, recalling them to the ways of God. On a lower level fit for their role as subjects (God works on them through the Vikings) the Franks therefore repeat what was true of Ludwig (God works directly on him). In showing penitence and returning to God the Franks also conform to the example set by their ruler. The punishment demanded of them as penance is of a twofold nature, secular and ecclesiastic: secular in that they are to suffer *haranskara* (14), a legal punishment (the word occurs in this sense as a vernacular term in Latin legal texts of the period), but also ecclesiastic in the form of fasting. Both are summed up in the verb *buozen* (18), denoting legal satisfaction as well as religious penance. In stressing this double aspect the poem agrees with contemporary sources' report of reactions to the Northmen's depredations (Berg 1964:188 f., 195). For example, in 862 Charles the Bald saw an improvement in their ways as an indispensable precondition for Frankish success in the field, ordering his bishops to impose penance for sins and his counts to punish with the full rigour of the law. In the year of Saucourt Hincmar of Reims demands *satisfactio* and *poenitentia* in a comparable context.

The testing to which Ludwig (and through him his subjects, too) is subjected as a trial of his worth shows his superiority to rival claims in yet another way, once more with an implicit, but barbed reference to Boso (Kemper 1989:5). Boso's investiture in Burgundy included a public ceremony in which he underwent an aptitude test conducted by his bishops, asking searching questions to which he had to give binding responses. In our poem, however, the *examen rigorosum* takes place on a higher level, for the testing of Ludwig is arranged by God himself. The author repeats here what we saw of the contrast between Boso as the spiritual son of the pope and Ludwig as the adopted son of God: in both cases Ludwig's claims derive their authority from the highest conceivable level.

Before battle is joined the *Ludwigslied* depicts the king encouraging his men (31-41), pointing out that God has sent him there to save them at whatever the cost to himself, and that he expects the same willingness to face death from his followers, but promising rewards to those who survive and to the families of those who may fall. The encouragement of his troops takes a different form in the historical sources: at a decisive point in the course of the battle, when all could have been lost, he sets an example by force of arms and wins the day (Berg 1964:190, 194). By replacing active encouragement by words and by giving these prominence before the battle, thus dictating its course, the poet accentuates his view of these events. In summoning his followers to battle the king repeats God's earlier call to him. Where Ludwig had sworn his readiness to do as God commanded at any cost (25: "Lord, I shall do this, all that you command, unless death prevent me"), he expects the Franks to submit themselves likewise to God (37: "Our time on earth is limited for as long as Christ wills. If He wishes our death he has the power"). Where God's reward awaits Ludwig for his service (2), Ludwig commits himself to reward his followers for their service. By means of such parallels the relationship between God and Ludwig is reduplicated on another level by that between Ludwig and the Franks, to whom he could be said to stand in for God. This religious heightening of the ruler's position is of a piece with what we shall see of the Christian elements with which the poem is imbued, but this gain is not even bought at the price of forgoing the main advantage of the historical sources (their depiction of Ludwig's decisive example on the battlefield), for when the poem describes the battle it, too, stresses that none fought as bravely as he and it describes the battle largely in terms of his fighting, as becomes a work eulogizing a ruler's victory (50-54).

Largely because of this concentration on Ludwig's role in the fighting the poem compresses the course of the battle by contrast with what is reported elsewhere (Berg 1964:188 f., 195). In the *Annales Vedastini* the course of the battle was by no means straightforward, for after what looked like an initial Frankish success the Vikings managed to make a counter-attack, driving some of the Franks to flight and threatening them with defeat but for Ludwig's decisive intervention. Of this military to-and-fro there is no trace in the poem whose narrative proceeds in an untroubled straight line from Ludwig coming across the Northmen through his singing his battle-song and setting a heroic example at the head of his army down to gaining victory. Simplifying events in this way leaves no room for doubt as to the outcome or the fact that victory must be divinely ordained in the case of a leader who serves God and has persuaded his followers to do likewise in serving him. Praise for this victory is therefore due to God, but also to the king (55: "Praised be the power of God, Ludwig gained the victory"). The straightness of this narrative line, passing over the ebb and flow of the fighting which might have called the providential result into question, repeats the technique we saw in connection with Ludwig's succession to the throne, where opposition and rivalry were similarly passed over in silence. Seeing God and the king acting in concert in this way on the battlefield of Saucourt is not peculiar to the German poem, however. The *Annales Blandinienses* report of this battle between Franks and pagans that Ludwig was the first to go into battle and that by the gift of God victory was won (Berg 1964:190).

Inevitably, given the theologically inspired nature of the reaction of contemporaries to these events, we have more than once touched upon Christian elements in seeing how the *Ludwigslied* agrees with or diverges from what can be reconstructed of events from historical sources. However, these religious elements must now be looked at for themselves and more systematically. The basis on which they for the most part rest is the fact that the Franks, regarding themselves as God's chosen people, are represented in terms which recall God's attitude to Israel in the Old Testament (Green 1966:203 ff.). Already in the prologue to the *Lex Salica* the Franks are referred to as founded by God, inspired by Him in the formulation of their laws and shown His favour in the conversion of Clovis. In the conclusion of the prologue Christ is depicted as loving the Franks in particular and as guarding their realm with the care which Jehovah had lavished on the Israelites. Only shortly before the battle of Saucourt a vernacular author writing in South Rhenish Franconian, Otfrid von Weissenburg, twice suggests the same link between Israel and Franks (I 1, 65 ff.; *Ad Ludovicum* 1 ff. and 59 f.). In a programmatic passage he describes the territory of the Franks and its abundance of natural resources in terms taken from Moses' description of the Promised Land (Deuteronomy 8. 7 ff.). In his dedicatory preface Otfrid also depicts Ludwig the German in words reminiscent of the prologue to the *Lex Salica*: he is protected from his enemies by God who grants him assistance, his health and the peace of his kingdom are likewise a divine gift profiting both the ruler and his people. That Otfrid had the Old Testament in mind as his model is suggested by his comparison of the East Frankish king with David. For him both kings show the same exemplary patience in face of the afflictions which God imposed on them as a trial (to these rulers the West Frankish Ludwig could be added) and Otfrid even suggests that his Frankish ruler must be of the same descent as David. The more Ludwig the German is equated with David, however, the more obvious is the similarity between the two peoples over whom they rule. Otfrid says: "The one [David] ruled over God's people in a lofty and lordly manner, the same is also done truly by the other [Ludwig] constantly in a manner pleasing to God". In this comparison between the two kings the term *gotes liuti*, "God's people", is common to both, so that the Christian Franks of Otfrid's day stand in the same relationship to God as did the Israelites. That the same attitude informs our poem is clear from the way in which the battle between Vikings and Franks is presented as one between pagans (11: *heidine man*) and God's people (23: God commands Ludwig to bring assistance to His people: *Hilph mînan liutin*). On the basis of this underlying view of God's special interest in the Franks we may consider the various ways in which the battle of Saucourt, as treated in the *Ludwigslied*, was presented in Christian terms.

We start with God's function as Ludwig's *magaczogo* (4), adopting him while still a young man after the death of his father, looking at it no longer with regard to its historical context (the death of Ludwig the Stammerer, the rivalry of the usurper Boso), but rather in the light of the bible. The obvious precedent for this detail is the young Solomon whom God, speaking to David advanced in years, promises to bring up in his stead (II Samuel 7.14: "I will be his father, and he shall be my son") (Ehlert 1981:31; Wehrli 1969:76). When Ludwig is said to be 'fetched' by the Lord for this purpose (4) this, too, is reminiscent of the frequency with which the Old Testament refers to God calling, choosing or taking someone, particularly a ruler, for His own ends (e.g. Isaiah 41.9; 42.6). If in view of this frequency the connection of Ludwig's divine adoption with Solomon in particular may seem too pointed, later allusions to the example of Solomon may help to remove this doubt. The main rival to regarding Solomon as the precedent does not take us all that far from him, for David, his father, was also adopted by God and placed on the throne by Him (Psalm 88.20 and 27f.) (Yeandle 1989:69). Precisely this model for divinely blessed kingship had underlain Otfrid's praise of his East Frankish ruler, just as Charles the Great was pointedly referred to as David. Whether the parallel is with David or Solomon, the Old Testament background is clear.

The purpose of God in calling someone in the Old Testament is often to enthrone him. This is the case with Ludwig (5 f.: "He [God] gave him...the throne here in *Francia*"), but it is also true of Solomon in the immediate context of God's adoption of him (II Samuel 7.13: "I will establish the throne of his kingdom for ever"; cf. also 7.16) (Ehlert 1982:32; Wehrli 1969:76). The close conjunction of these two features (adoption and enthronement) both in this biblical passage and in the German poem suggests that the former was in the author's mind and that Solomon was indeed the model he saw for Ludwig. The relationship between God and Ludwig is also depicted in a way characteristic of the Old Testament, where repeatedly God speaks to Hebrew kings and prophets directly and personally (Haubrichs 1995:140; Yeandle 1989:73). Such direct contact is repeated in the direct speech with which God addresses Ludwig and gives him commands (23f.: "Ludwig, my king, help my people. The Northmen have sorely oppressed them").

However important the presence of Old Testament allusions may be, they serve the Christian function of acting as prefigurations of what was achieved by Christ (the words "my people" in the last quotation no longer designate the Hebrews, but Christians, more specifically the Christian Franks). Seen in this light Solomon is a prefiguration of Christ (Ehlert 1981:34 f.). Christ sees himself in this way (Matthew 12.42: "and behold, a greater than Solomon is here"), as the actual Son of God He surpasses Solomon who was only adopted by God, and just as Solomon was called to the throne of his father David by God, so will God also place Christ on that throne (Luke 1.32), but in a metaphysical sense going beyond Solomon (Luke 1.33: "and of his kingdom there shall be no end"). Applying this conventional typological exegesis to the German poem we recognize that the connection established between Ludwig and Solomon also amounts to one between Ludwig and Christ, *not* in the sense that, as was true of Christ, Ludwig was a typological fulfilment of Solomon, but rather that, as a Christian king living in the fullness of time brought about by Christ, he incorporates an *imitatio Christi* (Ehlert 1981:35; Haubrichs 1995:141). Just as Christ was tested by being tempted in the wilderness, so is Ludwig tested by God in the battle with the Vikings (9 f.: "God wished to test him, to see if one so young could endure afflictions"). Where God sent Christ to redeem mankind, He also sends Ludwig to free His people, the Franks, from the Vikings. Just as Christ complied with God's will even in the face of death (Matthew 26.39: "nevertheless not as I will, but as thou wilt"), so does Ludwig accept the risk of death in battle in obeying God (25: "Lord, I shall do this, all that you command, unless death prevent me"). When Ludwig later voices before his assembled troops his readiness to obey God's command (34 f.: "...that I should fight here and not spare myself until I saved you") the verb used for "to save" (*gineriti*) is one used in Old High German of Christ as Saviour (Yeandle 1989:74 n.322). Verbally as well as in these parallels in the narrative action Ludwig is therefore presented in his christomimetic function, an obligation placed on rulers in many a *speculum principis*, but here converted into a literary commemoration of a topical history.

The author, by placing the Frankish king in connection both with Solomon and with Christ, has embedded the historical event at Saucourt in a larger framework and has presented it as part of the history of salvation. The *imitatio Christi* which is theoretically demanded of the Christian ruler as a representative of God has been converted in the case of Ludwig into actual practice, a fact which, even more than his victory in battle, served to legitimize his kingship, threatened not merely by external foes, but also by internal dissension (Ehlert 1982:32).

God's active intervention in this poem extends beyond the person of Ludwig, however much the focus of events he may be. The testing in which he has to prove himself is the battle made necessary by Viking attacks on his people, an affliction which they have brought on themselves by their sinfulness and which is presented as the sign of God's anger (20). To the testing of Ludwig we therefore have to add the punishment of the Franks; God has the Vikings come for no other reason than to admonish the Franks (11 f.). That is a view common in contemporary sources, but its origin lies clearly in the Old Testament, where the same sequence of events as in the *Ludwigslied* is attested repeatedly: God's chosen people breaks away from Him; God punishes them by allowing a foreign power to oppress them; Israel calls to God, who takes pity on them and sends someone to save them (Berg 1964:180).

How closely Ludwig is seen to act in concert with God as His representative can be seen in the details of his absence from *Francia* (while assisting Karlmann in Burgundy) and his return (Berg 1964:193 f.; Yeandle 1989:72). When he mentions the king's absence (19: "The king was far away, the kingdom in confusion") the author follows this in the next line with a reference to Christ's anger (20: "Christ was angry"), so that Ludwig's absence is equated with a withdrawal of divine grace. When Ludwig comes back to his people they express their gratitude for one for whom they have been waiting so long (29 f.: "They who had been waiting for him thanked God, they all said: 'My lord, so long have we been waiting for you'"). The messianic overtones of this greeting, seeing Ludwig's arrival as a token of restoration to God's grace, should be clear, for these words, addressed to the king, were applied equally to Christ, especially by those who await his coming to release them from Hell (*Venisti desiderabilis quem expectabamus in tenebris*) (Wolf 1995:39). It has been suggested that the German poem can be interpreted as an *adventus*, meant to be sung in praise of the victorious king after, even perhaps soon after the battle (Haubrichs 1995:142 f.). If we can also apply this *adventus* reading to this particular scene where Ludwig returns to *Francia* it is significant that, according to the historical sources, he returned from Burgundy to Compiègne to celebrate Christmas there (and sought out the Vikings only in the following year) (Kemper 1989:8). The poem's compression of events into a simplified narrative is nothing new to us, but the historical fact that Ludwig returned before Christmas, in time for the liturgical Advent, gives added force to the words with which those waiting for him greet him. His return to them, like Christ's coming, is seen as the arrival of a saviour.

The battle itself, following on with a compression of time more fitting to the literary needs of a short poem than in conformity with historical chronology, is seen as directed by God's authority. When Ludwig succeeds in finding where the Vikings are he gives thanks to God (44 f.) and then sings a "holy song" (46: *lioth frâno*) to which all his followers respond with a *Kyrieleison* (47) (Berg 1964:189 f.; Ernst 1975:374 f.; Haubrichs 1979:177 f.). We know from historical reports on battles with the pagans in the early Middle Ages (although admittedly not in the sources for the battle of Saucourt) that *Kyrieleison* was used as a battle-cry by

Christian warriors. Given this sequence of events under God's control leading up to this encounter it is no surprise that God should also be seen as granting victory, not to the exclusion of the praise due to Ludwig for his bravery and leadership, but still in such a way that priority is given to where it belongs. This is brought out twice in quick succession. First, after the description of the king's skill in fighting praise is given to God and then to Ludwig (55: "Praised be the power of God, Ludwig gained the victory"), but secondly thanks are given to all the saints before it is repeated that victory came to Ludwig (56). In each case metaphysical power is acknowledged first, but not so overridingly as to diminish the praise also due to the Frankish king (Berg 1964:195). These lines, attributing victory to God's power working through the medium of the ruler, are in agreement with what the *Annales Vedastini* in quite a different way report of the temporary setback which nearly cost the Franks their victory at Saucourt (Berg 1964:188 f.). When the Franks at first realize that they are gaining the upper hand they boast that this success is due to themselves and do not attribute it to God, which immediately brings its due punishment when God once more exposes them to the renewed attack of their enemy. Only when the Franks mend their ways and, moreover, thanks to the example set by Ludwig is victory finally assured.

The poem concludes with praise of Ludwig (57: "Hail once more Ludwig, our king blessed with fortune") and with a prayer to God to preserve him in His grace (59). The fact that the king is blessed (*sâlig*) is a final confirmation that God has assisted him, while his enjoyment of God's grace (*Bî sînan ergrehtin*) sums up that he is indeed *rex Dei gratia*. For the author, and presumably for those who joined in this praise of the victorious ruler, the doubts which clouded Ludwig's accession to the throne have finally been dispelled.

To these doubts and to the opposition which Ludwig encountered we must now return. So far I have only mentioned the general dissension which the claims of Ludwig and Karlmann called forth and the particular case of Boso's rivalry. Another centre of opposition lay even closer to hand, for Hincmar of Reims, whose name has been mentioned in passing, but not in this respect, was involved in conflict with Ludwig over the question of episcopal investiture (Yeandle 1989:18 ff.). As a result of this conflict Hincmar expressed his doubts in a number of respects about the fitness of Ludwig for kingship and it is in regard to these that the *Ludwigslied* presents, if not an explicit response, then at least a view favourable to the ruler.

In the first place, Hincmar seized upon the king's youth, quoting *Ecclesiastes* 10.16 as an argument for disqualifying him: "Fear the opinion of Scripture which does not lie: Woe to the land whose king is a young man" (Yeandle 1989:49). The German author cannot deny Ludwig's youth (he twice refers to it: 3, 10), but turns it to good effect by seeing in his orphaning as a young man the occasion for God's first decisive intervention in adopting Ludwig into His special care. What for Hincmar had been a disqualification is now seen as a token of divine protection and therewith as a sign of a divinely favoured kingship.

God's readiness to see to the upbringing of Ludwig, consequent on the latter's youth, also illustrates the difference between the archbishop and the poet-propagandist. Hincmar had proposed, against the advocacy of Ludwig and Karlmann as joint successors, that these two should be entrusted because of their tender years to the care of "mature and wise men" to take the place of their father, a sure way of sidelining them politically (Ehlert 1981:37; Kemper 1989:5). When the poet presents God Himself taking care of Ludwig as his *magaczogo* he is arguing on two fronts at the same time: against Boso, who could claim no more than that he was the "spiritual son" of the pope, and against Hincmar by outbidding his suggestion of finding someone to take care of Ludwig's upbringing.

The test to which Ludwig is put reaches its obvious peak in the battle itself, where he is to show the bravery which is the hallmark of the true ruler. The poem, for all its compression of events, makes it clear that he passed this test. All the Franks fought well, but none so bravely as the king (50), for he was endowed with bravery by his descent which he could trace back to Charles the Great (51: "Brave and bold, that was inborn"). Accordingly, the battle is depicted in terms of Ludwig's personal fighting (52 ff.). Despite differences in detail this is in agreement with the *Annales Vedastini* over the essential feature of bravery: the annalist describes how, at the critical point in the battle, when all seemed about to be lost, Ludwig leapt from his horse, put an end to the headlong flight of the Franks and gave them new heart until it was the Northmen's turn to be put to flight (Berg 1964:187 f.; Yeandle 1989:76). The picture is quite different, however, when Hincmar presents the king in negative terms, taking flight himself together with his men, but even, so it is added, when no one was pursuing them (Yeandle 1989:70). If *fortitudo* is an essential attribute of the ruler it is quite clear that the archbishop and the poet stand on different sides of the political fence.

Another attribute of the ruler is that he should dispense justice and here, too, archbishop and poet differ. In the *Ludwigslied* the king is shown dispensing it by punishing lawbreakers (14): *haranskara* denotes specifically legal punishment in the non-clerical sphere, in the ruler's sphere of responsibility. That offences should be punished and order in the kingdom restored in this way shows that *iustitia* is upheld in Ludwig's kingdom, in contrast to Hincmar's complaint at the synod of Fîmes that it was dead (a general statement which had, of course, a highly personal point) (Yeandle 1989:49, 71).

In view of these criticisms levelled at Ludwig by Hincmar it is not surprising that the archbishop should go so far as to say in a letter to the king in 880 that because of his immature years he was a king more by name than by quality or virtue (*ut nomine potius quam virtute regnetis*) (Berg 1964:182; Yeandle 1989:69). We have already seen how the poet deals with the criticism of immaturity, but there are other ways of meeting this argument. He pointedly stresses Ludwig's kingship, both at the beginning (1: "I know a king, his name is Ludwig") and at the close (57: "our blessed king") and says that the throne, the symbol of his authority, was given him by God (5 f.). However, God gave him more than that, for in the same stanza Ludwig was also divinely equipped with a lordly following (*frônisc githigini*), the means by which he passes the test in the battle, and given *dugidi* (5: *Gab her imo dugidi*). This Old High German noun later came to be the equivalent of Latin *virtus* (cf. modern German *Tugend*), but also denoted the qualities demanded of a man in a particular situation (e.g. in battle) or station in life. Since this stanza is devoted to Ludwig's kingship (his royal retinue and his throne) the word *dugidi* has been translated as *Herrschertugenden*, 'qualities or virtues becoming a ruler' (Haubrichs 1995:143). Whether intended as a specific response to Hincmar or not, the application of this word to Ludwig, as a gift bestowed by God, shows him in quite a different light.

We should be careful how we interpret these differences between the claims made for Ludwig in the poem and the criticisms voiced by Hincmar. It goes too far and anachronistically operates with terms of the Investiture Contest to elevate the contrast to a conflict between Church and state or to see in the direct relationship sketched between Ludwig and God a bypassing of the Church's role in mediating between man and God (Fouracre 1989:83 ff.). This does not mean that the contrast between poet and archbishop is devoid of any significance, but simply that the poet is involved in a task of image-boosting on behalf of Ludwig in the face of opposition to his claims in the succession struggle, clerical in the case of Hincmar, but secular in the case of Boso.

A last question to be considered is a purely literary one, more precisely one of literary history. For long the *Ludwigslied* was regarded as a survival into the Christian period of the Germanic *Preislied* or praise-song; one of the two leading genres which, alongside the *Heldenlied* or heroic lay, flourished in the period of the migrations. There are reasons to doubt whether it is justified to see our poem in terms of the Germanic past rather than the Frankish, Christian present (Wehrli 1969:73 ff.). The thoroughgoing presence of Christian features makes it difficult to argue for a Germanic origin, the more so since the Germanic praise-song, although attested in the North, is a hypothetical entity for southern *Germania*. The *Ludwigslied* is of course a song of praise, lauding God and a ruler, but poetic eulogies are common in the Middle Ages, in Latin as well as various vernaculars, without there being a trace of justification to identify them with the specifically Germanic *Preislied* (Georgi 1969). Interpreting the poem in terms of a postulated literary genre of the past, instead of seeing it within the ninth-century context in which its historical allusions clearly place it, has led inevitably to wishful thinking, a hankering after a genre which is otherwise not attested in the South and to forced interpretations (Wehrli 1969:78 f.). Ludwig's spear could even be seen as reminiscent of Odin's weapon; the saints to whom, as well as to God, thanks are given for victory, have been regarded as valkyries; the verb used for the Franks' fighting (19: *spilôn*, literally 'to play') has been claimed for the grim battle-humour attributed to Germanic warriors, without regard for the fact that the verb means primarily 'to move violently, actively' and as such need not be confined to a warrior context, let alone a Germanic one.

Instead of remaining prisoners of a past of which our knowledge is largely fragmentary we do better to place the *Ludwigslied* in its contemporary setting on which we are at least somewhat better informed. By doing this we can better judge the uniqueness of the *Ludwigslied* in the history of literature (not merely German) (Wehrli 1969:83 ff.). It is the first attested vernacular example of a military encounter depicted in Christian terms as its justification, but if it remains isolated for so long in German this is because the heroic lay in oral form, glorifying exploits of the Migration period, still remained in force and dominated the field. In France the position was different, where there was no competition from a native pre-Christian heroic tradition to challenge the literary supremacy of the *chanson de geste*, like the *Ludwigslied* combining Christian warfare against the pagans (more Saracens than Northmen) with an originally Carolingian background (Wehrli 1969:85; Wolf 1995:34 f.). Because of this similarity it may well be possible to see our poem profitably, not in a line with earlier Germanic literature, but instead, on the German side of a bilingual *Francia*, as an early forerunner of the later *chanson de geste*. It may not be by chance that the historical events on which it is based also gave rise to one *chanson de geste*, namely *Gormont et Isembart*, contaminated though it may be, like most works in this genre, with other literary and historical features.

In short, in assessing the *Ludwigslied* it is necessary to analyse the poem first and foremost for itself and in its contemporary setting, but in either case in terms of the ninth century to which it belongs. If we look beyond this setting at all then it is more rewarding to pay attention to the genesis of a future genre rather than to a past, hypothetical one, and to direct our inquiry towards the West Franks and France, rather than *Germania*.

References

Textual sources:

Annales Bertiniani: see Waitz 1883.
Annales Blandinienses: see Pertz *et al.* (eds.) 1844:20-34.
Annales Vedastini: see Simson 1909:40-82.
Hincmar of Reims
       Capitula Synodalia: see Migne 1852:1069-86.
Ludwigslied: see Haug & Vollmann 1991.
Otfrid von Weissenburg
       Evangelienbuch: see Erdmann 1882.
Sermo in tumulatione S. Quintini: see Waitz, Wattenbach *et al.* (eds.) 1887:271-273.

Bibliography:

Berg, E.
    1964   Das Ludwigslied und die Schlacht bei Saucourt. *Rheinische Vierteljahrsblätter* 29: 175-199.
Coupland, S.
    1995   The Vikings in Francia and Anglo-Saxon England to 911. In *The New Cambridge Medieval History, Vol. II: c. 700 - c. 900.* R. McKitterick (ed.), pp. 190-201. Cambridge: Cambridge University Press.

Ehlert, T.
1981   Literatur und Wirklichkeit - Exegese und Politik. Zur Deutung des
        Ludwigsliedes. *Saeculum* 32: 31-42.

Ehrismann, G.
1932   *Geschichte der deutschen Literatur bis zum Ausgang des Mittelalters. Erster
        Teil: Die althochdeutsche Literatur* (2nd ed.). Munich: Beck.

Erdmann, O. (ed.)
1882   *Otfrid von Weissenburg. Evangelienbuch.* Halle: Waisenhaus.

Ernst, U.
1975   *Der Liber Evangeliorum Otfrids von Weissenburg. Literarästhetik und
        Verstechnik im Lichte der Tradition.* Cologne/Vienna: Böhlau.

Fouracre, P.
1989   Using the background to the Ludwigslied: some methodological problems.
        In *Mit regulu bithuungan. Neue Arbeiten zur althochdeutschen Poesie und
        Sprache.* J. L. Flood & D. N. Yeandle (eds.), pp. 80-93. Göppingen:
        Kümmerle.

Georgi, A.
1969   *Das lateinische und deutsche Preisgedicht des Mittelalters in der Nachfolge
        des genus demonstrativum.* Berlin: Erich Schmidt.

Green, D. H.
1966   *The Millstätter Exodus. A Crusading Epic.* Cambridge: Cambridge
        University Press.

Haubrichs, W.
1979   *Georgslied und Georgslegende im frühen Mittelalter. Text und
        Rekonstruktion.* Königstein/Ts.: Scriptor.
1995   *Geschichte der deutschen Literatur von den Anfängen bis zum Beginn der
        Neuzeit.* Band I/1: *Die Anfänge: Versuche volkssprachiger Schriftlichkeit im
        frühen Mittelalter (ca 700-1050/60).* Tübingen: Max Niemeyer.

Haug, W., & B. Vollmann (eds.)
1991   *Frühe deutsche Literatur und lateinische Literatur in Deutschland 800-1150.*
        Pp. 146-149, 1135-1140. Frankfurt: Deutscher Klassiker Verlag.

Kemper, R.
1989   Das Ludwigslied und die liturgischen Rechtstitel des westfränkischen
        Königtums. In *Mit regulu bithuungan. Neue Arbeiten zur althochdeutschen
        Poesie und Sprache.* J. L. Flood & D.N. Yeandle (eds.), pp. 1-17.
        Göppingen: Kümmerle.

Migne, J. P. (ed.)
1852   Hincmar of Reims, *Capitula Synodalia, Patrologia Latina* 125. Paris:
        publisher in rue d'Amboise. [Repr. Turnhout: Brepols].

Nelson, J. L.
1997   The Frankish Empire. In *The Oxford Illustrated History of the Vikings.*
        P. Sawyer (ed.), pp. 19-47. Oxford: Oxford University Press.

Pertz, G. H., *et al.* (eds.)
1844   [*Annales et chronica aevi Salici.*] *Monumenta Germaniae Historica.
        Scriptores* (in Folio), 5. Hanover: Hahn. [Repr. Anton Hiersemann Verlag,
        Stuttgart, 1985.]

Sawyer, P. H.
1996   *Kings and Vikings. Scandinavia and Europe AD 700-1100.* London: Routledge.

Simson, B. (ed.)
1909   *Annales Xantenses et Annales Vedastini. Monumenta Germaniae Historica.
        Scriptores rerum Germanicarum in usum scholarum separatim editi.* [12.]
        Hanover: Hahn.

Waitz, G. (ed.)
  1883   *Annales Bertiniani. Monumenta Germaniae Historica. Scriptores rerum*
            Germanicarum in usum scholarum separatim editi. [5.] Hanover: Hahn.
Waitz, G., W. Wattenbach *et al.* (eds.)
  1887   *[Supplementa tomorum I-XII, pars III. Supplementum tomi XIII.]*
            Monumenta Germaniae Historica. Scriptores (in folio), 15. Hanover: Hahn.
            [Repr. Anton Hiersemann Verlag, Stuttgart, 1963].
Wehrli, M.
  1969   *Formen mittelalterlicher Erzählung. Aufsätze.* Zürich: Atlantis.
Wolf, A.
  1995   *Heldensage und Epos. Zur Konstituiering einer mittelalterlichen*
            volkssprachlichen Gattung in Spannungsfeld von Mündlichkeit und
            Schriftlichkeit. Tübingen: Gunter Narr.
Yeandle, D.
  1989   The *Ludwigslied*: King, church and context. In *Mit regulu bithuungan.*
            Neue Arbeiten zur althochdeutschen Poesie und Sprache. J. L. Flood &
            D. N. Yeandle (eds.), pp. 18-79. Göppingen: Kümmerle.

Discussion

AUSENDA: My question has little to do with Vikings; it concerns the various forms for Louis or Ludwig.

GREEN: Ludwig and Louis, the French form, are modern vernacular forms for Chlodwig which in turn becomes Clovis. The first element of the compound means 'famous' and the *wig* element here means either 'warrior', or someone who is of a warlike disposition. So the fundamental meaning of the name in Germanic would be 'a renowned warrior', or 'a renowned man of warlike disposition'. 'Chlodwig' is attested as the earliest Germanic form for the word. 'Clovis' would be explained by what early French does to Germanic loanwords which it takes over. The [s] comes in from the masculine nominative ending to -us, that's straightforward; the [ch] element before an [l] was reduced, in some French forms, to a [k] pronunciation, which gives you Clovis. In some forms it was lost altogether as in German, and that gives you in modern German Ludwig, and it also accounts on the French side for the modern French form Louis.

AUSENDA: I'll make the suggestion that all versions of this poem, some by minstrels, flourish until eventually one becomes transcribed. Could it not be that, whereas the historical introduction was assembled for the purpose, the epic description was taken from that of a previous battle which would have been sung for some time by minstrels?

GREEN: I would qualify that last point and say that the epic description in the poem is a very short one, four or four and half lines at the most. Only that is devoted to the actual battle, so that very little remains in the total poem of an earlier—if we can postulate that—epic description. I would see the earlier form, though, as not being an earlier poem celebrating a particular battle, but more importantly a formulaic diction used of battle descriptions in any number of poems from which the poet is drawing as from a reservoir of stock phrases which can be used in any battle description. In other words, I don't think it would be necessarily tied to a particular previous battle, but instead to a formulaic fund which was pre-existent.

And then in regard to what you call a historical introduction (page 281), I would say that the history or the historical references in this poem are present not merely as an introduction, they inform the whole poem at various points, so that they penetrate right through the poem and cannot be said to constitute really an introduction to it.

LUND: Yes, although we have had an ample introduction to the political context and to this interaction between the Vikings and the Franks, I would like to suggest that there is an even wider context of political interplay between the Danes and the Franks, which started in the early ninth century, perhaps even earlier, when one pretender to the Danish crown, Harold Klak, entered into an alliance with Louis the Pious. He later went over to his sons and this led the king who ruled in Denmark, King Horic, to enter into much better relations with Louis, so that there was a political game in which some Danes supported some Franks and other Franks cooperated with other Danes; and they swapped partners. That would be worth looking into to have a more complete picture of this. It wasn't just Vikings seizing opportunities of political discord; they were very much part of Frankish politics.

DUMVILLE: There is a new discussion of some parts of that in Simon Coupland's paper this year, in *Early Medieval Europe*. Even if these simply affect the background to your argument, I think there are points that need raising.

GREEN: Let me make it quite clear that in the background to my argument I am totally dependent on others, on historians. I cannot claim any originality for the historical background.

DUMVILLE: For the sake of correctness, I would like to point out that while "Scandinavian raids on Continental coasts may have occurred before 790" (page 281), they are not known.

LUND: I think probably Ian Wood has given us a more fruitful lead to the eighth century. That was not a time of raiding, but, according to Ian, a time of Scandinavian dominance which may be what is reflected in the finds from Ribe when after the crumbling of Merovingian dominance in this area, somebody appears to have stepped in and there is no other candidate than a Danish king to have secured peace in the southern part of the North Sea. So, it is not a matter just of raids unrecorded, different things went on in the eighth century. When we get renewed conflict, this may have to do with the Frankish revival under the Carolingians, but in the meantime others had established interests in Frisia and Saxony and among other rights, that of taxation. And of course they weren't happy to be put out of business again by Charlemagne. I think that's the core of the conflict between Charlemagne and Godfrid.

GREEN: I hope you realize that my phrasing and, even more so, with David's corrections, I am not trying to make a sudden switch from no Viking Age to Viking Age and leaving the door of continuity to be opened.

DUMVILLE: You are talking (page 282) about Vikings being "encouraged by political difficulties among the Franks", and I think it is wider than that. Within the Frankish area of interest, or sphere of influence, are other groups who may be in rebellion against Frankish dominance. The people I think of particularly in this context are the Bretons, who appear in Carolingian political discourse as rebellious provincials, but who in Breton political discourse appear as freedom fighters.

LUND: I was waiting to hear whether you would swallow the claim that *Francia* was the main target in a period extending to 875.

DUMVILLE: I wasn't going to quibble about ten years [laughter].

GREEN: I acknowledge your generosity [laughter].

DUMVILLE: I wince every time somebody uses the phrase "written down" (page 283) but I restrain myself from saying anything about it. Why could it not have been written down during the process of composition? Why not written in the process of composition?

GREEN: From what we know of this, in early literacy in the Middle Ages, a poem was first composed in writing on a wax tablet, bit by bit, and then transferred to parchment at a later stage. I am talking about the final stage, and I use the wording "writing down" for the parchment which we have in Valenciennes.

DUMVILLE: Yes, but what you appear to be arguing is that the Valenciennes manuscript was not the original, was not the first written version.

GREEN: No, I don't argue that, I don't even express an opinion on that.

DUMVILLE: But you have to have an opinion in order to offer answers to me as you just did. I cannot see why you are leaving out the possibility that there was a parchment version within hours of the composition?

GREEN: I am not excluding that possibility.

DUMVILLE: You appear to be. You are allowing so much latitude, about twenty years latitude.

GREEN: No, I am saying that the copy we have, which is what I am basing myself on, was written down at that stage. I am making no claim about when the poem was composed in writing. Well, I am making no claim about the latest date possible of the composition, apart from the year in which Louis himself died.

DUMVILLE: But the manuscript is dated by a script. The script is of the last third of the ninth century and, therefore, comprehends the date that you are concerned with. And, therefore, I take it that your convinction that the poem is later, significantly later than the event, derives from this phrase *piam*. Twenty, thirty years ago Christopher Brook compiled a list of uses of phrases like *memoriae...civili*. In other words, this can be a way of referring to somebody politely.

GREEN: Yes, but we have other evidence that Louis III died in that particular year.

DUMVILLE: Yes, I am not doubting that, I am simply saying you could refer to someone of pious memory, while he was still alive.

GREEN: No, what you mean then is that the external evidence we have that Ludwig died in 882 should be the point to make here.

DUMVILLE: Yes, in other words, I simply cannot see why you appear to be excluding the possibilities a) that the poem is the earliest possible date, and b) that the manuscript is the closest date as it possibly could be to that.

GREEN: I am not excluding that possibility.

DUMVILLE: I said you appear to be.

JESCH: When you say something is "written down", you are not excluding any possibilities about what might have happened before that moment when that text was written down, but if you say "written", then you would be excluding the possibility that the poem had been composed at least several hours before, because the meaning of 'written' includes 'composed'.

GREEN: That is precisely why I used the phrase "written down". There you started by objecting to that phrase.

DUMVILLE: You say "poetic compression of events, also to be found in the heroic lay and unavoidable in a genre for oral recital of a restricted length" (page 285). Do you mean "such a lay may not have more than 107 lines"?

GREEN: There is no specific number [laughter]. The lay was recited at a specific occasion when the ability to hold audiences' attention was a factor to be taken into account. One reckons a south-Germanic lay at this time as being not much longer than 160 to 200 lines at the most, so of considerable shortness. This is one of the generic distinctions between the epic and the heroic lay, that the lay was of such a concise short length.

DUMVILLE: Is there a sufficient number of examples to justify any such supposition?

GREEN: It is a theoretical argument.

DUMVILLE: Which may be circular.

GREEN: Which may be circular, yes. Simply because of the lack of the evidence. I would say that what evidence we have for heroic lays has in effect surprisingly little scope in the sense of the number of lines in actual battle description. What they are mainly concerned with, is the ethical conflict which lies behind this battle, and when talking about actual battle descriptions, not merely in this poem, but in others, the actual scope given to the description of figthing is reduced in the extreme.

BRINK: I am interested in the background of the word *haranskara* (page 287).

GREEN: Possibly *harm*: the more common form would be *harm* in the sense of harm or damage, and *skara* in the sense of meting out damage in the form of punishment.

BRINK: So, it means *harm*.

GREEN: Possibly, we are not sure.

BRINK: And what does *buozen* mean?

GREEN: *Buozen*, modern German 'büßen', in the sense of 'to do penance' in the religious sense, but also to 'take punishment for a secular legal misdemeanour'.

BRINK: It has a cognate in Swedish *bot*, a penalty to be paid.

HERSCHEND: There is an obvious conflict between their religious way of looking at what a king ought to be in this age and then the other side of the coin (page 288); and I think of Ludwig's inborn qualities to be a king, and also the fact that since his father's death we must take God as the only king worthwhile to give them the kingship. And he also gives it to a small collective, namely his retainers, to prove his ability to be a king. That reminds me very much of what I would say from the old Scandinavian sources, a typical Germanic king.

GREEN: German scholarship of a time now almost entirely past tended to see this poem not in Christian terms at all, but as a survival of the pagan Germanic past and make reference to these farfetched and untenable associations with Odin and the rest. I am not denying that there are possible links between the Christian conceptions and native Germanic conceptions, but I think it is overwhelmingly a Christian interpretation in the case of these events.

HERSCHEND: I just pointed to a slightly greater world, as a more ideological way of understanding the meta-history of this period.

GREEN: You are using the Scandinavian evidence as being exemplary of what was common Germanic and therefore as lying behind a thought world which could be applied to Christianity in *Francia*.

HERSCHEND: Actually I don't think that it was difficult for Scandinavians to understand High German.

GREEN: That Scandinavians could have understood the poem I very much doubt.

ARRHENIUS: Yes, I wanted to observe that it could be dangerous to infer pagan syncretism or meaning, as it was one of the strategies of the Christian missionaries to use a measure of syncretism. But I think that it is dangerous to talk about the pagan one. We really don't know anything about it.

GREEN: Well, I hope you noticed that in my own paper, I made no distinction between pagan and Christian among the Franks. I have left that on one side. Enough damage has been done in past interpretation from that point of view.

JESCH: I wonder if it is worth mentioning the battle of *Brunanburh* in that context (page 290). The battle of *Brunanburh* is also the celebration of a defeat of the Vikings, also a poem which some scholars have thought perhaps represented in some way a tradition of English praise poetry, also placing the particular battle not so much in a Christian context but more in the history of the Anglo-Saxons.

GREEN: I think one is bringing in two different approaches to history here. The one I was concerned with was the Christian interpretation of events in this world under the aegis of God's domination. You are talking, when you are referring to the *Brunanburh* example, of historical in the wide sense of earthly history. I am talking about 'Heilsgeschichte' as an interplay between earthly history and the divine plan which is being worked out in earthly history. I think these are two different approaches.

JESCH: No, I thought that perhaps the 'Heilsgeschichte' approach was implicit in *Brunanburh*, but that certainly is something that could be discussed.

DUMVILLE: I had a question here (page 295) about your word "pagan" and attitudes to the various groups of outsiders who were attacking the sub-Carolingian world. How much was being discussed about Saracens, and about heathens and religion, to enable a distinction to be made between *pagani* on the one hand in areas of Scandinavia, and *Saraceni* on the other, who could not be described in those terms.

GREEN: You are talking on the level of learned clerical discourse. I am talking on the level of 'chanson de geste' where frequently enough Vikings are referred to as 'Saracens'.

NIELSEN: No!

GREEN: Yes. [Laughter]. You are not in agreement that the Vikings are Saracens, but in the chansons de geste that equation comes up often enough.

References in the discussion

Textual sources:

The Battle of Brunanburh: see Dobbie 1942.

Bibliography:

Dobbie, E. van K. (ed.)
   1942   *The Anglo-Saxon Minor Poems*. (The Anglo-Saxon Poetic Records 6). New York: University of Columbia Press. .

HARALD BLUETOOTH – A SAINT VERY NEARLY MADE BY ADAM OF BREMEN

NIELS LUND

Institute of History, University of Copenhagen, Njalsgade 102, DK-2300 Copenhagen

When Christianity spread in the Roman empire it was a popular religion that first caught on among the citizens of the towns; it became a state religion only when there was a popular pressure strong enough to persuade the emperor that it could no longer be ignored or repressed. In Scandinavia, however, although Widukind (iii 64) makes the enigmatic statement that when Harald Bluetooth was baptized the Danes were already Christians of old, they only continued to worship their old deities, Christianity seems to have been introduced from above. In Norway kings Olav Tryggvason and Olav Haraldsson the Saint are both credited with having converted their compatriots by means of the sword, and although many Scandinavians must have been acquainted with Christianity all attempts to introduce it in Denmark also seem to have gone via the head of society rather than via its members.

The first reference to an attempt to spread the Word in Denmark is in Alcuin's life of St Willibrord, the Anglo-Saxon missionary in Frisia, who, when his efforts there were frustrated, tried to extend his field of mission to Scandinavia but found King Ongendus in Denmark impermeable to the Truth. A century later a Danish king adopted Christianity in the hope of securing imperial support against his rivals in Denmark, and throughout the ninth century the success of the missionaries clearly depended very much on their relations with the kings. This was so also in the tenth century when Denmark was finally officially Christianized. Although there are hints that Christianity had gained some foothold earlier in the century,[1] the decisive event was the baptism of Harald Bluetooth at the hands of the missionary Poppo. This made Denmark an officially Christian country although we have little idea what sort of foothold it had gained among ordinary people.

To study the way Christianity was adopted we need to define a number of concepts but first of all we need to know our sources, their purposes and their bias. One of the most important sources is Adam of Bremen's *History of the Archbishops of Hamburg,* the German archsee that claimed responsibility and exclusive rights to evangelize Scandinavia and to organize its Church. The Swedish historian Sture Bolin described Adam as a singularly truthful author who,

---

[1] Since the conference was held in 1998, archaeologists have repeatedly claimed that they now had Christian graveyards, individual Christian burials and churches that predated Harald's baptism. It has even been claimed that Harald's offence, for which his son rebelled against him, was not that he replaced the ancient pagan cult with Christianity but that he replaced one form of Christianity with another. None of this is based on sound evidence.

unlike most of his contemporaries, was concerned to provide a historically accurate account, not to write a political pamphlet vaguely based on historical evidence but designed to influence contemporary events (Bolin 1960:284). The following will demonstrate that this judgment is ripe for qualification.

Some years ago Peter Sawyer demonstrated what a pragmatic understanding of truth Adam of Bremen displayed in his account of Sven Forkbeard's career (Sawyer 1991). In so doing he inevitably also cast doubts on Adam's information about Sven's father Harald Bluetooth, against whom Sven rebelled, but, equally inevitably, he did not carry out a full investigation of this part of Adam's history. A closer study reveals that very little of the picture of Harald that emerges from Adam's pages merits any confidence.

Adam's account of Harald's reign may be summarized like this: During the reign of Harald's father Gorm Christian missionaries were not welcomed in Denmark. However, Unni, archbishop of Hamburg-Bremen 918-36, managed to persuade Harald, and although he was not immediately baptized he permitted Christianity to be practised openly and he supported Unni's work. Unni was able to consecrate clergy for all the churches in Denmark and to leave the faithful in his care (i 59).

Defeated in battle by Otto the Great, king of Germany 936-73, emperor since 962, Harald paid homage to Otto and took baptism together with his wife Gunhild and his son Sven, who was given the name Sven Otto. In Jutland three dioceses were created and submitted to Hamburg. Documents in the church of Bremen show that Otto's power in Denmark was such that he appointed the bishops, and papal letters show that Agapitus granted Adaldag, archbishop 937-88, everything that his predecessors had granted, as well as the right to consecrate bishops for Denmark and the other Scandinavian peoples (ii 3).

Harald remained a pious king and a staunch defender of Christianity. Therefore he was able to extend his power over Norway and England (ii 25).

Towards the end of Adaldag's life the Danes rebelled against Harald, rejected the Faith and swore allegiance to Harald's son Sven. Defeated in battle by the rebels Harald got on board a ship and made his way to the town of Jumne among the Slavs (ii 27).

Harald was given a friendly welcome by the Slavs, more friendly than could be hoped for since they were pagans, but soon died from his wounds. His body was then taken to his *patria* by the army and buried in Roskilde in the church that Harald himself had built in honour of Holy Trinity. Adam expresses the wish that Harald, who first introduced Christianity among the Danes and filled all Scandinavia with clergy and churches, and who was innocently wounded and driven out because of Christ, will not miss the crown of martyrdom. He ruled fifty years. He died on All Saints' day. He and his wife Gunhild will be remembered eternally in Bremen (ii 28)

After this follows the story of the divine punishment that Sven suffered for betraying the true God who had protected his father. He was exiled twice seven years, he was twice captured and ransomed, and Adam makes the nice point that while his Christian father had been welcomed by the pagan Slavs, the pagan Sven was rejected by the pagan Norwegians and could only find refuge among the Scots. If Adam knew anything about the Scots he probably found them to be congenial company for Sven: their kings normally succeeded after killing off their predecessor.

Some of this has enjoyed the general acceptance of later historians. It is normally accepted that Harald acknowledged the archbishop of Hamburg-Bremen as metropolitan of the church in Scandinavia and supported his work in Denmark wholeheartedly; that he admitted German bishops into his country; that, when Sven rebelled, Harald sought refuge with friends in Jumne and died there on the 1st of November sometime around 985, and certainly no later than 987; and that he was afterwards buried in Roskilde in a Trinity church that he himself had begun to build. There is, however, little reason to believe any of this or anything else in Adam's story. Adam's *History of the Archbishops of Hamburg* was conceived and written as part of Hamburg's struggle to preserve its position in Scandinavia; it served the same purpose as the forgeries produced at about the same time by Adam's colleagues in the archiepiscopal *scriptorium*, those very documents that he refers to in his text.

An analysis of Adam's information leaves little to be trusted. When Harald is first mentioned he is not yet king, but we are informed that he was much more favourably disposed towards the Christian missionary Unni than his father Gorm and even in defiance of his father permitted the Christian cult to be practised in public (i 59). Adam never informs us of Harald's accession. When he is next mentioned he acts as a king of the Danes, fighting and losing a war against the Germans and consequently submitting to the emperor. After this Harald was baptized and bishops were appointed to the sees of Slesvig, Ribe and Aarhus (ii 3-4). We should, therefore, infer that Harald's accession, submission and baptism took place before 948; in this year these bishops were appointed at Ingelheim (Fuhrmann 1964). Unfortunately, the invasion that Adam reports never took place. He has transferred the wars fought in 973-74 between Otto II and Harald Bluetooth and in 983, when after the death of Otto II Harald Bluetooth with Slav allies attacked Hamburg, to this earlier time, thus concealing the uncomfortable fact that his would-be saint accepted Christianity at a much later stage in his career and, worse, not from Hamburg-Bremen. He also, and this was no less important, established a claim that Hamburg deserved all credit for introducing Christianity in Denmark against claims made by Hamburg's arch-enemy the archbishop of Cologne that his see had a share in it. Cologne was, of course, demanding the return of Bremen to the archdiocese of Cologne from which it was taken after the sack of Hamburg in 845. This would severely threaten the very existence of the archdiocese of Hamburg.

Adam's next information on Harald relates to the 980s; it is basically a lot of fanciful information, among it a claim that Harald conquered England (ii 25). This particular information is given to demonstrate the contrast between kings on God's side, who expand and conquer other nations, and those who are against God and therefore lose their lands and suffer miserable exile, or worse. It is a clear example of Adam's putting the higher truth before historical truth, the latter of course being that Sven, not Harald, conquered England. After this comes the information about Sven Forkbeard's rebellion against Harald and in this context the claim that Harald reigned fifty years (ii 27-28). Adam, clearly, was unable to substantiate this claim. He manipulated the date of Harald's accession as well as of that of his Christianization, both in order to make Harald a more convincing candidate for sainthood and to give an enhanced impression of Hamburg-Bremen's efforts and influence in Denmark in the tenth century.

The oldest source to afford any information on the events that led to Harald's death is the *Encomium Emmæ Reginæ,* written in Flanders about 1040. This tells us that Harald, envious of his son, was going to bar Sven from the succession. Disaffected by this, the Danish army sided with Sven and protected him from his father. As a result the two sides met in a battle in which Harald was wounded. He then fled to the Slavs, *ad Sclauos,* and there died shortly afterwards (i 1).

Although the Encomiast is obviously biased against Harald and is careful to stress that Sven had done nothing to incur his father's disfavour, there is nothing implausible about this story. Whatever the.cause of the rebellion may have been, whether the encomiast's distribution of the blame for the sore relationship between father and son is fair or not, a rebellion is believable, and it should not surprise us that Harald should have fled to the Slavs. The encomiast does not tell to what Slavs, but it is well known that Harald was married to an Abodrite princess, the daughter of prince Mistivoi. She put up a runic monument, now sitting in the wall inside the church of Sønder Vissing in Jutland (*DR* 55) to her mother and in the inscription manages to mention her own name and that of her husband as well as that of her father, but not that of her mother.

Harald and Mistivoi were close allies. They had fought a series of wars against the Germans together, culminating in the attack in 983 when, after the death of Otto II, Harald regained what he lost in 973 and the Abodrites sacked Hamburg. It seems quite plausible, therefore, that Harald, having lost the battle with his son and his followers and having been wounded, should seek refuge with his Slavic father-in-law.

However, from the next source that records this event, Adam of Bremen's *History of the Archbishops of Hamburg,* we learn that after losing the battle Harald got himself on board a ship and found refuge in the Slavonic town of Jumne. There are many other differences between Adam's account and that of the encomiast. According to Adam, Sven had placed himself at the head of a pagan rebellion against Harald, and the Danes were falling from the faith on a great scale. Such differences matter little. They are easily enough explained by the different bias of the two authors.

Adam's continuation of the story, however, is intriguing. In the first place, Adam expresses surprise that Harald should find a friendly reception in Jumne because its inhabitants were pagan. They received him *contra spem.* But this very paganism is probably the reason why Adam chose Jumne as a place of refuge for Harald rather than the Christian Abodrites. His friendly reception here served to demonstrate what a good Christian Harald was and to stress his innocence in the conflict with Sven: he was a man who would find refuge even among pagans, while his pagan adversary was rejected by them, very suitable for a king whose recognition as a martyr Adam was preparing for (ii 28; Lund 1998:59-68).

In the second place Adam claims that after his death Harald was taken to Denmark for burial by his army and was buried in Roskilde in the church of the Holy Trinity which he himself had begun. This raises several questions, the most serious of which is not that archaeologists have been unable, in spite of extensive excavations, to locate this church. Who took the body of Harald to Roskilde? Harald had fled because his army was unable to keep him in power, so it could hardly bring his dead body back in spite of the victors. And it hardly makes sense to assume that Sven, being responsible for his father's death, would be able to go to Harald's supporters and just claim his fathers's body, whoever these supporters may have been. If they were Harald's friends they were presumably Sven's enemies.

And is it at all believable that Sven would be interested in the erection of a monument to his father so soon after rebelling against him? Would it not be more in his interest as far as possible to eradicate the memory of Harald? If Harald's supporters in Denmark had not been completely crushed his tomb might give them something to rally round, and this would be potentially dangerous for Sven. It is possible, of course, that it mattered to Sven Forkbeard, as it mattered to Sven Estridson, to be able to point to the tombs of his ancestors, but this would be a powerful argument for his enemies to deny him the body. Adam does not explain this. According to him, Sven was a pagan, therefore should probably not bury his father in a church even if he wanted, because of the implications for his own legitimacy, to venerate his father's tomb. In fact, Adam does not imply at all that Sven was involved in Harald's burial, and if Adam's further story is true, he could hardly have been.

According to Adam, Sven was twice captured by his enemies and ransomed by the Danes, and later he was exiled by the Swedish king Erik the Victorious and miserably travelled far and wide in search of shelter.

If these stories were true, Harald's body might have been taken to Roskilde by someone other than Sven, although Adam's information that Sven was ransomed by the Danes does imply that, in Adam's own view, he was the ruler of Denmark soon after the war with his father. There is, however, little reason to accept Adam's account of Sven's early years (Skovgaard-Petersen 1966; Sawyer 1991). A martyr presupposes a tormentor, and in this contradictory story Sven is the villain by contrast to whom Harald is recognized as the hero. It is well known that while, according to Adam, Sven is supposed to have been a miserable exile, he was, in fact, successfully attacking England and extorting Danegeld there. The Viking raids on England were resumed, and grew to what has been termed "England's second Viking Age", from about 980 when Southampton was attacked by a small fleet. Sven himself is first mentioned as a participant in 994 but there are good reasons for believing that he was also the leader of the raid in 991 on, among other places, Maldon (Lund 1991:132-33).

Thietmar of Merseburg also has the information that Sven was captured by his enemies, although he mentions only one captivity, and since it cannot be proven that Adam knew Thietmar, their accounts have been treated as independent evidence. The fact that there is no positive proof that Adam knew Thietmar does not, however, exclude the possibility that he did, and it seems very unlikely that Adam should not have been familiar with Thietmar's work. As Svend Ellehøj remarked, there is in fact a remarkable agreement between Adam's and Thietmar's accounts of Sven (Ellehøj 1953:37, n.1). Adam did, however, have little occasion to quote anything from Thietmar in his own text (Sawyer 1991:34). The story that Adam tells of Sven is a tale of divine punishment that out of Christian necessity had to be meted out to a king who neglected the rights of the archbishops of Hamburg-Bremen to the extent that Sven had, expelling bishops consecrated in Hamburg-Bremen—so that Otto III had to permit them to acquire privileged lands in the Empire (MGH. Dipl. Reg. II:440, No. 41)—and calling in bishops from elsewhere instead. It is also an attempt to create a Danish royal saint and to make Roskilde the centre of this cult. A claim therefore had to be made that his grave was in Roskilde—and it no doubt did not help these endeavours that the body could not be produced and that no wonders were worked. The only place where Harald is commemorated, apart from Jelling, is at Tamdrup which seems to have been the centre of a cult to Poppo, the cleric who converted Harald. The golden altar—or, more probably, the remains of a reliquary later fitted on an altar—from Tamdrup depicts his ordeal and Harald's baptism. But this is twelfth-century (Christiansen 1968).

The history of this period has, however, to a large extent been based on Adam's account, and much effort has gone into fleshing it out from other, mostly rather late, sources.

We would like to know what friends Harald might have had at Jumne that made him seek refuge there rather than with his father-in-law. Adam's own information about Jumne is, however, of no great help to us. He clearly never went there himself and gives us a sanguine description of a town which, he claims, was the biggest in Europe (ii 22).

Although this is going over the top, Jumne or Wolin certainly was an important port of trade, and it reached its peak in the second half of the tenth century, when its number of inhabitants approached 10,000. An exhibition of finds from Wolin has been touring the Scandinavian countries and in an excellent catalogue Wladyslaw Filipowiak puts before us the archaeological facts about Wolin (Filipowiak 1991).

Later legend turned this port of trade into a fortress manned by the Jomsvikings and it was even claimed that Harald Bluetooth had founded it himself. In spite of brave attempts by great scholars like Svend Ellehøj (Ellehøj 1953) to make sense of these legends it must be realized now that Jumne was not a Danish stronghold manned by a force of Danish vikings that could serve as Harald's allies. It was a sizeable port of trade in the territory of the Wolynians, and towards the end of the tenth century it was trying to defend a precarious independence against the expanding Polish kingdom. As part of this defence Wolin may, of course, as Filipowiak suggests, have availed itself of Danish mercenaries or auxiliaries (Filipowiak 1991:39).

At this time Scandinavian chieftains took service with foreign princes in a number of cases. It is common knowledge that a number of Swedes served in Russia, where Russian princes repeatedly sent for reinforcements of their varangians. They also served in Byzantium (Blöndal 1978), and in the West king Æthelred of England hired a complete viking army to serve him in 994; later he hired Thorkell the Tall, who is supposed to have been connected with the Jomsvikings. Thorkell's army is referred to in the *Anglo-Saxon Chronicle* as an *unfrithhere,* and if this expression is not simply tautological, it is probably to distinguish this *here* from those armies with which the English had a *frith,* like the agreement they concluded with the army at Southampton in 994 and which they got with Thorkell's army in 1012. Scandinavian mercenaries also appear to have served the first Piastr rulers of Poland and to have found their graves in Western Poland.

If there is any truth in the claims about Thorkell's connection with Jumne it may be that the services of his gang of thugs, so valued in the 980s, were no longer required at Wolin twenty years later, when Wolin had apparently found an ally in the German emperor Henry II, and Thorkell therefore sought a fortune elsewhere.

Be that as it may, we must return to our question of the plausibility of Harald's seeking refuge in Wolin, or *Jumne,* as Adam calls it. It is difficult to establish the political position and sympathies of this community in this period. It has been much discussed whether it was independent or it was under Polish domination, or whether it had sought itself allies among other powers in the Baltic, be it Danes or Swedes. Leopold Sobel has shown that at the time Harald is supposed to have sought refuge there, Wolin formed part of the Lutitian federation, which was independent of Poland and remained so, strengthened by an alliance with Bohemia, well into the eleventh century (Sobel 1981:56-85). Filipowiak, on the other hand, has stressed the expansion of Poland in this area (Filipowiak 1991:35-37). Suggestions that the Danes might have played a significant role, either in the shape of Jomsvikings or even, as Sven Aggesen would have it in the late twelfth century, that Harald Bluetooth was the founder of Jumne and that it could be regarded as a Danish base (Sven Aggesen, *Brevis Historia*) have been ruled out of court. The Danes would also have liked to extend their influence in these parts but because of the Poles they had to look further west, and here Danish and Saxon interests clashed.

Although Leopold Sobel's case for Wolin's independence of the Poles under Mieszko is convincing, it seems likely that Polish influence was making itself increasingly felt. To the extent Polish presence is a factor to be reckoned with in Wolin at this period it should serve to discourage Harald from seeking refuge there. Throughout his reign Harald had been on hostile terms with the emperors of Germany. Harald may have been a co-regent of his father Gorm the Old, who died in 958, but after Gorm's death Harald was sole king. A few years later Wichmann the Younger, a Saxon rebel, sought Harald's support and took refuge in Denmark. Even if Wichmann did not get much active support from Harald, this shows that Harald was counted among the enemies of the Empire. Soon after, Harald accepted Christianity under German pressure. Otto the Great had appointed bishops to Denmark and looked like supporting their work in practical terms, so Harald took baptism—and soon after began extensive works on Danevirke, very likely to be prepared for a conflict with Otto. In 948, when bishops were appointed to three Danish dioceses, bishoprics were also established among the Slavs in Brandenburg and Havelberg. Harald Bluetooth surely had made the same observation that Timothy Reuter has recently restated: "Conversion meant in the first instance political submission and the obligation to pay tithe; it cannot easily be distinguished from conquest" (Reuter 1991:165).

Following Otto I's death in 973 Harald attacked the Germans, probably in an attempt to exploit their apparent weakness during succession disputes to restore Danish influence among the Slavs, but with little success. He lost part of south Jutland, exactly how much we cannot tell—it may in fact have been only that the Saxons were able to build a fortress just north of the border (Hoffmann 1984:120- 21)—and only got it back ten years later when, following the death of Otto II soon after his defeat at Crotone in Calabria, he attacked the Germans once more and was able to restore the ancient boundary at the Eider. In both these wars Harald's father-in-law Mistivoi was his ally. The Abodrites wished to break loose from domination by the Billung dukes of Saxony and sacked Hamburg in 983. They reverted to tributary status, however, the following year (Reuter 1991:257).

In the same period, however, Mieszko of Poland was an ally of the Germans. Having christianized Poland in 966 he stayed on good terms with the emperor and sided with him in his wars against the Wends. As an ally of the Germans he ought to have been an enemy of the enemies of the Germans: the Danes and the Abodrites. Doesn't Adam owe us an explanation why Harald should seek refuge in a town that was in any case dangerously close to the Poles? If the Poles were not a problem, then what Adam ought to have explained is why Harald should have bypassed his Christian father-in-law and gone to the other major confederation of Slav tribes, a confederation with which he did not, as far as we are informed, have any relations? And to a place that seems even to have been a leading center of pagan religion and cult. The explanation probably is that Jumne, not the Christian Abodrites, offered Adam the opportunity to make the point that Harald, saintly Harald, was well received by the pagans, while pagan Sven was not.

There are certainly more arguments than just the one based on source-critical fundamentalism: always prefer an older source to a younger one, for doubting Adam's information. The Encomiast does not suggest with what Slavs Harald took refuge, but from our own knowledge Mistivoi and his Abodrites is a much more plausible suggestion than Jumne. This implies that if we want to find Harald's grave, Mecklenburg is the place to start.

This means calling Adam into question on yet another issue, and there must be grounds for serious doubts about his whole account of Haralds reign. Could Harald really have been such a zealous protagonist of Christianity and the interests of Hamburg-Bremen, or is this whole thing a story made up by Adam and Sven Estridsen for their own purposes a century later?

Hamburg-Bremen was kept out when Harald adopted Christianity, having been persuaded by Poppo's ordeal—Poppo did not come from Bremen and this is no mere coincidence — and is it likely that Harald should have invited bishops from Hamburg-Bremen, a recognized agent of German imperialism, immediately after, or, indeed, at any time during his reign, if he was constantly hostile to emperors Otto the Great and Otto II? Later on we see Adam painting a rosy picture of Sven Estridsen's relationship with Hamburg, although the grim fact, also revealed by Adam, was that Sven was negotiating with the pope for the creation of an independent Danish archsee, the very catastrophe that Hamburg was fighting so hard to avert.

If we doubt Adam's information on the relationship between Harald and archbishop Adalgar, this increases our difficulties in assigning a year to Harald's death. It has been argued, persuasively it would seem at first glance, that Otto III's letter of immunity to the Danish bishops of 988, permitting them to acquire privileged lands in the Empire, should be seen as a prompt reaction to the troubles they had been plunged into by Sven's rebellion. According to Adam, we remember, Sven was brought in by a pagan reaction and was an apostate himself. He consequently drove out the suffragans of Hamburg-Bremen from Denmark. This would be an argument for dating Harald's death as late as possible before Otto's letter, i.e. 987 (Refskou 1985).

There may be that core of truth in this that Sven did not want German bishops in his kingdom, agents as they were of German imperialism, but he was no apostate and there is no evidence that there was a pagan reaction in Denmark. But is it not reasonable to question the presence of German, or, more specifically, Hamburg bishops in Denmark in Harald Bluetooth's own reign?

Harald endorsed Christianity, no doubt about that, but Hamburg could take no credit for it. In fact, his conversion took place by virtue of a violation of Hamburg's missionary privileges for the North. Poppo was no representative of the archsee and Adam is at great pains to conceal this regrettable fact: he moves the Poppo episode into a different context. But ever since his conversion Harald was on such terms with Germany that it seems unlikely that, while his programme of Christianization clearly required a clergy, he would ever have admitted such imperial agents as Hamburg bishops were. And there is, in fact, no evidence that any of the bishops appointed in 948 ever set foot in Denmark—although it is perhaps puzzling that a fourth diocese should be added in 988 to those mentioned in 965 in Otto the Great's letter of immunity.

Erich Hoffmann has suggested that the war in 983 might have been the occasion for the expulsion of the bishops (1984:122) but this event does not seem to mark any turn of the tide in relations between Denmark and Germany.

There are many more problems related to this. One is the apparent alliance between Poland and Sweden, as expressed in the marriage between a Polish princess and a Swedish king. Adam mentions an attack by the Swedish king on Denmark, and he makes it part of the divine punishment that Sven has to take for his wicked deeds. If this attack ever took place it would have made sense in Harald's time—but this would obviously ruin Adam's point. We may suspect that if Adam did not invent it, he moved it out of its proper context (Sawyer 1994).[2]

According to Adam, Harald Bluetooth died in the ultimate days of Adaldag, *novissimis archiepiscopis temporibus,* who died 29 April 988 (ii 27), and the metropolitan church of Hamburg-Bremen commemorated Harald on All Saints' Day, the 1st of November (Adam ii 28). The year of his death is uncertain, however, and much debated. He could, trusting Adam and accepting the 1st of November as the actual day of his death, have died no later than 987, and some prefer this year (Refskou 1985). It has been customary to give a cautious *ca* 985, or 985-986, but it has also been argued that Adam's information is so vague that Harald's death could even have occurred as early as 980 (for example Olsen 1980).

The traditional date of his death is based upon Adam of Bremen's information that Harald ruled fifty years, very nearly the same length of time as Adaldag occupied the see of Hamburg-Bremen. Adam claims that Adaldag died in his 54th year in office. In fact he was appointed in 937 as successor to Unni who had died in September 936, and he died 29 April 988, in his 52nd year in office, *i. e.* Harald is said to have died in the ultimate days of Adaldag, and as he could not have begun his rule before 935 or 936, when his father Gorm the Old is last mentioned by a narrative source, adding fifty years was a simple calculation. However, it is now known that Gorm was not placed in his burial chamber in the north mound in Jelling until 958, and therefore presumably died about this time. Adam's information can, therefore, be no clue to the year of Harald's death.

If we accept the information that Harald died in the ultimate days of Archbishop Adalgar, how wide a margin does this leave us? Adalgar held his see for more than fifty years, he was appointed in 937 and died 29 April 988, so would five years seem reasonable, or ten? Or should we discard this information too, on the grounds that Adam has constructed parallel biographies of Harald and Adalgar, and been proven wrong on the beginning of Harald's reign? The best reason not to believe Adam's information is, that he contradicts it himself. He informs us that after Harald's death Sven was deprived of his kingdom by the Swedish king Erik the Victorious and was fourteen years an exile among the Scots. His kingdom was given back to him only after the death of Eric. We can put an approximate date to Erik's death. He died *ca* 993, and since, according to Adam, Sven was twice a captive with the Slavs and spent some time trying to find refuge in Norway and England before finally ending up in Scotland, we must deduct at least fifteen years

---

[2] This point has not been included in the printed version of Peter Sawyer's paper but it was made at the seminar in Kopervik.

from this year to arrive at the year of Harald's death; this takes us back to 978. Chronological precision was obviously not Adam's concern.

If Adam's years cannot be trusted, can we at least trust his day, All Saints' Day? Hardly: Adam was trying to build up Harald's sainthood; it served this purpose admirably to claim that he was venerated on All Saints' Day. This date, however, was not the actual date of the death of those venerated on it. All Saints' Day was the feast day of all those saints whose actual death date was *not* known.

What has been said here is far from exhausting the problems posed by Adam of Bremen. Much more work needs to be done before we understand Adam's work, its purpose and its context. And it has to be done before we can hope to understand the problems involved in the introduction and adoption of Christianity in Denmark.

References

Textual sources:
[Abbr.: *DR = Danmarks Runeindskrifter.*]

Adam of Bremen
 Gesta Hammaburgensis ecclesiæ pontificum: see Trillmich & Buchner (eds.) 1978.
Danmarks Runeindskrifter: see Jacobsen & Moltke (eds.) 1941-42.
Encomium Emmae reginae: see Campbell (ed.) 1949.
Ottonis III. Diplomata: see Sickel (ed.) 1893.
Widukind
 Res Gestae Saxonicae: see Bauer & Rau (eds.) 1977.

Bibliography:

Bauer, A., & R. Rau
 1977 Widukind, *Res Gestae Saxonicae. Quellen zur Geschichte der sächsischen Kaiserzeit.* Ausgewählte Quellen zur deutschen Geschichte des Mittelalters. Freiherr vom Stein-Gedächtnisausgabe. R. Buchner & F.-J. Schmale (eds.) Band VIII. Darmstadt: Wissenschaftliche Buchgesellschaft.
Blöndal, S.
 1978 *The Varangians of Byzantium. An aspect of Byzantine military history,* transl., rev. and rewritten by Benedikt S. Benedikz. Cambridge: Cambridge University Press.
Bolin, S.
 1960 Gesta Hammaburgensis ecclesiae pontificum. In *Kulturhistorisk leksikon for nordisk middelalder*, vol. 5, pp. 283-289. Copenhagen: Rosenkilde og Bagger.
Campbell, A.
 1949 *Encomium Emmae Reginae.* Ed. for the Royal Historical Society by A. Campbell. Camden third series, vol. LXXII. London: The Royal Historical Society 1949. Reprinted with a supplementary introduction by S. Keynes. (Camden Classic Reprints 4, Cambridge 1998).
Christiansen, T. E.
 1968 De gyldne Altre I. Tamdrup-pladerne. *Aarbøger for nordisk Oldkyndighed og Historie* 1968: 153-205.

Ellehøj, S.
1953   Olav Tryggvesons fald og venderne. *Historisk Tidsskrift* 11 (4): 1-53.
Filipowiak, W.
1991   *Wolin-Jomsborg. En vikingetids-handelsby i Polen.* Roskilde: Roskilde
            Museums forlag.
Fuhrmann, H.
1964   Die "heilige und Generalsynode" des Jahres 948. In *Ingelheim am Rhein.
            Forschungen und Studien zur Geschichte Ingelheims.* J. Autenrieth (ed.), pp.
            159-164. Stuttgart: Klett. [Also in *Otto der Grosse.* H. Zimmermann (ed.),
            pp. 46-55. (Wege der Forschung Band CCCCL, 1976). Darmstadt:
            Wissenschaftliche Buchgesellschaft].
Hoffmann, E.
1984   Beiträge zur Geschichte der Beziehungen zwischen dem deutschen und dem
            dänischen Reich für die Zeit von 934 bis 1035. In *850 Jahre St.-Petri-Dom
            zu Schleswig. 1134-1984.* C. Radtke & W. Körber (eds.), pp. 105-132.
            Schleswig: Schlesinger Druck- und Verlagshaus.
Jacobsen, L., & E. Moltke
1941-42   *Danmarks Runeindskrifter* Text og Atlas. Udg. af Lis Jacobsen og Erik
            Moltke, under medvirkning af Anders Bæksted og Karl Martin Nielsen.
            Copenhagen: Ejnar Munksgaards Forlag.
Lund, N.
1991   The Danish perspective. In *The Battle of Maldon AD 991.* D. Scragg (ed.),
            pp 132-133. Oxford: Basil Blackwell.
1998   *Harald Blåtands død - og hans begravelse i Roskilde?* Roskilde: Roskilde
            Museums Forlag.
Olsen, O.
1980   Tanker i tusindåret. *Skalk* 1980 (3): 18-26.
Refskou, N.
1985   "In marca vel regno Danorum". En diplomatarisk analyse af forholdet
            mellem Danmark og Tyskland under Harald Blåtand. *Kirkehistoriske
            Samlinger* 1985: 19-33.
Reuter, T.
1991   *Germany in the Early Middle Ages, 800-1056.* London: Longman.
Sawyer, P.
1991   Swein Forkbeard and the historians. In *Church and Chronicle in the Middle
            Ages.* I. Wood & G. A. Loud (eds.), pp. 27-40. London: The Hambledon
            Press.
1994   Rikssamlingen i England og Sverige sammenlignet med den norske
            rikssamling, *Rikssamlingen og Harald Hårfagre.* Historisk seminar på
            Karmøy 10. og 11. juni 1993. Utgitt av Karmøy kommune. Pp. 131-146.
            [Kopervik 1994]
Sickel, T.
1893   *Die Urkunden Otto des III. (Ottonis III. Diplomata). Monumenta Germaniae
            Historica. Diplomata regum et imperatorum Germaniae* 2,2. Hanover:
            Hahn. [Rep. 1980, MGH].
Skovgaard-Petersen, I.
1966   Sven Tveskæg i den ældste danske historiografi. En Saxostudie.
            *Middelalderstudier. Tilegnede Aksel E. Christensen på tresårsdagen 11.
            september 1966.* T. E. Christiansen et al. (eds.), pp. 1-38. Copenhagen:
            Munksgaard.

Sobel, L.
1981   Ruler and society in sarly medieval Western Pomerania. In *Antemurale*
            XXV, pp. 19-142. Rome: Institutum Historicum Polonicum Romae.
Trillmich, T., & R. Buchner (eds.)
1978   *Quellen des 9. und 11. Jahrhunderts zur Geschichte der hamburgischen
            Kirche und des Reiches.* Ausgewählte Quellen zur deutschen Geschichte des
            Mittelalters. Freiherr von Stein-Gedächtnisausgabe, Band XI. R. Buchner
            (ed.). Darmstadt: Wissenschaftliche Buchgesellschaft.

Discussion

AUSENDA: From field experience in eastern Sudan, Moslem sufi sects gained a foothold in areas where there was incipient urbanization. It seems that traditional religion, vulgarly called 'paganism', is difficult to undermine unless the corporate group based on kinship can be transcended. In fact, in the absence of urbanization, corporate groups, even when sedentary, are held together by kinship ties on which their traditional religion is based and where the main officiant is generally an elder of the group itself. In such a cultural environment conversion to a supra-familial religion has little appeal and even less of a possible foothold. So I agree with you.

Two pressures appear to favour the taking hold and subsequent spread of supra-familial religions: one from the top down and one from the bottom up. The top down pressure is effected by chiefs or kings, in turn under pressure from neighbouring groups at a higher level of socio-cultural integration, in the need to have at their command a collection of the least possible autonomous corporate groups, especially as due to their cohesion which is fostered both by kinship and traditional religion. The pressure from the bottom is generated by the presence of different social groups in settlements where there is incipient urbanization. Embracing a supra-familial, 'universal' religion gives them the possibility of enhancing their status vis-à-vis the dominant group, which is generally attached to traditional religion. It does not seem a coincidence that the spread of Christianity to Scandinavia occurred after the neighbouring Saxons had become a kingdom and later an empire. The above remarks also explain the relatively few episodes of intolerance on the part of some corporate groups, which arose out of their reaction to what appeared to them—and indeed was—an initiative tending to reduce their independence. I think this supports your perspective.

LUND: Yes, there is a difference between introducing Christianity in countries where you have political power and countries where you don't. We had a conference many years ago now, where we started having called the conference on the conversion of Scandinavia, but ended up publishing the proceedings under the title of *The Christianization of Scandinavia.* Because what we could elucidate was the process by which the Christian apparatus was introduced in Scandinavia, but we couldn't say anything about conversion, understood as the permeation of society and people by the Christian faith. You suggested yesterday that that was a long drawn out process, some people even say that it isn't completed yet. We also have comparisons with what happened in Africa, but in British colonies the English had the political power and their missionaries could work there. It wasn't a major issue for the governor at a place to convert the local population, but of course the Churches went in and wanted to do it. And what persuaded many to become Christians was that they got fed and they got to go to school. In these circumstances, many other things creep in to explain why Christianity could gain a foothold. It is difficult to take these, more or less, ethnological situations and compare them with the situation in Denmark a thousand years ago.

GREEN: In your first line, you say of Christianity in the Roman empire that it was a popular religion. I suspect that there is an ambiguity here. I may be wrong, but I suspect that what you mean here is that it was the religion of the common people, because 'popular' has the other sense that it was enthusiastically received by all and sundry, and you don't mean that. So, would it not be better to say "a religion of the common people", rather than "popular" to avoid that ambiguity?

Further below you say "In Scandinavia...Christianity seems to have been introduced from above". Certainly true, but I think that to avoid another false impression, I would say "in Scandinavia, as in many other places", because this conventional Christianization from the top down, is by no means confined to Scandinavia.

LUND: Well, I am not discussing any other places [laughter].

DUMVILLE: And while the experience in Scandinavia may indeed have been very different from how it was elsewhere, it surely was not in terms of this being introduced from above.

BRINK: It started various times again and again especially both in southern and central Scandinavia. The christianization of Scandinavia went from the upper to the lower level of society. This does not make Scandinavia unique in that sense, but the traditional view in Scandinavia has been that christianization went the other way round, from the bottom to the top social level. That has been the traditional view of christianization in Scandinavia for the last thirty to fifty years.

MEULENGRACHT: Your main point (page 304) is that we cannot trust Adam as a historical source, and I think you excellently demonstrate that, but if I am relating your paper to Professor Green's paper about the *Ludwigslied*, I would say that they demonstrate very nicely two different points of view on a text from this period, apparently a spurious text. Professor Green goes a step further than you when you are calling Adam of Bremen's text a political pamphlet. Dennis Green is talking about the text in a meta-historical framework that is as part of the history of salvation. Would you think that it is possible to see Adam's text and to understand it better as part of the history of salvation at this meta-historical level?

LUND: I think we would take leave of the ground if we did that. I have no doubt that Adam had a different perception of historical truth from what we have. He may well have believed that if the information he gave served a good cause, then it was true in that sense.

GREEN: Talking about Harald introducing Christianity amongst the Danes, do you consider at all the Jelling stone, would you find that useful for your purpose?

LUND: Well, no, it doesn't tell us anything that we didn't know. He [Harald] simply makes the claim that he introduced Christianity in Denmark and in Norway as well.

GREEN: I don't know what the conditions for erecting the stone were. If we knew them, it might help your case.

LUND: Well, I would say it demonstrates that he was serious about it, and that he set some store by this. And there are good reasons why he should, because that demonstrated that he was in control in Denmark, and not the Germans.

GREEN: Yes. And in that same context in the next line, I am not quite sure what you mean when you say that Harald "was innocently wounded", a funny conjunction, or it is for me.

LUND: Yes, it may not be a very elegant way to put it. It is paraphrasing Adam, who says that he was innocent and therefore wounded by his son. Or Adam wants to stress because he wants to make him a saint later on, that he was innocent and he was wounded, and we have a model for that.

AUSENDA: Could you kindly explain who Unni was and his antecedents?

LUND: Unni was a former archbishop in Hamburg who did a missionary journey into Denmark in the 930s.

ARRHENIUS: What is the source of the *Encomium Emmae* (page 306)?

LUND: The *Encomium Emmae* is also known as *The Deeds of King Knut*. It is a text that was written in Flanders about 1040, on behalf of Emma, who wanted to explain her family's claim to rule after Knut's claim to England. She was the queen first of Æthelred II, then of Knut.

DUMVILLE: Could I add to that one? A new paperback of A. Campbell's edition, bilingual (Latin and English), has just been published by Cambridge University Press, and there is a long introduction by Simon Keynes and some question about the precise time and also about the place of composition. But it is a very important, very interesting, though not a straightforward source.

LUND: It is a virtuoso piece in half truths, not actually exactly lying, but never telling the full truth.

GREEN: Can I come in precisely at that point, because it is there, I think that there is a slight danger in using a source like this as your historical source, because in the prologue to this *Encomium* we read, that "when writing the deeds of any one man one inserts a fictitious element, either in error or, as is often the case, for the sake of ornament, the hearer assuredly regards facts as fictions when he has ascertained the introduction of so much as one lie". And a comment has been made on this fairly recently by Ruth Morse. She says: "This functions as a rhetorical ploy: having attempted to establish an ethos of veracity, the author inserts elaborate imitations of/and explicit references to the usual figures: Virgil, Lucan, and Sallust. The successful writer achieved an art that is an art that hid art".

DUMVILLE: And here the model is Sallust.

GREEN: Well, more and more I think it grows from Virgil and Lucan and they were both known as historians and poets. So veracity as well as elaboration and fictitious additions. Further down, you say that Adam put the higher truth before historical truth. I don't want to get into meta-history again, but do you mean by 'higher truth' something like Harald's aura of sanctity?

LUND: No, the 'higher truth' in this case is Adam of Bremen's cause.

GREEN: You say "The fact that there is no positive proof that Adam knew Thietmar does not, however, exclude the possibility that he did." (page 308) It doesn't exclude it, you are logically correct, but how convincing is that?

LUND: Well, if he had obviously missed points that he could have used from Thietmar, I would have concluded he didn't know him, but he doesn't have any reasons to quote him. He would have either had to have reasons for an argument from silence to be effective.

AUSENDA: What does *frith* (page 309) mean?

LUND: Yes, *frith* means an agreement, a peace agreement. Chris Fell did a very good paper on that some years ago when she interpreted a passage in Ohthere who didn't dare to go on beyond a certain point in the White Sea for *unfrithe*, the text said. And the standard interpretation, until her paper, was because of enmity, but she demonstrated that it was for lack of an agreement of peace with them.

DUMVILLE: That might also put in a reference there is rather good article by somebody called Lund on the same subject [laughter].

AUSENDA: Is it possible to say that there was an entity called Poland as early as the tenth century (page 310)?

LUND: Well, there was an entity called Poland, or a Polish duchy. I don't think there is full agreement when Poland became a kingdom and when it was a duchy, but there certainly was an entity called Poland, which was expanding westwards at the expense of the Pomeranians in this particular period. And it had intimate political relations with the Germans and certainly there was a change of political relations in 1002 when the German emperor reversed his policies.

AUSENDA: A 'pagan reaction' (page 311) is in the order of things when mass conversions occur; it would be surprising if there were none!

DUMVILLE: A whole clutch of them in the seventh century.

LUND: No, there is no evidence that there was one.

DUMVILLE: Well, carrying on on Giorgio [Ausenda]'s point, does that mean that there had been a mass conversion?

LUND: Quite probably yes.

DUMVILLE: Could I tack on something? For lack of knowledge more than anything else, I got a bit confused as to the situation. Could you give a quick summary of what you think in the ninth century was the relation between the German crown and the bishops in Denmark? You are hedging your bets here, perhaps for very good reasons. I would be grateful if it could be talked through just a little more.

LUND: My point of departure is an interpretation of both the appointment of these bishops and of the whole relationship between Hamburg, Bremen and Denmark. The archbishopric had been created in 832 and it had never grown to a proper archbishopric with suffragans. This was a great problem for them, because after 845 Bremen had been taken away from the archbishopric of Cologne to be added to Hamburg. And their friends or foes, as they were in Cologne, never forgot this, and as Hamburg still didn't develop into a proper archbishopric, the archbishop of Cologne pressed for Bremen to be returned to Cologne and Hamburg to come with it, in fact for Hamburg to be quashed. But in the middle of the tenth century, the archbishops of Hamburg had very good relations with the Empire, close family relations and that kind of thing. And when Otto the Great took up missionary work, evangelizing his neighbours, creating new bishoprics along the Slav borders, and warming up work on the Danish side as well, the archbishop of Hamburg got to appoint three bishops to their sees, Schleswig, Ribe, and Aarhus. Well, I think they just mentioned some places, and the point of having them, was simply that the archbishopric could now function. He needed two suffragans when he consecrated new bishops. And he could have synods now if he had three suffragans, which gave him a defence against Cologne, and gave him a basis for a fresh start in Scandinavia. But on this background, it's unlikely that these bishops ever set foot in Denmark, and when we add that Harald Bluetooth fought wars with these emperors, and fortified Danevirke against them, there are these two diplomas in which first Otto the Great, and later Otto III gave these bishops privileges which amount to releasing imperial control of the Church in Denmark. It may be that he got his hands full on the Slavonic border and was happy to let the Danes suit themselves from this point of view, as long as the archbishop could handle them. It meant effectively that Harold Bluetooth replaced the emperor in his function as protector of the Danish Church.

AUSENDA: Is it fortuituous that the date of Harald's death (page 312) should coincide with the day when all dead are remembered and celebrated?

LUND: I think that is one of Adam's small inventions. He wanted to make Harold a saint and, in order to place him in a saintly context, he put his day of death on the same day with all other saints. This means that they didn't know the exact date of his death. That's the day when All Saints are celebrated, whose death dates are unknown. I think it was a way of giving him a saintly quality.

BENDER: If Harald died in 978 (page 313), I wonder how to interpret the Trelleborgs [a number of circular fortresses in Denmark that are quite famous] and the Ravning Enge Valley bridge near Jelling? These have been dated to the winter of 980.

LUND: Well, I put in this calculation to please Olaf Olsen or to displease him, whichever he likes. The Trelleborgs used to be interpreted in the context of Sven Forkbeard's conquest of England. And when they were re-dated or were properly dated, they were moved into the reign of his father. And Olaf was so reluctant to give up the connection with Sven Forkbeard and their interpretation as garrisons, that he set about interpreting the final days of the archbishop expanding them so that they could encompass 980; so he tried to finish off Harold Bluetooth as early as this. But he overlooked the possibility of dating it on another basis in Adam, which I have then attempted somewhat here. If you calculate as I have done this back from the death of Erik the Victorious of Sweden, you come back to 978. I am not suggesting that this is a better solution than the other one, I am only doing it to show that we cannot base that kind of dating on Adam. Because he puts in the information that suits him and has no bearing on what we would regard as historical truth.

BENDER: I wondered whether you have any idea whether the fortresses and the bridge could have been built by Erik the Victorious.

LUND: I wouldn't think so.

BENDER: Or would you rather not involve those constructions?

LUND: I don't think they are relevant to the questions I am dealing with here. But it was very simple in the good old days when we could link them up with this conquest. Now, with these dendro-datings they have in fact been moved out of the political contexts that we knew into a context that we don't know at all; therefore, we don't know what purposes they served.

References in the discussion

Bibliography:

Campbell, A.
    1949   See References at end of paper.
Fell, C. E.
    1982-3   *Unfrið*: an approach to a definition. *Saga-Book of the Viking Society* 21: 85-100.
Sawyer, B., P. Sawyer & I. Wood (eds.)
    1987   *The Christianization of Scandinavia*. [Report with summaries of discussions during a seminar held on the topic in 1985]. Alingsås: Viktoria Bokförlag.

GIORGIO AUSENDA

C.I.R.O.S.S., 6 C.da San Francesco, San Marino (Rep. of San Marino)

Location in space and time[1]

North and South

Having discerned a difference between northern and southern Scandinavia while making a survey of rural economy, *Bender Jørgensen* believed that the comparison could also be extended to northern and southern Europe and to sea and land. *Ausenda* asked where one could draw a line between North and South and there were several suggestions on the basis of which *Herschend* sketched a borderline.

Fig. 13-1: Sketch of borderline between climatic 'North' and 'South' in Scandinavia.

---

[1] The sequence of topics follows S. C. Hawkes's scale of inferences.

Arrhenius noted that there was also a climatological borderline between the pine forest and the lower region and that the northern part was much larger and scarcely inhabited.

Jesch pointed also to a division between "historical Denmark" and the rest of Scandinavia, she added that a philologist had in mind a "very clear distinction between East and West, depending on the types of sources he or she had as well as the language", and she would have liked to suggest that the partition "ought to be North-South-East-West".

Ausenda reminded the audience of the suggested dichotomy between 'land' and 'sea' as it showed also on the map. *Green* noted that the differentiation between North and South had been limited to an "internal Scandinavian scope" whereas "the same [was] not true when it [came] to sea and land, because there one [opened] up into a sea context rather than a land context across the Baltic and across the North Sea. So there [one moved] into an extra-Scandinavian dimension".

For *Herschend* one should take into account also the partition of the landscape where there was a "mountain-shore-sea" differentiation, and *Green* concluded that "this second aspect opened up a wider dimension that the first one [did] not".

Eleventh century in Scandinavia: Viking Age or something new?

Jesch, who had suggested the topic, explained that she had done it out of a "personal interest, as [she] happened to find the eleventh century more interesting than any others", admitting, however, that it may have been "because of the kind of sources" she was interested in, which were "particularly copious in that century", but she thought that the question had not been much debated, unlike the debate about the beginning of the Viking Age. She noted that archaeologists liked to "draw a line under the year 1000 and forget everything that [happened] after that" whereas, if one was looking at the Viking Age, perhaps from an Irish context, and perhaps other parts of the British Isles, one would see it "going into the twelfth century". She stressed that the eleventh century seemed a century of transition where "a lot of things change[d]: Christianity [was] established, writing became a fairly regular activity", and other people might suggest other areas in which they could "see changes in that century". She thought of suggesting that "chronological area" as it hadn't been covered in the symposium although some participants had "unavoidably streched into it".

Brink commented that the chronological aspect was so interrelated with the geographical one that it was difficult to "pick out one from the other"; this meant that there was a slow change that made it impossible to pinpoint the end of the Viking Age when looking "at Scandinavia as a whole". *Herschend* noted how the 'Viking Age' could be stretched even later as, in the Baltic, people didn't "get into church until the eighteenth century" and buried their dead on the farms. *Brink* reckoned that even in mainland Sweden there were some "Iron Age economies and communities that [went] up to the fourteenth century".

Nielsen noted how one of the two fundamental sources concerning Denmark in the eleventh century, Adam of Bremen, had been demolished during the discussion of the previous day and suggested relying more on the archaeological material which was more abundant in Denmark than in Norway and Sweden; he averred that it was "a strange period in between history and archaeology". *Jesch* added hopefully that one could "encourage archaeologists to find a few things before the next symposium".

Arrhenius stressed the fact that a lot of dendrochronological datings were available from about 980, plus an interesting dendro date in the eleventh century, so that one could "tie up that part which [one] had in the beginning and the end and see what happen[ed] in between". *Jesch* acknowledged seeing the eleventh century as "stretching roughly from 960 to 1120".

Realistic assessment of population numbers in the three inhabited areas at different time intersections

Ausenda had suggested the topic thinking that "one [could] not talk intelligently of a situation without having a fair idea of the people interacting". He thought that it would be useful to bring in someone specialized in the demography and population studies of the period. He noted how strange it was that scholars had "an idea of the population numbers during the Neolithic, whereas they had no idea of the population numbers in more recent ages".

Brink objected that it was impossible to have an idea of such a figure and that when Norwegian historians tried to assess the population in Norway "in the middle of the Middle Ages" it became "one of the largest debates in Norwegian history". He cautioned that the figures suggested were completely "off, because unimaginable" as one had only reached the stage of trying to understand "how the subject work[ed]", and *Olausson* admitted having used population figures that she had found in the literature. *Herschend* thought that it was difficult to "read or remember" estimates of the population of Scandinavia, but that regional surveys were not impossible; for instance, the population of the southern part of Jutland could be estimated from the remains of farms, also obtaining an idea of the "average farm size and the average byre size...and the areas of living quarters of people", e.g. 27 m^2 on Iron Age farms, so that it became "just a matter of counting the farms". His opinion was seconded by *Arrhenius*.

Dumville said: "Can I say that I have not been impressed by the occasional points which have been made of population sizes in the discussions over the last few days, where there seems to be a level of relative specificity both as to numbers and to methods. When this questions come up, if I may make a comparison with Britain from the Roman period onwards, the literature is full of estimates, guesstimates as to population size, which is thrown out on quite extraordinary topics and where the population of Roman Britain has increased dramatically over the last half or three quarters of a century. And this is in a context of a long period, a huge archaeological work, a great deal of survey work and a huge amount of excavation. And yet the discussion is extraordinarily primitive; it is very crude, it's estimation of numbers where people are working on the back of cigarette packets, dreaming up numbers. And at moments of major change, therefore, discussion can be skewed by having these estimates floating around. And one of the things that happened is that, because the population of Roman Britain has grown and grown, estimates of the number of incomers at the beginning of the Anglo-Saxon period, the Migration period, depending on the tendency of the people making the suggestion, have had a tendency to climb dramatically reaching 4 million Britons, against which one would have 5,000 Germanic invaders, settlers. In order to have an impact in terms of numbers on that remarkable British population, one has to increase dramatically the estimates. And these estimates also have been fixed crudely. The starting point appears to be statements now such as whichever direction you go from whichever point in Roman Britain, you will find a settlement within half a mile. And it may be that the archaeological record can demonstrate something like that. But it doesn't seem to be a satisfactory rule from that point to specific numbers, and specific numbers are still, as far as I can make out, utterly impressionistic, because I don't see any counting of the number of settlements in spite of this characterization of the general pattern. A similar thing could happen to the Anglo-Saxon period, whereas we look into a historically documented period for the Roman period in one sense, but not in the way that the early Middle Ages are. And there, even when we have something like Domesday Book to assist us, it certainly doesn't assist us in all manners and sorts of ways. Nonetheless it has become clear, not least through Peter Sawyer's work, in another division of his activities, that estimates which had been used, which had been made on a rather less crude basis for the population at the end of the Anglo-Saxon period are agreed to be defective, because of the nature of the record and overreliance on the nature of that record. There is a sign of archaeologists and historians and demographers getting together on that end of things, but it doesn't seem to me yet to be having a useful feedback into the earlier period. My impression is—it may be my fault—my impression is that in Scandinavia archaeologists in particular have a much better handle on the nature of the problems and how to proceed than colleagues working in the British Isles do".

Magnus pointed out that "regional differences in Scandinavia [were] huge" concerning population sizes. There were very few farms from the Vendel-Viking period in western Norway, and in cemeteries there seemed to be only "one grave for each generation". She acknowledged that Bjørn Myhre had made an estimate for southwest Norway based on the number of deserted farms from the Migration period: he had concluded that the population "had decreased so much at the end of the Migration period that it only came up to that level again in the seventeenth century", and that was only in southwestern Norway where there was certain "specific material" throughout time which allowed such an estimate.

Nielsen admitted that there had been considerable problems concerning medieval demography also in Denmark, especially in the first millennium AD. One finding was that there were many more settlements during the Roman period than there were in the Middle Ages. The problem was that the houses could not be dated more closely than within one hundred years or so, which meant four generations and four houses, because "the house could not stand for more than one generation" and, furthermore, it was almost impossible to tell which houses were coeval. Another possible departure was to work from anthropological material by estimating how many people could be fed by the "combination of grain agriculture and cattle breeding" present; the objection was that the figures suggested by anthropologists were so rough that they didn't make sense. He concluded that it was very difficult to make demographic estimates based on the Danish evidence.

Lund agreed and mentioned a problem which had arisen concerning the population of medieval York where one knew with a fair approximation the number of plots in the town, but there was no agreement on the number of people that each plot could feed, so that the population could vary from 10,000 to 30,000.

Herschend conceded that there were difficulties but observed that anyhow the estimates had confirmed that "the population of the late Migration period was as large as the Viking-Age and early medieval population" [having decreased considerably from the Roman period] a result which confirmed the enormity of problems in Scandinavia in the sixth and seventh centuries. He also suggested tying the carrying capacity to the number of "gold finds...in connection to the ruined farms" to get an idea of how many hectares correspond to one gram of gold thereby reconstructing the whole settlement and obtaining the number of farms. *Brink* admitted having tried to use that method for an estimate of the population in northern Sweden and *Herschend* conceded that it was probably not applicable to peripheries.

Kinship and marriage

European kinship structures

Vestergaard had suggested the "study of kinship structures" which had been "conducted along the same lines and the same interpretations for the last fifty years...and [had taken] no advantage of the...boom in anthropology of the last years" not only concerning "kinship and the various socio-political structures linked" to kinship, but also the "explanatory functions that kinship might have for other social phenomena". She averred having suggested Europe as a whole to have "a comparative element introduced".

Arrhenius expressed her agreement with *Vestergaard*'s suggestion adding that it was necessary to have "better source material", and that that could be accomplished through DNA studies which were being made even though handicapped by their high costs; this meant that an effort was to be made to raise the necessary funding: she thought that such a study should touch on the family structure based on DNA studies in Merovingian or Migration-period Europe.

Vestergaard insisted on "combining the latest developments" in anthropology "and see", while *Arrhenius* said that explanatory models also had to be developed.

Herschend supported *Vestergaard*'s position saying that there was "a point in starting with kinship and lineage from an anthropological point of view bearing in mind that in ten years the corrections [were] bound to come from the genetic perspective".

Magnus mentioned a new doctoral thesis (Ethelberg 2000) on cemeteries of the early Roman Iron Age in Zealand, Denmark, connected with a very important centre, Stevns, where there were "very good skeletal remains in the graves", all of them were graves of females or small girls with only one man, which implied that they were related. Their relationship was proven by the fact that they all had a specific dental deficiency pointing to a genetic origin which meant that physical anthropologists could "instantly see that they were related" and "in spite of the differences in the furnishings of the graves, they did appear related".

Social relations

Aristocracy and other classes

Herschend explained having suggested the topic by saying that "the general idea [was that]...one of the things happening in Scandinavia [was] the transformation or remaking of aristocracy, based on a slightly different background than in the early Iron Age" and that he didn't "believe there [were] any lower classes (an expression *Ausenda* had used in a preceeding discussion) but lower strata". He thought that in the late Iron Age one got "the first idea of class in society", but there was "a point in sticking to aristocracy...as [they] put their mark on society even today". He insisted on the fact that there was "a very long line of development before there [were] any words known".

Dumville thought that 'aristocracy' was "a very troublesome word" and that there were parts of Europe where "historians were unwilling to use it", so that some "definitions" were necessary about what was invented in late Iron Age Scandinavia.

Herschend answered that he referred to the individuals that *Brink* had listed in his excursus in 'political relations' on terms concerning presumably higher positions in Scandinavia (see page 338). Those were some of the indications, as he went on to concede that "first there [was] the moral idea of what it meant to be an aristocrat and some norms, and then [came] the functional things".

Lund remarked that *Herschend*'s clarification came very close to his point [the following one to be discussed] on the 'Social structure in northern Europe 400 AD - 1200 AD' [concerning the existence of a power structure] which he had recognized in his "work on military organizations", based on "one of the things one was told about St Knud...[was] that he alienated the chieftains by trying to reduce their power", and scholars had no idea of the privileges of these chieftains and how they could react "when kings began to encroach" on their use of power. A clue concerned a chieftain, a relative of the king, in the mid-twelfth century, who "was able to relieve a monastery that he was founding of taxes". Did this mean that chieftains had a right to tax their "subordinates"?

Answering *Dumville*'s question as to how these chieftains were referred to in the sources, *Lund* said that Latin terms were used such as *duces, meliores,* and *optimates,* terms which *Dumville* thought belonged to "a language of aristocracy".

Arrhenius asked whether one could say that individuals buried with the "richest grave finds" or in a big mound belonged to "the upper classes", and could one do "systematic work on this" basis? *Herschend* countered that graves "[were] difficult" whilst it would be easier with farms. *Arrhenius* suggested focussing on grave goods found around farms, but *Herschend* insisted that it was very difficult, promising that he would "come back to that [in the discussion of the topics in the category] 'Rural economy and surplus', as he thought that surplus production was "a very odd phenomenon in the Iron Age".

Magnus being interested in the problem of tribute because a source on Scandinavia in the tenth century asserted that King Alfred "extracted tribute from the Saami in the North" asked what was the term used. *Lund* answered *gafol* which *Green* said meant 'tribute', but not only that, as it depended on the context. To a further request for a general meaning, *Green* answered that the verb's stem meant 'to give', which to *Magnus* meant that the king might have been extracting 'gifts' from the Saami, and there should have been other people "adjacent to the Saami" from whom he also extracted gifts, and she asked whether there were any other ways of finding out than through the written sources. *Herschend* suggested numismatic studies.

Arrhenius noted that there were "a lot of treasure finds in the Saami area [which meant] that it [was] not tribute", because they got something back. *Green* said that one "got protection back on a tribute", but *Arrhenius* insisted that the "Saami people got things from the West" that were found in the treasure hoards. In *Lund*'s opinion the hoards could "have seemed more likely to be the result of raiding than of trading" as the sources, especially Ohthere in his report to King Alfred he Great, told that the Saami often conducted raids on the Norse. *Herschend* pointed out the difference between the east-Scandinavian hoards in the border zone between Åland and the mountain areas, which were "typical ethnic markers", whereas in west Scandinavia the Norwegian fiords made it possible for single individuals "to go into Saami areas...and the interaction [would be] obviously personal" where one could find "all kinds of Migration-period gold rings and spears and arrows". *Arrhenius* asked whether in the West it was tribute because there was a "system there"; *Herschend* answered that it "was much more a tribute system...an interactive system" rather than "marking [themselves] as either Saami or Germanic" [as was the case for the east-Scandinavian hoards].

Dumville observed that "reciprocity in relationship to giving [didn't] necessarily imply that there [was] balance" as it could be seen as incomplete reciprocity. In *Green*'s words: "It [was] reciprocity but not equality".

The Scandinavian bœndr - social structure in northern Europe 900-1300

Lund explained that he was thinking of "the sort of development that [took] place within that group" which was very wide. He thought that they had gone through a development which was linked to the development of the settlement. Settlements became fragmented which meant that from a position of "fairly substantial landowners", their possessions being fragmented, "only part of them could go on and stand up to their original obligations, military or other of this class"; this part was later called the *hermenn* class (squires) while those who could not stand up "formed a humbler peasantry", concerning which there followed a debate among scholars as to "whether it meant that they were the men of some lord, or that they were members of the army".

Lund added that "those that could keep their possessions together...continued the old form of *leiðangr* (akin to a *comitatus*), whereas those who couldn't were reduced to a newer form of *leiðangr*" known from the provincial laws, which was introduced in the second half of the twelfth century as a system of naval mobilization to muster "a kind of coast guard".

Dumville asked for the explanation for "what [set off] this particular change in the relations of *bœndr*". *Lund* averred that the phenomenon required a "complex of explanations" which needed looking into. While he could not explain it as yet, he thought that it was "part of the process by which agriculture took over from pastoral farming" and also the cessation of "migrations within bounded areas" [such as transhumance] and became settled "in a number of smaller settlements" that became permanent.

Dumville mentioned as a parallel the "changes affecting the *ceorl* class in Anglo-Saxon England" asserting that it sounded as if *Lund* had developed a different complex of explanations...to explain essentially the same end results". *Lund* agreed that there were many similarities in both developments.

Brink noted again that north Scandinavia was different from south Scandinavia: in the Middle Ages there were estates with tenants and free farmers in Sweden, whereas in the north of Sweden there were only free farmers. In Norway there was also a somewhat different situation from the south-Scandinavian one. He concluded that Scandinavia was complex and quite interesting and as yet unexplained, e.g. as to what happened when Scandinavia got "the new 'European package'" whereby southern Scandinavia got tenants and as to why there were those differences in the later Middle Ages.

Jural relations and conflict

Scandinavian law - indigenous or imported? Langobardic law may be a very important source

Lund explained that he had "sponsored a point on which we didn't know where we are". He was well aware of the difficulty of the subject and of the disagreement among scholars about it, but he thought it was "worth having a go". He stressed the necessity for a consensus of opinion on what "one could use these laws for: could they be regarded as "an expression of the time they were written in Scandinavia", did they "reflect customary law", were they based on what could be "scraped together of [ancient] laws from...Scandinavia", or were they, as also complained by Elsa Sjöholm (1977), "simply based on what their authors had picked up in schools in Oxford, in Bologna, in Paris or wherever they had learned law"? The problem was to find the best fit between the "old idea that the laws [resembled] each other because they [went] back to a common Germanic source", a collection of laws called the *'Lombarda'* according to Sjöholm, and her implication that they resemble[d] each other also "because their authors had gone to the same schools and studied the same texts".

Dumville asked what was "this theoretical underlying source" and how it was connected to the Langobards; *Lund* answered that a collection of Langobardic laws, called the *Lombarda*, was studied at *studia,* later in universities, in Bologna and Pavia in the eleventh and twelfth centuries, he explained that "Danish ecclesiastics [had gone] abroad to study" and back home "had codified these laws on the basis of what they had learned", as in fact their work required "great legal training". *Dumville* thought that it was a process which was "common right across Western Europe in that period" whereby one sought to "verify the local law" and at the same time "bring it within broader concepts"; he asserted that "there were parallel processes elsewhere in Europe" and that the study "had gone farther and less far in different countries". *Lund* agreed and added that the same "had to be done in Scandinavia" as the Scandinavian laws hadn't been placed in a European context. Saxo Grammaticus's text was put into a European perspective, and he believed that the Scandinavian laws "belonged very much in the same context as Saxo" who had written to "give Denmark a past" that could match Rome's past. Scandinavian "laws were made very much in the same circles".

Green cited the work, done especially by people in Münster, on Germanic terminology in Germanic laws which had been codified in Latin where there was no exact Latin equivalent; he was seconded by *Ausenda* who recalled a few of the many Germanic words in Rothari's Edict, e.g. *wadia,* 'gauge', *aidi,* 'oath-helpers', *gamahalos,* 'affine', etc. and *Arrhenius* concluded that those laws "must have [had] a Germanic origin".

Brink said that he and other scholars had tried to convince legal historians to take up similar studies to those made by Sjöholm, in which she had "placed the Scandinavian provincial laws in a European context". In her opinion the European influence was more important than the old view that it was only indigenous and her view was vindicated during the last "ten or twenty years" when scholars of Scandinavian legal history in Norway agreed that local laws had been written on the basis of European laws. According to *Brink* it was "obvious that there [were] many examples of ancient Scandinavian legal customs in...provincial laws, and not only those but perhaps also from Langobardic laws", which became evident when one read these laws. In his opinion the problem was that no "trained legal historian" was interested in these provincial laws, and it was difficult to make them interested in them.

Ausenda asked why he had to make those people interested and *Brink* replied that it was indispensable for someone who embarked on such a study to be "legally trained". *Green* recalled that in Germany there was a scholar, R. Schmidt-Wiegand, who was both legally and linguistically trained, who had been doing such studies for West Germanic but, so far, hadn't been persuaded to do it for Scandinavian laws.

Ausenda suggested that the study should be carried out not only by a "legal expert" but also by a cultural anthropologist familiar with kinship and jural relations among pre-industrial populations. He told how he had been able to understand Langobardic laws on oath-taking only after reading how "the Bedouin of the Eastern Desert and Sinai took oaths according to the importance of their crimes and how they chose their oath-helpers". He pointed out that such procedures were quite "involved" and that "legal people [had] little or no idea of how customary law function[ed] in contemporary societies", which was more the field of [cultural] anthropologists. *Brink* replied that he had been working on the subject for 15 years and was certain that "legal knowledge was essential" for that kind of research, and that philologists or archaeologists or historians "could not venture on this extremely problematic material by themselves". *Bender* cited a Danish doctoral dissertation by Annette Hoff (1997) on *Lov og Landskab* (Law and 'landscape') in which she is looking for traces of customary law in the *Landskab* laws of Denmark.

Dumville ventured that a "certain range of competences" was needed; in England a "reasonable number of people" was interested in early law, however, none with philological competence. *Jesch* added that scholars were looking for early forms of law in the North "where the English material would [have been] quite relevant". *Dumville* and *Jesch* concluded that the study could be done and that competent scholars should be encouraged to embark on such studies.

Ausenda asked for the meaning of the word *landskab*; *Vestergaard* said that it could be translated as 'provincial (law)'. She was seconded by *Brink* who said that one had always used 'provincial', because the *landskab* were equivalent to provinces; *Jesch* suggested the term 'regional'. *Lund* recalled having advocated that they should be called 'land laws' "because they were in fact laws for different lands and [one] didn't want to imply...that those lands belonged together: they were independent legal lands, not provinces". *Dumville* objected that the expression 'land law' had "such a specific contemporary usage that one would run into difficulties".

Law, poetry and art - public discourse in the Viking Age

Jesch had suggested the topic because she had felt that there were "two...important things missing" in the papers discussed, which were 'law' and 'art'; she was glad that *Magnus* had suggested 'art' as she [*Jesch*] was not qualified to talk about it. In the course of the discussion she had noted that a lot of the topics which had been proposed for further research were "well worn" and one could "pick away at them and find new insights and so on", but the one proposed by *Brink* which she thought needed urgent attention was "the question of law". She affirmed to be "just supporting the previous suggestion" but remarked being "a bit worried in case it turned out into purely a legal thing", because if one was "looking at traces of customary law, or law before the written *landskab* laws" one had to "see them in a broader context" because of the scarcity of written evidence and the need to bring in "indirect evidence from other sources" including English laws, as it would be very useful to have them considered in connection with Scandinavian laws by some qualified scholars. "Just to broaden it out" she had thought of "bringing in other kinds of public communal speaking activity, and poetry [had] sprung to...mind".

Green asked *Jesch* whether in her threefold title she was placing the emphasis on law, as it might also be placed under 'Symbolic life', or as a "borderline case between 'Jural relations' and 'Symbolic life'". *Jesch* replied that for her own personal interest she would have preferred to have it discussed in the category 'Symbolic life' but, "in the interest of what she thought needed doing, she thought law should be the focus and the other subjects should be satellites around it".

Meulengracht noted that "the most important words in her line [were] 'public discourse' and that "law and poetry [were] two kinds of public discourse in the oral society of the Viking Age"; however, one didn't know much about either law or formalized discourse at that time, but "there might be an interesting relationship between the two", which, according to *Jesch*, was worth exploring.

Warfare, defence and forts in late Iron Age [Scandinavia]

Holmquist believed it was "obvious that armed conflict, warfare, and violence, played an important role in late Iron Age in Scandinavia". She had said something about it during the discussion of her paper, and she wanted to discuss the presence and use of not only forts but also fortifications that she thought were an interesting aspect to study. She recalled that the first stone building in Sweden was dated to around 1150 and there was a gap between the Iron Age and that date, and there were 150 years during which one didn't "know anything about fortifications". Perhaps one could date the hill-forts into the Viking Age, or there were other kinds of fortifications which had not been seen yet. She mentioned one, the palisade outside Old Uppsala, which she thought was important.

Nielsen cited a dissertation by Thomas Højrop (1995), an ethnologist at the University of Copenhagen, who discussed warfare from an ethnological point of view; a main point in his work was that the "prerequisite for the existence of any society [was] simply that it must be able to defend itself"; he cited a research project sponsored by the Danish Research Councils for the Humanities dealing with both theoretical and empirical issues, in which both archaeologists and other experts on armies and war participated in a study which he thought would lead to interesting results {see, e.g., Jørgensen & Clausen (eds.) 1997: *passim*). In studying Iron Age warfare the very important bog finds in Jutland with their many sacrificed objects appeared to be the equipment of small foreign armies, probably consisting of a few hundred warriors, which had been defeated. The analyses in some cases made it possible to tell their provenance from this or that region in northern Scandinavia (Ilkjær 1990; 1993), throwing light on "warfare and political history in southern Scandinavia from the late Roman Iron Age onwards" and also on the probable presence at that time of "political formations larger than chiefdoms".

Arrhenius continued recalling that in the Mälaren area there were "more than 500 hill-forts from the Bronze Age to the end of the Viking Age", proving that there must have been "some kind of [political] organization", whereas in Denmark there were "almost no hill-forts at all". To a request for clarification by *Dumville*, she added that "not every hill-fort [went] from the Bronze Age to the upper Viking period" because many were burnt down, as could be ascertained from the ruins. *Holmquist* made the point that 'hill-fort' was "an antiquarian name" and that they "could be different types of enclosures, not all of them used for defence".

Brink wished that everyone should reach agreement because, in his opinion, the late Iron Age "was a time of war and fighting". *Arrhenius* agreed with *Brink* but could not help remarking that where there were those "rich warrior graves" there wasn't a "single hill-fort". *Nielsen* explained that, in Norway and Sweden, hill-forts were in thinly populated areas where hunting was mostly practiced, which prompted *Dumville* to ask whether those hill-forts were simply settlement sites, and *Holmquist*'s reply was that only some of them were, he then asked how defensible they were, and *Herschend* pointed to a "correlation, a rule of the Iron Age" that: if [one took] the hundreds of ^{14}C tests made, one would ascertain that "when hill-forts were being built, there were not as many ^{14}C finds in the settlements", which meant "the more houses, the fewer hill-forts" and conversely "the fewer houses, the more hill-forts"; this to him meant that their presence may have been due to "ideological" considerations, that "they [had] the largest Swedish fortifications ever" which went on for hundreds of years and were never used, which allowed him to think that they were "a show-off". *Holmquist* agreed adding that "part of the idea was the threat" and *Brink* seconded her by adding that it was "a kind of manifestation of a new...power", to say to people in those areas: "Look, there is a new power in your 'landscape' now'", and their presence had nothing to do with defence or aggression.

Rural economy

Foods eaten and their caloric spectrums at different time intersections

Ausenda introduced the topic stressing the fact that the food that people ate was a very important aspect and that one should try to find out "what they ate, what they relied most on, why they relied on it, and how they cooked their food", all questions linked to several other aspects. He cited the example of the silver spoons found in Merovingian Age graves which meant that those individuals had their personal spoons, as those populations ate mostly with their hands, so that having a spoon meant that they were becoming "refined" and their presence could have been a sign of an incipient aristocracy. He explained that there was a "normalized" figure in food research called the Body Mass Index (BMI), defined as

$$BMI = W \ (kg)/h^2 \ (m^2)$$

The borderline between sufficient food intake and malnutrition was about 17, and was quite important because it afforded an idea of the working capacity of a given group.

The present knowledge about ancient Scandinavian food habits, according to *Magnus*, concerned "what was grilled on farms in the Iron Age" but little was known about "what kind of food people ate or how they prepare[d] anything; whether...they had their daily bread or was porridge their stock food". Even the ordinary public wanted to know "what people in the Viking Age ate". In conclusion, one could say "what kinds of raw material they had for their settlements, but how they prepared their food and their daily meals...[was] a much more difficult question".

Arrhenius observed that, by looking at remains near sea ports one could tell that fish was eaten and surveys were made concerning nitrogen and phosphorus contents of remains that could disclose the "food chain" the people were using, and also taking trade into account; she noted that among Scandinavians there was a great difference "between women's and men's food". She mentioned a project in Upper Svealand which was "working on these aspects and doing tracers with isotopes", which would also go on skeletons. *Ausenda* agreed saying that it was fairly common that in pre-industrial societies women were less fed than men, presumably because men were supposed to work harder. *Herschend* noted that even simple measures on skeletons could tell how tall people were and how long they lived; it was found that "upper-class women in the early Roman Iron Age in Jutland were as 'large' and well-living as the [later] Viking Age women of the Mälaren region" which meant that it took the latter 800 years to reach the same standard of living as the upper-class Jutish women of the Roman Iron Age. He jokingly said that there "were a lot of unpleasant things" to be gotten out of those studies, but also some interesting results, such as the "shift" in the Iron Age all over Scandinavia from "cooking in a pit, and the different objects where [one] put [hot] stones into, to the idea of the hearth, the slab and the bowl in cooking", and eating with a spoon, which were "coming in" in "better graves in the Roman Iron Age". *Magnus* mentioned that spoons were found in Iron Age hoards, and there were also decorated ones in the medieval period; she asked whether there were any wooden spoons in between. *Arrhenius* averred that during that intermediate period "spoons were not used" and *Herschend*, seconding her, stated that he "had always advocated that the great problem [for Scandinavia] was in the middle of the [first] millennium" where it went "down to hell".

Nielsen remarked that there were calculations of daily caloric intakes, numbers of domestic animals needed for one person, and so on—a most disputed topic. As far as medieval Iceland was concerned, where the consumption of milk and milk products played a very important role, Frieðriksson (1972:785 ff.) made some interesting calculations, for instance that each individual needed the caloric production from the milk of six ewes or half a head of cattle; he also discussed what this meant for grazing areas and hay production; he finally used his figures to reconstruct the demographic vicissitudes of the island. In Jutland, preserved traces of stall partitioning made it possible to see how many head of cattle there could be in an Iron Age longhouse, noting, however, that one could not tell whether those facilities were fully or only partially used, causing a considerable uncertainty.

An increase, *Herschend* remarked, would mean more children; in the late Roman Iron Age the dwelling area was something like 100 m^2 and the byres could contain 30 cows; the osteological material was also interesting disclosing, e.g. that very few sheep were the norm in Jutland as against four times as many in Gotland.

Role of the Saami

Arrhenius recalled discussing the Saami, a subject which was linked to the topic 'Rural economy' adding that it was also linked to politics; the Saami could be easily recognized because of selenium, a very good tracer element, in the bones, as selenium was found both in the soil and in the reindeer which got it from bark which had a high selenium content; she thought that the relations between the Saami and the Svear were even stronger than in Norway, as the Svear "constantly had problems and political discourses about the Saami" and the same was true with the Russians, the Finns and the Norwegians, so that the relationship of the Saami was very important, to be taken more seriously, "not just as a small marginal thing".

Asked by *Dumville* about how that relationship could be characterized, *Herschend* said that the whole idea behind work on the Saami seemed to be "how [did one] suppress people without killing them". *Meulengracht* contributed his observation that "one never read of Saami slaves...something to think about". *Arrhenius* explained that in the North there were many court cases because the Saami "[claimed] that they had a right to the forest...to graze their reindeer, whilst the private owners said they had no rights"; at the end of a very "hot debate" the private owners won. At present this was going on as it had become a political issue and as such was never concluded. *Ausenda* asked whether the Swedish museums were required to give back for burial the Saami skeletons, *Arrhenius*' answer was: "Not yet, but it will come". *Magnus* asked *Meulengracht* what he thought about the story told in the saga of King Harald Finehair that he was married to a Saami. He answered that the main source was Gro Steinland's dissertation (Steinsland 1991) which he considered as "a way of interpreting history" but, in his opinion, also had a "real foundation".

Rural economy, subsistence and suplus

Herschend introduced the topic: "I think there is an interesting aspect of Scandinavian society, that the subsistence was relatively good; there was enough food, the population was growing during the Roman Iron Age. When the Roman empire disappeared there was a decrease in population and different kinds of crises, both material and intellectual, and then slowly it started back up again. During that period, at least up to the sixth century, the traditional subsistence production was able to produce a surplus, mostly in the form of hides, wool and commodities that one hasn't really become used to see in the trading of the Middle Ages. In fact my idea is that, as long as there is an urban community, there is always need for any kind, any form of commodity that could be brought there. I think that they were able to export some goods into the Roman empire and get money or gold for them; in Scandinavia they were not interested or were only interested to a very small degree in silver. That's one way of achieving prosperity in a subsistence economy, the other one is the surplus production of men, which made it possible for them already in the Roman Iron Age, in the second, third, fourth and fifth centuries, now and then to engage in a 'pillage economy'. From time to time it was a huge success, for instance in the middle of the third century with the Goths in the Balkans and notably in the Baltic islands in the fifth century, between Valentinian III, around 420, and up to 500 and perhaps to 516. It is not a matter of a continuous influx of *solidi* into these lands, it is a matter of perhaps six or seven locations where the bulk of these coins came. That's the way I see the economy at large: a favourable subsistence economy producing a surplus that might from time to time be distributed into a market network, and also producing a surplus of people which could, from time to time, be used in a pillage economy. And that is why we have the bog finds and several other finds of an aggressive type. To my mind this is a typical theme to create a discourse about the backbone of development perhaps from 300 to the Viking Age; in many ways in less developed northern Scandinavia, the Viking Age was nothing more than a renewed late Roman Iron Age. So that nothing has happened on the social side of things. I mean in Jämtland it was more or less the same as during the Roman Iron Age".

Arrhenius agreed that surplus was a very important aspect of economic life in Scandinavia and suggested that "one of the important surpluses in Scandinavia where there [was] so much wildlife [was] fur", as in fact in northern Scandinavia tax was paid in fur both of foxes and squirrels; she knew that it was traded all the time and must have "meant much more than [one could] imagine" as pieces of the bones of foxes were found also in the ancient trading place of Birka; she explained that there must have been furs with a short "special type of hair", in addition to that of beaver, which must have been obtained by a special combing technique called *drop pani* described also in Arabic sources; the importance of fur trading was testified by the quantity of names for the different furs of animals such as beavers, so that it must have been quite important.

Magnus remarked that one could consider it a surplus economy "with a surplus of goods and a surplus of people" based on "many levels of production...as [there were] several levels in the society where [there was] production of different goods" that could be bartered for other goods at higher levels. She recalled that Martens (1989) and others had shown that in the Viking Age some people could live "in the mountains in ordinary longhouses all year round without producing grain at all", which meant that they were so sure of obtaining their livelihood "from nature" or, "if it was a commodity which [was] wanted somewhere else, [they could] get what they wanted" from trading it; she held that such a level [of wealth] could not be seen as early as the Roman period and "with the kind of distribution economy [available] in the Migration period", so that higher levels were attained in later periods.

Herschend insisted that during the Roman Iron Age there were "houses or farms" on Åland where there was the possibility of extensive pasture, which he thought one "should see...as the beginning of a manorial economy, rather than people working on a market basis". Did he think that this model applied everywhere, asked *Magnus,* and, to his affirmative reply, *Dumville* mused that "it was a 'possible' estate" economy.

Herschend listed also iron production which was always present. However, he thought that "there was no organized way of bringing goods into market" but it was more or less a happenstance event, a subsistence economy with a region actually "exporting and getting [in return] precious prestige goods, not on a regular basis, but more or less by chance". [This process must have required that the exportable goods be long-lasting so that they would be available on the arrival of the trader or merchant who came by more or less unexpectedly, whereas trade in large numbers of livestock almost certainly required some kind of pre-arrangement].

Ausenda suggested that another form of surplus might be represented by young men going into the Roman army and bringing back money, loot and prestige goods, but *Herschend* doubted that that could have been possible saying "that it was a very bad idea to go into the Roman army if [one wanted] to get rich".[2] *Arrhenius* remarked that there were many scholars studying that possibility, but *Herschend* insisted that it was "easier to obtain money through pillage in large groups and tribute from Roman sources", he stressed the fact that the hoards of "*solidi* were obvious tribute payments from the central Roman administration to...a tribal entity"; *Dumville* reminded the audience that service in the Roman army lasted 20 years, at the end of which, *Herschend* remarked, they would have died shortly thereafter or "use[d] their money on whatever women" there were there.

---

[2] But see Morten Axboe: "Both the material and the spiritual imports may have become possible in a variety of circumstances, among which may have been service in the Roman army (1995:225)", and "The chieftains had a retinue of warriors which can be traced, through weapon graves, back into the later pre-Roman Iron Age; a phenomenon which might have been reinforced by contact with the Roman empire and service in the Roman army (1995:228)".

Ausenda explained that he had suggested that possibility on the basis of what he had seen in Sudan, where young men from nomadic tribes go to the towns and work there for three or four years and "come back with enough money to buy their dowry" and then they settle down to their traditional life, but also they bring back the things they have learned in the course of their experience, which represent a cultural surplus no less beneficial to the community. *Herschend* said that in the study of coin hoards even small numbers of coins showed "coin distributions with very many die links..." that [could have been] made with the same die...so that they had "never been out in Roman markets".

Arrhenius suggested that the most fitting model was that of a "chieftain [who] took his men and filled his boats with fur and leather" and sought a trading place; this, she thought was true especially amongst Germanic soldiers where there were "a lot of people around", and then he got money or prestige goods and went home with his men. *Herschend* confirmed that "there were examples where the coin types in a large hoard [were] reflected in small hoards around that" which fitted the model suggested by *Arrhenius*.

Urban economy and trade

Logistics and supply of non-agrarian settlements

Holmquist introduced the topic saying that it was closely connected to the previously discussed 'Rural economy, subsistence and surplus', as the question was "how to support a non-agrarian settlement...and to supply a population that..." came together for given periods of the year; she thought that there were farms, but surely not sufficient for the population; there were several questions connected with the issue, "not only about ways of milling wheat...and storage, but...also how to handle the garbage" in those settlements. *Ausenda* suggested that it could be put back in the fields as manure, while *Holmquist* held that it was not possible at the Birka stage but may have been in the Viking Age. *Arrhenius* agreed considering that that could be a reason why they had cultivable areas and didn't use them; *Holmquist* thought that that was the first proto-urban settlement in mid-Sweden, whereby the inhabitants, most of them not permanent, were not used to live so close together and, therefore, not organized to handle that much garbage. Later medieval towns learnt to use manure and to transport it to the fields.

Changing the subject, *Dumville* asked when bridges started being used in Scandinavia. *Herschend* answered that Denmark had begun in the tenth century while in trans-Baltic Scandinavia they started to be built in the eleventh, there were three bridges which would be considered as such today. *Arrhenius* and *Holmquist* thought that the category referred to bridges made of stone; *Herschend* said that they were connected to "eleventh-century fashions connected to Christianity, at least in Sweden"; "and harbour constructions" added *Arrhenius*.

Political relations

Terminology designating 'leaders' in early Scandinavian society

Brink acknowledged the importance of "the sphere in Scandinavia during the early and late Iron Age" and how many new aspects had been discovered in recent years, but mostly from archaeological and historical contexts, while there was "one dimension that one [had] to bring into these discussions as well, the terms [designating] the leaders" of that period, and also those for the existing social classes, a topic also linked to the category 'Social relations'; he thought that the study of such terms would be "rewarding from an etymological point of view" and could be conducted on runic inscriptions and the few written sources available for that period. *Green* remarked that, although "not a very linguistic matter", the issue turned up in language, history and ethnography; he was sure that it could not be confined to Scandinavia as there must have been links to the Germanic world of the period; in his view this would be a worthwhile but "highly technical discussion". *Arrhenius* agreed that the topic should be extended to the whole of Germanic Europe including the *Alamanni*, the Anglo-Saxons and *Francia*; she pointed out that a "new kind of aristocracy" was being formed and there were different names; such a study would have to be based on linguistics and literary evidence. *Green* suggested that there might be "peculiarities to the...Scandinavian positions" but that "many links would be necessary...to differentiate" and compare.

Ausenda having asked *Brink* to give an example of what he meant, he answered: "Let's start from the top. We have the word 'chief', *konungr* which is not a single term, there are different kinds of *konungar* in early Scandinavian society. And then in the political or military sphere we have leaders like *jarl*, *þegn*, and even some kind of élite leaders of perhaps warriors; we have *rinkar*, *karlar*, *sveinar*. We also have the *þulr*, probably corresponding to OE *þyle*. And we have *goði*, of course, in the east Scandinavian form, *guþe*. Some place-name evidence shows a *lytir*, probably meaning 'the one who throws lots'. They seem to indicate that, in this early Scandinavian society, there were some kind of cult leaders, whereas, according to the old hypothesis, there were no priests in early Scandinavia: it was the resident farmer or chief who conducted all these duties in the society. There too we have to look at the terms, we have them there. So, by doing this overview we can get an insight into the early Iron-Age society in Scandinavia".

Dumville pointed out that, before one starts, there is the problem of drawing up usable models of medieval vocabulary, and then vocabulary invented to respond to aspects of the record which then produced the vocabulary, such as 'chiefdoms' and that sort of thing. On this point he referred back to the paper he had given for the Anglo-Saxon volume, which was a study of the terminology of kingship and particularly overkingship. The difficulty he had faced for a long time with that subject was, first of all, trying to find a suitable terminology for all these parades of kings and overkings, and, secondly, historians assuming there was something which they would call a 'real king', and anything that didn't meet modern expectations of what a real king was, would have to be deliberately downgraded slightly in a modern discussion. There was a determinism which had been inherent in much historical writing, which was now being questioned and disposed of in different parts of Europe, but which still controlled the thinking of scholars, sometimes not obviously so; the big problem was not really finding what these terms meant, which Stefan [Brink] had introduced the participants to, but finding a terminology in one's respective modern language which whould enable some sense of that to be conveyed. He thought that that was where the real, very serious difficulty started to arise.

Jesch raised a methodological question linked to the preceding remarks by *Brink* who had mentioned etymology, and by Green who had mentioned links with other Germanic languages, and that "both methods [had] a very long history in the study of vocabulary"; she asked whether there were any new methods to avoid "going around in the same circles". *Vestergaard* suggested that such a study "should be combined with social studies, what [one knew] theoretically about social institutions, social organizations in various places...together with the history of religion"; it was apparent that there was no "agreement about the meaning of the word 'kingship'" as such institutions differed in time even in the same society; her suggestion was "to combine the more classical studies in this area...language and religion, with social theoretical studies" and new information should come out. *Herschend* was of the same opinion saying that one would have to look at the "archaeological material in *Vestergaard*'s perspective of broader sociological terms", as he thought there was "absolutely no solution to the linguistic perspective to the problem"; he recalled that *Brink* had said that "there must have been priests as there were terms for priests", but that was not necessarily true as there were many roles in that society and one could be in one role one day and in another the next; he thought the study might be fruitful on that transition period in which "there were more terms than men".

Arrhenius did not disagree with *Herschend*'s statements but insisted that one would have to do also a very careful comparative study regarding such terms and functions as they were "connected with the same use in England and the Frankish area", and at the same time look very closely at "how the graves are situated in the cemeteries" and for those which have a prominent position compared to others.

Brink concluded that it would certainly be fruitful "to put the terminology in this new framework...and to use this methodological policy" and, at the same time, that it was obvious that one could not forego the etymological approach.

Kinship in Europe 400 AD to 1200 AD

Vestergaard acknowledged that the topic coincided with the previous one, so that it could be considered closed. *Dumville* noted that what was known today about royal genealogies had been helped considerably by "classical social anthropology" which had thrown light on genealogical practices that were useful "so as not to be blundering out in a hopeless way, as it were, before that comparative material in hand".

Scandinavia and Anglo-Saxon England from year 0 to the year 1500

Dumville specified that he had suggested the topic 'Scandinavia and Britain in the Migration period' in the context of relations with Scandinavia, because previous discussions had focussed on the Viking Age rather than on the earlier period.

Green noted that *Dumville*'s paper on the British Isles dealt more "with the periphery than with the Anglo-Saxon world", and that he had not "covered Anglo-Saxon England and its relationship to Scandinavia", of which he proceeded to give four examples, two on the literary side, i.e. the battle of Maldon, which "cried out for more attention" and "also the Scandinavian affiliations...to be found in *Beowulf*, specifically the correlation between East Anglia and Jutland"; secondly, there had been no "discussions of the problems of the Danelaw, linguistic, political and legal"; thirdly, "more work had to be done...on the presence of OE loanwords in Old Norse, in...poetic as well as pragmatic" fields, and "conversely Old Norse loanwords in OE".

Jesch proposed to take "the relationship between Scandinavia and England for a very long chronological period, from the year 0 up to about the yeat 1500" as there had been no discussion of such relationship after the Norman conquest "which might influence a lot of...evidence for aspects like language, place-names" and so on. *Dumville* complained that saying "Scandinavia and England" would bring the beginning "half way through the period", and *Green* added that the topic could not be confined to England but should also include Normandy. *Jesch* agreed and proposed that it should "include Frisia as well".

Magnus cited John Hines as having "used the art of the Migration period to link up Scandinavia and East Anglia" which proved very hard; she believed that one needed to look into "all the publications that [pointed] to Anglo-Saxon influence on the late Style 1 in Scandinavia to see "whether there [was] something there as well", something which had not been done for some time; she thought that there was a tight relationship between southwest Norway and England, and that archaeological material in southwest Norway was "so very colourful...rich and abundant" that she "[felt] that there [was] something there to look into". *Lund* asserted that "work [was] going on", as Peter Sawyer was completing a paper on English influence on early Norwegian administrative terminology and there had been suggestions by Danish historians that "a lot more [was] to be found if [one] looked closely for it in the way of English influence on twelfth-century Danish administration".

Settlement of Faeroes and Iceland: sources and dates

Dumville had noted that during the discussions one had gone through approximately a century of Icelandic proto-history and that there would be "much merit in integrating it...with what [one] will be doing". He was also struck by the fact that knowledge of the Faeroese historical thinking, quite certainly related to the sources concerning settlement in Iceland, was inadequate, so much that he suggested "a new survey on that question"; he was aware of the difficulties concerning the date and source of the settlement on the Faeroe Islands because, if the date of about the year 900 for settlement in the Faeroes was correct, then "the context of that settlement would need to be focussed on the relationship...between Britain, Norway and Iceland", rather than if the settlement in the Faeroes were considered "immediately antecendent to the settlement of the Orkney and Shetland" islands; he thought it was a "big subject" to which a "huge amount of attention" had been dedicated over a long time, but it seemed useful to take a new look at "that triangle, with Iceland perhaps the ultimate focus of it".

Arrhenius confirmed that there had been a lot of debate in recent years concerning Iceland and that there was to be "an overview of the whole problem of the settlements".

Scandinavia, Baltic lands and Russia

and

Rus and the eastward expansion

Green noted that similar topics had been proposed both by him and by *Dumville* even if the titles were not identical, they had considerable overlap. He introduced the topic: "I come on to this geographical and cultural direction because I have been at work on precisely that direction with an earlier problem, namely the expansion of the Goths from the Baltic down towards the Black Sea. So that this immediately struck me as a continuation which has been almost absent from our discussions, and I'll be brief and kind of heading for a topic I would suggest could use a lot more information, 'Trade and warfare' together or separately — I think it is almost impossible to separate them entirely, so that I mention them together. Secondly, not just the route followed from the South to the North or from the North to the South, but the routes, in the plural, followed by Scandinavians. Thirdly, the foundation of the — shall I call it 'entity' and avoid any hint of the word 'state' — the foundation of the entity of Rus and, lastly, a vast problem which no one man could deal with, but nibbling at it can only help: Old Norse loanwords in various languages to the east, the Baltic languages, the Finnic ones, and the Slavonic ones. There is a lot of material there and a useful comparative discussion would help. You may wonder why, whereas on the Anglo-Saxon side, when I came to you with loanwords, I said Anglo-Saxon loanwords into Norse, Norse loanwords into Anglo-Saxon, you may wonder why I have not got a reciprocal relationship here. I think the answer to that is simple, that in the other direction from Baltic, the Baltic languages, Finnic and Slavonic, the direction of loanword traffic to Scandinavia is so minute by comparison with the other way round, that although it could be included, I don't think that much would come out".

Magnus acknowledged that a lot had been done on Viking expansion eastwards, but felt that the "meeting had lacked exactly that part" which had acquired new significance since the fall of the Iron Curtain and she thought there was a lot of fresh new material that "a scholar like Dr. Ingmar Jansson would be interested in"; her feeling was a consequence of "the revelation she had had when she had come from western Norway to Stockholm" having found out that she had had the same idea, i.e. "part of the spirit of the Viking Age eastward which...linked up with earlier expansion which started...long before in the Iron Age".

Dumville admitted that one had the right to complain about the many books called *The Vikings*, although "very often written by very fine scholars", because they failed to satisfy the need of "any kind of survey or textbook account, to take into account what [was] going on in the East with equal knowledge and sensitivity to the evidence"; he realized that an investigation of the eastward expansion needed a "great range of different specialists"; he hoped that the next book on *The Vikings* would have that overview.

Lund suggested that one should stop "writing general reports about the Vikings and dig a little bit deeper in more limited areas" and that it would be worthwhile to "encourage somebody to replace the very dated surveys...of eastward expansion". *Jesch* felt like supporting that, she thought that it was a "fascinating area" and that "one could go even further east and take in the Arabic sources" that no one had worked on since Harris Birkeland.

Symbolic life

Decorative arts of the Vendel period and Viking Age and their social implications

Magnus introduced the topic asserting the need to "say something about...arts" in Scandinavia during the periods in discussion as nothing had been offered during the seminar; in fact "the study of animal ornamentation...[weighed] heavily in the research of these periods in Scandinavian countries" and was indispensable for typological and chronological research; she thought that the influence of that style came from east of the Danube and was very important, and that the symbolic value of those representations was exemplified in the Jelling stone. She thought that the use of *lim* [the glue that holds garnets in place in cloisonné jewellery] and of precious stones should also be the object of such a study.

Arrhenius reminded the audience that the material was very useful to "relate to workshops" as one could see that they "[used] the same stamps and shared or exchanged the same commodities; in Svealand one found many Frankish coins, almost certainly diplomatic gifts, and also things from Denmark; hence there was also a "political view" if one looked carefully. *Herschend* agreed that gift giving was an important prime mover; concerning stamped artefacts he noted that the studies of stamps for gold rings in the Roman Iron Age had shown that, even though they looked alike, they were not made with the same stamp, which was typical for that period, during which "the exchange of gold [was] so fast and the need for prestige rings so big, that one never got a goldsmith who made two rings alike"; there was a considerable slow down during the Migration period and then once more mass production in the Viking Age, and the interesting result was a revival of decorative arts. *Magnus* assented adding that both in Gotland and in the lakes region there was "a sort of revival of Migration-period art in the Viking Age", and that there seemed to be a sort of "retardation of style on some prestige objects like the big Gotlandic box brooches", as found in a woman's burial where she was buried with her brooches between which there was a "Migration-period square brooch" indicating some sort of revival which affected art as well.

Costume as a social, political and ethnic marker

Bender Jørgensen explained that, in her opinion, "costume or clothing were one of the most direct ways of signalling who [one] was, what [one] was, who [one] wanted to be, etc."; research on that subject was relatively limited for many reasons but now was on a growing trend; she mentioned Ulla Mannering's thesis (1998) from the University of Copenhagen which was a study of costume based on *guldgubber* (gold foil) figures, in which "she managed to sort out the kind of clothing represented in those figures", she had also made a chronology, a study of their distribution and of the people represented and what the clothes signalled. *Dumville* thought that that was an area where "social anthropological material could be brought to bear", while *Arrhenius* cautioned that there was a problem with gold foils due to the fact that one thought of a regional 'folk dress' which, however, was a rather late trait, hence this kind of information could be obtained only beginning from a relatively late date. *Arrhenius* further noted that one had to be cautious when looking for ethnic markers in clothes as, for example, seventh-century Svea people would have preferred to look like Franks. *Bender Jørgensen* agreed that it could have been a "signal to be sent" as it was obvious even from the "textile remains of northern Europe" through which one could recognize "periods when textiles were uniform all over Europe and periods when they were not".

Herschend was reminded of the instance when the Visigoths left Aquitaine for Spain and "why they were not in Aquitaine for a generation since there [were] no fibulae there"; he noted that costume could reflect either the ethnic or the social category [or both] and that "one should be aware of social fashion, not just ethnic". *Magnus* acquiesced but remarked that in art there were all kinds of variables including the time factor as "there were parts of the dress like brooches and buckles...that [could] be inherited" which constituted a great problem, as it would be difficult to tell which part of the costume [was] influenced by contemporary fashion and which [was] an heirloom. *Bender Jørgensen* related how this problem was brought up a couple of years before during a discussion on "what did women bring with them when they married", certainly their jewellery, but did they also bring the clothing that they wore at home? The consensus of opinion was that they probably did not, because "when moving to a new place [one wanted] to look like the others", wich meant adopting the costume and habits of the place where one had moved, but continuing to wear the inherited jewellery. *Dumville* rightly remarked that "that would be the case only with a high status marriage". *Arrhenius* added that such brooches had been found also in Russia, however, there they were combined with the local ones.

Ausenda offered both a historical and an ethnographic parallel to the adoption of more civilized dress as a part of the process of acculturation: in Langobardic law unmarried women were termed as being "*in capillis*" because their hair was visible in that they did not wear a veil, a habit taken over from Roman fashions, and in eastern Sudan Beja (a nomadic pastoralist group of tribes) married women wore a *top*, i.e. a long coloured veil covering their body and over their head, whereas unarried ones left their head uncovered, both costumes having been adopted from Arabic-speaking sedentary populations in towns; he thought that the same trend would probably have been present also in northern Europe, and that possibly the increase in the quantity of brooches in the archaeological record might be related to the adoption of Roman-style tunics by Germanic women.

Bender Jørgensen told about the analysis of fragments of ancient Scandinavian textiles made a few years before by a British expert who had also done work on British and Irish textiles, she had found that Scandinavians tended to wear blue, Britons tended to wear red and the Irish wore purple.

Herschend concluded that dress was a very promising field of research but that the extension of the field was unknown and whether there existed "generalities that *Bender Jørgensen* would like to see in it" and whether general social ideas were applicable to the subject.

Genesis and function of writing before and after Christianization

Ausenda introduced the discussion on the topic: "This morning a path-breaking paper was discussed on the fact that when cultures are not ready for something, it is very difficult to enforce it. And that was very convincing. What was not convincing was how writing was introduced into Scandinavia. And the reason for that is because writing was used only in a limited and symbolic way, so that it would have been very unrealistic for a chief or a priest to have invented or adopted it and induced other people to learn it and use it albeit sporadically. So, I thought that a good way to investigate the problem would be to set up models and then test them against the facts. This is one issue. The other issue is how to find out how runes came into being. I would suggest two models which sprung from the recent discussions: the first one is the Roman army. Preben [Meulengracht Sørensen] said that wooden tablets were found with runes inscribed on them. It is presumable that the Roman army didn't have a widespread medical service for disease, although there were surgeons to treat wounds, but in all probability there were also witch doctors or soothsayers following the army and selling their tablets to soldiers as philacteries to protect them against sickness and wounds, as is the custom even nowadays with very many populations around the world. In the beginning they may have used Latin or Greek scripts with magical formulas. In fact I heard an aspect of the runic alphabet that seemed interesting in relation to the proposed model, that runes seem particularly adapted to being cut in wood because they privilege straight lines as against round ones. The model proposed is based on the idea that some Scandinavians came to the Roman army whether soldiers or mercenaries and became acquainted with this kind of treatment that appeared to be 'potent', and they helped in spreading the art to their countries of origin. Is it quite possible that some of them learned the art while campaigning or that they persuaded some witch doctors to come back with them to their lands. This seems a possible method of diffusion and it would also account for the fact that the original Latin and/or Greek scripts were gradually distorted into 'runes', i.e. a 'mysterious script', to make their 'magic' more 'effective' as it became adapted to the magical rites performed among Germanic populations, e.g. by replacing some alphabetic letters with simplified symbols of Germanic or other popular gods and goddesses. This model would also have had the advantage of an 'economic' explanation, insofar as it would not require a population of thousands of rune writers and/or readers, but only a few itinerant practitioners who would teach their apprentices, presumably their own sons, by rote. The second possible, and perhaps parallel, model is that of traders; it stands to reason that traders made contracts concerning 'future' deliveries with their counterparts in the various emporia which have been discovered along the coasts of Scandinavia, especially if their visits were periodic and, in the absence of intervening communication between visits, it was important for both seller and buyer that these contracts be kept. It is quite possible that both the 'magical' route and the 'trading' route to the origin of runes, eventually merged, and it is even possible that they may have been practised by the same individuals doubling as witch doctors and as writers of contracts, especially in order to make them magically 'inviolable', if one bears in mind that written documents must have also had a 'magical' potency vis-à-vis those who were bound by them. I don't think it should be difficult to work on these models and follow the diffusion of these forms into Scandinavia. For instance, it would be interesting if one found that in Roman military encampments they had such 'magical tablets' with letters inscribed on them, or, even better, with runes. The second part of the problem is finding out how the various characters came about. As I understand, some runic characters are based on Latin and others on Greek letters, whilst some were based on other alphabets. It is possible that these characters were modified when people started working with them, as they found, for instance, that the name of an important god started with a given sign or had a symbol and they adapted that sign or symbol to their formulas. It would be interesting to track the conversion of these signs to their earliest sources. I know that tablets with signs on them were found in Roman encampments and, if these signs were magical formulas, that would be a symptom of something that could have had a wider diffusion. I am also suggesting setting up other possible models as well, that could be studied, compared, and gradually refined.

Meulengracht Sørensen said that his thinking was based on the recognition that so-called 'pagan' Scandinavian or Germanic spiritual or intellectual culture before conversion to Christianity had been underestimated. Two phases in the knowledge of writing in Scandinavia materialized, there was "this early creation of runes, which was highly interesting, for which the sources [were] very few, and then the other period after Christianization"; he turned to *Ausenda* according to whom there was a "transformation of the society to a writing culture", whereas he himself would call it "the textualization of the society...of its social institutions, history and daily life"; he thought that "writing was so important and so 'odd'...and...language was so closely connected to social life, that [one] should try to look at the society from that point of view".

Magnus pointed to a possible connection with "early Roman inscriptions of one word and what Tacitus [had] said about these people's priests drawing lots and that there were signs on these chips of wood and from that they could tell the future", she asked whether there was any possible connection with runic inscriptions.

Meulengracht Sørensen admitted that it was a possible direction. *Herschend* cautioned on the credibility of Tacitus by contemporary historians, whilst *Ausenda* affirmed that there were many observations made by Tacitus which had been confirmed by later documents, e.g. the wedding cortege which was much the same as described in Langobardic law.

Meulengracht further remarked that "Italy [was] the place where [one] should go first to study the origin of runes", whereby *Dumville* asked him to explain and *Meulengracht* continued saying that "the Etruscan alphabet or one of these pre-Roman alphabets seemed to be the closest possibilities of inspiration for the runes, but...the Greek and other Mediterranean alphabets [had] been suggested too" (Moltke 1985).

Comment

This last statement by Meulengracht that the runic script may have been based on Etruscan or other pre-Roman alphabets appears to confirm the spreading of runes via philacteries either through the Roman army or through witch doctors knowledgeable in former Roman magical formulas adapted to north Germanic populations. In fact in Roman circles the Etruscans and probably also other pre-Roman societies enjoyed a reputation of having superior magical know-how, as in fact even nowadays magic is connected to antiquity, e.g. the sources of astrology, a form of magic, are tied to ancient Mesopotamia. *Arrhenius*'s remarks on gnostic amulets and tablets found in late Roman times in the border zone also seem to go in the direction of a Roman army origin, or at least a Roman origin for runic script via magical applications. In any case more needs to be done to obtain a clear picture of the genesis of runic script.

Scandinavian languages and dialects

Nielsen said that he thought that Danish, Icelandic, Norwegian and Swedish were "much closer to each other than they [were] today...an important [phenomenon] because he [thought] that when languages [diverged], cultures [followed]. He admitted his difficulty in understanding the trend characterizing the development from Old Norse, once spoken in Iceland, Norway, Sweden and Denmark up to the Viking Age, to the formation of individual languages in each of the countries mentioned. He understood that, according to common linguistic conceptions, divergence occurs when communication and contacts decreased among the regions involved, but he thought that this trait could not be applied to the Scandinavian countries in the Middle Ages because "close relations existed between Denmark, Norway and Sweden".

Meulengracht Sørensen acknowledged that one started talking about dialects in the Viking Age, he recalled "one definition of language...'a dialect with an army'" and he agreed that Scandinavian languages were very close to each other, although the term 'Danish tongue' was very much discussed, possibly because Danish was the best known of these tongues from a Continental point of view. Scandinavia as a whole was divided into many dialects, which were close and often quite similar to each other, and there were gradients from North to South and from West to East: a person coming from far North to the South (like Ohthere to Hedeby) was able to understand the dialect there, but "a short distance south of Hedeby maybe they couldn't understand what he said". He added that the most discussed was the "division between north Germanic and west Germanic...and [he thought] that there [was] enough evidence to maintain the same division between North and West".

Dumville mentioned a related point: the "major intelligibility between Old English and Old Norse, which [was] much harder to imagine and was discussed principally in relation to poetry"; he asked *Jesch* whether she had any ideas "about taking this from a question of borrowing into the ability...of poetic texts to spice Old English poetry with Old Norse words" and whether there was a possibility of mutual intelligibility between these two languages. *Jesch* answered that she had not thought much about the issue and "wasn't sure that [one] had enough evidence", but to her it was...the opposite, "that people were linguistically aware because they had to learn each other's languages"; she offered the example of Ohthere "explaining an animal whose name he didn't know, but knew that the Old Norse word *steinn* meaning 'stone' had an Old English equivalent' *stan*, so when he heard the Old Norse word *hreinn* he created an Old English word *hran*", showing that he was "philologically aware".

History and written texts - the source problem

Meulengracht Sørensen introduced the topic saying that three papers had discussed "the question of criticism of textual sources, Stefan Brink, Dennis Green and Niels Lund...other papers [had] implicitly been based on the opinions of written texts...and others still [had] unconsciouly implied a knowledge of texts"; he thought that the time had come to discuss the problem, "how did [one] use written texts in the study of historical time, [and even] pre-historical time". He had two qualifications, 'history' and 'written texts'; by 'history' he meant 'concepts of the past, as seen by historians, archaeologists, historians of religion, and so on; when he alluded to source problems he declared that he didn't really like the word 'source' used about texts, but by saying 'text problems' he meant something else. By source problems he designated those implied in the texts, i.e. "how to read and understand them" which meant "understanding the 'genre', the dating, the social context, the interpretation and so on".

Dumville added that, talking about 'genre', it was important to discern how historians and perhaps archaeologists used text; what was wanted was 'narrative information' much of which came from annalistic chronicles "where the information implies a story but doesn't tell one" as it could be an entry of a few words, from which one has to deduce a story, "sometimes according to a repetitive pattern...or by converting it into our conventions of historical writing", but once it had "been through a couple of history textbooks" they had become 'narrative', whilst chronicles were not 'narrative'. Answering *Arrhenius*'s question about the meaning he gave to 'narrative', he cited the example of an entry of an Irish chronicle saying that Clonmacnoise had burnt at some date, if comparable entries were spread over several years they would be interpreted as meaning perhaps that the Vikings had come, so it became a story and "very rapidly the immediate information was lost and the story replaced it"; if needed, one could go back to the primary sources, but even then one would have the textbook in mind and one didn't "realize...how sparing in wording a chronicle source could be...[he had] been struck how much a chronicle [was] almost monosyllabic" and then there would come a later chronicler or the historian "using that material and reading a lot into it".

Jesch noted how there were different kinds of sources implying a story, i.e. mythological poetry where something was deduced "from the poetry that refers to aspects of the myth", skaldic poetry was "a bit like...monosyllabic chronicles" until the thirteenth century when "it was [turned] back into a narrative" which, however implied an earlier narrative, "which was not told but only implied". She thought that the archaeological material reflected the same process, as there were "various bits and pieces which archaeologists [turned] back into some kind of story".

Herschend concluded that "reading a text [was] a matter of taking the different layers from relatively formal systematic or...annalistic structure" and "coming closer and closer to what the real" narrative was meant to be. *Meulengracht Sørensen* clarified that one "never [should] take a detail from a text before [one] understood the text as a text".

Ausenda wanted to add the anthropological background to the study of the significance of chronicles: he recalled how in pre-industrial societies most people didn't count years, and they didn't know when they were born as they had no calendars nor accounts of time; the only way to reckon time was to start from personally known important events in the past, such as floods, plagues, wars that they could remember from given stages in their youth. Thus chronicles supplied sequences of important events that people would have a knowledge of and allowed them to reckon their age and transition ceremonies or when they made agreements or alliances with other parties starting from the time of an important event that they had witnessed; in other words, chronicles punctuated life and supplied a temporal infrastructure to reckon from.

Religion

The process of Christianization in West-, South-, and East-Scandinavia, a comparative archaeological study

and

Role of German and Anglo-Saxon Churches in the Christianization of Scandinavia

Magnus considered the topic timely as Christianization had been the object of much study during recent years, especially with "those two large projects in Sweden and Norway" and a quantity of archaeological material being presented; she was interested in "some sort of comparative study" where one could "assemble what was achieved so far...where there were the differences and where the narrative". *Brink* explained that the "topic was huge", that "two huge projects" were in progress "in Scandinavia with lots of theologians and [backed by the] governments of Norway and Sweden", financed in part by the European Commission, which had given rise to many questions. He referred to *Lund*'s paper as a possible departure for the discussion of the "earlier German phase", and then continuing to highlight the developments in the eleventh and later centuries in Scandinavia in an "ongoing process where [there was] an...impact from both Germany and Anglo-Saxon England" in which the English contribution became increasingly important; the time required was an important factor but also the new archaeological material had to be taken into account as it placed the whole subject "in a different light".

Jesch extended the argument begun by *Magnus* and hinted at previously by *Dumville* who had said that there were "an awful lot of books interpreting things for us" and sometimes mentioning the evidence; she thought that both as scholars and teachers one "needed very, very badly a kind of compendium bringing together the evidence from different types of sources" taking an overview of all the archaeological evidence and placing it beside the written sources and using footnotes to explain what was thought of it: a "first start [could be] just presenting the evidence and...the contexts without too much interpretation".

Dumville wished to express a caution and mentioned what had happened to Scottish history at the beginning of the twentieth century when a source book was put together for the period from 500 to 1286, in which there were "very good translations from different languages, very cleverly organized...and historians stopped referring to primary sources thereafter" as they always referred to the compendium; to some extent the same had happened to Anglo-Saxon history because of the "production of *English Historical Documents*"; and another question was testing "the written evidence of documents". He agreed with *Jesch* that one needed "readier access to evidence without...a heavy interpretation that sometimes one may not understand" but one had to be careful not to "go too far in the other direction".

Herschend brought back the discussion to the two projects on 'Christianization' and asked *Brink* if he could comment on his work in those projects. *Brink* recalled that the Swedish project had gone on for six years when they "finally got together" with the most prominent scholars [in the group] who wrote a 'Stand der Forschung' on the subject in a 600 or so page-long book by the title *The Christianization of Sweden: Old Sources, New Interpretations* (Nilsson 1996), written in Swedish. He continued saying that by now the 'Stand der Forschung' was already outdated, which was "a good thing, because it [showed] that research [was] going on". Instead the Norwegians were unable or unwilling to make a 'Stand der Forschung' and instead had a final symposium in which some presentations were very good. *Meulengracht Sørensen* confirmed that there was no final report and there would be none, but "papers and articles here and there"; he thought it was misleading to consider the Norwegian project on the same level as the Swedish one, while the Norwegian one "probably [had] been at least as expensive".

References

Textual sources:

Brennu-Njáls saga: see Gunnarson & Kyrre (eds.) 1960.
Beowulf: see Klaeber (ed. & trans.) 1941.
Edictus Rothari: see Bluhme & Boretius (eds.) 1868:1-90.
Saxo Gramaticus
        Gesta Danorum: see Olrik & Ræder (eds.) 1931.

Bibliography:

Anderson, H.
    1992   De glemte borge. *Skalk* 1: 19-30.
Axboe, M.
    1995   Danish kings and dendrochronology: archaeological insights into the early history of the Danish state. In *After Empire: Towards an Ethnology of Europe's Barbarians*. G. Ausenda (ed.), pp. 217-252. Woodbridge: The Boydell Press.
Birkeland, H. (ed.)
    1954   *Nordens historie i middelalderen etter arabiske kilder*. (Skrifter utgitt av det Norske Videnskaps-Akademi i Oslo, II. Historisk-Filosofisk Klasse, No. 2). Oslo: Jacob Dybwad.
Bluhme, F., & A. Boretius (eds.)
    1868   *Leges Langobardorum. Monumenta Germaniae Historica. Leges* (in Folio) 4. Hanover: Hahn. [Repr. 1984, Stuttgart: Anton Hiersemann Verlag].
Ethelberg, P.
    2000   *Skoovgarde: ein Bestattungsplatz mit reichen Frauengräber des 3. Jhs.n.Ch.* (Nordiske Fortidsminder 19). Copenhagen: Det kgl. Nordiske Oldskriftselskab.
Friedriksson, S.
    1972   Grass and grass utilization in Iceland. *Ecology* 53 (5): 785-796.
Gunnarson, G., & H. Kyrre (eds.)
    1960   *De islandske sagaer I-III*. Copenhagen: Gyldendal.

Hastrup, K.
1985   *Culture and History in Medieval Iceland: An Anthropological Analysis of Structure and Change.* Oxford: Clarendon Press.

Hines, J.
1997   *A New Corpus of Anglo-Saxon Great Square-Headed Brooches.* Woodbridge: Boydell for the Society of Antiquaries.

Hoff, A.
1997   *Lov og Landskab. Landskabslovenes bidrag til forståelser af Landbrugs - og Landskabsudviklingen i Denmark ca 900 - 1250.* Aarhus: Aarhus University Press.

Højrop, T.
1995   *Omkring livsformsanalysens udvikling.* (Stats- og livsformer 1). [English summary: Theoretical Foundations of Life-mode Analysis]. Copenhagen: Museum Tusculanums Forlag.

Ilkjær, J.
1990   *Illerup Ådal 1-2. Die Lanzen und Speere.* (Jysk Arkæologisk Selskab Skrifter 25, 1-2). Aarhus: Jysk Arkæologisk Selskab.
1993   *Illerup Ådal 3-4. Die Gürtel. Bestandteile und Zubehör.* (Jysk Arkæologisk Selskab Skrifter 25, 3-4). Aarhus: Jysk Arkæologisk Selskab Skrifter.

Jørgensen, A. N., & B. L. Clausen (eds.)
1997   *Military Aspects of Scandinavian Society in a European Perspective, AD 1-1300.* (Papers from an International Research Seminar at the Danish National Museum, Copenhagen, 2-4 May 1996). (Publications from the National Museum. Studies in Archaeology & History, Vol. 2). Copenhagen: The National Museum.

Klaeber, F.
1941   *Beowulf and the Fight at Finnsburh.* New York: Heath.

La Cour, V.
1972   *Danske borganlaeg til midten af det trettende århundrede 1-2.* Copenhagen: Nationalmuseet.

Mannering, U.
1998   Guldgubber. Et billede af yngre jernalders dragt. Unpublished Master's thesis, University of Copenhagen. [For a short published version see: U. Mannering, 1999, 'Sidste skrig', *Skalk* 4: 20-27].

Martens, I.
1989   *Bosetning og ressursutnyttelse i Norge - Et marginalitetsproblem?* Universitets Oldsaksamlings Årbok [Oslo] 1986-1988: 73-80.

Moltke, E.
1985   *Runes and their Origin.* Copenhagen: National Museum.

Nielsen, S.
1999   *The Domestic Mode of Production and Beyond. An Archaeological Inquiry into Urban Trends in Denmark, Iceland and Predynastic Egypt.* (Nordiske Fortidsminder 18). Copenhagen: Det Kongelige Nordiske Oldskriftselskab.

Nilsson, B. (ed.)
1996   *Kristnandet i Sverige. Gamla källor och nya perspektiv.* (Sveriges kristnande. Publikationer 5). Uppsala: Lunne.

Randsborg, K.
1995   *Hjortspring. Warfare and Sacrifice in Early Europe.* Aarhus: Aarhus University Press.

Sawyer, B., P. H. Sawyer & I. N. Wood (eds.)
1987   *The Christianization of Scandinavia.* Alingsås: Viktoria Bokförlag.

Sjöholm, E.
1977   *Gesetze als Quellen mittelalterlicher Geschichte des Nordens.* (Acta Universitatis Stockholmiensis 21). Stockholm: Almqvist & Wiksell International.
1988   *Sveriges medeltidslagar. Europeisk rättstradition i politisk omvandling.* (Rättshistoriskt bibliotek 41.) Stockholm: Nordiska bokhandeln.
Schmidt-Wiegand, R.
1978   Stammesrecht und Volkssprache in Karolingischer Zeit. In *Aspekte der Nationenbildung im Mittelalter. Ergebnisse der Marburger Rundgesprache 1972-1975.* H. Beumann & W. Schröder (eds.), pp. 171-203. Sigmaringen: Thorbecke Verlag.
Steinsland, G.
1991   *Det hellige bryllup og norrøn kongeideologi.* Oslo: Solum.
Wormald, P.
1977   Lex scripta and Verbum regis: Legislation and Germanic kingship from Euric to Cnut. In *Early Medieval Kingship.* P. H. Sawyer & I. N. Wood (eds.), pp. 105-138. Leeds: University of Leeds Press.
Zachrisson, I.
1997   *Möten in gränsland: samer och germaner i Mellanskandinavien.* (Statens Historiska Museum Monographs 4). Stockholm: Statens Historiska Museum.

INDEX

Jacket photo: *courtesy of*
Statens historiska museum, Box 5428, S-114 84 Stockholm;
showing Viking Age picture stone from Gothland.

Page setting: *Bene e Presto, I - 20144 Milano*
Phototype setting: *Fotoedit S.r.l., Serravalle (RSM)*
Printers: *Studiostampa S.A., Serravalle (RSM)*